Guardians of the Holy Grail

The Knights Templar, John the Baptist, and The Water of Life

Guardians of the Holy Grail

The Knights Templar, John the Baptist, and The Water of Life

By
Mark Amaru Pinkham

Guardians of the Holy Grail:
The Knights Templar, John the Baptist & The Water of life

ISBN 1-931882-28-2

Printed in the United States of America

Published by
Adventures Unlimited Press
One Adventure Place
Kempton, Illinois 60946 USA
auphq@frontiernet.net
www.adventuresunlimitedpress.com

Other books by Mark Amaru Pinkham
THE RETURN OF THE SERPENTS OF WISDOM
CONVERSATIONS WITH THE GODDESS
THE TRUTH BEHIND THE CHRIST MYTH

Guardians of the Holy Grail

The Knights Templar, John the Baptist, and The Water of Life

Dedicated to the

Sinclairs

without whom
the Holy Grail Mysteries of the Knights Templar
could not have survived

Table of Contents

Foreward

by
Chevalier Ian Sinclair

I deem it an honour to be asked to write the Forward for Mark's new book, and I am trying to remember where it all began. There I was on this lovely evening, enjoying a glass of fine whisky and reading the manuscript for a new book that a friend from the USA had sent me to cast an eye over before she sent it off to the publisher. The telephone rang and I thought, "should I just let it ring?," but something was saying to me, "you need to take this call Ian." When I answered the call Mark Amaru Pinkham from the USA introduced himself to me and requested that I grant him an interview for a new book he was writing. On enquiring what the content of the book was, he began to tell me about being guided to try and find the Sinclair contacts who may be able to add greatly to his knowledge base regarding the Sinclair-Templar connections.

After making the date for the telephone interview, I began flicking around some of the books in the library that contained information Mark had spoken about, such as Kundalini, which was a totally unknown word to me when I first became aware of its power.

The interview date duly arrived and I made sure that there would be no disturbances during our telephone conversation when Mark rang. I was not sure just what to expect, but his questions were direct and to the point, and I was impressed with his knowledge about the Sinclairs and their Masonic and Templar/Rosslyn Chapel connection.

We arranged for Mark and his wife, Andrea, to fly over to Scotland and spend some time at the Clan Sinclair Study Centre. This would allow him the use of the library and it would give me chance to have a face to face contact with him. We also arranged for Mark and Andrea to deliver a lecture at the Prince Henry St Clair Preceptory. When it was later given, the lecture was extremely well received.

One day we sat at the Study Centre and talked for hours about the dream that Mark and Andrea had of setting up an International Order of Gnostic Templars. When first asked if I would play a part in its creation, I was cautious, only because I am involved in other Templar organizations and I thought there could be a clash of interests. But my role as the Sinclair Archivist and Librarian was to assist people and organizations wherever and whenever I could. So the more I thought about it, and after recognizing their determination and the results of many years of hard, dedicated study, I decided to accept the challenge and help them create a ritual for opening and closing their Commandary. I also assisted in framing a ritual for the admittance of Squires and the Accolade of Knighthood. These rituals were **personal and tailored** to the requirements of the **I.O.G.T.**

I am encouraged by the creation of the I.O.G.T. and its potential to revive the early practices of the Knights Templar. At the time of their trial, the Templar's were accused of magical and diabolical practices, although it seems unlikely that they as a society were all guilty as charged. There is, however, little doubt that the Templar's were the possessors of real and important magical powers, powers perhaps even greater than the ones they were accused of.

Far from being ignorant monks of war as some authors have labelled them, a great number of Knights were gifted with Gnostic knowledge and served as custodians of the wisdom tradition from ancient times. Their wisdom included elements of Gnosticism, Hermeticism, and alchemy. Their hidden knowledge and practices were almost certainly learnt from their sojourn in the East.

True to all possessors of great skills and knowledge, concealment of their great accumulation of riches was of paramount concern to the Templars, and it is my belief that a great host of these Gnostic secrets are on view to us all, every day, in that magnificent Sinclair structure they call Rosslyn Chapel. As for the physical treasures - we are already aware that Sir William Sinclair had removed from Holyrood Abbey the Holy Reliquaries and rich chalices that had been donated by the second St Clair Earl of Orkney, a generous benefator who had also previously endowed the Abbey with vestments of gold and silver and enough land to graze seven thousand sheep. The reason William removed them was to prevent them from falling into the hands of the Calvinist radicals and Protestant English forces who had already sacked Edinburgh, Melrose, and Rosslyn Castle two years previous.

In 1545, the Lords in Council ordered William Sinclair to return all jewels, vestments and ornaments back to the Abbey, but he still would not yield them. It is reputed that they were part of the blessed hoard hidden in the vaults of his chapel. These treasures probably included the piece of the True Cross in it's reliquary of silver, gold and jewels, the Holy or Black Rood of Scotland, which had been guarded by St Margaret's cupbearer and the St Clair family for five centuries as Scotland's most precious holy symbol. What secrets still remain down below the chapel, in the Sinclair vaults, has been the speculation of many writers and researchers, only time will reveal the true facts.

The new **International Order of Gnostic Templars** created by Mark and Andrea will, in my opinion, help solve some of the mysteries and secrets that have been lost to us for centuries. And what better place to start the order than **Rosslyn Chapel, cradle of the Sinclairs.**

Having read Mark's other publications, I wish him well with this one. I am left in no doubt that he is an extremely dedicated and enthusiastic individual, supported by an equally talented and dedicated Andrea.

Chevalier Ian Sinclair KCTpl.

W. Commander of The Prince Henry St Clair Commandary

Archivist to the Clan Sinclair Study Centre

Foreward

Introduction

For the past fifteen years I have been actively working to promote and reintroduce the ancient Goddess Tradition to western culture through my books and the esoteric schools I direct. This has been my contribution to the current revival of the Goddess principle that is occurring on a planetary scale. Now I have been guided to take another step and reintroduce Gnostic Templarism, which includes those rites and practices of the ancient Knights Templar that the Order adopted from the Goddess sects of the East. The revival of the Gnostic and esoteric wisdom of the Templars is the underlying reason I now offer you *Guardians of the Holy Grail.*

I received the initial "call" for my current work some time ago while hiking along a rocky trail in the upper reaches of the Andes Mountains with a Canadian man, who with his shoulder-length hair and long beard perfectly fit the stereotype of the classic mountainman. My friend also displayed the anomalous characteristic of having both his arms completely covered with tattoos, an apparent vestige of his days riding with a motorcycle gang. At one point on our journey in the elevating and psychic air of the Peruvian Andes we both looked at the other in tacit acknowledgment, just as if we were agreeing on something we had been discussing even though neither of us had spoken a word. I then volunteered to be the spokesman for the "aha" we were mutually feeling. "We were Templar Knights before together," I affirmatively stated, "and we have returned to complete the work of the Knights, that of uniting East and West." And then, while the veil of our future was still lifted, I added, "We need to begin by reviving Gnostic Templarism, the original tradition of the Knights Templar." My Canadian friend cackled with delight and approval. He then informed me of his ostensible connection to the Templars. Both his parents were from Scotland, the country that the Knights Templar had, for hundreds of years, adopted as their own. Another flash of intuition enveloped me as my inner vision beheld the image of my friend sitting upon a tall horse and riding with a group of Templar Knights someplace in Europe. Apparently things hadn't changed much since this past existence. He was still a bearded warrior, large in stature, and he moved with a gang. He had simply traded his horse for a Harley-Davidson!

When I returned home to the USA from Peru I began to give interviews to prominent members of the Templar and Freemasonic communities, which you will find at the end of this book. My hope was to gain insight into the contemporary manifestations of these organizations and perhaps discern where I might fit in. One of the Templars I contacted to interview at this time was a Scottish man named Ian Sinclair who had his own Templar center in the north of Scotland. I knew enough about the Knights Templar to know that the Sinclair name had played an important role in the history of the Templars, and that the Clan had built the "Mecca" of Templarism and Freemasonry, Rosslyn Chapel.

When I first heard Ian's voice over the phone it seemed strangely familiar. I felt very comfortable talking with him, and my interview with him continued for nearly two hours. We discussed the history of both the Sinclairs and Knights Templars, as well as the Templar organization Ian is currently a member of, the Militi Templi Scotia. I felt so comfortable with Ian and what he told me about his order that I immediately wanted to become a member. Ian was amenable to the idea and even encouraged me to move ahead with application process. But the decision was not only his to make. The ruling council of the Order needed to agree to accept a member from outside of Scotland. But Ian felt sure that that was not going to be a problem.

So my wife, Andrea, and I sent in our applications to the Militi Templi Scotia and waited patiently for a reply. Months flew by and no word came. Ian had brought up the issue of international membership at the Order's meetings, but the consensus seemed to be that the Scottish Templars were not ready to expand internationally. This disturbed Ian greatly, and he decided that by remaining circumspect the Order was hurting itself by not staying true to the goals and international ambitions of the original Templars.

Feeling very frustrated myself by what I perceived as nationalistic prejudice on the part of the Scottish Templars, I chose a day to get insight into what my next step would be by participating in an intensive shamanic ceremony at one of the Sedona vortexes. My answer came quickly during the rite. An understanding came to me that I was not to become a member of an existing Templar order, but was instead to create or revive a completely new Gnostic order. Templarism has gotten away from its Goddess roots over the years and taken on a veneer that is patriarchal and fundamentalist Christian. The Goddess influence, which included the esoteric practices of Gnosticism and Alchemy, had all but been expunged from the Knights Templar during the Order's persecution and dissolution in the 14th century.

When I later told Ian of my revelation he was very supportive and even volunteered his assistance in helping to create the Templar order. So Andrea and I hastily made plans to visit Ian's Prince Henry St. Clair Preceptory for intensive instruction, and we were in Scotland a couple months later.

Ian welcomed us with open arms and we both felt as though we had returned home. Ian had created a Templar retreat around an existing lighthouse on a promontory overlooking the North Sea. In the center of all the buildings of his retreat was a statue of Ian's ancestor, Prince Henry St. Clair, who had been a Grand Master Templar and one of the early discoverers of America. Many of the buildings were adorned with images of the distinctive Engrailed Cross of the Sinclairs. This special cross, I was to learn, revealed an intimate link between the Sinclairs and the Holy Grail Mysteries.

During our time at Ian's preceptory we laid the groundwork for our new Templar order, and I even gave a formal lecture related to it to the members of Ian's Templar Preceptory. For the most part, the concept of an International Order of Gnostic Templars was well received by them and there were even a few knights who recognized that our work was not so much about founding something new and different as much as it was to reinfuse Templarism with what it had lost.

We also met with Niven Sinclair. Niven, one of the leaders and spokespersons for Clan Sinclair, is a very tough individual that sees clearly how spirituality has been "hijacked" by fundamentalist religions and how it needs to return to its roots. This, apparently has been the stance of the Sinclairs for hundreds of years, beginning before the dissolution of the Templar Order in the 14th century. According to Niven, William Sinclair had built Rosslyn Chapel to be monument to the Goddess and Her nature religion, and he had even made seats attached to the outside of the Chapel so that worshippers "could identify God and Nature." Although the Sinclairs lost possession of the Rosslyn Chapel five generations ago, they would like to reclaim it and reactivate it. Its reactivation is part of the current planetary Goddess revival.

After I returned home the pieces of the puzzle began to fall together in my mind and it soon became crystal clear why I had been led to Ian and the Sinclairs. Like myself, they have long been proponents and caretakers of the Goddess Tradiiton. I told myself that the adherents of the Goddess path must now be returning and regrouping during Her time of revival, a notion that became even more pronounced a couple months later when I gave a lecture on Gnostic Templarism at the *Prophets Conference* in Palm Springs, California.

Persons from all over the US and Canada attended that *Prophets Conference* in order to learn about the Goddess-related roots of the Templars and the revival of the Order's Gnostic practices. When I began my lecture I felt compelled to speculate that all of us in the packed hall were reincarnated Templar Knights returning to "finish the job" of uniting East and West forms of spirituality. A moment of complete silence and reflection followed and it became obvious that the notion had not been taken in jest. Instead, as some of the participants informed me later, I had "hit the nail on the head."

For me, the most exhilarating turn of events at the *Prophets Con-*

ference was a chat I had with one of the speakers, a woman orignally from Russia and now living in California. For many years this woman had been associated with the Goddess Tradition in Russia and involved in extensive research studying the influence of the Goddess among the tribal peoples of Siberia. She had also recently been to Rosslyn Chapel, a journey she had undertaken following an instructive vision that revealed some special work she needed to do in the Chapel in order to assist in its recativation. With great faith in her connection to the Goddess, she had traveled to Rosslyn as requested and duly completed her mission.

This woman had responded to a call from the Goddess just as I had. And it was not long afterwards that I understood what her mission had been about. Niven informed me that he had previously invited a Feng Shui master to Rosslyn Chapel in order to measure the energy flow within and around the structure. The master discovered that an outer wall was obstructing the energy flow into the Chapel from a neighboring glen, but he still found the energy of Rosslyn to be very unique and predicted that the Chapel would soon become a major center of world peace. The Russian woman had obviously been led to Rosslyn to assist the Chapel in meeting its destiny.

The book you are about to read is the history of Gnostic Templarism, beginning with its foundation when the Knights lived for more than one hundred years in the Middle East. This text reveals the maelstrom of esoteric wisdom and practices that shaped Gnostic Templarism during the Templars' years in the East, as well as the specific rites they assimilated into their Order. Of these, the most important are the Mysteries of the Holy Grail, which originally came to the Middle East from the Far East many thousands of years before the arrival of the Knights Templar in the Holy Land. This Holy Grail tradition became rooted in the West by John the Baptist, who passed it on to Jesus, who in turn tranmitted it to John the Apostle and Mary Magdalene. After the Knights were initiated into this tradition in the 12th century they returned with it to Europe, where it became the foundation of numerous secret societies, including the Rosicrucians and Freemasons. The European Grail Mysteries were subsequently preserved within the numerous Holy Grail legends that surfaced throughout Europe, and these legends still remain the best source of wisdom we have regarding the Holy Grail Mysteries. They reveal their Eastern origin, as well as how the Templars knew the Mysteries.

Please read the following pages with an open mind and willing heart. Quite possibly you will be the next person called upon to assist in the rebirth of the Goddess and Her wisdom.

Mark Amaru Pinkham
Sedona, Arizona April, 2004

Part I
The Mysteries of the Holy Grail

1
The Eastern Origins of the Holy Grail Mysteries

When you think of the Holy Grail your mind probably conjures up the image of a golden chalice that Jesus and his Apostles drank out of during the Last Supper and later caught the blood of the crucified Messiah. Perhaps you envision this legendary Cup of Christ in the hands of a distinguished knight, possibly the Knight Percival, its eternal guardian. Have you ever pondered where your image originates? No doubt it is related to the legend of King Arthur and his Knights of the Round Table, whose reputed goal was to find the location of the Holy Grail, drink from the golden chalice, and then receive the sought-after prize of immortality. But King Arthur and his knights is an anachronism; no such person or persons ever existed, at least not in the way we are made to believe. According to historical fact, there were two royal figures living in the 6th centuries, an Arthur of Dalriada and an Arthur of Wales, both of whom currently contend for the honor of being *the* King Arthur even though neither lived during the beginning of the second millennium when the age of knights in shining armor began in Europe. Thus, we have been lead down a garden path of half-truths. But regardless of the historical deceit, the search for the Holy Grail has been a real one and it was indeed embraced by a order of intrepid knights. These were the members of the *Pauperes Commilitones Christi Templique Salomonis*, the "Poor Soldiers of Christ and the Temple of Solomon," who are better known today as the Knights Templar. This brotherhood of knights were the first of the chivalrous orders that existed in the Middle Ages and the model by which all others later patterned themselves. They were the inspiration and later became the authors of the captivating European legends of the Holy Grail, including those involving King Arthur and his Knights of the Round Table. Thus, the Holy Grail Mysteries of Europe truly begin with the Knights Templar.

The Order of the Knights Templar was founded in 1118 A.D. to ostensibly protect Christian pilgrims traveling to and from the Holy Land. Its first nine members, including Hughes de Payen, Godfroi de St. Omer, Rossal, Gondamer, Geoffroi Bisol, Payen de Montdidier, Archambaud de St. Aignan, and André de Montbard, had arrived in Palestine during the First Crusade, which is famous for extricating the Holy Land from the clutches of the infidel Moslems. The first Templars came from France, the European birthplace of knights in shining armor, where they had been known as *chevaliers*, meaning "knights," a term derived from *cheval,* the French word for horse. The equestrian *chevaliers* became famous for their chivalry and noble behavior, which included both sportsmanship and the protection of women, while their worldly sustenance flowed from the feudal kingdoms they were avowed to protect. The main differences between the French *chevaliers* and the Templars is that the Knights Templar were in service to the same lord, the Pope, and each took a lifelong vow of celibacy. The Pope instituted the monastic Rule of the Templars, which was drawn up by St. Bernard, the head of the Cistercian order of European monks, but other than the occasional mandates coming from the Holy See the Templar Knights were exempt from any worldly authority.

Leading the first Templars to Palestine as part of the First Crusade was the Count of Lorraine, Godefroi de Bouillon, who was subsequently chosen as the first King of Jerusalem although he never officially accepted the crown, preferring instead the designation of "Defender of the Holy Sepulchre." Godefroi's rulership of Jerusalem eventually passed to his younger brother, Baldwin I, who graciously accepted the title of King of Jerusalem and later passed it to his nephew, Baldwin de Bourg, the historical King Baldwin II, who is noted to have given the Knights Templar a permanent residence in the al-Aqsâ Mosque. This small mosque had previously been built by the Moslems over "Solomon's Stables," a part of Solomon's Temple that the Knights believed contained the hidden treasure of the ancient Jews and Hebrews.

Following in the wake of the Knights Templar was another spiritual brotherhood of fighting monks, the Knights of St. John, or "Knights Hospitallier," which had originated as a relief organization in Palestine years before the First Crusade. The Knights of St. John allied with the Knights Templar in their battles against the marauding Saracens, who sought to recapture Jerusalem and the Latin territories of the Middle East for Islam, and together the two sister orders of European knights founded the kingdom of Outremer, meaning "Across the Sea," which eventually extended up and down the coast of Asia Minor. Both orders constructed or acquired magnificent castles in the mountains and seacoast regions of Asia Minor, such as the still-standing Krak des Chevaliers in Syria and the commanding Beaufant Castle in Lebanon. It has been estimated that by 1187 the two orders of knights oversaw thirty-five percent of the lands comprising Outremer, including the divergent principalities of Antioch, Tripoli, Jerusalem and Edssa.[1] According to an existing census from 1180, at that time there were at least 600 Knights and 2000 "Sergeants" of the Templar Order stationed in the fortresses dotting the territories of Outremer.

But the knights of Outremer were not just warriors; they possessed a spiritual temperament and a penetrating intellect that the world is just now becoming aware of. The spiritual disposition of the Knights Templar was encouraged by their patron and mentor, St. Bernard, who not only constructed the Templar Rule but was intimately related to the Order by being the nephew of the Templar André de Montbard, as well as a spiritual brother to the Cistercian monks Rossal and Gondamer, whom he had released from their vows so that they could become two of the original nine Knights. In the Middle East, the Templars' Cistercian heritage combined with the mystical wisdom and mentoring they received from the numerous Asian mystics they encountered, thereby engendering the incipient European knighted brotherhood of the Holy Grail Mysteries.

Eventually the European knights of Outremer, especially the Knights Templar, became committed to the discovery of and protection of the Holy Grail in all its myriad forms. They learned from their Asia teachers that the Holy Grail included not only the Cup of Christ, but a multitude of other Grail manifestations, including the holy bloodline of Jesus, which one ancient legend maintained had survived after the death of the Messiah through Jesus' wife, Mary Magdalene. The Knights prodigious wisdom of the Holy Grail Mysteries was principally acquired from the Sufis, the enlightened mystics of Islam and the founders of numerous eclectic schools of wisdom that covered the sprawling territory of Asia Minor. Under the guidance of their Islamic mentors, states Barbara Walker in *The Women's Encyclopedia of Myths and Secrets*, the Templars made their first headquarters at the al-Aqsâ mosque a temple of the Holy Grail Mysteries. She states:

"Western Romances, inspired by Moorish Shi'ite poets, transformed this Mother-Shrine (the al-Aqsa mosque) into the Temple of the Holy Grail, where certain legendary knights called Templars gathered to offer their service to the Goddess, to uphold the female principles of divinity and to defend women."[2]

Eventually, all the Templars' castles in Asia Minor became Temples of the Holy Grail Mysteries. Then, during the more than one hundred years that followed while the Templars resided in Outremer, the Knights became Holy Grail adepts by becoming fluent in Arabic and translating the scrolls of occult wisdom regarding the Holy Grail Mysteries owned by their Sufi mentors. These priceless Holy Grail scrolls had been gathered from all parts of Asia, Europe, and Africa by the conquering Moslems, who then deposited them in libraries in the Middle East under the direction of the Sufis. For some Templars, these Sufis were the only adept teachers of *any* religious tradition, including Christianity, they would have the good fortune to deeply study profound spiritual subjects with. Such was the case of the Templar Grand Master Philip of Nablus, who was born and educated by Islamic teachers in Moslem-inhabited Syria. Philip's daily interactions with the Moslems made him friendly and protective towards the Saracens, and this tendency rubbed off on the Templar Knights that served him. The Templar sympathy for the Saracens is illustrated in an entry from the diary of one Usama ibn Mungidh, a Syrian Arab and the Amir of Shaizer, who while on pilgrimage in Jerusalem took time to worship at the Templars' al-Aqsâ mosque. Usama initially refers to the Templars in his diary as *acquaintances and friends*, and then states that after kneeling to pray in their mosque:

"...a Frank (a Christian pilgrim from France) threw himself on me from behind, lifted me up and turned me so that I was facing east. "That is the way to pray!" he said. Some of the Templars at once intervened, seized the man and took him out of my way, while I resumed my prayer. But he did it again and the Templars apologized again and said "He is a foreigner who has just arrived today from his homeland in the north, and he has never seen anyone pray facing any other direction than east."[3]

The vision of religious equality that the Templars acquired towards their Islamic neighbors was in large part acquired from their enlightened Sufi mentors. According to the Freemasonic and Templar historians, Mackey and Higgins, the equality consciousness of the Sufis had enabled them to perceive the same universal truths running through all the major world's spiritual traditions, including Christianity, and their universal vision eventually inspired them to unite the elements from Islam, Egyptian mysticism, Persian dualism, alchemy, Gnosticism, and the knowledge of the Greek philosophers into a host of well-oiled and erudite mystery traditions that subsequently blossomed throughout the Middle East. The Sufis also assisted in the creation of numerous Islamic sub-sects that similarly cultivated a universalist perspective, including the Druses, the Assassins, the Yezidhi, and the Ishmaili. Much of the arcane wisdom promulgated within these syncretic Sufi sects flowed into the Templar Order and was later taken by the Knights back into Europe where it became the backbone of many westernized mystery traditions, including Freemasonry and Rosicrucianism. In reference to the secret wisdom the Templars acquired in the Middle East from the various Moslem, Jewish and Gnostic sects, Manley Palmer Hall, the founder of a Rosicrucian study and research center in California, states:

"To a few of the Knights Templar, who were initiated into the arcane of the Druses, Nazarenes, Essenes, Johannites, and other sects still inhabiting the remote and inaccessible fastness of the Holy Land, part of the strange story was told (the esoteric mysteries)."[4]

A good example of an eclectic mystery school tradition fabricated by the Sufis in the Middle East is the Ikhwan al-Safa, the Brethren of Bosra, which was founded around 959 A.D. in Syria with the goal of uniting Arabic science with Islamic, Greek, Persian, Hebrew, Chinese and Hindu mysticism into a planetary mystery school. The Brethren, who were also known as the "Philosophers of Purity," compiled all the planetary wisdom available to them in the Moslem Empire to create the *Rasa'il Ikhwani s-Safa*, a collection of 52 Epistles, some of which later served as the foundation for a multitude of eclectic schools that subsequently mobilized in the Middle East, Africa, and Europe. This synthetic wisdom amalgamated by the Brethren mirrored the archetypal wisdom of the ancient Jewish Essenes, and it also foreshadowed the curriculum promulgated by the European Freemasonic Lodges.

One of the electic Islamic sects that had a significant influence on the Knights Templar was the Druses, a sect founded in the 10th century with the help of Sufi missionaries from Cairo's House of Wisdom. The Druses, who existed in mountainous compounds proximal to the Templar fortresses of Lebanon, observed a mystery religion that began as a synthesis of Judaism, Islam and Christianity. The structure and rites of the Druses, including the sect's foundational three degrees, reflected those of the Templars and betrayed a connection between the two organizations. When the Freemason Colonel Churchill, author of *Ten Years Residence on Mt Lebanon,* spent years studying the Druses in the 19th century he found their rites to be nearly identical to the observances of European Freemasonry, a later organization founded by the Knights Templar that was based upon their ancient rites. Other irrefutable links between the Druses, Templars and Freemasons include a reference to the Druses within the rite of initiation into the 22nd degree of the Ancient and Accepted Scottish Rite of Freemasonry, as well as the fact that the highest leader of the Druses was once averred to reside in Scotland, the northern land of Templarism. States the 33rd degree Freemasonic historian Mackey:

"The Druses hold the residence of their Supreme Head to be Scotland; a tradition which has been evidently handed down from the times when the Templars were all-powerful in their neighborhood."[5]

Another Sufi-inspired sect of the Middle East that greatly influenced the Templars is the Yezidhi, a cult of Kurds reformed by the Sufi Sheikh Adi in the 11th century. Although now principally in northern Iraq, the Yezidhi culture once spread through much of Asia Minor, including areas in Syria and Lebanon anciently inhabited by the Templar Knights. The religion of this sect, which amalgamates elements of Judaism, Zoroastrianism, and Islam, was, through its principal deity, Melek Taus, an important contributor to the Templars' Holy Grail Mysteries. The Yezidhi priests claimed that Melek Taus, the "Peacock Angel," was the infamous angel of the Garden of Eden who refused to bow to Adam and fell from pride to become Lucifer. The story of Melek Taus is the basis for the legend of the Fisher King within the Holy Grail Mysteries, who similarly fell from pride like the Peacock Angel and is portrayed as living in his Grail Castle while wearing a hat made of peacock feathers. The Templars' practice of wearing a sacred cord under their clothing may have also been influenced by Melek Taus, whom the Yezidhi remained eternally allied with through the symbolic red and black wool cord they wore around their necks.[5] The Templar predilection for wearing their sacred cords was exposed during their infamous French trail of the 14th century, when some of the Knights confessed to having been given cords previously wound around an idolatrous head named Baphomet, which as you will discover later in this text is a name for Melek Taus.

The Yezidhi could have also influenced the Holy Grail Mysteries through their membership in the Cult of Angels, an organization which includes two other Islamic sub-sects. The Cult of Angels' veneration of a deity represented by a sword or knife inserted vertically into the ground may have provided a model for the later Arthurian image of the Sword in the Stone. Moreover, the Cult's annual October celebration of the Festival of Jam, the Festival of the "Cup," may have inspired the later European authors of the Holy Grail legend to endow their mysterious Holy Grail Cup with supernatural powers. This Persian holiday, which celebrates the Golden Age of the immortals ruled over by the legendary Persian King Jamshid, the "Resplendent Cup," may have engendered a belief in the immortality-bestowing powers of the Holy Grail Cup.

Another Middle Eastern sect that apparently had a profound influence on the Knights Templar and their Holy Grail Mysteries is the Mandeans, a sect currently residing principally in southern Iraq but which has in the past colonized regions all over the Middle East, including Palestine. The Mandeans subscribe to an eclectic religion comprised of the Persian mysticism of the Sufis, as well as the doctrines of their neighboring Druse and Yezidhi communities. Like the Yezidhi, the Mandeans also have a tradition regarding Melek Taus, whom they refer to in their sacred texts as Malka Tausa, although their link to the Peacock Angel predates any contact they may have had with the Yezidhi sect by many thousands of years. Melek Taus (or Malka Tausa) was present at the birthplace of the Mandean culture, the island paradise of Sri Lanka, the Garden of Eden of the Arab world, wherein he was known not only as the Peacock Angel, but also as Murrugan or Sanat Kumara. The Mandeans diverge from the Yezidhi, however, by not only associating Melek Taus with Lucifer, but also ostensibly referring to him as Adam, the first Mandean prophet of Gnostic or intuitive wisdom. According to legend, the personality of Adam-Melek Taus or Adam-Murrugan anciently climbed down from Sri Lanka's highest mountain, Adam's Peak, and then taught the Mandeans their Gnostic wisdom. It is because of his seminal influence that the Mandean tribe was later able to forge a bridge between East and West spirituality once they had migrated to the Middle East. From the Mandean culture eventually emerged St. John the Baptist, the Father of Gnosticism in the West, who is reputed to have established a Gnostic tradition known as the Church of John, which is also referred to as the Johannite Church. John's Church was the "Hidden Church" that A.E. Waite later later wrote about in his *The Hidden Church of the Holy Grail*, claiming that it had played a significant role in establishing the Holy Grail Mysteries in Europe. Hughes de Payen, the first Templar Grand Master who is also reputed to have been initiated into John's Church as one of its Grand Masters, succeeded in amalgamating the Johannite wisdom with the eclectic knowledge of the Sufis in order to produce a European version of the Holy Grail Mysteries.

Of all the Middle Eastern Sufi-inspired sects that have influenced the Knights Templar none is more important than the Assassins, an Islamic sect of Nizari Ishmailis that was founded by Sufis attached to Cairo's House of Wisdom. The Assassins, like the Templars, were an order of Asian knights who built formidable castles in the mountainous regions of Syria and Lebanon, sometimes within view of the Templar fortresses. The Assassin tradition of knighthood and chivalry was, however, much older than that of the Templars' and came from Persia, the home of Hasan-I-Sabbah, the founder of the Order. Hasan had been raised on the legends of chivalrous Persian monarchs, such as the famed King Kai Khosrow, a ruler whose court of devoted knights is recognized to be an earlier Persian counterpart to, and possibly the inspiration for, King Arthur and his Knights of the Round Table. King Khosrow, who is said to have possessed a magical cup similar to the Holy Grail Chalice of legend, may have also provided the model for the character of Percival, the principal protagonist of the European Holy Grail Mysteries. Like Percival, Khosrow is portrayed as an idiot at the outset of his legend, and like his European counterpart, Khosrow is similarly inspired to travel to the king's court following the death of his father and a pivotal meeting with a valiant knight.[7]

It is historically documented that the Assassins were just as antagonistic to the fundamentalist Islamic factions in the Middle East as were the Templars, and it is known that at times both orders allied against a common Saracen enemy. One of their mutual foes was the indomitable Moslem general Saladin, who is credited for having wrested Jerusalem from the Christians in an attempt to create a homogenous Islam state of fundamentalist worshippers throughout the Middle East. Another common enemy shared by the two orders was the inimical Atabeg of Mosul, a Syrian chieftain, whose command of the Moslems of his country continually threatened both the Templars and Assassins with exile from his Middle Eastern country. Against the Mosul and other potential conquerors, the Templars and Assassins assisted each other by passing between themselves secret information gathered from their extensive intelligence networks in the Middle East.[8]

But the Assassin-Templar bond goes much deeper than any superficial alliances or treaties. This is because the two orders were, in many ways, mirror images of each other. The Assassins wore long white robes with a red sash wrapped around its center to compliment their high red boots and their bright, red turbans, while the Knights Templars' costume consisted of a white gown with a red sash and a red cross emblazoned over the heart area, surmounted with a red hood. From a distance it must have nearly impossible to tell the members of the two orders apart. The Templars and Assassins also reflected each other through their three degrees of advancement. The three Assassin degrees, Fedai, Rafik, and Dai, corresponded directly to the Templar degrees of Novice, Professed and Knight, respectively. The Templars and Assassins were, in fact, so closely related that some authors have even speculated that they were one united order. Waite in *A New Encyclopedia of Freemasonry*, for example, declares that the Assassins were "the intellectual and religious kinsmen of the Sufis," while the esoteric historian Godfrey Higgins concludes in his seminal text *Anacalypsis*:

"As the society of the Assassins and Templars were (I have no doubt) of the same philosophy and religion...I believe the Templars were Assassins"[9]

Higgins unites the Assassins and Templars under the singular classification of "Sophees," a term that denotes a connection to the Sufis, the Gnostics, as well as a proficiency in the art of alchemy, the science of transformation that has been called the "Sophic Art." The practice of both Gnosticism and alchemy has been repeatedly linked to both the Templars and Assassins, and the Grand Master Assassin, Hasan-I-Sabbah, is reputed to have been one of the foremost alchemists in all of Persia.

Like the Templars, the Assassins also enrolled in the quest for the Holy Grail. The Assassins, however, identified the Holy Grail with not a cup or secred object, but with the transformative power generated externally in their alchemical laboratories and through the intake of special herbs and the daily practice of yoga and meditation. One of the Assassins' external alchemical sacraments that may have intimately influenced the rites and ideology of the Knights Templar was a very strong concoction of hashish (the name Assassin is said to be derived from hashish). This herb had, for ages, been known by the Sufis as the "Flesh of Khadir," which is a name for the ubiquitous Green Man and a legendary initiator of the Sufis. Among the Templars, Green Man Khadir became known as St. George, the archetypal knight and Templar patron who was similarly recognized as a manifestation of the Green Man (George is from Geo, meaning Earth). Both St. George and Khadir were also known by the Sufis and Assassins to be Green Man manifestations and synonymous with the Yezidhis' Melek Taus, which was a manifestation of the Green Man in the Garden of Eden scenario. Supposedly, during the induction rite of an incoming Assassin, the "Flesh of Khadir" would transport the candidate into the Green Man's paradise of Eden, after which Hasan would try to convince his students that Paradise would be theirs for eternity if they would only commit to serving him alone as one of his Assassins.

Hasan built his principal fortress upon the "Eagles Nest" of Alamut in the Elbourz or Albourz mountains of northern Iran, an area famous for its ancient links to a lineage of Persian Fisher Kings, who were probably the model for the Fisher Kings in the European Holy Grail legend known as *Parzival*. Another Holy Grail rendition, *Peredur*, which describes the Holy Grail as a severed head upon a platter, may have been influenced by an unusual rite Hasan observed at Alamut and alluded to by Arkon Daraul in *A History of Secret Societies*:

"Hasan had a deep narrow pit sunk into the floor of his audience chamber. One of his disciples stood in this in such a way that his head alone were visible above the floor. Around the neck was placed a circular disk in two pieces which fitted together, with a hole in the middle. This gave the impression that there was a severed head on a metal plate standing on the floor. In order to make the scene more plausible Hasan had some fresh blood poured around the head, on the plate.

"Now certain recruits were brought in. "Tell them" commanded the chief, "what thou has seen." The disciple then described the delights of Paradise. 'You have seen the head of a man who died whom you all knew. I have reanimated him to speak with his own tongue."

"Later, the head was treacherously severed in real earnest and stuck for some time somewhere that the faithful would see it. The effect of this conjuring trick plus murder increased the enthusiasm for martyrdom to the required degree."[10]

It was not Hasan, however, but a Syrian Assassin chief known as Rashid al-din Sinan, the legendary Old Man of the Mountain, who had the majority of contacts with the Knights Templar. Not only were Sinan's castles in closer proximity to the those occupied by the Templars than were Hasan's, but in some regards it was safer for the Templars to interact with this Assassin chief because he had shown signs of wanting to allie his order with the Templars. He had even sent a special message to King Amalric of Jerusalem in order to create an alliance between the Assassins and Christiandom, but the messenger was murdered and Sinan's potentially momentous gesture came to naught. Moreover, Sinan was safe to deal with because he was an ardent student and admirer of the Christian *Gospels*. His scholarship regarding the *Gospels* is presented in the classic text *Chronicles of the Crusades*, wherein the Assassin chief is portrayed in a debate about the *Gospels* with a certain Brother Yves, a Christian emissary who had been sent to the Assassin chief by the Templars. In one comical moment, Sinan, who was very psychic by nature, took a Christian book in his hands and proceeded to tell the flustered Brother Yves the past lifetimes of St. Peter.[11]

Sinan was even more influential in the development and dissemination of the Holy Grail Mysteries than was Hasan. His principal message was that his birth heralded the prophesied Day of Resurrection, the day when the power of the Holy Grail would transmute his followers into immortal humans. He maintained that he was the long-awaited Mahdi and an incarnation of Khadir. He wielded the power of the Holy Grail and all persons could achieve immortal life through him. He was thus a "Human Holy Grail" and probably one of the principal inspirations for the character of the Fisher King of the European Holy Grail Mysteries. Like the Fisher King, Sinan was not only full of supernatural power but he also possessed a permanent limp, which he sustained after a boulder fell upon his leg during a severe earthquake in Syria.

The Holy Grail Mysteries from Persia

As has been shown in this chapter, most of the mystery traditions that thrived in the Middle East were in some way influenced by the Sufis. The Sufis, in turn, derived the bulk of their wisdom from the East, especially Persia, a country that the Freemasonic historian Mackey calls the true home of the Sufis.[12] The Sufis infused their Persian heritage into the mystery sects they helped to found in many identifiable ways. For example, they introduced the observance of both the Persian New Year, Nuroz, as well as the celebration of the Persian Festival of Jam, and they also advocated the regular practice of certain Persian religious rites, including the daily morning worship of the rising Sun, which in Persia had been dedicated to Mithra, the god of light. Much of the Sufis' Holy Grail wisdom from Persia was eventually conveyed to Europe via their students, such as the Knights Templar, who incorporated it into their European Holy Grail Mysteries. An irrefutable Persian influence can currently be found in the European Holy Grail legend known as *Parzival,* wherein the lineage of the Fisher Kings is said to have descended from Mazadan, a distinctly Persian name and a close relative to Mazda or Ahura Mazda, the greatest deity of the Persian pantheon. It has been speculated that the name is a synthesis of Mazda and Yazda or Yazadan, the Persian word for "God." Other characters in *Parzival* also have Persian epithets, including Parzival or Parsifal, the chief protagonist of the legend whose name is a Persian for "Persian Fate;" Parzival's half-brother, Feirefiz, whose name resembles many common Persian appellations; and Parzival's father, Gahmuret, whose epithet could have been derived from Gayomart, the name of the first human being in the Persian *Avesta.* Not to be overlooked is the Holy Grail astrologer with the Persian name, Flegetanis, whose name is Persian for "Familiar with the Stars." Even the term Grail, which is commonly written as Graal or Gral in the various Grail myths, could have been derived from the Persian gohr or gohar, a term denoting "precious stone," which is the form taken by the Holy Grail in *Parzival.* It is interesting to note that when translated into German the Persian gohr becomes Perle, which is the prefix of Perlesvaus, Perceval's name in another Grail rendition known as *Perlesvaus*. It has been conjectured that Perceval may be called Li Gallois, meaning "the Foreign Knight," in some Grail legends because of his Persian origin.[13]

Recently, the authors of *From Scythia to Camelot* have revealed through their prodigious research that history also supports the migration of Holy Grail wisdom from ancient Persia. Authors Littleton and Malcor reveal that the legends of King Arthur and the Holy Grail arrived in Europe via Scythian tribes known as Sarmatians and Alans, whose equestrian knights that rode out of the Caucasus Mountains and parts of northern Iran during the first five centuries after Christ and became assimilated into the Roman provinces of Europe. These Central Asian tribes brought with them legends of swords, chalices, and knights, which collectively could have provided the raw material for the Holy Grail legends of Europe. This appears probable since the Arthurian-Grail legends did not surface in Europe until well after the neo-Scythian tribes had become established on the continent.

Perhaps the most convincing evidence of a Holy Grail migration from Scythia are the *Nart Sagas*, the "Knight Sagas," which are chivalrous legends which were passed down among the Scythian tribes of Persia and Central Asia. Littleton and Malcor suggest that Baltraz, one of the principal figures in the *Nart Sagas*, could have evolved into the character of King Arthur via the migration of the Sarmatians into Great Britain during the Roman Empire. They cite many similarities between the two figures, including the fact that both commanded a stable of knights, which for Arthur were his Knights of the Round Table and for Baltraz were his "Narts." Both figures also possess almost the exact legend regarding their last moments on Earth. While dying on the battlefield both Arthur and Batraz asked their assistants to toss their swords into specific bodies of water, and in both cases their couriers returned without completing the mission but lied and claimed that they had. Both Arthur and Batraz detected the deception of their messengers, and when their swords were later truly plunged into water as asked extraordinary results occurred just as they had expected. When Baltraz's sword reached the sea, the water boiled and turned blood red, and when Arthur's sword of Excalibur returned to the body of water it originated from it was caught by the upraised arm of the Lady of the Lake, who carried it to the bottom of the lake.

The *Nart Sagas* also reflect the European Holy Grail legends on one very crucial point. They refer to a magical chalice, a Holy Grail, that can only be touched and owned by a "knight without flaw." The Scythian Holy Grail is the Nartmongue, the "Revealer of the Narts," which continually refills itself with drink at the banquets of Scythian knights, just as the European Holy Grail is reputed to do at the table of the Arthurian knights. And just as the Arthurian Grail will only appear to the most righteous of knights, the Nartmongue elevates itself only to the lips of those knights who are "without flaw." The Nartmongue also parallels the European Holy Grail in that it was passed down within lineages of special kings while eternally protected by an order of knights.

The influence of the Scythian Alans may still be in evidence through the names of some the characters of the European Holy Grail legends, many of which incorporate "Alan." A couple of such names include Alain le Gros, who is Percival's father in *Perlesvaus*, and Elaine, who is the mother of Lancelot. The name Elaine is especially interesting because it may be a direct evolution of "Elainus," which was the name of the Alan tribe in northern Britain. But the Alans' most conspicuous contribution may be the name of Lancelot, which according to Littleton and Malcor, could be an evolution of Alanus a Lot, or "Alan of the River," thus making the fictitious knight a blood relation of the Alans.

While Littleton and Malcor were conducting their fascinating research for *From Scythia to Camelot* they discovered many other researchers who had arrived at similar conclusions regarding the Persian origin of the Holy Grail legends. The German researcher Frederick von Suhtsheck, for example, "maintained the Arthurian cycle to be of Iranian origin" and many of its various texts to be "a free translation from the Persian." Suhtsheck also asserted that Wolfram's *Parzival* was derived from the Iranian epic *Barzu-Name,* and Montsalavat, a name of the location of the Grail Castle of the Fisher King of European Grail myth, was an evolution of *sal-wadshe,* the name of a Parsee holy place.[14] Closs, another well-known researcher of Grail legend, maintained that the European Grail myth had been derived from "a long forgotten source of Persian origin," while the scholar Jean Markale and his like-minded peers added that Wolfram's entire work may have been no more than a re-writing of the Iranian *Conte de la Perle,* and definitely "Germano-Iranian."[14]

The Knights Templar

A secret code of the Knights Templar.
Does it contain the Holy Grail mysteries of the East?

A Templar Knight and an Assassin play chess.

An Assassin chief and his knight.

A Knights Templar Castle.

2
The Evolution of the European Legend of the Holy Grail

Most of the European Holy Grail legends were written during the years between the founding of the Knights Templar Order in 1118 A.D. and its dissolution in 1307 A.D. This, and the fact that these European legends were authored either by acknowledged Templar Knights or their associates, suggests that the European legends evolved from the Holy Grail Mysteries the Templars brought with them from the Middle East. This has been the conclusion of numerous researchers of the Holy Grail myth, including the 18th and 19th Templar historians Dr. F.H. von Hagen, Dr. Karl Simrock, Eugene Aroux, and J. von Hammer-Pugstall, who collectively concluded that either the European Holy Grail legends were either directly based upon the Knights Templar and their Holy Grail Mysteries, or that the Templar Order had somehow emerged out of the mysteries and discovery of the Holy Grail.[1]

The first notable European version of the Holy Grail legend was *Perceval ou le Conte du Graal*, meaning "Perceval or the Story of the Grail," written by Chrétien de Troyes, a poet living in the palatial city of Troyes, a city of northern France that modern Templar historian Karen Ralls refers to as the Templar "Order's spiritual heartland."[2] Troyes was the residence of the nobles of the royal House of Champagne, who became intimately tied to Templar history when Hughes de Champagne became the tenth Templar Knight in 1125 and then lived among the Knights in Jerusalem for two years before returning home. Hughes de Champagne is credited for having been a generous benefactor of the Templar Order and the noble patron of Hughes de Payen, the first Grand Master of the Templars from Payens, a city 8 miles north of Troyes. It was in the city Troyes that the Council of Troyes met in 1128 when the reigning Pope Urban II ratified the official rule of the Knights Templars. The Templar Rule had been designed and authored by another associate of Hughes de Champagne, Saint Bernard of Clairvaux, who, along with the Cistercian monks he presided over, also received sizable land grants from the House of Champagne. As mentioned, Bernard was closely tied to the Knights

Templar through three of the original nine Knights, his uncle Andre de Montbard, and the two Cistercian monks Gondemar and Rossal.

During his formative years in Troyes, aspiring poet and author Chrétien de Troyes was exposed to a variety of philosophical ideologies and controversial mystical sects, including the Templar Knights, who along with other European knights made themselves visible twice a year during the famous 49 day Fairs of Champagne. Chrétien, who was a scholar by nature, assimilated all the Templar lore he could lay his hands on while also expanding his worldview through the intensive study of the important Greek and Roman classics, ultimately becoming one of the premier translators of the works of Ovid. In order to round out his education, Chrétien also studied most of the world's great religions, including the meditative paths of the East, and esoteric Judaism, which was taught in Troyes by some of the foremost Talmudic scholars of his era, including the famous Rabbi Solomon ben Isaac. Chrétien also dabbled in the study of Celtic history and mythology, which had arrived in France during the 5th and 6th centuries when the British settled the western province of Brittany. Because of his prodigious study, Chrétien ultimately became such a wealth of religious and esoteric information that the moment he put pen to paper reams of diverse information would inevitably flow out of him. It is for this reason that it has been difficult to conclusively ascertain the sources he used for *Le Conte de Grail.*

During Chrétien's life the province of Champagne was ruled by Marie de Champagne, the daughter of Eleanor of Aquitaine. Marie had spent most of her earlier years at her mother's castle in Poitiers, where she was exposed to the romantic poetry of the court bards. When she subsequently met Chrétien, who was famous at the time for being one of the most foremost romantic poets of Europe and the author of *Erec and Enide*, an incipient Grail romance, Marie immediately hired him to write the Grail romance she most desired to see in print, *Lancelot.* But being of a feminist disposition, Marie tried to impress upon Chrétien to make Guinevere the dominant partner in the famous illicit affair between Arthur's queen and Lancelot, and in the process completely alienated him. Chrétien's aversion toward Marie's feminist coaching regarding *Lancelot* would not allow him to complete the poem, and the task was finally given over to another poet of Marie's choosing.

Chrétien felt much more comfortable with an assignment given him later by Philip of Alsace, the Count of Flanders and a prince of the Holy Roman Empire, who was like Chrétien a great scholar with an insatiable appetite for knowledge. Philip contracted Chrétien to author (or some say translate) the poem on the Holy Grail Mysteries that was later published as *Le Conte de Grail.*

Count Philip's desire to learn everything about the known world mirrored that of Chrétien's. He was a voracious reader and traveler, whose wanderlust had previously compelled him to travel throughout Europe and take a pilgrimage to the Middle East in 1177. In the Holy Land, he paid homage to the shrines of Jerusalem and also visited his mother, who had previously accompanied Philip's father, Robert II, to the Holy Land and then remained there as a nun at the Convent of St. Lazarus of Bethany. Philip's family was, at the time of his visit thoroughly ensconced in the political and spiritual milieu of the Kingdom of Jerusalem, and many of his cousins had ruled the kingdom as its monarch. Because of his familial ties, Philip was offered the throne as King of Jerusalem while his cousin, the incumbent monarch Baldwin IV, recovered from leprosy. But although the Count from Flanders declined the royal assignment and returned to his home in northern Europe, his interest in the Holy Land and its mysteries never waned. He returned there with the Third Crusade in 1190 and subsequently died in battle a year later during a siege of the Asia Minor city of Acre.

Philip was no doubt exposed to the Holy Grail Mysteries in the Holy Land, where he is known to have had continued interaction with the Templar Knights, even leading them into an important battle against the Saracens. But the Count's initial exposure to the Templars probably began well before that, since he was related by blood to two of the original nine Knights, Payen de Montdidier and Archambaud de St Aignan. Philip's fascination and support of the Knights Templar remained steadfast during his years in Flanders, and it became even more solid when when his country joined into an intimate alliance with Scotland, which from the time of Hughes de Payen's first European tour in 1127 had become a bastion of Templar strength and ideology. Beginning with the reign of the Scottish King David I (1153-65), a steady stream of immigrants from Flanders settled in Scotland and vice versa, thus engendering an exchange of both resources and ideas between the two countries that would continue for hundreds of years to follow.

Phillip would have also had a continuous exchange with the Knights Templar while in France, which became the Count's second home in Europe. Philip's deep connections to the country included becoming godfather, tutor and Regent to King Philip Augustus of France, who himself became a patron of the Knights Templar. King Philip eventually distinguished himself as a lay Templar Knight by leading a regiment of Templars into battle during the Third Crusade.

It was during a period between his visits to the Holy Land that Philip contacted Chrétien de Troyes. According to legend, the Count gave Chrétien an obscure book on the Holy Grail that he apparently wanted translated. It is the content of this book which, along with some editing and additions by

Chrétien, became what we know today as *Perceval: The Story of the Grail.* Since Chrétien never clarifies in his text where Philip acquired the book, we can only speculate as to its origin, but it appears to have contained distinct influences from both Middle Eastern and Great Britain. A Scottish influence in Philip's manuscript is evidenced by the Scottish place names, albeit somewhat distorted, that Chrétien used in *Le Conte du Graal.* Scottish Galloway is thus Galois in the text, Caerlaverock becomes Roche de Canguin, and Carlisle evolves into Cardoeil. A Welsh influence is also discernable, beginning with the name of Chrétien's main character, "Perceval the Welshman." Since Chrétien's *Le Conte du Graal* reflects the Welsh Grail classic *Peredur* in much of its characters and storyline, scholars have suggested that Philip's manuscript was simply a spurious copy of *Peredur.* However other academics assert that the reverse is true, that *Peredur* borrowed from *Le Conte du Graal,* and support their theory with the fact that *Peredur* was not published until 1325 A.D. as a component of the *Mabinogen,* a compilation of ancient oral Welsh myths. They also emphasize that *Peredur's* inclusion of chivalrous knights in glistening armor is far from consistent with the old Welsh legends, and that the numerous Christian references in *Peredur* do not accord with the Celtic myths of Wales, such as references to the celebration of Good Friday.

The Evolution of the Holy Grail Legend

What did Count Philip know about the Holy Grail? Perhaps Chrétien tells us in *Le Conte du Graal* when he describes the Holy Grail not as a cup or chalice, but as a platter. Unfortunately, we will never know exactly where this information came from since Chrétien died before finishing *Le Conte du Graal* and the series of Continuations that later attempted to complete the poet's work principally echoed Chrétien's original identification of the Grail. In the *First Continuation*, for example, the Holy Grail is again a platter, although now it is said to float around the Grail Castle while filling up the guests plates with delectable food, thus becoming synonymous with the Horn of Plenty of European myth.

It is not until *Joseph d' Arimathie,* which was written around 1200 A.D. by Robert de Boron from Burgundy, that the Holy Grail is first associated with the Cup of Christ that Jesus and the Apostles drank from during the Last Supper. In his anomalous rendition of the Holy Grail legend, Boron explains that Joseph left Palestine with the Cup of Christ to lead certain members of his family to England, where Joseph's brother-in-law Hebron or Bron became Guardian of the Grail and hid the cup in Glastonbury. Boron's legend was not able to survive the vicissitudes of time, however, as it was later rewritten as the *Estoire del Saint Graal*, one of a series of Grail myths comprising the

Vulgate Cycle, and the Holy Grail chalice was again portrayed in its original form as a plate or platter.

Around 1210, with the publication of *Parzival*, Wolfram von Eschenbach's masterpiece, yet another manifestation of the Holy Grail is introduced. Wolfram, who claimed to be a knight himself and probably a Templar, was explicit in stating that the true Guardians of the Grail were *Temparies*, i.e., Templar Knights, and that the Holy Grail was the "Stone of Heaven," also known as the Lapsit Exillis or Philosophers Stone, which had the power to both produce an unending supply of banquet food and alchemically transform a base metal into gold, or a person into a god. Wolfram claimed that Chrétien and the other Holy Grail authors had distorted the Holy Grail legend, so according to him the true form of the Holy Grail was a stone.

Wolfram claims that he received his wisdom regarding the Holy Grail Mysteries from a man from Provence, France, named Kyot. Kyot, who was probably a Templar Knight or associated with the Knights, had discovered the story written in Arabic in Toledo, Spain, which at the time was a center for Arabic, Persian, and Judaic studies. Although his identity remains a mystery, many Holy Grail scholars, including Albert Shulz in 1837 and Dr. Karl Simrock, the author of *The Parzival of Wolfram von Eschenbach* in 1857, have speculated that Kyot was one Guiot de Provins, a Templar Knight and frequent visitor at the court of Frederick Barbarossa who at one point is reputed to have taken a pilgrimage to Jerusalem and learned firsthand the most secret Templar mysteries. According to the authors of *The Holy Blood and The Holy Grail*, Guiot may have met Wolfram during a gathering of knights in 1184:

"Guiot is known to have visited Mayence, in Germany, in 1184. The occasion was the chivalric festival of Pentecost, at which the Holy Roman Emperor, Frederick Barbarossa, conferred knighthood on his sons. As a matter of course the ceremony was attended by poets and troubadours from all over Christendom. As a knight of the Holy Roman Empire, Wolfram would have almost certainly have been present; and it is certainly reasonable to suppose that he and Guiot met."[3]

While correcting what had become a distortion of Kyot or Guiot's manuscript, Wolfram "returned" it to its original Persian roots. Among the "corrections" he made was the addition of characters with Persian names, including Parzival, or Parsifal, the Fisher King Mazadan, and the astrologer Flegetanis. He also implied that the true legend of the Holy Grail had originated in the East long before being taken to Toledo, and he stated that it had initially been written 1200 years before Christ by a "pagan" astrologer of the

Middle East called Flegetanis. Wolfram also explicitly connects his legend to the East by beginning *Parzival* in a Middle Eastern setting with the Angevin prince Gahurmet, Parzival's father, enrolled in the service of Baruc of Balduc, the Moslem Caliph of Baghdad and "the most powerful man in the world."[4] Gahurmet continues his adventures among the Saracens by traveling south and marrying a black Moorish queen from the African country of Zazamanc, with whom he has a child, Feirefiz, who is half black and half white. Gahurmet later returns to Europe to complete his family by marrying Herzeloyde, the reigning queen of the royal lineage of Mazadan, with whom he has Parzival, thus making the lineage of Holy Grail Guardians a union of East and West families.

Wolfram's identification of the Holy Grail with a stone did not remain definitive for long. On the heals of *Parzival's* publication emerged the *Grand St. Graal,* a Holy Grail rendition that maintained that the Holy Grail was a book given to a 7th century hermit by Jesus, who had appeared to the monk in a vision. The book described the Cup of Christ and the entire history of the Holy Grail, but makes it clear that the chalice is not necessary for enlightenment. Just by reading the book the hermit received the same transformative effect he would have acquired from holding the Cup of Christ.

The answer as to the true identification and caretakers of the Holy Grail ostensibly arrived with the publication of *Perlesvaus,* or *The High History of the Holy Grail*, which is a rendering of the Holy Grail legend written between 1220-1230 by an anonymous author that some scholars contend was a Templar Knight.[5] *Perlesvaus* unites elements of Robert de Boron's *Joseph d'Arimathie* with Wolfram's *Parzival* while jointly placing the Templar Knights and the family of Joseph of Arimathea as co-Guardians of the Holy Grail. In fact, they seem to be one and the same. Joseph himself appears to be a Templar Knight in the text by bearing a Templar-like white shield embossed with a large red cross. The author of *Perlesvaus* also reveals that the Holy Grail is not restricted to one definitive shape by having King Arthur beholding five different forms of it in rapid succession. The author has these forms emerge out of and then dissolve back into an energy field or aura, thereby apparently identifying the true Holy Grail to be the pure, etheric life force, the substance that precedes all physical form. In reference to Knight Gawain's vision of this amorphous energy field, the author of *Perlesvaus* states:

"Sir Gawain gazes at the Grail, and it seems to him that there is a chalice within it, although at the same time there is none."

3

A Multitude of Holy Grails

Taken as a whole, the various European Holy Grail legends that evolved out of the Holy Grail Mysteries of the East are explicit in revealing that there is not one, but numerous forms that the Holy Grail can take. Collectively, these legends assert that the Holy Grail can be anything from the platter championed by Chrétien de Troyes, the Cup of Christ alluded to by Robert de Boron, or the Stone of Heaven promulgated by Wolfram von Eschenbach in *Parzival*. Although it may seem confusing to those who equate the Holy Grail solely with the Cup of Christ, the Holy Grail was *never* meant to be only one object. In fact, states Grail researcher Emma Jung, Chrétien de Troyes was explicit in the very first Holy Grail rendition, *Le Conte du Graal*, when he stated that his Grail platter was "*a* Grail, not *the* Grail," thereby opening the "doors of perception" to the existence of many Grails.[1]

The San Greal

In this chapter we will cover many of the important Holy Grail manifestations that have historically manifested around the world. But first we will present the criteria for determining a true Holy Grail. First of all, and perhaps most importantly, a Holy Grail must possess the power to bestow health and immortality on those who come into contact with it. Secondly, it must conform to some definition of the term "Grail." The first of such definitions was popularized in the 13th century by Helinandus, a Cistercian chronicler and therefore possibly a Templar affiliate. He maintained that the word Grail was derived from the Latin "Gradale," and then stated:

"Gradalis or Gradale means a dish (a scutella), wide and somewhat deep, in which costly viands are wont to be served to the rich in degrees (gradatim), one morsel after another in different rows. In popular speech it is also called "greal" because it is pleasant (grata) and acceptable to him eating therein."

Thus, Helinandus' interpretation of a Grail or Gradale reveals that it is not only a platter, but anything that is greal or agreeable. This unusual notion is corroborated by the author of the European Holy Grail legend known as the *Didot Perceval*, who in reference to the Holy Grail states "...we call it Grail, because it please us men."

But Helinandus' definition only holds true if the word Grail had a Latin origin. By contrast, some scholars assert that the word is originally derived from the Persian gohr or gohar, a term denoting "precious stone." Thus, the Holy Grail can, from this perspective, also be a Stone of Heaven or Philosophers Stone.

In more recent times another definition of Holy Grail has become popular with the publication of the book *The Holy Blood and The Holy Grail.* Through careful research and etymology the authors of this text discovered that San Greal, the "Holy Grail," could (or perhaps should) be written as Sang Real, which would thus give it the meaning of "Royal Blood" or "Holy Blood." The holy blood referred to is, state authors Baigent, Liegh and Lincoln, the sacred bloodline of Jesus Christ.

Thus, all sources of etymology point to there being a multitude of possible forms a Holy Grail can take. But there are a few standard manifestations of the Holy Grail, which have been identified in the Grail text known as *La Folie Perceval*. Collectively known as the Holy Grail Hallows, these four forms of the Grail include a cup or chalice, a sword, a spear, and a platter or a stone. This chapter will present the most important manifestations worldwide of these four primary forms of the Holy Grail..

The Holy Grail Chalices

The most famous historical manifestation of all Holy Grails is the **Cup of Christ** or **Joseph of Arimathea's Cup**. This is the vessel that Joseph of Arimathea used to catch the blood and sweat of the Messiah after he was taken down from the Cross, and it is also the chalice that Jesus passed among his disciples as part of the first communion during the Last Supper. According to Robert de Boron's version of the Holy Grail legend, *Joseph d'Arimathie*, Joseph traveled to England with the Cup of Christ right after being incarcerated within a Jerusalem prison, where the Jewish authorities had placed him after the body of Jesus suspiciously disappeared from its tomb. During one day in his cell Joseph found the Cup of Christ suddenly and miraculously placed at his feet by God, who then proceeded to explain "the secrets of the Grail," which are the secrets of the Eucharist and how the rites of that sacrament reflect the Passion of Christ. Joseph was kept alive for many years by food and drink that would spontaneously manifest in he Cup of Christ, and he continued to do so until Jerusalem was conquered by the Roman Emperor Vespasian and he was suddenly released from prison. Fearing re-imprisonment and renewed torture from both the Jews and Romans, Joseph escaped with his family to the desert, where both he and they were continually sustained by the sacred Cup of Christ. Joseph died soon after this exodus, but not before placing the Cup into the care of his brother-in-law, Bron, whose inner guidance subsequently lead him north to Glastonbury, Britain, where he was told to deposit the Grail.

Thus, in de Boron's version of the Grail it is Bron that carries the Cup of Christ to Glastonbury, however more popular versions of the same legend claim that it was Joseph himself who brought the chalice to the sacred city in England. According to the myth's popular rendition, when Joseph was still in Jerusalem the Archangel Gabriel appeared to both him and eleven other missionaries and then instructed them to travel to Glastonbury in order to build a church in England dedicated to Mary, the mother of Jesus. Leaving Palestine with the Cup of Christ in tow, Joseph and his entourage finally reached the coast of Britain after a very long journey. Then, after sailing down an inlet leading to Glastonbury, which at the time was a marshland covered with water, they finally disembarked on an island now known as Wearyall Hill, which refers to the weary state the group arrived in. It was here that Joseph planted his famous staff into the ground and watched with jubilation as it immediately sprouted leaves and flowers, thus signaling to himself and his companions that they had completed their journey. Today, Wearyall Hill is part of a "Zodiac Landscape" that is comprised of terrestrial landmarks mirroring the twelve Zodiacal signs of the heavens. Within this terrestrial Zodiac Wearyall Hill is located in the twelfth and last sign of the astrological Zodiac, Pisces, which represents both Piscean "fish," including the fish symbol of Christ, as well as endings, such as the ending of Joseph's journey.[2]

Once settled in their new homeland Joseph and his companions followed Gabriel's instructions and constructed St. Mary's Chapel, which became the first Christian church in Europe.12 dwellings were thereafter built in a circle around this chapel, each of which faced the central temple, which thus became building number thirteen, the number of the Christ. It is believed that the Cup of Christ was placed within this central Chapel, thereby uniting the Grail Cup with its owner, the spirit of the Christ. Joseph's little Chapel was eventually torn down and a larger chapel rose to take its place, one that would later be incorporated into the structure of Glastonbury Abbey. But before Joseph died, it is said that he buried the Cup of Christ in one of the mounds of Glastonbury now known as Chalice Hill. Or, states an alternate myth, Joseph secreted his Holy Grail in the Chalice Well, where today blood-stained, iron-rich water, symbolizing the blood of the Messiah, continually flows out to nourish and heal all who bathe in it or drink it.

But more contradictory legends abound, including one that states that Joseph did not die in Britain, but that he left Glastonbury soon after constructing St. Mary's Chapel and sailed south to Spain with his Holy Grail. Supposedly he landed at Barcelona and then proceeded overland to either Montserrat in the Pyrenees or Montsegur in France, two mountain refuges that later became linked to the Cup of Christ or some manifestation of the Holy Grail. Since Joseph's era, both of these mysterious mountains have often been equated with Montsalavat, the holy mountain of Grail legend upon which the Holy Grail is said to be interred in the Grail Castle of the Fisher King.

Which of the legends regarding Joseph can be relied upon? Discerning the truth becomes an even more odious task in light of the growing body of evidence that asserts that Joseph did not bring a cup to Britain as thought, but arrived instead with two cruets or small flasks of "white and silver." The image of Joseph and his two cruets containing the blood and sweat of Jesus has become a popular theme of poets, historians, and artists, who have placed stained-glass images of Joseph with his two vials in strategic British churches, such as the Church of Saint John the Baptist in Glastonbury and All Saints Church in Langport. And even though one legend asserts that the flasks remain buried with Joseph in Glastonbury, some scholars claim that they have since been located and remain in the care of private collectors or in museums. According to them, Joseph's vials currently exist as the **Hawstone Park Vial** and the **Zingaro Templar Vial**. The Hawstone Park Vial, which is a small onyx flask found hidden within a statue in Hawstone Park in Shropshire, England, has the size and shape of Joseph's legendary cruets. It is also nearly identical to the Zingaro Templar Vail, Joseph's supposed second vial, the location of which first came to light in a 1995 article featured in *The Boston Globe* that proclaimed that "the Holy Grail had been discovered in Italy."[3] The newspaper described the Zingaro Vail, which has since proven to be a close match to the vials depicted with Joseph, as a small green flask, two to three inches in length, that had for sometime been in the possession of Rocco Zingaro di San Fernando, the Grand Master of an Italian branch of the Knights Templar [4] Supposedly the vial had been given to Zingaro by Antonio Ambrosini, another Templar, who discovered it in a Coptic monastery in Egypt. It is probable that the Zingaro Templar Vail arrived in England with Joseph and was later taken to Egypt; or perhaps Joseph deposited the vial in Egypt after leaving Palestine on his way to England. Either way, *The Boston Globe* is conclusive that at least one Holy Grail manifestation was in the protection of the Templars just as Grail legend suggests.[5]

But even Joseph's two cruets must be considered suspect as manifestations of *the* Holy Grail since another set of dual cruets filled with the blood and sweat of Christ are also reputed to have been taken out of the Middle East following the Messiah's death. The owner of these vials was Nicodemus, who, like his close friend Joseph, similarly gathered up the blood and sweat that rolled off the Messiah's body while assisting in the preparation of Jesus' body before its internment. In order to hide his precious cruets, Nicodemus is said to have secreted them inside an image of the crucified Christ that he carved himself, which many scholars today claim is still in existence as the **Volto Santo**, a wooden crucifix that currently hangs in Saint Martin's Cathedral in Lucca, Italy. Identified as a legitimate Holy Grail manifestation in the Grail rendition known as the *First Continuation*, the Volto Santo arrived in Italy after being hidden for many years in Palestine, during which it was in the care of the descendants of one Isaac or Isaachar, a member of the early Church whom Nicodemus hand picked to guard the Volto Santo just before he died. Following the arrival of the Volto Santo in Italy its two cruets of blood were quickly discovered within the image's head by the bishops of Luni and Lucca, each of whom took one and placed it within his respective cathedral.

Complicating things even further is a third person who is reputed to have assisted Joseph and Nicodemus in wiping down the crucified body of Jesus before capturing his blood and sweat in a vessel. This was Mary Magdalene, whose Holy Grail vessel is her famous white alabaster jar. The legend of Mary's jar begins in France, where it was initially discovered alongside her skeletal remains and supposedly holding a few drops of Jesus' dried blood. According to the *Golden Legend* written by the French Archbishop Jacobus de Voragine, Mary had completed her life in France after having arrived in the country years before in a boat crewed by her sister Martha and her brother Lazarus. They were accompanied to France by Jesus' aunts, Mary Jacobi and Mary Salome, and one of Jesus' seventy-two disciples, St. Maximim. Apparently Mary and her companions originally set sail in Palestine right after the Ascension. Against their will they were set aimlessly adrift by "heathens" on the turbulent Mediterranean Sea "without any tackle or rudder…for to be drowned." Fortunately, states the legend, "by the purveyance of Almighty God" they eventually landed safely in the French coastal city of Marseilles.

Today, especially since the publication of *The Holy Blood and The Holy Grail,* Mary's Holy Grail has become synonymous with her own body, which became the vessel for the blood of Christ when she was supposedly impregnated by the Messiah previous to his crucifixion. Mary may have been pregnant with a child when she left Palestine, or she could have already given birth to a daughter when she left the Holy Land.

Although radical in light of traditional Christian theology, the notion that Jesus married Mary Magdalene and had a child with her is entirely possible since it was common for Jewish Rabbis, such as Jesus, to marry. In fact, to mate and bare offspring was their obligation to society. Although it is little known, some of Jesus' Apostles, including Saint Peter, fulfilled their Jewish obligation by marrying.[6]

According to Margaret Starbird, author of *The Woman with the Alabaster Jar*, Jesus and Mary Magdalene did have a child together and her name was Sarah, whom some traditions assert was a black-skinned servant girl that accompanied Mary on the boat to France. In France, Sarah supposedly married into the Frankish line of kings and thereby became a matriarch of French royalty. Perhaps Sarah, which is Hebrew for "Princess," was specially chosen to mate with the French monarchy because of her own royal blood.

There are, however, numerous objections to this theory. Why would Jesus and Mary have given birth to a black-skinned girl? And why are there no references to historical black-skinned Frankish kings? It is thus possible that rather than Mary and Jesus having conceived a physical child, black-skinned Sarah, who is known by gypsies everywhere as Sarah Kali, the "Black Queen," may instead be a personification of the "black" or destructive/transformative aspect of the female power of the Holy Grail that moved from the Master Jesus into his disciple Mary. This alchemical power, which is known as synonymous with Kali in India, could, from a metaphorical perspective, be conceived of as the Magdalene's "handmaiden" or "servant girl." The first Black Madonnas of France, whose proliferation corresponded to the arrival of Mary and Sarah and probably represented the mother and child, could be proof of this. These incipient Black Madonnas were carved from highly charged meteorites, the fallen stones that embodied the Holy Grail power, thus possibly denoting the alchemical power wielded by the Magdalene. Because of the alchemical power ascribed to her, Mary was eventually acknowledged by her worshippers to be an incarnation of Venus, whose Asiatic forms were also meteorites and who was venerated as the patroness of alchemy.[7] Besides her association with Venus, Mary's special affiliation with the power of the Holy Spirit might also be intrinsic to her name, Magdalene, which is derived from the town she was born in, Magdala, the "Village of Doves."[8] The dove is the eternal symbol of the power and wisdom of the Holy Spirit.

The accepted French legend has it that Mary Magdalene died around 75 A.D. after spending the last forty years of her life as a hermit in a cave in the hill region of Saint Baume even though current depictions of her in southern France portray her evangelizing to the masses during that time.[9] After her transition, Mary's body was interred by her brother disciple, St. Maximin, in the chapel he administered in the village of Villalata, which was later renamed St. Maximin in his honor. Between the 3rd and 4th centuries, Mary's body was placed in an ornate white marble coffin, where it remained until 710 A.D., when Saracens invading southern France compelled Cassian monks to move her remains into a less ostentatious coffin and bury it. Finally, in 1279, Mary's tomb was rediscovered by Charles, a nephew of King Louis IX of France. Her bones and accompanying sacred objects were dug up and became part of her Sacred Relics, which were subsequently interred in the Basilique Sainte Madeleine. Today, Mary's Relics reside within in the French village of Vezelay, and her skull is the centerpiece of an annual procession through the streets of St. Maximin.

Unfortunately, the whereabouts of Mary's alabaster jar currently remains a mystery. One legend suggests that it eventually became one of the prized possessions of the Cathars, a group of Gnostics who were exterminated in 1244 by a crusade organized by Pope Innocent and his Inquisition. According to this legend, leading up to their final decimation on March 1, the Cathars took their most sacred books and artifacts, which included both the Holy Shroud and a version of the Holy Grail – possibly Mary's alabaster jar and/or Joseph's Cup of Christ – and then sought refuge in their nearly impenetrable mountain-top fortress of Montsegur, the principal seat of the Cathar Church since the year 1230. While their fortress was under siege by soldiers of the Inquisition, two or more Cathars are believed to have clandestinely escaped with many of the Cathar treasures, including both the Shroud and Mary's Holy Grail, and then to have hid them in the surrounding countryside. The recovery of the Cathar relics in southern France has been an obsession of treasure hunters ever since.

Could Mary's Holy Grail still exist somewhere in the south of France? As strange as it sounds, Mary's Grail may have been discovered and moved to another location by Hitler's Nazis. In 1931, Otto Rahn, a German who believed himself to have been a Cathar in a previous incarnation, was sent to Montsegur by Hienrich Himmler to search for the lost Cathar treasures. Rahn discovered tunnels and caverns beneath Montsegur, but he died mysteriously before he was able to extract any of the treasure interred within them. Another SS officer, Otto Skorzeny, was then dispatched by Himmler to complete the job, and according to one eye witness account he was later seen leaving Montsegur with a plane load of relics headed for Himmler's secret mountain fortress of Berchtesgaden. Then, states an additional eye witness account from the end of World War II, a German Heinkel 277 V-1 left Salzburg, Austria, bound for the East, possibly Nepal or Tibet, with a plane load of cargo believed to include the ancient Cathar relics. According to Howard Buechner, a retired U.S. Army Colonel, on board the German plane were also "twelve stone tablets of the Germanic Grail, which contained the key to ultimate knowledge." [10]

Mary's Holy Grail could, therefore, currently either reside in southern France or in the East. But, like so many legends of its kind, the final destination of Mary's alabaster jar is still open to debate. One alternate ending of its odyssey asserts that the Nazis eventually transported Mary's Holy Grail from Berchtesgaden to Antarctica by a clandestine submarine and it now resides within a stone obelisk marking a cave in the Muhlig-Hoffman Mountains. This mysterious cave, known as the Emerald Cave, is supposedly linked by tunnels to caverns inside the Earth, where a subterranean civilization my even exist. Interestingly, the Antarctic cave's association with an emerald links Mary's Holy Grail with the Stone of Heaven, a large emerald referred to by Wolfram Eschenbach in *Parzival* as being the true Holy Grail.

Further complicating the current whereabouts of Mary's Grail are rumors that her vessel was not a jar but a cup, and that it never even left Palestine. Some scholars content that it was part of the **Arma Christi**, the "Weapons of Christ," which is a name for the relics of the Passion that were discovered in Jerusalem where Jesus was supposedly crucified. According to the 5th century historian Olympiodorous, Mary's Grail, referred to as the **Marian Chalice**, was discovered by excavators working for the Empress Helena, the mother of King Constantine, as they sifted through the earth in the area of Golgotha, the reputed location of the Crucifixion. After its retrieval the cup was first taken to Constantinople and then to Rome, where it resided until the city was sacked by the Visigoths, at which point it was transferred to a secret location in England, possibly Glastonbury. According to the Brit Graham Philips, author of *The Search for the Grail*, the Marian Chalice was taken to the English Midlands, where for centuries as a stone cup made of onyx it was carefully preserved by the Peverel family of Whittington Castle. Sometime in the mid 19th century, a Peverel descendent transferred the cup to a hidden stone grotto, where it was later found by Walter Langham in the early 20th century and kept by his family. When Philips discovered the location of the Langham family nearly one hundred years later, he also found the onyx vessel. Since then, the jar has been dated by the British Museum and found to be a spice jar used during the first century after Christ.

But Philips' conclusion that the Peverel cup is one and the same as the Marian Chalice has not gained wide acceptance. Many Grail scholars maintain that after reaching England the Marian Chalice became known as the **Nanteos Cup**, which is a vessel made of olive wood and therefore a better candidate for being a household drinking cup used in Jerusalem during the time of Jesus than one made out of metal or stone. Supposedly the Nanteos Cup, currently owned by the Powel family of Wales, was hidden within one of the walls of Glastonbury Abbey for many years after arriving in England from Rome, where it had previously resided for hundreds of years following its sequester in Palestine. When Glastonbury Abbey was threatened with complete destruction at the hands of the iconoclastic King Henry VIII, the wooden cup was taken by the Abbey's monks to the Nanteos Manor in Wales and kept there by them for safekeeping. When the last guardian monk was near death he asked the Lord of Nanteos Manor to safeguard the wooden cup "until the church claims her own."[11] Later, in 1878, the Powels of Nanteos Manor put the Nanteos Cup on public display and it has since become a national treasure.

Another chalice reputed to be a Holy Grail that remained in Palestine for many years after the Ascension is the **Great Chalice of Antioch**. This chalice, which was discovered in Antioch during the last century along with a smaller chalice and a cross could be the true Marian Chalice, or if not, it may be Joseph of Arimathea's Cup of Christ. Dated from the first to the fourth centuries and now residing in the New York Metropolitan Museum of Art, the Antioch Chalice has been set into an ornate silver reliquary and decorated with images of Jesus and the Apostles. Some antiquarians maintain that the Chalice of Antioch arrived in the city of Antioch via the Crusaders, who were returning a sacred chalice, perhaps Joseph's cup, to its rightful place in the Holy Land. But although the cup is very old, most experts have concluded that the Chalice of Antioch is too large and not antiquated enough to be the original Cup of Christ.

According to the Vatican, as well as to certain Templar historians who emphasize its historical links to the Knights Templar, the true Cup of Christ is currently in the possession of the Catholic Church and known as the **Santo Caliz of Valencia**. The Santo Caliz, meaning "Holy Chalice,"currently resides in the Cathedral of Valencia in Spain. It is a stone cup made out of a type of red agate called "Oriental Cornerina" that sits upon an ornate base studded with 27 pearls, 2 rubies, and 2 emeralds.[12] While the agate cup dates from the time of Christ, its decorative base was added much later.

Like most of the western Holy Grail manifestations, the history of the Santo Caliz of Valencia is full of capricious twists and turns. According to its accepted history, after Joseph of Arimathea filled it with the blood and sweat of Christ the Santo Caliz was first taken to Antioch and then to Rome by St.

Peter, where it became the principal cup used by the early popes during the Eucharist or Holy Communion. Then, in approximately 258 A.D., or around the time that the Roman Emperor Valerianus was regularly persecuting many bishops and other high-ranking Catholic Church officials, a Vatican soldier took the Santo Caliz to Spain with an accompanying letter that read: "Please give this to Orencio and Paciencia," two priests of the Church of Huesca.[13] The Holy Grail safely resided in Huesca until 713, when the Moslems invaded Spain and the cup was quickly removed to a more inconspicuous location. First it was taken to a cave in the Pyrenees, and later it was embedded in the wall of the Chapel of San Pedro de Siresa. Then, approximately a century later, the Santo Caliz was passed around again, this time to the Cathedral of Jaca and then to the Monastery of San Juan de la Pena, an abbey that was built inside of a nearly inaccessible cave. Here in this hidden cave Don Alfonso, a revolutionary warrior who sought to conquer Spain, mobilized a group of neo-Templar Knights to fight in his service. Legend has it that all these knights swore an oath of fidelity to Don Alfonso and his cause while kneeling in front of the "Grail."[14]

The Santo Caliz remained within the Monastery of San Juan de la Pena until 1399, when Martin V, the King of Aragon, removed the cup to the chapel of the Royal Palace of Zaragoza. There it remained until 1424, when King Alfonso V took the cup to the Palacio Real in Valencia. Finally, in 1437, the Santo Caliz found its final resting place when King Alfonso's brother, King Juan I of Navarra, transported the cup to its present location in the Cathedral of Valencia in Spain.

But while the Santo Caliz fits the historical criteria of the Cup of Christ, it does not meet the criteria established by many Grail authors. Some of these authors, such as Wolfram von Eschenbach, were Templar Knights or neo-Templars who claimed that the true Grail was made of emerald. Of the surviving Holy Grail manifestations, only one cup meets their criteria. This is the **Sacro Catino**, which for many hundreds of years was believed to be carved directly out of a huge emerald although recently its composition has been determined to be that of glass. Now on display in the Treasury of San Lorenzo in Genoa, Italy, its eight-sided octagonal shape also makes it an alchemical vessel with the ostensible power to bestow immortality.

Another legendary cup believed to have been carved out of pure emerald but now lost to history is **Solomon's Chalice**. Solomon's Chalice is reputed to have been carved from the emerald that dislodged from Lucifer's crown during the war in Heaven and then fell to Earth where it was discovered by sailors after it plunged into the Mediterranean Sea. The sailors took the emerald to King Solomon, a world renowned alchemist, who then had it carved into an alchemical chalice. Although not much more is known of Solomon's Chalice, according to the famous Russian explorer and painter Nicholas Roerich, legends of it abound in Russia's Solovetz Monastery. After studying these legends, Roerich remarked: "Great is the Chalice of Solomon, fashioned from precious stone. On the Chalice are inscribed three verses in Sumerian characters and no one can explain them."[15]

Holy Grails Worldwide

Besides Palestine, Holy Grails have also been accounted for in many other parts of the globe. One such Holy Grail, the **Sumerian Grail**, was discovered in that part of the Middle East that was previously the cultured land of Mesopotamia. In *The Holy Grail, Its Legends and Symbolism*, author Arthur Edward Waite asserts that he learned of this Grail vessel by one of his colleagues, Dr. Waddell, who apparently had a piece of it in his possession that he had acquired from excavators working in conjunction with the Pennsylvania University Expedition in the Middle East. Waddell claimed that his fragment of the Sumerian Grail had been discovered in the foundations of a tower belonging to "the oldest Sun Temple in Mesopotamia,"[16] where it had anciently been hidden by King Udu of Kish, the "King of the Hidden Vessel." King Udu was the great-grandson of King Dur or Tur, the first Sumerian king and original owner of the chalice, who had apparently captured the cup from "aboriginal Chaldean Serpent-Worshippers"[17] when he replaced dragon worship with a Sun-Cult. King Dur then engraved the vessel with "the oldest known historical inscription in the world," which contained a genealogy of the ancient Sumerian kings.

One of the renowned Holy Grails of Central Asia is today known as the **Jami-Jamshid**, the Cup of Jamshid, which was found by the legendary Persian King Jamshid when he was excavating the city of Istaker in central Asia. Jamshid's radiant chalice, which was "made of turquoise and filled with the precious nectar of Life,"[18] could both reveal the future and transform a human being into an immortal god. King Jamshid is averred to have lived twenty thousand years ago, so the Jami-Jamshid is at least that old.

The existence of Holy Grails in the Far East have been recorded by many western explorers, such as the Russian Nicholas Roerich. When the famous artist journeyed across China and Mongolia in the 1920s, the existence of one of these magical Grails, the **Chalice of Buddha**, was revealed to him by Buddhist monks. The monks maintained that the history of the chalice was contained within a *Jataka*, an anecdotal story extracted directly from the life of Buddha, which Roerich recounts in the diary of his journey, *The Heart of Asia*:

"…from the four lands came the four guardians of the world who offered chalices made of sapphire. But the Buddha refused them. Again they offered four chalices made of black stone (muggavanna) and he, full of compassion for the four wise men, accepted the four chalices. He placed one inside the other and ordained, "Let there be one!" And the edges of the four became visible as outlines. All the Chalices formed one. The Buddha accepted food in the newly formed Chalice and, having partaken of food, he offered thanks."[19]

Roerich acquired additional information about the Chalice of Buddha as he passed through Asian territories that had at different times been sanctuaries to the cup, such as the eastern Chinese city of Karashahr. In regards to the cup's various resting places, Roerich states:

"Karashahr is …the last resting place of the Chalice of Buddha, as cited by the historians. The Chalice of the Blessed One was brought here from Peshwar and disappeared here. It is said, "The Chalice of Buddha will be found again when the time of Shambhala approaches."

"Purushapura, or Peshawar, was for many years the City of the Chalice of Buddha. After the death of the Teacher, the Chalice was brought to Peshwar, where it long remained the object of deep reverence. About 400 B.C., during the time of the Chinese traveler Fa-hsien, the Chalice was still at Peshwar, in a monastery especially built for it. It was of many colors, with black predominating, and the outlines of the four chalices that composed it were clearly visible.

"In about 630 A.D., during the time of Hsuan-tang, another Chinese traveler, the Chalice was no longer at Peshwar. It was already in Persia or in Karashahr."[20]

Another legendary Holy Grail of the Far East is China's **Royal Cauldron**, which is a large golden pot known to have once brought long life and prosperity to some of the early Chinese emperors. The Royal Cauldron was especially renowned for its alchemical properties; and in this regard legends assert that the pot magically manifested within itself the ingredients of the elixir of immortality for the righteous Emperor Hung-ti and the beneficent Emperor Wu of the Han Dynasty. But the Golden Cauldron would only assist those emperors who followed a righteous path and governed their kingdoms in a way that was in harmony with the Divine Will. Otherwise, as in the case of the evil Emperor Shi Huang-ti of the Chin Dynasty, the Royal Cauldron would mysteriously disappear and remain hidden until a more well-disposed ruler ascended the throne of China.

The Holy Grail Spears

Another one of the Grail Hallows that has multiple manifestations worldwide is the Holy Spear. Like the Holy Grail Chalices, some of the Holy Spears have similarly been ascribed special powers related to healing and longevity. And just like the Holy Chalice that belonged to the Fisher King of the European Holy Grail Mysteries and was a composite of Holy Cups everywhere, all Holy Spears were synthesized into a composite Holy Spear which, as part of a "Grail" procession that included all the Holy Grail Hallows, was regularly paraded through the Grail Castle in front of the Fisher King and his guests. This Holy Spear of legend possessed the power to heal the wounded thigh of the crippled Fisher King, and was alternately used by both Percival and Gallahad in various Grail legends for this purpose. Certain renderings of the Holy Grail legend, such as Wagner's opera *Parsifal*, even elevate the Holy Grail Spear to a position superior to that of even the Holy Grail Chalice.

There are currently four historical Holy Grail Spears located in Europe and Asia, each of which has submitted its own claim for the right to be called the **Spear of Longinus**, or the **Spear of Destiny**, which the Roman centurion Caius Cassius, a.k.a. Longinus, used to pierce the side of Christ during the Crucifixion. The most credible claimant currently lies interred within one of the massive columns supporting St. Peter's Basilica in Rome. Supposedly this manifestation of the Holy Spear came into the possession of Pope Innocent VIII after the Holy See received it in exchange for a prisoner, the brother of the Turkish Sultan of Bajazet. This spear, which is believed to have originally been part of the Arma Christ, was initially put on display in the Holy Sepulchre, where the historian Arculpus is reputed to have seen it in 670. Then, sometime between the 8th century and the year 1375, when it was seen there by Sir John Mandeville, the spear was taken to Constantinople and interred in one of the city's fabulous palaces. There it remained until the 15th century, when marauding Turks claimed it as there own.

It is, however, acknowledged that the spear at St. Peter's Basilica only possesses the lower portion of the blade of the Spear of Longinus. The upper portion of the lance was broken off and began a separate destiny in 615 A.D., when Jerusalem was raided by the Persian King Chosroes. Then, states the historical account known as the *Chronicon Paschale*, the tip came into the possession of one Nicetas, who took the relic to Constantinople and interred it within the Church of St. Sophia, which at the time was the greatest church of Christendom. Later, during the Crusades, the tip was acquired by King Baldwin II, the second monarch of Jerusalem and patron of the Templars, who gave it to St. Louis in hopes of garnering military support from the French king for his territorial holdings in Outremer. After King Louis had the tip specially interred within the Church of Saint Chapelle it remained untouched until the French Revolution, when it was transferred to the Bibliotheque Nationale in Paris. After that time the whereabouts of the tip after the French Revolution becomes shrouded in mystery, and so for now it must lamentably remain one of history's great loses.

But not all scholars are in agreement that the spear interred in a column of St. Peter's is the true Spear of Longinus. Some academics claim that the Vatican's pretentious spear is really the Holy Spear known as the **Antioch Spear**, which was discovered by the Crusaders in the city of Antioch. Legends have it that the Crusader Peter Bartholomew was shown the location of this spear by St. Andrew in a dream and told it would lead his brethren to victory in a pivotal battle with the Saracens. The Crusaders, who found the spear the following day after prying up floor stones in the basement under St. Peter's Cathedral in Antioch, were convinced that they had discovered the prized Spear of Longinus and subsequently offered it to the Emperor of Constantinople, who at the time possessed one of the three other Holy Grail Spears and thus believed that he was already in possession of the true lance. History is vague on whether the Antioch Spear eventually ended up in one of St. Peter's columns after leaving Constantinople, but many Armenian Christians are convinced that it is currently in their church of Etschmiadzin, Armenia. However, to many experts the point is moot. It has recently been determined by them that the Antioch Spear cannot possibly the Spear of Longinus because its blade is the head of a Roman standard, not a lance.

A third claimant for the distinction of the Spear of Longinus is the **Lance of St. Maurice**. This is the spear that is commonly known today as the Spear of Destiny, which is the Holy Spear recently made popular by Trevor Ravenscroft in his book *The Spear of Destiny.* Ravenscroft maintains that a lineage of 45 emperors of the Holy Roman Empire used this spear to empower and authenticate their reigns as world monarchs. He also states that this is the spear that Hitler plundered from the Hapsburg Treasure House Museum in Vienna as part of his plan to resurrect the Holy Roman Empire in the form of his Third Reich.

The long history of the Lance of St. Maurice begins with the incipient Holy Roman Emperor, King Constantine, whom legends maintain created the blade for the Holy Spear out of one of the three nails found by his mother Helena among the Arma Christi. After its creation, Constantine made his replica of the Spear of Longinus his constant companion, and it is said that he won many battles with it by his side. Besides linking it to Jesus, Constantine also apparently related the spear to Mithras, the patron of all Roman kings and soldiers, whose symbol, a burning spear with attached Labarum, the Chi-

Rho, appeared to the monarch previous to the decisive victory on the Milvan Bridge outside Rome that catapulted him into the office of Roman emperor.

Following Constantine, the Spear of Destiny was passed down through a long line of Holy Roman emperors that included Charlemagne, Otto I, Frederick Barbarossa, and Frederick II, an enlightened monarch who moved the lance to Nuremberg, the spiritual center of the Holy Roman Empire. When the line of Austrian Hapsburg kings subsequently ruled the Empire, the Spear of Destiny was taken from Nuremberg and placed in a museum in Vienna, Austria. This is where it remained until the time of Third Reich, when Hitler decided it was essential to return it to Germany in order to resurrect the empire.

According to Ravenscroft, who received the bulk of his information from Dr. Walter Johannes Stein, a personal acquaintance of Hitler's during his earlier years, the future Fuehrer of the Third Reich would often spend entire afternoons in the Hapsburg Treasure House Museum admiring the Spear of Destiny. His plan to found a new Holy Roman Empire may have first taken hold of him one day when a museum tour stopped next to him and paused to examine the spear. He recollection of the event is recorded in his autobiography, *Mein Kampf*:

"These foreigners stopped almost immediately in front of where I was standing (in the Treasure House), while their guide pointed to an ancient Spearhead. At first I didn't even bother to listen to what this expert had to say about it, merely regarding the presence of the party as an intrusion into the privacy of my own despairing thoughts. And then I heard the words which were to change my whole life: "*There is a legend associated with this Spear that whoever claims it, and solves its secrets, holds the destiny of the world in his hands for good or evil.*"

Other Holy Grails of the Arma Christi

Besides the Marian Chalice, the Lance of Longinus, and the nails of the True Cross that became the Lance of St. Maurice, other relics comprising the relics of the Passion discovered in Jerusalem have similarly been accorded the status of Holy Grails. These articles include wooden pieces of the True Cross, the sponge that the Roman soldiers used to give the crucified Christ a drink of wine and vinegar, and the Crown of Thorns. These objects became Holy Grails by absorbing the Holy Grail power radiating from the body of the Messian.

The Crown of Thorns

After its discovery in Jerusalem by the excavators of Queen Helena, the Crown of Thorns was interred within a church situated upon Mt. Sion. Later, during his reign as King of Jerusalem in the 12th century, Baldwin II presented both the crown and the tip of the Spear of Longinus to St. Louis, who placed them both in the Church of Saint Chapelle, an edifice built especially for them in 1248. The relics were later placed in the Bibliothéque Nationale for safekeeping during the French Revolution, but unlike the tip of the Holy Spear, the Crown of Thorns did not disappear from the world stage but found safe haven in the Cathedral of Notre Dame, the sanctuary which continues to protect it today. Some of the Crown's thorns were, however, removed at different times during the relic's capricious history, so it is currently not completely intact. The Emperor Justinian, for example, is reputed to have given a thorn of the Crown to St. Germanus, a Bishop of Paris, to be used as a sacred talisman, and the Empress Irene is remembered for having sent several thorns to Charlemagne, who in turn deposited them in his "Grail Castle" at Aachen, France.

The True Cross

Legends state that the Empress Helena was lead to the True Cross by a Jewish Rabbi named Judas, who was threatened and starved by the Empress' soldiers until he disclosed its location. Jesus' Cross was subsequently found hidden under a Temple of Venus along with the two crosses of the robbers who had been crucified with him. In order to differentiate which of the three crosses was the True Cross, Helena is said to have had the body of a dead man dug up and placed on each. She knew she had the True Cross when one of them miraculously brought the dead man back to life.

The True Cross, along with some of the other relics of the Passion subsequently discovered by Helena, was divided into two parts, one of which found interment when the Empress built the first version of the Church of the Holy Sepulchre in 335 A.D., and the other, along with the three nails of the Cross, was sent to Constantinople, where King Constantine had it enclosed in the statue of himself in order to bless the city with impregnability. But soon after its discovery pieces of the True Cross were cut away and distributed as diplomatic gifts, some so tiny that Paulinus, who was given a piece in a golden vial, maintained they were nearly as small as an atom. By 350 A.D., St. Cyril of Jerusalem claimed that the wood of the True Cross was already profusely distributed throughout the known world. The part of the True Cross in the Holy Sepulchre survived, however, until 1187, the year legends claim the victorious Moslem general Saladin tied it to the tail of his horse and dragged it behind him as he rode triumphantly through the streets of Jerusalem. Its location following this irreverent event is lost in the mists of time, although it was probably divided up into innumerable fragments.

According to St. John Chrysostom, when they were separated from the main body of the True Cross most of the wooden fragments were carefully protected by being encased in golden reliquaries and worn as talismans. Among the better-known fragments that circulated in Europe during the 1st millennium, one was taken to Venice where it is reputed to have healed a madman of his psychosis and other convalescents of their fatal illnesses. Another was given by Juvenal, the Patriarch of Jerusalem, to Pope St. Leo in 455 A.D. A third fragment was presented by King Constantine to the Sessorian Basilica in Rome, and another piece was given by the Emperor Justin II to Radegunda, a Queen of the Franks, in 569.

There are currently many surviving fragments of the True Cross in the world today. In the United States alone there are currently 10 or more fragments scattered in parishes around the country. Some of the churches they can be found within include: St. Helena Catholic Church in the Bronx, the Holy Angels Catholic Church in Mt. Airy, North Carolina, Boston's Cathedral of the Holy Cross, and the Chapel of St. Nicholas of Myra in Columbus, Ohio. In Scotland, a fragment known as the Holy Rood or "Black Rood of Scotland" previously resided in Holyrood Abbey, which was built especially for it by King David I in 1128, but its current location is a secret to all but a few. This piece of the original cross was brought from Hungary with the dowry of Queen Margaret, who became King Malcolm Canmore's wife. Margaret placed the Holy Rood in the safekeeping of her Cupbearer, William de St. Clair, and it is known to have spent sometime in the living monument of the St. Clairs, Rosslyn Chapel.

The Nails of the True Cross

When the three nails of the True Cross were discovered by the Empress Helena she sent them to her son, the Emperor Constantine, who is said to have used them in the creation of a statue of himself, as well as in the making of the iron blade of the Lance of St. Maurice. One of the nails also became the foundation of the **Iron Crown of Lombardy**, which Constantine and many European emperors were subsequently crowned with. Currently residing in the Cathedral at Monza in Lombardy, the Iron Crown consists of a very thin band of iron formed from one of Arma Christi nails, to which is attached sheets of gold and precious stones.

Over the years the Iron Crown of Lombardy, which is said to give its owner the power of world domination, has been in the possession of many formidable Italian and German kings. Its most famous owner was the Emperor Napolean, who on 1805 crowned himself with it in a ceremony in Milan, Italy. While placing it upon his head, Napolean, in the tradition of the Lombard kings before him, proclaimed: *Dieu me la donne, gare à qui la touché*, "God gives it me, beware those who touch it."

When Napoleon was crowned he founded the Order of the Iron Crown. His order was later revived by the Austrian Emperor Francis I, who also had himself coronated with the Iron Crown. Then, after the war between Austria and Italy, the Iron Crown was taken to its present location.

The **Santo Caliz de Valencia**

Mary Magdalene and her jar
Mary Magdalene by Frederick Sandys (1862)

The Pope and the **Santo Caliz de Valencia**

Presentation of the **Zingaro Templar Vial**

The **Nanteos Cup**

Joseph of Arimathea and his two cruets

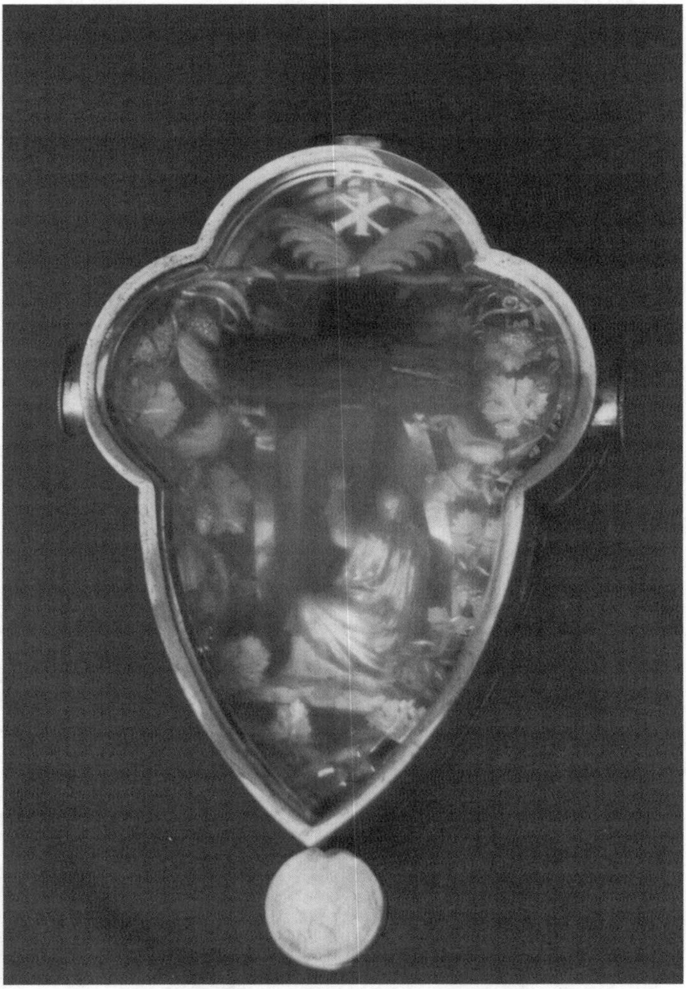

The Holy Rood of Scotland. A piece of the True Cross.

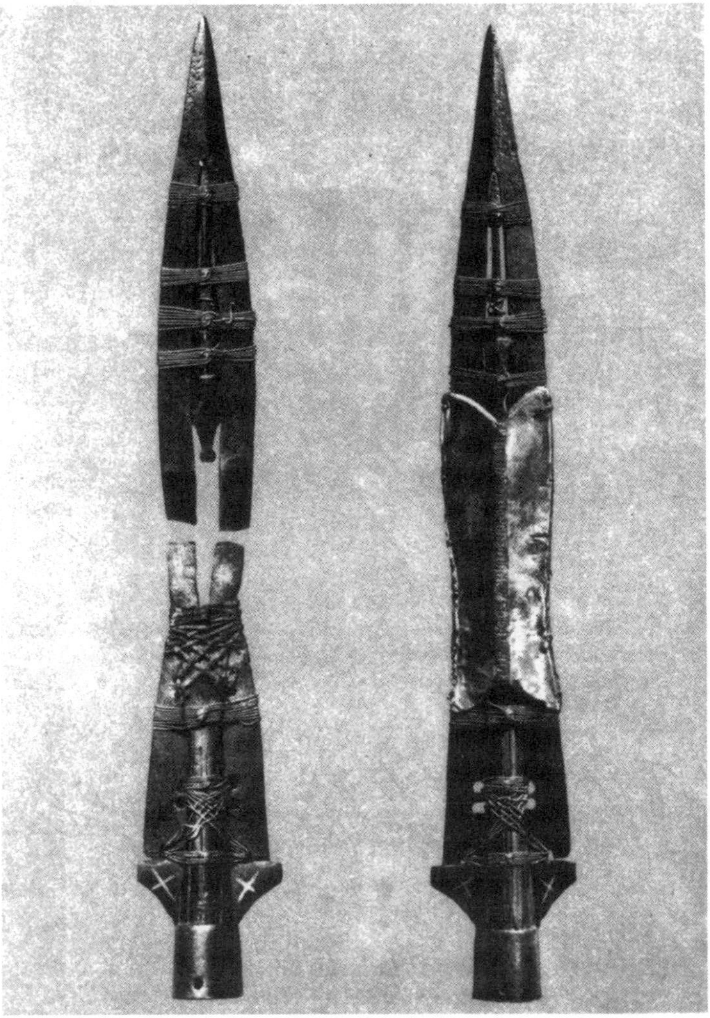

The Spear of Destiny

4
The Stone of Heaven

"By this Stone the Phoenix is burned to ashes...however ill a mortal may be, from the day on which he sees the Stone he cannot die for that week, nor does he lose his colour...Such powers does the Stone confer on mortal men that their flesh and bones are soon made young again. This Stone is also called "The Grail."[1]

Of all the legendary Holy Grail manifestations, the "Stone of Heaven" written of in *Parzival* by Wolfram von Eschenbach is certainly one of the more mysterious and intriguing, which is why an entire chapter is now devoted to it. One of the four Holy Grail Hallows, this manifestation of the Holy Grail has been ubiquitous throughout history and versions of it have existed throughout the world for many thousands of years.

When Wolfram von Eschenbach identified the Holy Grail as a Stone of Heaven he knew he was alluding to a Holy Grail tradition that had extended far back into the mists of time. The tradition began with primitive man, who experienced a distinct physical and/or emotional change just by being in proximity to certain stones. Later, during the time of early Egypt, India, China, and Sumeria, entire cults of alchemists grew up around certain stones, both natural and synthesized, which were ascribed the property of transforming a base metal into gold and a human into a god or goddess. Many of their early texts were eventually catalogued during the time of the Moselm Empire by the Sufis, who then added their own alchemical data to the developing art before transmitting it to their students, including the Knights Templar, who took the wisdom back into Europe. In this way, not only Wolfram, but all European authors and students of the Holy Grail Mysteries were eventually indoctrinated into the wisdom of the Alchemical or Philosophers Stone, including Chrétien de Troyes. Littleton and Malcor point out in *From Scythia to Camelot* that in some of the translations of Chrétien's *Conte del Graal* the Holy Grail platter or bowl has been portrayed as full of precious stones.

Whence the name "Stone of Heaven"?

Wolfram's "Stone of Heaven" is a European translation of the alchemical term Lapsit Exillus, which is closely related to Lapis Elixir, an appellation used by the Sufis that denotes "Philosopher's Stone."[2] Lapsit is derived from lapis, meaning "stone," and related to the Latin lapsus, meaning fallen, thus denoting "fallen stone." Since the term Exillus is intimately related to exillis stellis, meaning "from the stars,"[3] the entire moniker Lapsit Exillus literally translates as "The Stone of the Heavens" or "The Stone which came down from the Stars."

The name Stone of Heaven can also be derived simply from the word Grail. According to etymologists, the term Grail may have been derived from the French grés or the Persian gohr, both of which denote some kind of stone. Grail of Greal could also be related to the French grêle, meaning hailstone, which is a "stone" from heaven. Thus, from this linguistic perspective any Grail can be defined as a Stone of Heaven.

The legend of the Stone of Heaven

According to the Grail scholar Arthur Edward Waite, another interpretation of Lapsit Exillus is "Exiles Stone."[4] This surprising interpretation ostensibly affiliates the Stone of Heaven with Heaven's most notorious exile, Lucifer, which is an association Wolfram von Eschenbach continually alludes to in *Parzival.* The Stone's Luciferian heritage is explained in the German poem known as the *Wartburgkrieg,* the "Wartburg War," which was popular during Wolfram's time. This poem, which succinctly summarizes the heavenly battle between Lucifer and St. Michael, identifies the Stone of Heaven as a large emerald that became dislodged from Lucifer's crown and descended to Earth:

"Shall I then bring the crown
that was made by 60,000 angels?
Who wished to force God out of the Kingdom of Heaven.
See! Lucifer, there he is!
If there are still master-priests,
Then you know well that I am singing the truth.
Saint Michael saw God's anger, plagued by his insolence.
He took (Lucifer's) crown from his head,
In such a way that a stone jumped out of it,
Which on earth became Parsifal's stone.
The stone which sprang out of it,
He found it, he who had struggled for honor at such a high cost."

This scenario illustrated within the *Wartburgkrieg* is a synthesis of many ancient Luciferian motifs taken from a variety of legends. It contains elements from the arrival of the Sons of God encapsulated in the *Book of Enoch,* as well as the War in Heaven described in *The Book of Revelation.* It also relies on the derogatory comments made by the irascible Prophets Isaiah and Ezekiel when commenting on the Kings of Babylon and Tyre and their Luciferian characteristics.

Lucifer's fall from Heaven that is incorporated into the *Wartburgkrieg* was a theme first popularized by the Prophet Isaiah during his harangue against the King of Babylon in *The Book of Isaiah.* When describing the decline and fall of the megalomaniacal King of Babylon, Isaiah used the metaphor of the Morning Star's "fall" or descent below the horizon at sunrise, an image that subsequently became linked to Lucifer when the *Torah* was translated into Latin by St. Jerome and the name for Morning Star was translated as Luz-I-fer or Lucifer, the Light Bringer. Previous to its translation as Lucifer, however, Isaiah's Morning Star would have been known as *Shahar* or *Helel*, which were the names of Venus' dawn appearance among the coastal cultures of Asia Minor. Thus, Lucifer was originally associated with both Venus and *Helel*, a name that appears to have evolved into Hell, Lucifer's underworld home.

In *The Book of the Prophet Ezekial,* the Prophet Ezekial expanded upon the meaning of Lucifer's infamous fall. While comparing the King of Tyre with Lucifer, Ezekiel identifies Lucifer as the "anointed" cherub and forever-young boy who once walked in the Garden of Eden while covered in precious stones, including the emerald, and was "perfect in (his) ways from the day that (he) was created, til iniquity was found in (him)." Ezekiel thus perpetuates the tradition of Isaiah by making Lucifer's fall the product of his pride.

The images of the fallen Lucifer promulgated by Isaiah and Ezekiel were subsequently incorporated into *The Revelation of St. John the Divine* by the Apostle John, wherein Lucifer's resolve to rule Heaven culminated in his eventual expulsion from Paradise. When St. Michael and his angels fought with Lucifer over his right to rule, states St. John, "that old serpent, called the Devil, and Satan, which deceiveth the whole world...was cast out (of heaven) into the earth, and his angels were cast out with him."

The remainder of Lucifer's legend in the *Wartburgkrieg* states that during his battle with Michael an emerald became dislodged from Lucifer's crown and fell to Earth. This theme is ostensibly based on Ezekiel's description of the gems – especially the emerald - that adorned Lucifer's regalia in the Garden of Eden. It was also influenced by the Knights Templar. But, as you will see in the foregoing, the association between Lucifer and the emerald predates the Prophet Ezekial and the Templars by many hundreds and thousands of years. Before their time the emerald had been recognized within Earth's earliest civilizations and their Holy Grail Mysteries as the esteemed Stone of Venus, the "fallen star" of Lucifer.

Venus' Stone

Could Ezekial have known of Venus' very ancient association with the emerald? It seems fairly conclusive that he did since not only emerald, but the stone's color green and its associated planet Venus were all known about and interrelated in Egypt when the Jews resided in ancient Khem, and this wisdom was also part of the canon of arcane knowledge taught within the Mesopotamian temples by Babylonian priests during the Jewish captivity. In ancient Egypt the emerald was the stone of Hathor, the Egyptian Venus, and in Mesopotamia the color green was the stone of Venus in her manifestation as Inanna or Ishtar. Venus was associated with the color green in these ancient cultures because she was the Goddess of Love, which is produced through the union of the polarity represented by Her dual manifestations as the Morning and Evening Stars, and green is the color in the middle of the spectrum that denotes balance, union and love. In order to represent the duality of Venus, the Egyptians portrayed the goddess as a two-headed deity, and in Babylonia she was a goddess that ruled over the polar opposite activities of both love and war. Later, as the Greek Aphrodite, Venus was sometimes represented as an androgynous female with a long beard.

Since Venus is the union of the polarity, the planet was anciently accorded the epithet of the Star of Alchemy. Alchemy is the scientific process that unites the polarity to produce the fire of transmutation, which is then used to transform a base metal into gold and/or a human into a god or goddess. Within the mineral kingdom, this fire can transform a common stone into the most evolved of minerals, the emerald and the diamond, both of which are ruled by Venus and noted to be precious gems of the highest vibration.

The wise alchemists of ancient Greece, Egypt, India, and Mesoamerica venerated Venus as the Star of Alchemy. Her stones, including emerald and diamond, were the original Stones of Heaven and the incipient Philosophers Stones. Her rulership over these stones incompassed their color and crystalline matrixes, but most importantly She was the alchemical power within the stones. Thus, Venus was not only the patroness of alchemy, She *was* alchemy. She was the fiery power that induced alchemy and brought it to fruition. It was She that transformed a base metal into gold, and it was She as the evolutionary force that made a person immortal. In reference to Her fiery, transformational nature, Venus was portrayed by Her Egyptian priests and priestesses as a Phoenix, the mythical firebird that arises reborn and transfigured from its own ashes.

Venus taught the ancient sacred scientists the process of human alchemy through Her planetary cycles. Venus' "alchemical" cycle of eight years begins with its sunset position when it is just above the horizon, an event that symbolizes a person's spiritual darkness preceding his or her alchemical transformation. Venus' subsequent transit below the horizon and "under the Earth," represents a person's passage through the hellish underworld regions of their own subconscious and his or her corresponding "death." And finally, the planet's reappearance as the Morning Star that precedes the light of the rising Sun symbolizes the rebirth and "dawn" of the transfigured immortal.

In Egypt and Mexico, the sacred scientists created myths within which the could personify Venus as the archetypal seeker, which they duly named Osiris and Quetzlcoatl. Thus, when the planet went under the Earth, it was said that Osiris or Quetzlcoatl was visiting the underworld, and when it rose at dawn it was said that the archetypal initiate was reborn, etc.

Three very important "alchemical" numbers eventually occured to the alchemists from observing the cycles of Venus. The first number was eight, which is the number of years it takes for Venus' cycle to elapse; the second number was five, the number of times the planet becomes the Morning and Evening Stars during the cycle; and the third was thirteen, the number of times Venus revolves around the Sun during the span of eight years. Of these three numbers, the Arabic numeral 8 was adopted by the alchemists as their definitive symbol for polarity union and the infinite state of immortality it engenders. The number 8 symbolized polarity union as two united circles, and it also revealed that alchemy was the union of two circular "worlds," Heaven and Earth. The number and symbol 8 became so important to the early alchemists that they made it the sacred number of their eternal patron, the Egyptian Thoth-Hermes.

The Venusian number of 13 was also very important for the alchemists because it denoted the number of stages in the alchemical process leading to death and rebirth. Legend has it that these 13 stages were inscribed by the sage Thoth-Hermes as 13 precepts on a tablet called the Emerald Tablet that was made of solid emerald; thus, the stages leading to the creation of the Philosophers Stone were themselves inscribed on a version of the Philosophers Stone. These 13 precepts became the foundation of Egyptian alchemy, and they were later inculcated within the Islamic Universities of Constantinople and Seville in Spain.

Some researchers have asked the logical question: Could the Emerald Tablet be Lucifer's legendary emerald? Could it be Wolfram's Stone of Heaven, his Holy Grail? It could be if "al" is added to the Persian word for Grail, gohr, to become gohr-al, which carries the meaning of "engraved stone." But emeralds do not normally fall from the sky, especially engraved ones. So perhaps Lucifer's legend did not begin with a falling emerald but another kind of precious green stone that fell to Earth from the heavens. There is such a green stone known as Moldovite, a Tektite, which in some New Age circles is being touted as *the* Stone of Heaven. Moldovite is created by the intense heat of a high velocity meteorite colliding with a deposit of earth's minerals, thereby producing a green hybrid species of mineral. Moldovite, which comes from Moldavia in Czechoslovakia, has become popular around the globe because of its synergistic and enhancing effect on spiritual disciplines, such as the arts of alchemy and meditation. But Moldovite was initially a black meteorite, which begs the question, was Lucifer's stone originally a meteorite? There is certainly evidence pointing affirmatively in that direction, including the fact that Goddess Venus was once believed by the ancient cultures to periodically come to Earth in the form of a meteorite. She was the legendary genitals of Uranus, the Lord of Heaven, whose fiery sexual organs transformed into a meteorite after splashing down in the Mediterranean Sea. Since Lucifer is synonymous with Venus, the meteorite must thus be taken into serious consideration as Lucifer's Stone of Heaven.

In classical times, the Venusian-ruled iron core meteorites were considered the most alchemically active of stones. They were so active that alchemists considered them "stones with a soul."[5] They were often used in many of the most ancient Mediterranean mystery schools for initiation purposes because of their ability to precipitate the awakening of the inner alchemical forces within a spiritual seeker, eventually leading him or her to immortality. Simply by placing them upon the back of a candidate for initiation they were known to stimulate an electromagnetic current strong enough to awaken the alchemical force in the body, the Kundalini, and move it from its home at the base of the spine to the crown of the head. On Crete, these initiatory meteorites were known as "Thunderstones" and used for inductions into the Thunders of Nocturnal Zeus. When the Greek sage Pythagoras had a thunderstone placed upon his back during his initiation by the Dactyloi priests of Crete, he lay "as if dead" for an entire night with his face buried in the earth. The Thunderstone initiation of Crete caused another initiate, the famous sage Epimenides, to drift into a profound dream-sleep that lasted just a few minutes of Earth time but was experienced by him as lasting for 57 years. Iron-nickel meteorites were also used in many other parts of the world for initiation and spiritual purposes because of the profound effect they have upon the human electromagnetic field. Andean priests and shamans, for example, have been using meteorites in their work for virtually thousands of years. These shamans hold a "male" and "female" meteorite in their right and left hands to unite the inner polarity and stimulate an electromagnetic impulse strong enough to move any energy blockages impeding health and spiritual progress.

In order to explicitly identify their sacred meteorites as manifestations of the Goddess Venus, the early venerators of the Patroness of Alchemy carved them into the form of a cone or pyramid, the geometrical form that generates the Venusian Fire of Alchemy, and sometimes they even molded them into the shape a human female. A cone or pyramid (pyr-a-mid, fire in the middle) shaped meteorite was venerated as the Goddess Venus in Her main temple in Paphos on Cyprus, and a huge cone shaped meteorite was also worshiped as Venus in Her form of the Phoenix in Heliopolis, Egypt. In Ephesus, where she was worshipped as Artemis/ Diana, Venus manifested as a huge meteorite carved into the shape of a beautiful woman, thus denoting Her role as the Queen of the Heavens and the Universal Goddess.

The Stone of the Kaaba

When the fundamentalist religions of the Middle East captured the sacred sites of Venus and Her worshippers, they also inherited some of Venus' meteorite forms and then constructed their own temples for worship around them. Such is the history of the famous Stone of Heaven interred within the great Kaaba, or "Cube" of Mecca. The Kaaba, which was designed by the Prophet Abraham with the assistance of his son Ishmael, the patriarch of Arabs, and then later rebuilt by the Prophet Mohammed, was erected in the center of Mecca's principal shrine area, wherein Venus as a meteorite had been worshipped for thousands of years. The cube shape of the Kaaba incorporates the alchemical number eight by having two four-sided squares, one above and one below (4+4), thus emphasizing and enhancing the alchemical properties of its indwelling form of Venus. According to a descendant of the Sufi builders of the Kaaba, Idries Shah, "Eight symbolizes the number of perfect expression, the octagon, representing among other things, the cube."[6] As mentioned, the alchemical number of 8 denotes both enlightenment as well as the union of the two "worlds," Heaven and Earth, a point made explicit by the builders of the Kaaba, who, according to Shah, incorporated into its structure thirty-one courses of stone and wood, and then added two more, symbolizing Heaven and Earth, thus making thirty-three, the number of enlightenment.[6]

Sticking out from one corner of the Kaaba is the sacred meteorite that devout worshippers of the Middle East once worshipped as the Goddess Venus. At first a solid rock, time has since split this meteorite into many pieces that are now held together by a silver ligature. One legend has it that this Stone of Heaven was brought from Heaven by the Angel Gabriel right after the Kaaba was completed, while an alternate legend states that the stone was presented directly by God to Adam and Eve in the Garden of Eden. The rock was white at the time Adam received it but has since become black from the sins of humanity. This latter myth becomes ever more intriguing (and potentially accurate) in light of an Islamic belief that holds that the original Garden of Eden was in another world or in another dimension and that Earth's Garden of Eden, which the Moslems today locate on the Island of Sri Lanka, is but a reflection of the first Eden. What if the original Eden had been on another planet, such as Venus? The rock in the Kaaba would then be truly an authentic piece of the body of the Goddess Venus.

A legend from the opposite side of the world from Mecca supports the notion that the Kaaba's stone could indeed have come from the planet Venus. This is a Peruvian myth that the Incas disclosed to their Spanish conquerors. It states that approximately six million years ago a small spaceship from Venus landed on the Island of the Sun in the center of Lake Titicaca. Emerging from the craft was a woman with an elongated head, long ears, and four fingers on each hand. With her were plants, animals, and "other things" from her home planet, including some black stones. Supposedly she proceeded to mate with a tapir and their progeny became the ancestors of the Andean people. When the Spanish conquerors heard of this unusual woman with long ears they nicknamed her Orejones, meaning "Big Ears."

After the departure of Orejones, continues the Peruvian legend, the god Tvira built a temple over the spot that she had landed and placed the black stones she had brought from her home planet within it. These stones, called Kala, were worshipped for many thousands of years, but unfortunately they disappeared from the temple long before modern science could analyze them. According to Robert Charroux in *One Hundred Thousand Years of Man's Unknown History,* information compiled from ancient Andean records convinced the Spanish chronicler Garcia Beltran that one of the Kala stones was taken to Mecca where it became the stone of the Kaaba.

Is the legend of Orejones just a myth or could it be based in fact? Its legitimacy could help resolve certain Andean mysteries, such as why the Inca royalty artificially elongated their skulls and wore large, heavy earrings to enlarge their ears. They may have been simply emulating the appearance of their ancestress. A Venusian visitation in the distant past would also explain why at Tiahuanaco, an ancient temple city built many thousands of years ago on the shores of Lake Titicaca, one can currently find stone effigies of otherworldly, extraterrestrial-looking entities. Perhaps they represent Orejones and other extraterrestrials before and/or after her that played a significant role in the storied past of the Incas. Moreover, the arrival of Orejones from Venus could additionally shed some light on how the people of Tiahuanaco could have understood the cycles of the planet Venus as well as they did. One of their remaining chiseled artifacts at Tiahuanaco is the fabulous Gate of the Sun, upon which is carved a series of hieroglyphic images that have been interpreted by some scholars to represent a Venusian calendar that perfectly calculates many of the planet's normally confusing cycles.

The Chintamani Stone

Orejones' rock might be more suspect if legends of extraterrestrial rocks did not also exist in other parts of the world outside of Peru. Of these exotic and mystifying Stones of Heaven the most famous is probably the Chintamani Stone of the East, which was made popular during the last century by the Russian mystic

Nicholas Roerich. According to legends complied by Roerich and other travelers in the East, the Chintamani Stone was brought to Earth by missionaries from another star, possibly Sirius, and it is composed of a mineral that exists on one of the planets that revolves around their home star. The Buddhists of Mongolia and the Buryat shamans of Siberia maintain that the bulk of the rock currently resides in the magical country of Shamballa, which is somewhere in the area of the Gobi Desert, although pieces of it can spontaneously manifest at any locale around the globe, especially now during the time leading up to the "Great Advent" or beginning of a new Golden Age. Roerich maintains that the stone or fragments of it have been in the possession of King Solomon, as well as the chiefs of the conquering Mongol tribes, including Tamurlane, Ghenghis Khan, and Akbar the Great. Among these ancient rulers the Chintamani Stone was popularly known as the "Treasure of the World" and ascribed the power to elevate its possessor to the position of King of the World. Supposedly by the changes in its temperature, color, and weight it was also supposed to empower its caretaker with the ability to both see into the past and predict the future. While commenting on this property of the stone, Roerich remarks:

"When the stone is hot, when the stone quivers, when the stone is cracking, when the stone changes it weight and color – by these changes the stone predicts to its possessor the whole future and gives him the ability to know his enemies and hostile dangers as well as happy events."[7]

Supposedly one piece of the Chintamani Stone was gifted to the founders of the League of Nations in order to help their planetary organization efficiently and effectively govern the world. When the League eventually dissolved, Roerich was chosen to carry the piece back to Shamballa and reunite it with its parent stone. During his subsequent long trek across Asia Roerich made the stone the subject of many of his most famous paintings.

Another Russian adventurer who traveled throughout the East in the early 1900s and similarly acquired legends regarding the Chintamani Stone was Ferdinand Ossendowski. According to Ossendowski's journal of his travels in *Men, Beast and Gods*, the Russian listened with rapt attention while visiting a Buddhist monastery in Mongolia when the Bogdo Gheghen, the chief Lama of the abbey and an incarnation of the most famous Buddha, the Buddha Shakyamuni, had one of his attendant Lamas read a history of this magical stone. At the Bogdo's request, the Lama began:

"When Gushi Khan, the chief of all the Olets or Kalamucks, finished the war with the "Red Caps" in Tibet, he carried out with him the miraculous "black stone" sent to the Dalai Lama by the "King of the World." Gushi Khan wanted to create in Western Mongolia the capital of the Yellow Faith; but the

Olets at that time were at war with the Manchu Emperors for the throne of China and suffered one defeat after another. The last Khan of the Olets, Amursana, ran away into Russia, but before his escape he sent to Urga the sacred "black stone." While it remained in Urga so that the Living Buddha could bless the people with it, disease and misfortune never touched the Mongolians and their cattle. However, about one hundred years ago someone stole the sacred stone and since then the Buddhists have vainly sought it throughout the whole world. With its disappearance the Mongol people began gradually to die."[8]

Since Urga, the capital of Mongolia, is near the Gobi Desert, the legendary home of Shamballa, Ossendowski's stone appears to be synonymous with Roerich's Chintamani Stone. Perhaps Ghenghis Khan had this stone in his possession when his great Asian juggernaut of Mongols rolled westward into Europe, which is why he was so remarkably successful in his quest to conquer the known world.

Could the Chintamani Stone alluded to by Roerich and Ossendowski be synonymous with Lucifer's Stone of Heaven? There are a couple important reason why it could be. First of all, Ossendowski maintains that the stone belonged to the King of the World, and according to legend, when Lucifer arrived on Earth he assumed that role. Secondly, according to various Buddhist legends of the East, including one popularized by the American Robert Dickhoff, a Buddhist Lama who traveled in the East, the King of the World came from Venus and is reputed to have acquired a predominantly dark and self-serving temperament after becoming our planetary monarch. This appears to be a direct reference to Lucifer, the first King of the World, who continues to rule from his self-serving ego.

Another important reason why the Chintamani Stone owned by the King of the World may be Lucifer's Stone of Heaven is that it is interred in the palace of the world's monarch located in the center of Shamballa. For centuries, one of the most consistent places mentioned as the true location of the Holy Grail has been the center of the human heart, and Shamballa is to the Earth what the heart chakra is to a human being. Like the human heart, Shamballa possesses eight sections or "petals" surrounding it, and within its center is the spirit of the Earth, the legendary King of the World. So, just as we all possess a personal soul and spirit that resides within our heart, the King of the World is the spirit and soul of planet Earth residing in Shamballa.

The *Even ha'Shettiya* and the Dome of the Rock

Thus, Shamballa may the home of Lucifer's Stone of Heaven, but, surprisingly, there is another Stone of Heaven candidate residing in the Middle East that is also associated with the center and heart of the world. This is the *Even ha'Shettiya*, the "Stone of Foundation," which resides within the eight-sided Dome of the Rock in Jerusalem, the Holy City that the early Christians and incipient European mapmakers placed at the center and heart of our Earth. The *Even ha'Shettiya* is famous for being the rock upon which the patriarch Abraham made his legendary attempt to sacrifice his son Isaac in the sight of God, and the place where Mohammed was lifted to Heaven by the angel Gabriel. Since the *Even ha'Shettiya* was known about by the early Knights Templar who resided nearby it in the al-Aqsâ mosque, the Stone of Foundation may ben an even better claimant than the Chintamani Stone for being *the* Stone of Lucifer. Lucifer's European legend was, no doubt, greatly influenced and enhanced by the returning Knights of the Temple.

Since the *Even ha'Shettiya* is located in the exact middle of the Earth, it is part of an axis mundi, a pre-existent column that unites Heaven and Earth, or Earth human to God. This feature of the *Even ha'Shettiya* was not overlooked by King David, who purchased the rock from the native Jebusites to serve as the location for the Ark of the Covenant, the power object that served as a vehicle for communication with Lord Yahweh. Later, David's son King Solomon, a renowned alchemist, similarly acknowledged the stone's alchemical property as a Heaven/Earth mediator when he used the rock as a foundation for his famous Temple, which was designed to be an alchemical cauldron that could unite the polarity and thereby produce the presence of Yahweh as the androgynous Yod He Vau He.

The value of the *Even ha'Shettiya* as a natural unifier of the universal polarity was apparently known by the Moslem Caliph Abd al-Malik, who between 687-691 A.D. built the eight-sided Dome of the Rock over it. His octagonal structure, which is more explicitly a Heaven-Earth mediator and alchemical chamber than even the sacred Kaaba, significantly enhanced the stone's power as an alchemically charged Stone of Heaven. Each of the eight sides of the Dome of the Rock were painted dual colors representing Earth and Heaven. The bottom half of each of the eight panels was painted the same whitish color of Earth that the temple rests upon, and halfway up each panel the color was changed to blue, the color of the upper sky and Heaven. This dual motif symbolized the two polar-opposite "worlds" of Heaven and Earth and their alchemical union that is engendered by the Dome of the Rock.

While living next to the Dome of the Rock in the al-Aqsâ mosque, the Knights Templar came to understand the Dome's unique octagonal design and how it is a natural unifier of Heaven and Earth. The Sufi teachers that helped them arrive at this understanding were members of an order of builders known as the Al-banna, a Masonic organization of Sufis that had inherited its wisdom from Persia, the Asian country that consistently utilized the octagon in its enclosures. Because of their in-depth Sufi tutorials, many Templar Knights became builders themselves and participated in the construction of the octagonal Church of the

Holy Sepulchre and the eight-sided Church of the Ascension.

The Templar understanding of the alchemical effect of the esoteric number 8 no doubt played a contributing role in their adoption of their distinctive eight-pointed Cross Pattee. Along with the image of the Dome of the Rock that they inscribed upon their official seal, the eight-pointed cross served as a telling emblem of their Order. The Templars were schooled in the eight-pointed star's very ancient associations and knew that it had been a symbol of not only the Moslems, but also the Persians and Mesopotamians. All these early civilizations had recognized it as the symbol of the Goddess Venus. Thus, by adopting the eight-pointed star as their definitive cross design, the Templars were revealing their own special affiliation to the Goddess Venus and Her ancient path of alchemy.

Thus, the *Even ha'Shettiya* appears to meet most of the criteria for being Lucifer's Stone of Heaven, except two. It is not an emerald, nor was it dropped from the sky. There are, however, Islamic and Persian legends that ostensibly assign it these characteristics. These intriguing myths refer to a mountain in the center of the Earth, called Mt. Kaf by the Arabs and Mount Albourz by the Persians, that may be synonymous with the *Even ha'Shettiya* and the Temple Mount it sits upon. Mt. Albourz, state the Persian scriptures, was the first stone or mountain on Earth; it was the original "Holy Mountain of God" and the axis mundi in the center of our planet. From Albourz evolved all the other mountains around it, like saplings sprouting from a central tree. In this regard, the *Bundahishn*, the Persian Book of Creation, states: "First Mount Albourz arose…in the middle of the Earth; for as Albourz grew forth all the mountains remained in motion, for they have all grown forth from the root of Albourz."

The Moslems central mountain is Mount Kaf, which is considered by most researchers to be an alternate name for Mt. Albourz. Mount Kaf is mentioned in some of the important scriptures of Islam, such as the *Araisu't Tijan*, which states: "GOD Most High created a great mountain from a single emerald. The greenness of the sky is derived from it. It is called Mount Kaf." Thus, when taken together, the Islamic and Persian legends anoint Albourz-Kaf as the primal mountain in the center of the Earth that was formed out of an emerald. But if *Even ha'Shettiya* is not pure emerald could it be synonymous with Albourz-Kaf? Perhaps. Since a mountain made of solid emerald has never been found, the green mineral matrix of the primal mountain of the Persians and Moslems may simply refer to its alchemical property of uniting the polarity of Heaven and Earth as an axis mundi just as the color green unites the polarity within the color spectrum. Thus, from this perspective, the *Even ha'Shettiya* and the Temple Mount it sits upon qualify is both an "emerald" mountain in the center of the Earth and Lucifer's mythical Stone of Heaven.

The Philosophers Stone

All the Stones of Heaven so far mentioned are naturally occurring, but strickly speaking, a Philosophers Stone is synthetic. This fabricated version of the Stone of Heaven has the same alchemical properties as its naturally made cousins, and it can even be said to have come from Heaven to Earth. This is because part of the process of its creation in a lab involves sending the lighter parts of an alchemical compound to "Heaven," a name for the top of a test tube, and then reuniting it with its heavier parts on "Earth," the bottom of the vial.

In brief, the process of creating the Philosophers Stone involves the classic thirteen stages of alchemical processing, during which a material substance called the Philosophical Mercury that contains properties that reflect the universal male principle and Spirit is united to a second substance, called the Philosophical Sulphur, which possesses properties that reflect the universal female principle and Earth. These polar opposite substances are mixed together into an alchemical compound, which is then placed in a test tube and heated until "dead." At that time its watery, Mercurial Spirit rises to "Heaven" at the top of the test tube while leaving a lifeless ash on "Earth" at the bottom of the vial. This remaining inert mass, known as the Prima Materia and acknowledged to be a reflection of the "First Matter" of the universe, continues to remain on ""Earth" until the test tube cools and the vaporous Spirit comes back from Heaven to unite with it, thus completing the alchemical union. The final steps of this alchemical process is cryptically detailed by Thoth-Hermes on his Emerald Tablet as:

"...The Impalpable (is) separated from the palpable. Through wisdom it rises slowly from the world to heaven (from base to top of the tube). Then it descends to the world, combining the power of the upper and the lower. Thus you shall have the illumination of the world, and darkness will disappear..."

The result of the Heaven/Earth reunion is the Philosophers Stone, a rock-like substance that is normally red in color and fiery like the blazing conflagration that was kindled at the time of the Big Bang. Among the alchemists of Medieval Europe, the Philosophers Stone was usually fiery red, the color of purification and destruction, but in ancient Egypt it was often black, which is another color associated with destruction. Alchemists in both areas normally ground up their Philosophers Stone and scattered the dust over a base metal so that its transformative power could "kill" the metal and transmute it into gold. By this practice many Medieval alchemists of Europe, including Raymond Lully, Nicholas Flamel, and Wenzel Seilor, are reputed to have converted base metals into gold. Flamel, as well as the alchemists Saracen Artephius and the Knights Templar chief, Saint Germain, also used the Philosophers Stone to engender human longevity and immortality by making it into an Elixir of Immortality, or by simply placing the Philosophers Stone in proximity to the human body just as the ancient mystery schools had once done with their stimulating meteorites. Similar to a meteorite, the synthetic Philosophers Stone would engender heat within the Root or *Muladhara Chakra*, thereby awakening its indwelling Kundalini and beginning the process of alchemical transformation.

Although a Philosophers Stone is efficacious in the awakening of Kundalini, almost any red or black mineral has, to a certain degree, the same potential for activating the inner alchemical power. Naturally occurring minerals with the strongest stimulating influence of this nature include black tourmaline, which strongly activates the electromagnetic field, and obsidian or volcanic glass. Since it is made from red-hot magma from the bowels of the Earth, obsidian possesses both a black color and the "vibration" of heat and transformation. It is the Stone of Vulcan, the smith god and patron of alchemy who lives within volcanoes.

Crystal Skulls

Clear quartz crystals also possess an electromagnetic influence that is stimulating and transforming like a Philosophers Stone and must therefore also be recognized as manifestations of the Stone of Heaven. These rocks can be conceived of as coming from the Heavens because they are captured and solidified clear white light. Like white light, crystals have a full spectrum of properties, including alchemical transformation, a property that is enhanced by their atomic matrices of silicon dioxide molecules combined into tetrahedrons, the sacred geometrical forms that generate transformative fire. The terminations of crystals, which often slant at the same alchemical angle of the Great Pyramid of Egypt, 51° 51', also contribute to their transformational property.

Quartz Crystals have an ancient association with the Knights Templar, who were reputed to have used crystal skulls in their rituals. According to author and researcher Frank Dorland, one of the most famous crystal skulls on Earth today, the Mitchell-Hedges Skull, may have once been in the possession of the Templars. This skull, which is reputed to be one of thirteen crystal skulls that once resided on the continent of Atlantis before becoming the property of occult priesthoods and secret societies around the globe after the continent sank, somehow ended up with the Templars who transported it to Belize where it was later found by Mitchell-Hedges, an initiate of Freemasonry. Dorland's assertion of an ancient visit by the Templars to the Western Hemisphere may not be as outlandish as it seems since stone slabs carved with Templar crosses were recently discovered in Patagonia that reveal that the Knights Templar may have visited North, South, and possibly Central America in the past.[9]

The Templars' ritual skulls are said to have been made of precious metals and human bone covered in gold and/or silver. Some of their skulls may have been those of their own deceased brethren, a notion implied in the Holy Grail rendition *Perlesvaus*, wherein a Grail maiden is portrayed leading a cart that holds the heads of 150 knights sealed in gold, silver and lead. We may never know the nature and extent of the Templar skulls, however, because most of them were hidden previous to the Knights' arrest in the 14th century and the closest the Inquisition's raids on Templar commandaries came to finding an intact skull were two silver-encased skull bones. These were found in the Order's Paris temple and were supposedly those of a small person, perhaps a female. They were encased in gilded silver and then wrapped in a cloth of white linen, with another red cloth covering the white linen.

There are, however, references in the Templar documents and the Knights' own testimonies extracted by the Inquisition that allude to the skulls possessed by the Order. A skull of gold or silver was mentioned in the testimony of a Knight from Burgundy in 1307, who claimed to have seen it when it was being taken out of its cupboard during an important Templar ceremony at his temple, which was a daughter lodge of the Grand Priory of Champagne at Voulaine. Another metallic skull of the Templars, apparently came from Asia Minor, is alluded to in the following unusual legend:

"A great lady of Maraclea was loved by a Templar, a Lord of Sidon; but she died in her youth, and on the night of her burial, this wicked lover crept to the grave, dug up her body and violated it. Then a voice bade him return in nine months time for he would find a son. He obeyed the injunction and at the appointed time opened the grave again and found a head on the leg bones of the skeleton (skull and crossbones). The same voice bade him "guard it well, for it would be the giver of all good things." It became his protecting genius, and he was able to defeat his enemies by merely showing them the magical head. In due course, it passed into the possession of the (Templar) Order."[10]

The famous skull and crossbones motif normally associated with pirates is often said to have originated with this skull from Sidon, but it was probably much older. This haunting motif, which we today associate with poison, was most likely a symbol related to the earlier alchemical rites of the Templar Knights. During these early rites, skulls were used representing "Caput Mortumm" or "Dead Head," which refers to a stage in alchemy preceding creation of the Philosophers Stone.[11]

The most important skull or head used in the rites of the Templar Knights was known within the Order as Baphomet. This most sacred of heads, which many of the Knights' alluded to during their depositions preceding their French trial, may have been that of John the Baptist, whose head was acquired by the Templars as part of treasure they looted from Constantinople during the Fourth Crusade. More will be said about Baphomet in later chapters.

The Goddess of Love, Venus-Ishtar, with Her eight-pointed Star of Alchemy.

The Persian eight-pointed cross, ancient symbol of the Goddess.
Could this have been an inspiration for the Templars' Cross Pattee?

Nicholas Roerich's Chintamani Stone returning to Shamballa .

Roerich's depiction of the King of the World.

Shamballa, the 8 petalled Heart Chakra of the World.
TheChintamani Stone & King of the World are in its center.

The Octagonal Dome of the Rock.

Pieces of Moldavite Tektite. The Stone of Heaven?

5
The Celestial Grails

In a separate category of their own are a group of Holy Grails known as Celestial Grails. These are star configurations that resemble cups, platters and spears. According to Wolfram von Eschenbach, the original legend of the Holy Grail was first conceived by Flegetanis, an ancient astrologer, who while observing the nighttime sky supposedly discovered "a thing called the Grail, whose name he read in the stars..." Thus, the initial wisdom of the Holy Grail came from the stars. But what did Flegetanis observe in the heavens? In accordance with the maxim "As above, so below," it appears probable that he spotted a star configuration resembling some manifestation of the Holy Grail, either a cup, chalice, stone or spear. And if Flegetanis' Celestial Grail was truly a cosmic reflection of a terrestrial Holy Grail, could it have also emanated the same alchemical power ascribed to its physical counterpart on Earth? If so, then one could expect to receive some spiritual benefit by capturing the rays descending from certain stars. These are questions that will be addressed in the present chapter.

Flegetanis, Discoverer of the Holy Grail

According to Wolfram, the astrologer Flegetanis, whose name is Persian for "Familiar with the Stars," was Jewish and descended from Solomon on his mother's side but "heathen" on his father's side, meaning that he was probably either part Babylonian or of Persian descent. Many Grail scholars currently contend that the name Flegetanis refers to an historical astrologer and alchemist known as Thabit ben Qorah, a resident of Baghdad during the 9th century who is reputed to have translated Greek astrological and alchemical texts into Arabic. Perhaps during one of his nightly watches on top of an ancient Mesopotamian Ziggurat, Flegetanis (or Thabit) made his pivotal discovery of a celestial Holy Grail in the heavens. If his gaze fell on the starry outline of a cup, the Celestial Grail that taught him the secrets of the Holy Grail could have been either the constellations of Aquarius, Crater, or the Big Dipper. But if the astrologer spotted a starry spear in the heavens, he might have been informed of the Grail mysteries by the constellation of Bootes, the "Lance Bearer."

The Celestial Holy Grail of Aquarius

If Flegetanis received his inspiration from the stars of Aquarius, the "Water Bearer," he would have observed a constellation whose outline is that of an androgynous man/woman carrying a bucket that he/she appears to continuously shower water down to our world from. If he initially subscribed to its mundane interpretation, Flegetanis might have simply seen Aquarius as a person transporting water. But if he comprehended the constellation from a spiritual perspective, which he would have had to in order to gain an understanding of the Holy Grail, he would have beheld the form of an androgynous savior of humanity holding a special vessel, a Holy Grail, from which he/she continuously showered the world with the Water of Life or Elixir of Immortality.

Flegetanis must have deferred to the spiritual understanding of Aquarius because, like all Middle Eastern astrologers, he would have naturally recognized the androgynous figure in the sign as androgynous Enki, whose legendary function as the Sumerian and Babylonian savior was to uplift humankind by blessing it with the wisdom and transformative power contained within the Apzu, the cosmic Water of Life. Since Enki's vessel contained such a valuable elixir, Flegetanis may have concluded that his container was a holy container, and perhaps the archetypal Holy Grail.

If Flegetanis had made a survey he would have found his spiritual insight regarding Aquarius confirmed within many of the spiritual cultures that surrounded the ancient Middle East. The Hindus, for example, were known to have identified the constellation as the home of Varuna, a god of creation and the lord of the cosmic waters of life force that can both create and transform. The neighboring Egyptians also associated Aquarius with a creator deity, whom they new as Khnum. According to the common man, Khnum caused the Nile to overflow every time he dipped his water bucket into the great river, but the Egyptian priesthood associated Khnum with the Water of Life and its indwelling manifestation in the human body as the Kundalini power. Khnum resided in the temple of Elephantine of Upper Egypt that was associated with the root chakra, the dwelling place of the Kundalini power of the Lord of Egypt, the Green Man Osiris. It was to this temple of Khnum that the Egyptian priests and priestesses went for activation of their inner elixir of Kundalini.

It was left to the later Greeks to conclusively identify the cup of Aquarius as a Celestial Holy Grail. The Greeks recognized the constellation of Aquarius as Ganymede, a Trojan boy who had been carried to Mount Olympus to act as a cup or "Grail" bearer for the gods. Ganymede is reputed to have kept the chalices of the gods continuously overflowing with the nectar of immortality that flowed from his own holy vessel.

The Celestial Holy Grail called Crater

Of all the Celestial Grails Flegetanis could have studied within the heavens, Crater the Cup comes closest in shape to an actual chalice. And in conjunction with the two constellations that are contiguous with it, Hydra the Water Snake and Corvus the Crow or Storm Bird, it also contains an abundance of wisdom regarding the nature of the Holy Grail and Water of Life.

Crater, Hydra, and Corvus produce a magnificent celestial Holy Grail motif that resembles a snake supporting both a chalice and bird upon its curvaceous back. Crater, of course, represents the Holy Grail Chalice. Serpentine Hydra is associated with the Water of Life that travels through space like a spiraling snake. And the black bird of Corvus is symbolic of the process of death and the acquisition of secret, occult wisdom that emerges through imbibing the Water of Life. Flegetanis may have also conceived of Corvus, as many cultures did at the time, as a dove, which as you will discover in the next chapter is a much more common avian symbol associated with the Holy Grail and the Water of Life.

Although most Grail scholars can only speculate about Crater and the possibility of it being Flegetanis' celestial Holy Grail, Henry and Renée Kahane, authors of *The Krater and the Grail: Hermetic Sources of the Parzival*, are unequivocal in proclaiming that they are one and the same. The Kahanes base their theory on references to Crater in certain ancient alchemical texts, such as the *Corpus Hermeticum*, which refers to Crater as the celestial vessel that was sent down to Earth for humans to drink from and/or bathe within in order to acquire immortality and Gnostic wisdom.[1] But since the Hermetic text is not clear whether or not the earthbound manifestation of Crater is physical, the elixir it refers to could simply be a description of the descent of the Water of Life or Holy Spirit life force from above. Perhaps special alchemical rays are beamed to Earth occasionally from the constellation of Crater itself?

The Celestial Holy Grail known as the Big Dipper

Although the descent of the Holy Spirit "dove" from Crater must remain conjecture, certain legends are unmistakably clear in ascribing the Celestial Grail known as the Big Dipper with the reoccurring tendency of sending high frequency rays of spiritual light to Earth. The Big Dipper is thus truly the definitive Celestial Grail. Technically an asterism or group of stars that comprise part of the constellation of Ursa Major, the "Great Bear," the Big Dipper projects rays of immortality to Earth while creating the outline of a huge heavenly cup, pan or ladle.

There are many reasons why the Big Dipper has merited distinction as a Celestial Holy Grail. First of all, its association with immortals and immortality is implicit to its location in the heavens, the northernmost part of the sky. The Big Dipper is one of many residents of the northern sky known as the celestial "immortals," which are stars and constellations that are always overhead and never set below the horizon. They always pivot around the "immortal" North Star, the celestial pointer that shines directly over the Arctic regions and North Pole.

The disposition of the Big Dipper within the Great Bear also associates the asterism with immortality. The Great Bear has an association to immortality through its animal shape, the bear, which is an "immortal" animal that emerges renewed and reborn from its cave tomb every spring. In ancient times, the Great Bear was part of an even larger constellation associated with immortality that included Ursa Minor, the Little Bear, as well as Draco, the dragon. Together, they created the huge celestial configuration of *Arctoe et Draco,* the "Bear and Dragon." Throughout history the dragon, like the bear, has been a preeminent symbol of immortality.

The ancient astrologers venerated *Arctoe et Draco* as the form of the immortal Celestial Emperor of the Universe, who was always looking down upon the affairs of humanity. And according to the maxim of "as above, so below," they also knew that the Celestial Emperor had his terrestrial counterparts on Earth. These were the array of supernaturally endowed priest kings who once ruled our planet and are collectively alluded to in the Holy Grail Mysteries as the Fisher King. Like the Celestial Emperor, who incorporated into his cosmic form the Big Dipper and its potent Water of Life, many of these early kings possessed both remarkable inner power and spiritual insight, and some even achieved physical immortality.

When the Pole Star eventually shifted to become Polaris, which is currently located on the handle of the Little Dipper, *Arctoe et Draco* was subsequently divided into the two constellations of the Great Bear and Draco, and at the same time Earth's priest kings become known either as "Bears" or "Dragons." The lineages of priest kings who adopted the Bear and/or the seven stars of Ursa Major as their special emblems include the lineage of the Persian monarchs, the immortal kings of Arcadia in Greece, the Merovingian French Kings, and on the other side of the globe it became the symbol of the

Hopi Bear Clan, the ruling clan of the current or Fourth World.

The Great Bear and its indwelling Big Dipper also became famous as the celestial symbol of the emperors of China, who represented their affiliation to the stars by embroidering the seven stars of the Big Dipper and/or the image of a bear upon their ceremonial robes. Many of these legendary kings were even considered to be physical incarnations of the stars, such as the Emperor Yu, who revealed his connection to the Great Bear at birth by emerging from the womb with the image of the Great Bear engraved upon his chest. Another Chinese king, Huang-ti, is said to have been born from a ray of blinding light that emerged from the Great Bear and pierced the womb of his mother. Twenty-five months later Huang-ti was born with such an advanced intellectual development that he could speak moments after his birth and had mastered all the mundane and sacred sciences by the time he was in his teens. Huang-ti, who is now venerated as the "Father of Taoism," eventually became an adept alchemist and achieved the hallowed state of immortality. After completing his time on Earth, it is said that Huang-ti transformed himself into a great dragon and winged his way back to his celestial home in the heavens.

The powerful priest kings around the globe that have been associated with Ursa Major and the Big Dipper have been the preeminent Guardians of the Holy Grail. Like the composite Fisher King who repesents them, they have been terrestrial reflections of the Great Bear and have thus incorporated the power of the Big Dipper or Celestial Chalice right inside their own bodies. One manifestation of the Fisher King specifically affiliated with the Great Bear is the famous King Arthur of Britain. Arthur's form was once identified in the heavens by the astronomers of the north as the Great Bear, while his Knights of the Round Table could be spotted nearby as the stars that surrounded the constellation and moved together in a circumpolar fashion.

According to its etymology, Arthur is derived from, or intimately related to, the Welsh Arth Fawr and the Greek Arktos, meaning "Bear." The name also has a relationship to Arcturus, the "Guardian of the Bear," which is the bright star in the constellation of Bootes that points to the tail of the Great Bear. Arthur's intimate link to the Big Dipper, the constellation that in Britain is also known as the "Plough," can be gleaned from the name Artoius, "the Plough Man," which has been submitted as another possible origin of his name. King Arthur's intimate association with the Big Dipper is revealed in Grail literature by the scenario that follows his death, when the monarch's body is taken to the Island of Avalon, the paradise of the immortals now associated with Glastonbury, England. Glastonbury is a landscape temple that is a terrestrial reflection of the Big Dipper.

The Big Dipper was also the celestial reflection of the priest kings of the Toltec, Maya and Aztec tribes of Mexico and Central America, who were known to channel an abundant amount of life force or Water of Life to keep their kingdoms prosperous. The asterism was not, however, associated with a bear in Mexico, but the jaguar, an animal that in many shamanic cultures has been recognized as the royal symbol of kings. The Holy Grail power that moved through the shamanic kings of Middle America was represented by the monarch's ceremonial regalia, which included jaguar gloves, as well as a red jaguar throne, the most famous of which currently resides within the Castillo, the Temple of Quetzlcoatl, in Chichen Itza on the Yucatan Peninsula. The Mayan shaman kings released their jaguar power into their kingdoms through an annual rite during which they pierced their own flesh with sharp obsidian blades, thereby releasing their life force along with copious amounts of divine blood.

Bootes, the Celestial Holy Spear

If Flegetanis did not discover the mystery of the Holy Grail in the aforementioned Celestial Grails, perhaps he found it in the constellation of Bootes, which is a manifestation of the Celestial Holy Spear. Bootes is the celestial "Herdsman" and lance bearer, who carries a spear in one hand and the reigns of two leashed dogs in the other while closely following and guarding (or as some say, "herding") its adjacent constellation of the Great Bear. The lance borne by Bootes, who is also associated with Longinus, the Roman centurion reputed to have pierced the side of Jesus during the crucifixion, comprises part of the heavenly palace of the Celestial Emperor in the northern sky and is thus recognized to be a celestial version of the Holy Spear that the Fisher King keeps in his Grail Castle.

If Bootes was discovered by Flegetanis, perhaps it was the Middle Eastern astrologer who first associated the Holy Spear with the Holy Grail. If so, he may have then synthesized that wisdom with what he learned from the constellations of Aquarius, Crater, Corvus, Hydra, Ursa Major and Bootes, to produce the first rendition of the Holy Grail legend.

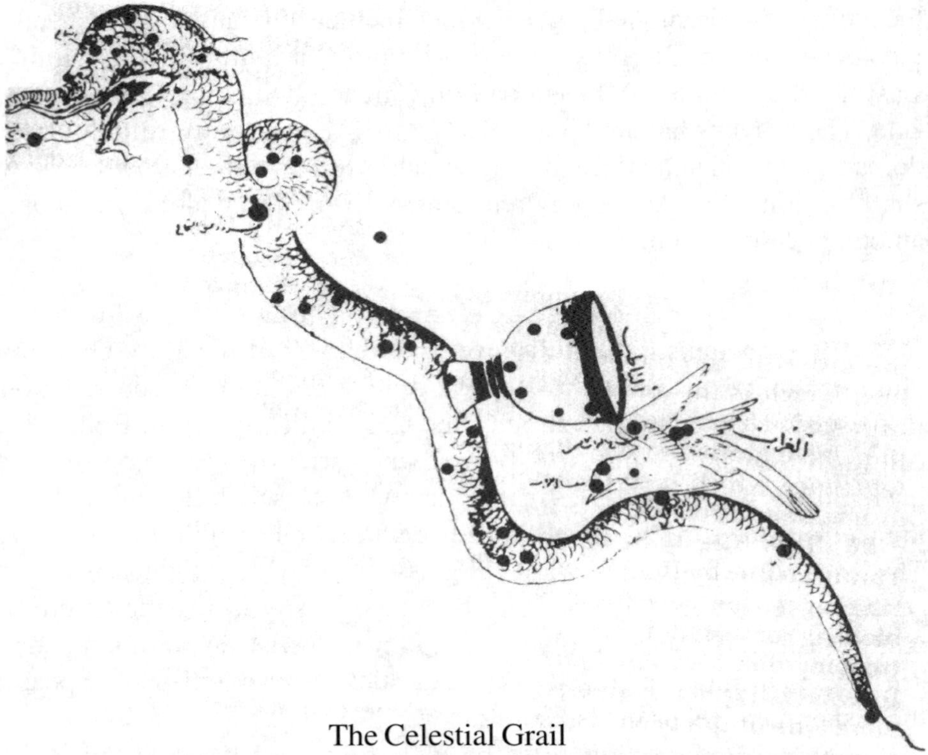

The Celestial Grail
Crater and Crovus ride upon the back of Hydra.

6
The Alchemical Power of the Holy Grail

The common thread that unites all the aforementioned Holy Grail manifestations, be they rocks, chalices, spears, or constellations, is the power to alchemically transform a human being into an immortal god or goddess. It can thus be stated that *the Holy Grail is not an object, but the power attached to that object.* The true Holy Grail is life force, the subtle, etheric energy that surrounds and interpenetrates an object and has the power to transform those who come into contact with it. In the Holy Grail Mysteries this power is referred to as the Holy Spirit and portrayed as a white dove, the symbol of pure, untainted life force, that descends to Earth from the heavens. The striking avian image of the descending dove, which had earlier been utilized by the authors of the *Gospels* as symbolic of the Holy Spirit descending upon Jesus Christ during his baptism, was later adopted by the German Wolfram von Eschenbach, who maintained in his magnum opus *Parzival* that on every Good Friday a dove would swoop down from the heavens and recharge the Stone of Heaven with the power of the Holy Spirit for the coming year.

The association between the Holy Spirit and the Holy Grail is very ancient and begins well before the era of Jesus. It is at least as old as ancient Persia, where the Holy Spirit in the form of a halo or nimbus surrounding the heads of saints was referred to by Persian epithets that denoted "Holy Grail."[1] The Persians' link between the Holy Spirit and the Holy Grail was also evident in their word gohar, a term that possibly preceded and evolved into the European graal or grail and denoted "fire in the water," which is an alchemical term for the Holy Spirit.[2] The Persians' understanding of the Holy Spirit was eventually taken west by the Sufi alchemists, who designated the Holy Spirit power as the *Azoth,* and they in turn passed it to the fledgling European alchemists, who likened *Azoth* to their *mecure igne*, which they represented in their texts as a Holy Grail chalice.[3]

The Holy Spirit is the Goddess

The dove that descended from the heavens and the Holy Spirit power it embodied was anciently venerated as a symbol of the Universal Goddess in the Middle East. According to Grail author Wolfram von Eschenbach, this association was assimilated by the Knights Templar during their sojourn in Asia Minor, and they in turn revealed their affiliation to the Goddess and Her Holy Spirit power by adorning themselves with symbolic turtle doves and representing themselves as Knights of the Dove.[4]

According to the ancient Goddess cosmology that the Templar Knights learned from their Middle Eastern teachers, the Goddess was understood to be the Holy Spirit life force that descended to our planet Earth like a dove at the beginning of time and thus became "Mother Nature." At that primal moment, the Goddess crystallized into the material forms that have since populated our world, and since that time She has continued to return to Earth daily as the life force in the air in order to nurture and sustain Her beloved creations. The Goddess' favorite time of the year is the beginning of the growing season in spring, when She returns in Her fullness to bring forth the fledgling buds and sprouts that will eventually grow into the lush vegetation to nourish Her terrestrial children throughout the coming year.

In most pre-Christian cultures the Goddess was venerated as an equal partner to the "male" God and given full membership in the primal Trinity of Father, Son and Mother (the Goddess), which is a grouping that later evolved into the trinity of "Persons" known as the Father, Son, and Holy Spirit (or Holy Ghost). Within these early Goddess-worshipping cultures the Goddess was known as the power and wisdom of the transcendental Spirit, the Father; so She was not only equal to God but a part of Him. Because of the Goddess' close association with the Father, Her worshippers depicted Her as locked in an eternal embrace with Him and designated God to be the Goddess' perpetual consort. These early Goddess worshippers understood that life could not begin or be sustained if it were not for the eternal coition of the universal God and Goddess.

But even though the God and Goddess are eternally united, they seem to be separate and disconnected in the cosmos. This is because God is technically invisible and transcendent, and all around us in the universe all we see are manifestations of the Goddess. But God *is* always visible; He is visible *as* the Goddess. At the beginning of the creative cycle, the transcendental God emanated a part of Himself in the form of life force that eventually crystallized into the myriad forms of the physical universe. This was the Goddess. So while it may appear that God separates Himself from the Goddess and dense matter, He simply evolves *into* the Goddess. This is the premise of the Eastern philosophy of Non-Dualism.

The Goddess is the Power and Wisdom of God

The wisdom that stipulates that the God *is* the Goddess has been adopted and embraced for many ages all around the globe by the worshippers of the Goddess. Specifically, these Goddess worshippers have venerated their beloved Goddess as the *Power and Wisdom of God*, and as such they have given Her names meaning power and/or wisdom. Many of Her names also begin with or incorporated the letter *s*, which represents the serpentine life force form that She traditionally travels throughout the universe within. Her Hebrew venerators, for example, referred to the Goddess as Shekinah, and She was known as Sekhmet, meaning "The Power," by the neighboring Egyptians. She was paid homage to by the Hindus as Shakti, a name denoting "power," and as Sophia, meaing "Wisdom," She was prayed to by the Gnostics of the Middle East, Egypt, and the coastal areas of the Mediterranean Sea.

In India, the Goddess Shakti is understood to be the power and wisdom of the "male" God, Lord Shiva, and traditionally portrayed as one or more snakes dangling from the neck of his anthropomorphic image. In Egypt, the Goddess as Sekhmet has been portrayed as both a red lioness and as a serpent, each of which have been said to emanate from the "Eye" of the primal God, Lord Ra. In the Jewish tradition, the Goddess Shekinah was venerated as the power emanating from Lord Yahweh, and among the early Gnostics the Goddess as Sophia was paid homage to as the personification of God's power and wisdom. Sophia was also worshipped in a serpentine form, which Her Gnostic devotees asserted was a reflection of Her manifestation as the Serpent of the Tree in the Garden of Eden. And She was also acknowledged by the adept Gnostics to be synonymous with the power of a Holy Grail chalice.[5]

The Three Powers of the Goddess

The worshippers of the Goddess knew that as the life force their deity wielded three powers, the powers of creation, preservation, and destruction. In Her form of the life force the Goddess creates this universe and sustains it, and at the end of time She destroys Her material creation and returns it to pure energy or life force. By extension, the Goddess' worshippers also recognized that when the life force attaches itself to an object, such as a manifestation of the Holy Grail, then that object also wields the three powers of the Goddess.

In the Holy Grail Mysteries the Goddess as the life force attaches Herself to an abundance of platters, cups, swords, and stones, thereby infusing them with Her three powers. It is the Goddess' creative power contained within a Holy Grail platter or cup that brings forth a continual supply of sweet liquids or tasty foods. It is the Goddess' creative power attached to the Holy Grail platter in *Parzival* that brings forth "the very fruit of bliss, a cornucopia of the sweets of this world." Wolfram's Grail manifestation was so plentiful, states the author, that "...whatever one stretched out one's hand for in the presence of the Grail, it was waiting, one found it all ready and to hand – dishes warm, dishes cold, new fangled dishes and old favorites, the meat of beasts both tame and wild..."[6]

By contrast, it is the destructive power of the Goddess that gives a Holy Grail the power to transform a human into a god or goddess, a process it accomplishes by destroying the physical and emotional impurities, as well as the false notions, that keep him or her from knowing their true self. The Goddess' power of destruction creates entropy, a process that eventually brings all things to their death, but in the end it reveals the transcendental and infinite God that underlies all physical form. The Goddess' destructive power was reflected by many of Her manifestations worldwide, including the Egyptian Sekhmet, who as the red lioness was known to destroy all the enemies of Lord Ra. The Goddess' destructive nature was also personified as the terrifying aspect of Shakti, known as Kali, the black and bloodthirsty goddess who was called upon by Her human worshippers to destroy their mortal enemies. Another manifestation of the destructive Goddess has been the numerous Black Madonnas that have been installed and worshipped within churches and chapels throughout Europe. This was one form that the Knights Templar venerated the destructive aspect of the Goddess. They, like their fellow alchemists and nature worshippers worldwide recognized that death leads to rebirth and that destruction and transformation are two sides of the selfsame coin.

The Goddess' three powers are most noticeable in Her role as Mother Nature. During the annual cycle of nature, She manifests the plants of spring, nourishes them during the summer, and finally destroys them in the fall. Thus, the Goddess' priests and priestesses knew Mother Nature as the triune or Triple Goddess, which they personified in iconography as a maiden, mother, and a crone. They also worshipped Her triune manifestation as the three phases of one of Her celestial manifestations, the Moon. Those Goddess worshippers desirous of drawing down and utilizing Her creative power to create abundance in their lives would normally perform their rites during the Moon's new or waxing phase; those worshippers desirous of attracting the Goddess' nurturing and sustaining power would revere Her during the time of the Full Moon; and those compelled to call upon the destructive aspect of the Goddess would summon Her during the dark or waning phase of the Moon. During the time of the dark Moon, alchemists and yogis seeking to utilize the destructive power of the Goddess might also invoke Her in a specific form, such as the vicious Sekhmet, the blood thirsty Kali, or as the grotesque Hekate of the Greek pantheon. As Kali, the Goddess might even appear etherically to them as a red or black skinned woman with long, disheveled hair, pointed fangs dripping with blood, a dismembered human head in one hand, a noose and axe in her other hands (she has many), and a garland of human skulls around her neck. But although Kali's grotesque form would inspire fear and loathing among the common populace, it was welcomed by those committed to the path of spiritual transformation because they understood Her macabre image to be symbolic of the Goddess' power to destroy both the ego and the physical, emotional, and mental impurities that prevent a seeker of wisdom from knowing his or her inner Spirit.

Kundry, the Dark, Destructive Goddess of Grail Legend

According to the founder of the Theosophical Research Organization, the esotericist Manley Palmer Hall, the destructive power of the Goddess is personified in the Holy Grail Mysteries as Kundry, a sorceress with grotesque features that is typically clothed in a black cloak embroidered with white doves, the symbol of the Holy Spirit she personifies. In *Parzival*, Wolfram graphically describes Kundry's Kali-like appearance thus: "Her nose was like a dog's, and to the length of several spans a pair of tusks jutted from her jaws...Kundry's ears resembled a bear's...in her hand she held a knot (perhaps part of a noose)...her fingernails were none too transparent...they looked like a lion's claws."[7] A particularly telling feature ascribed to Kundry by the author Wolfram is her "hat of peacock feathers," which ostensibly affiliates her with the destructive power of Lucifer, who is also known in the East as the Peacock Angel.

The name Kundry and its prefix of *kun* or *kund* point to Her special affiliation with Kundalini, the Sanscrit term for the destructive power of the Goddess that purifies a seeker and leads him or her to divine knowledge and empowerment. Thus, in the Holy Grail Mysteries the Kundalini is manifest as Kundry. As Kundry, the Goddess Kundalini transforms Parzival, the archetypal seeker, into an immortal Fisher King, and in the process She puts him through an intensive process of purification punctuated by lessons within which She assumes an abundance of diverse personalities. In the Grail rendition of *Peredur*, for example, Kundry is seen assuming the identity of Parzival's cousin, as well as the fair Grail Bearer in the Grail Castle of the Fisher King, and a young, blond haired youth. Near the end of the Grail legend, Kundry reverts to her original, repulsive form to convey the "news" that since Parzival has proven himself to be both courageous and integrous while meeting his challenges he has earned the right to become the new Fisher King.

Kundry is related to the German kunde, meaning "information" or "news." Thus, the personality of Kundry is a pure manifestation of the Goddess who is the wisdom or "news" of God. Kundry's association with "news" also makes Her a manifestation of the power of God, because in Arabic "good news" translates as Baraka, a name for the life force. Thus, Kundry is the pure life force, which means that She must wield not only the power of destruction, but also the powers of creation and preservation. This truth is conveyed in Book Nine of *Parzival*, wherein Kundry assists Sigune, Parzival's female cousin and a forest-dwelling hermit, by making sure that the Grail she possesses continually provides her with an abundance of sustaining food. Kundry plays a similar role in both *Peredur* and *Perlesvaus*, wherein she is depicted as the fair bearer of a food-producing Holy Grail chalice in the Grail Castle of the Fisher King.

In *Parsifal*, composer Wagner accurately portrays Kundry as Mother Nature and Her three powers by making Her synonymous with the cycle of nature. The German composer initially portrays Kundry in Her hag manifestation during which She is under the control of the evil king Klingsor. Meanwhile, the outer world, which reflects Kundry, is desolate and the cycle of nature is in its annual phase of death and destruction. When Parsifal eventually defeats Klingsor and reclaims the Holy Grail (which in this Grail rendition is in the form of the Holy Spear), Kundry is set free. The Goddess then magically turns from a decrepit hag into a beautiful girl while her liberated power simultaneously produces an abundance of spring flowers, thus transforming what had previously been a cold and barren world into a summer paradise.

Since Wagner made Kundry synonymous with Mother Nature, many scholars have compared Kundry to the goddess Eriu, a personification of Mother Nature in ancient Ireland. During the winter months, when the land was barren and cold, Eriu was conceived of by the Irish Celts as an old hag, but when spring arrived she magically transformed into an enchanting damsel. The Celts, who thus linked Mother Nature to the life force she personified, understood that, like the life force, she is radiant and creative in the spring and old and exhausted in the fall.

The Power of the Holy Grail is also Al-Khadir

Although many Goddess worshipping cultures, including the Celts, recognized nature as the product of the Goddess' life force, and thus synonymous with Her, other Goddess worshipping tribes took an alternate route and designated nature to be the progeny, child or "Son" of the Goddess. From their perspective, the Goddess was the solid ground of Mother Earth who gave birth every spring from Her barren womb (the surface of the Earth) to a son that took the form of the multudinous forms of green foliage that covered the countryside each spring and summer. The Goddess' Son, who eventually became known as the Green Man, was thus said to be born each year before maturing in the summer and finally dying with the deterioration of vegetation in the fall. And since he was an embodiment of the life force, he was ascribed the same three powers as his mother, the Goddess. But although he wielded the three powers of the life force, he did so *for* his mother. He was Her administrator on Earth. He wielded the Goddess' three powers while serving as the etheric King of the World.

When the Knights Templar were in the Middle East they were exposed to legends of the ancient Son of the Goddess and Green Man. The Son of the Goddess had been worshipped for thousands of years by the surrounding indigenous natives, who knew him as Dionysus, Tammuz, Adonis, and Attis. The Sufi and Assassin mentors of the Knights also knew the Son of the Goddess by the name of Khadir or Al-Khadir, which is an Arabic appellation meaning "Verdant" or "Green Man." Other cultures of the Middle East, including the Jews, Persians, and Turks also knew Al-Khadir, although they translated his name into their native vernacular and he thus became known to them as Hudr, Kisir and Hizer, respectively.

Al-Khadir was also venerated as the Goddess' adminstrator and King of the World, and in this function he was called by his regal name of King Melchizedek. He wielded the three powers of the life force, and like the life force, he was androgynous. The life force is androgynous because it unites the male and female principles to become life, just as a man and woman come together to produce life. To his venerators, Al-Khadir was the androgynous Lord of Nature who could be creative, but he could also be a destroyer. In his desctuctive aspect Al-Khadir was known as the "Initiator," the one who awakens the inner destructive force of Kundalini and eventually makes a human immortal.

To comprehend and directly experience Al-Khadir, the Sufis, Assassins, and most probably the Knights Templars, smoked or consumed hashish, a compressed cannabis resin that was referred to in the Middle East as the "Flesh of Khadir." Through the sacramental consumption of Khadir's own flesh they were able to adequately expand their consciousness until they found themselves transported into the presence of the Green Man. Their experience of Khadir at that moment, which had its counterpart in the experiences of the Greek revelers of Green Man Dionysus, would have no doubt assumed many nuances, such as a tangible feeling of an all-pervading consciousness or the presence of an eternal Witness who perpetually watches all third-dimensional existence from a transcendental realm. Such experiences of Al-Khadir have been alluded to by many Sufi and Arab mystics, as well as by some of the early Jewish prophets, who knew him as the eternal "Watcher." The experience of the Green Man has also been common in other parts of the world, especially among shamans, who for millennia have communed with nature through a ritual communion – possibly the earliest form of communion with the Son of God – using certain psychoactive plants, including the North American Peyote, the Mexican Cubensis mushroom, and the San Pedro cactus and Ayahuasca vine of Peru. The worshippers of Queztlcoatl, the manifestation of the Green Man in Mexico, have for centuries consumed a sacrament of mind-altering mushrooms that they respectfully refer to as the "Flesh of Queztlcoatl." And to experience Dionysus, the Green Man of Greece, the Dionysian revelers used hallucinogenic mushrooms along with draughts of very strong wine. Their liquid sacrament may have been borrowed from the cult of the Egyptian Green Man, Osiris, the "many-eyed one," who is averred to have invented the sacrament of the ascended grape many thousands of years ago and then spread it around the globe. In India and Sri Lanka, the worshippers of Green Man Murrugan directly experienced both their deity and Murrugan's father, the trident wielding Lord Shiva, through a flowering plant known as Datura. When Murrugan's Datura cult was later taken westward by Mascara gypsy dancers it became part of the sacramental cult of the European witches, and trident-wielding Shiva eventually became synonymous with the Devil of the Catholic Church.

How might the Knights Templar have experienced Al-Khadir? The many Green Man heads sticking out from the foliage decorating the interior of Rosslyn Chapel of Scotland, a bastion of Templar iconography, may give a clue. The Knights may have also experienced Khadir as one of their own, i.e., a knight. This appears probable since they identified Al-Khadir as synonymous with their patron knight, St. George, who was also an evolution of the Green Man (the name George is derived from Geo, meaning "Earth;" he was the Earth or Green Man). At some point St. George and Khadir merged into one, and today they share the same annual holiday, April 23. Perhaps the Templars experienced Khadir-George as the Green Knight, a figure from Grail legend who figures prominently in the Medieval poem known as *Sir Gawain and the Green Knight*.

If the Templars did conceive of Green Man Khadir as a spear or sword wielding warrior they were not alone. Other manifestations of the Green Man worldwide have been experienced similarly. Both Dionysus and Murrugan, for example, were experienced by their worshippers as spear-wielding warriors and even the commanders of extensive armies. In this context, Murrugan has been referred to as Karttikeya, the Commander of the Celestial Host, and Dionysus has been honored as a great chieftain who once led an army clear across Asia.

Of course, the Knights Templars' experience of Khadir could have also been consistent with how their Middle Eastern teachers experienced him, as an immortal sage and/or as the Initiator into spiritual life. In addition, there are other manifestations of Khadir that are intrinsic to his assorted names, most of which are derived from the same root, KHDR.[8] One of these derivations of KHDR, Khadar, is an epithet meaning palm tree, the towering plant that symbolizes Baraka or life force to the Arabs. Thus, the Templars and their Sufi mentors may have experienced Khadir as the consciousness and life force surrounding and interpenetrating the palm trees populating desert oasises. Another derivation of KHDR is ElKHuDRat, which means "the sea," a name that associates Khadir with Earth's largest bodies of water, as well as the subtle Water of Life. And a third variation, ElaKHaDir, carries the meaning of gold, meat and wine, thus linking Khadir to alchemy, as well as to the sacramental meal of meat and wine often consumed in various cultures as the blood and flesh of the Son of God. Therefore, the Knights Templar may have come to know Khadir as not only the Green Man, but as the power in alchemy and an ancient Son of God who preceded the Christian Son of God on Earth by many thousands of years.

When the Templars left the Middle East it is conjectured that they brought their hashish cult of the Green Man with them into Europe. Apparently a cult of hashish flourished in Europe after the Knights returned to France, especially in Paris, where the Templars built their principal French fortress. Later, after they had fled the inhumane brutality of King Philip the Fair and the French Inquisition, it is possible that the Knights may have taken their hashish rites into Scotland and continued them there. It is currently recognized that the production of hemp, the fibrous material of the plant that produces hashish, was widespread in the northernmost regions of Scotland near Sinclair Bay, a territory believed to have once served as a stopover for Templars fleeing France. Hemp was also cultivated in other Templar strongholds of Scotland, such as the Lammermuir Hills above Rosslyn Chapel.[9]

The Order of St. George

But even if they did not introduce their hashish cult to Scotland, the Templars could have continued their communion with the Green Man through the rites of the local pagan population of the country, who often celebrated the Green Man as their own "Green George." According to *The Golden Legend,* a sourcebook of medieval English legends, the British pagans derived the name George from Geo, meaning "Earth," and acknowledged that when a farmer tilled his land he was slicing through George's flesh.

The upper classes of Britain also celebrated Green George, but they did not embrace his form as the scruffy bumpkin of the country folk. For them he was St. George, the righteous warrior who was dedicated to perpetually protecting the kingdom of Great Britain. St. George's red cross became the foundation of the British flag, the Union Jack, and an Order of the Knights of St. George was duly founded under the auspices of King Edward III, who christened it the Order of the Garter. The Order of the Garter continues to meet annually in the Tower of London to reaffirm its allegiance to the British crown and its goal of protecting the Empire.

According to the Sufi Idries Shaw, the chivalrous Order of the Garter was actually modeled after the Middle Eastern Order of St. Khadir. Khadir, in his manifestation as Akhadar, the Spirit of Chivalry, had been the patron of an order of Middle Eastern knights known as *Tarika-I-Hadrat-I-Khidr*, the Order of St. Khadir, which in English directly translates as the "Order of St. George."[10] Shah maintains that the Order of Khadir had been a Holy Grail Order of Cupbearers overseen by the Sufis, who divided up the membership into circles of thirteen participants each, called *halkas.*

Britain's Order of the Garter not only copied the Order of St. Khadir by dividing into two groups of thirteen, but it also chose for its ceremonial robe an imitation of those worn by Khadir's initiates in the Middle East. The blue and gold robes of the Order of the Garter had originally been designed by Khadir's initiates to align them with Khadir, whose epithets of ElaKHaDir and ElKHuDRat associate the Green Man with "gold" and the blue "sea," respectively. The standard adopted by the British Order of the Garter, the "Greek" red cross with four equal arms placed in the center of an eight-pointed star, had also originally been symbolic of Khadir. The red cross is an ancient alchemical motif of Asia associated with the union of the polarity as the life force or Green Man, and the eight-pointed star is the ancient motif of the Goddess, who is the mother of Her Green Man Son. It is probably because of the Green Man's ancient connection to the number 8 that many Green Man heads currently decorating Rosslyn Chapel were set by the later Templars within the center of an eight-pointed star created by eight projecting vines.

The Initiator and Lord of the Two Rivers

Khadir's most important function among the Sufis, and possibly among the Templar Knights as well, was that of the primal "Initiator." As previously mentioned, since he was an embodiment of the life force, Khadir possessed the powers of both creation and destruction and he could initiate a seeker into the alchemical path of death that leads to rebirth and complete transformation. Khadir could awaken the destructive Kundalini because he *was* the Kundalini.

One of Khadir's names that relate to his function as Initiator is the "Lord of the two Streams." Khadir is the patron of those places on the Earth where two streams of water come together and produce an "androgynous" alchemical elixir. He is also the patron of the place in the human body where two streams of life force unite as the "androgynous" Kundalini. These two "streams," which flow through the Ida and Pingala Nadis, the subtle energy channels portrayed as the two snakes that spiral around the Caduceus of Hermes, come together at the base of the human spine as androgynous Khadir, the Kundalini power.

One of the places of confluence ruled by Khadir on the surface of the Earth is located on the island of Sri Lanka, which is one of the Green Man's favorite earthly abodes. Khadir is patron of a confluence of two sacred rivers on Sri Lanka known as the Menik Ganga, the "River of Gems," and the underground "Current of Grace." It was at this point of confluence on the island, states a popular legend, that many ages ago Al-Khadir discovered the *Abu-Hayat* or "Water of Life," which is, essentially, a name for Kundalini. The Green Man drank the Water of Life and instantly achieved immortality. Legend has it that he also tested the empowered water by placing a dead fish in it and then watched with wonder as it immediately returned to life. Since Khadir's ancient discovery of the Sri Lankan Fountain of Youth, people from all over the world, and especially the villagers from the nearby village of Hambantota, have continually searched for Khadir's Water of Life.

The place where the two rivers meet on Sri Lanka has been called the *Muladhara,* or Root Chakra, of the subcontinent of India, because it is Earth's counterpart to the two "streams" that unite within the root chakra of the human body. The *Muladhara* of Sri Lanka encompasses both the confluence of the two holy rivers as well as Khadirgama, the "Place of Khadir," which is a temple city sacred to the Buddhists, Hindus, and Moslems alike. Like the human *Muladhara*, the *Muladhara* of Khadirgama, which could thus be called the "Place of Kundalini," lies at the extreme end or base of the terrestrial "spine" of India. This earthly spine, which corresponds to the 81st parallel of longitude, has the Root Chakra of Khadirgama at one end and Mount Kailas of Tibet, the *Sahasrara* or Crown Chakra of the Indian subcontinent, at its other end.

It is interesting to note that when the ancient Greek cartographers drew up their early maps of the world they placed Sri Lanka at the extreme end of the world. It was placed at the eastern antipode, i.e., the easternmost end of the known world. The cartographers called the island Taprobane and claimed that it resided in a far distant place where day and night are of equal length. The island was thus the place of perfect balance and an ideal location for Khadir, the dual or "androgynous" Kundalini. Since the Greeks knew the Green Man as Dionysus, on their maps they designated Khadirgama as *Bachi Oppidum*, the "Town of Bacchus."

Besides Dionysus, Khadir has been known on Sri Lanka as Murrugan or Karttikeya, the Green Man of the Hindus, who thus refer to Khadirgama as Katirgama, the "Place of Karttikeya." One of Murrugan's other names is Melek Taus, with Taus meaning both "Peacock" and "Verdant Land."[8]

The Serpent on the Tree, the Lord of Wisdom

An additional appellation that has been assigned to Sri Lanka over many ages that relates to Khadir's manifestation as the serpentine Kundalini is the Garden of Eden, which is an epithet used by the Sufis and Arabs when referring to the paradisiacal island. The Garden of Eden was the original home of Khadir-Murrugan, who continues to reside there in his incipient form of the Serpent on the Tree. But, states the yoga master Paramahansa Yogananda, the Biblical authors never intended the Serpent on the Tree in *Genesis* to be taken literally. Instead, it was meant to be a motif representing the serpentine Kundalini power that ascends the "Tree of Life," a term used by yogis when referring to the human spine. Therefore,

Khadir-Murrugan is the Kundalini at the base of the spine of the Indian subcontinent.

As an embodiment of the serpent Kundalini, Murrugan of Sri Lanka has often been portrayed in iconography as a snake with one or seven heads and venerated as the bestower of Gnostic or intuitive wisdom, the knowledge of "I AM GOD" that arises following the spiritual purification engendered by the serpentine Kundalini. One of the names of Khadir-Murrugan is *Jnana Pandita*, the "Lord of Wisdom," because he is synonymous with the Serpent on the Tree of Life and its corresponding Gnostic wisdom, which in Sanscrit is Jnana (Yana). It is because Khadir-Murrugan was both the first physical teacher of Gnostic wisdom, as well as a manifestation of the indwelling serpentine Kundalini, that the Mediterranean Gnostics claimed that the premier teacher of Gnostic wisdom was the Serpent on the Tree of the Garden of Eden.

Among his Moslem venerators, Khadir's influence as a teacher of intuitive wisdom is well known and woven into anecdotes found in some of their scriptures, such as the *Surat al-Kahf*, which recounts the special instruction that the Prophet Moses received regarding Gnosticism from Khadir. During one special day they spent together, the Green Man is said to have performed some uncharacteristically destructive and insensible actions in order to compel Moses to use his intuition for understanding rather than his rational, intellectual mind. As Moses accompanied the Green Man he observed with horror as Khadir spontaneously killed a boy and later recklessly put a hole in someone's boat, seemingly for no good reason. Khadir also rebuilt a wall in a town populated with undeserving, cruel and inhospitable people, thus bringing to the surface Moses indignation. When in disgust Moses finally turned to walk away from the irrational Khadir, the Green Man called him back in order to explain himself. After stating "You must do what Allah guides you to do even if it is against logic," he then revealed to the Jewish prophet that Allah had intuitively communicated to him the reasons for his nonsensical actions. Allah had shown Khadir that the child was the son of followers of Moses and that he would have harmed his parents and caused them to leave the Judaic religion if he had been allowed to live. As for the boat, the vessel needed to sink so that it could be hidden from boat thieves, and the wall needed to be rebuilt so that the unrighteous persons of the town would not have found some treasure that had recently been buried underneath it.

Khadir is said to visit the shrine of his mother, the Goddess, in Mecca every year during the Hajj, the annual pilgrimage undertaken by the Moslem faithful to the Kaaba. Because of Khadir's annual presence during the Hajj, initiations occur and the Stone of Heaven in the Kaaba is re-empowered. It is said that Khadir arrives at Mecca with his "brother" Elias or Elijah, even though it is acknowledged that he and Elias are synonymous. The rest of the year the two "brothers" are separated, with Elias guarding the firmament of Earth, and Khadir governing its seas.

The Turks, who worship Al-Khadir as Hizer, maintain that the Green Man can manifest physically to worshippers during the Hajj, but he is more apt to appear to lost travelers or individuals that are in dire need of his assistance. Khadir as Hizer is thus honored as the patron saint of travelers, as well as *dues ex machina,* a "last-minute rescuer from disaster."

The Turks maintain that Hizer often manifests as an aged dervish with a long white beard and white turban, but they also allow that he can assume any form. One Turkish soldier claimed that when he was confronted by four Chinese soldiers in Korea, he shouted "Ya Hizer!" and Hizer instantly manifested in the form of one hundred Turkish soldiers. The Chinese were so frightened by the inexplicable appearance of the soldiers that they immediately laid down their weapons and surrendered to the enemy. According to another anecdote, Hizer as an old man once stopped a busload of people traveling from Ankara to Samsun. Hizer told the bus driver that he had a sick child at home that needed to be taken to the doctor. The driver waited for the old man to bring his child, but Hizer never returned. Eventually the occupants of the bus began to urge the bus driver to forget the old man and move on. But there was no answer from the driver. He had suffered a heart attack and died. Thus, Hizer had averted what would have been a tragic accident if the bus had been allowed to continue with the severely infirmed driver.

Since Hizer is an embodiment of the life force, the Turks believe that he can grant any request for material support. Thus, on May 6 of every year they conduct a silent ritual before sunrise with models of those things they most desire, such as a car, house, coat, shoes, etc. If Hizer is feeling generous towards them, they will get their desires met in the coming year. If not, they will try again the following year.

The Green Man and King of World. From an English priory.

The triple Green Man heads at Chartres Cathedral.

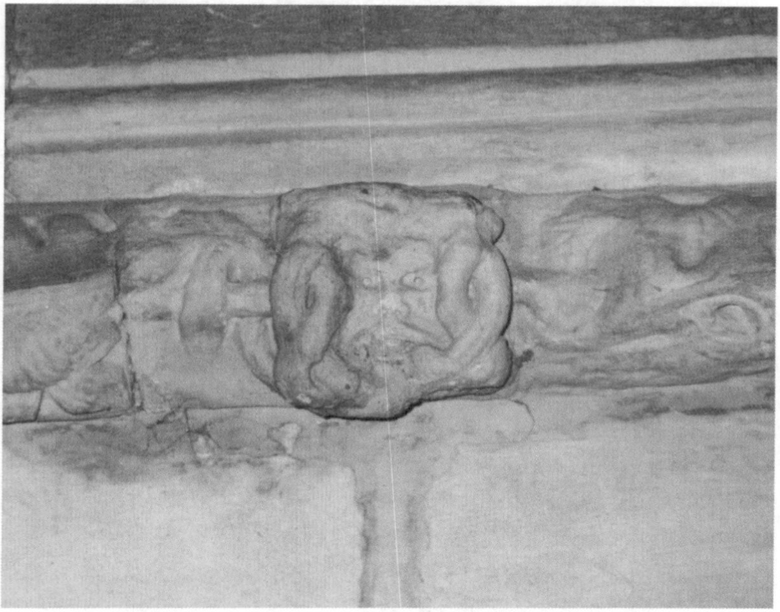

The dual Green Man. Left side of face is good, right side is evil. Rosslyn.

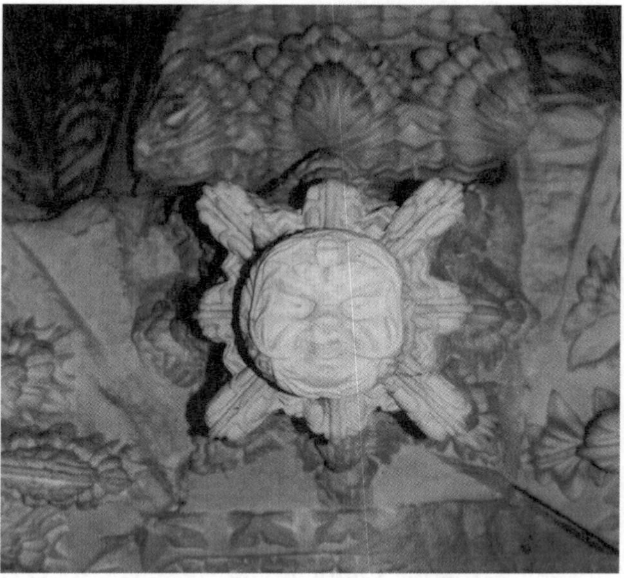

The Green Man in the center of the 8 pointed star. Rosslyn Chapel.

Kali, destructive/transformative power of the Goddess

Early symbol of the Knights Templar. The stars and crescent moon reveal affiliation to the Goddess Tradition of the East.

Part II:

The Human Holy Grails

7
Human Holy Grails

Part 1 revealed many Holy Grail manifestations worldwide and defined the power they possess as synonymous with the Holy Spirit power of the Goddess. Many of the Grail manifestations thus far presented are extremely powerful, and some have been known to produce unexplainable miracles. But there is a genre of Holy Grails that is immensely stronger than any so far presented. This class of Grails is known as the Human Holy Grails and comprised of spiritual adepts who move the Holy Spirit power of the universe through their very own bodies every second of every day. Because of their power, they wield the supernatural ability to create or destroy whatever they desire, as well as the ability to make a human being immortal. These Masters are the premier and archetypal Holy Grail vessels, and the Holy Grail Mysteries truly begin with them. It was their Holy Spirit energy that originally empowered the chalices, spears and stones that are today ascribed the power of Holy Grails. It was the Holy Spirit power flowing through the Human Holy Grail known as Jesus Christ, for example, that empowered the most famous of all Holy Grails, the Cup of Christ, even though Christ and not his chalice was the true Holy Grail. The truth of his status as a Human Holy Grail was conveyed by the Messiah to his disciples when he proclaimed "*of my cup shall you indeed drink.*"

The Human Holy Grails become embodiments of the Holy Spirit or Kundalini after they awaken the evolutionary power at its seat at the base of their spines. Then, as it moves throughout their physical, emotional, and mental bodies, it performs the task of destroying all the impurities that prevent him or her from knowing his or her innate divinity. Such Human Holy Grails are rare, even though they have existed all over the globe and during every historical era as enlightened priest kings, Kundalini Masters, and the heads of secret societies and mystery schools. In India, where the evolutionary force has been known as Kundalini, the "Serpent Power," the Human Holy Grails have manifested as Kundalini Masters, Siddhas (Perfected Masters) and as powerful Naga Kings, i.e., monarchs who wield the power of the naga, the serpent. Among the Jews, where the alchemical power has been known as Shekinah, the Holy Spirit, they have manifested as powerful prophets, including Elijah, Elisha, John the Baptist and Jesus Christ. John the Baptist identified the transformative power of the Holy Spirit that moved through the Jewish prophets when he stated that his disciple Jesus would baptize with both water and "fire." In the land of the Maya, the Human Holy Grails were known to be embodiments of K'ulthanilni, which they sometimes depicted as a fire serpent. The Peruvian Incas acknowledged the inner power of their Human Holy Grails as Kori Machakway, the "Golden Serpent," and the Chinese Taoists and shamans of the East recognized it as the transformed Jing or seminal fluid, which would rise like burning fire to the crown of the head through sacred ritual and yogic practices,and then fill their bodies with spiritual light. The power that the European and Middle Eastern Human Holy Grails embodied was referred to by them as the Astral Light and the Azoth and acknowledged to be the transformative power generated by their alchemical experiments that could both transform base metals into gold and humans into gods and goddesses. The Human Holy Grails of the Sufis knew their inner power to be the fiery, transformative Baraka, which could be transmitted from Master to disciple, and their predecessors, the Sumerian Human Holy Grails, recognized the power to be synonymous with their serpentine creator Enki and referred to it as the Water of Life.

The European authors of the Holy Grail legends were fully cognizant of the power that moves through a Human Holy Grail, having learned of it from the Templar Knights returning from the Holy Land. They represented it in their Grail legends as a dove descending from Heaven or as a dynamic radiance, although they also conceived of it in the form of a Black Madonna. The Templar affiliated author of the Grail legend known as the *Queste del Saint Graal* accurately portrayed this power as "A clap of thunder...followed by a brilliant ray of light."[1]

According to certain contemporary Johannite and Templar orders, the Knights became fully cognizant of the mysteries of Kundalini through the Gnostic sect of Middle Eastern Johannites, which had been anciently founded by the "two Johns," John the Baptist and John the Apostle. The Johannites currently maintain that most of the important occult wisdom regarding Kundalini activation and development passed from John the Baptist to Jesus and then on to John the Divine, whose symbol was a Holy Grail chalice entwined within the coils of the Kundalini serpent. The Johannites additionally claim that some of wisdom that John the Apostle received from Christ regarding Kundalini originated in Egypt, where Jesus had undergone an intensive initiation into the priesthood of Osiris. Egypt was, at that time, renowned the world over for its knowledge of both alchemy and Kundalini activation.

Partly because of its Johannite influence, the Day of Pentecost became the most sacred celebration of the year for the Knights Templar. It was on that day that the Knights would receive the Holy Spirit and then embark upon their quest of becoming Human Holy Grails.[2] Their observance of Pentecost is currently reflected in the legend of King Arthur and his Knights of the Round Table, the archetypal representations of the Knights Templars, who are similarly portrayed as designating Pentecost to be the most holy of days.

The Templars celebrated the Day of Pentecost in specially constructed temples that were designed to be energetically conducive to the activation and reception of the Holy Spirit. Such temples were built either in a circular design or as octagons, or sometimes they were a combination of these two alchemical forms. Such man-made crucibles of alchemy naturally united the universal polarity while simultaneously generating the transformative Holy Spirit presence of the Green Man. During their time in the Middle East, the Templars learned that the circular shape was especially sacred to the Green Man in his manifestation as Al-Khidr, whose sects included the El-muawwira, an epithet meaning "the Round Building."[3]

In the center of the Knights' alchemical temples were altars upon which sat effigies of the Green Man. Also gracing their shrines were Black Madonnas, idolized mummified human heads and skulls, and awe-inspiring skull and crossbone motifs. The walls of these temples were adorned with alchemical and Gnostic symbols, which have been intensively studied by certain European writers and researchers, like Baron von Hammer-Purgstall, and identified those venerated by the earliest Gnostics and alchemists of the Middle East and Egypt. Although the practice of alchemy cannot be conclusively stated as having occurred among the earliest Templars, we do know that it was observed within some of the later European branches of Templarism, including the German Strict Observance, whose membership included the greatest of European alchemists, Count Alessandro Caglisotro and Saint Germain.

Sexual Tantra observed by the Templars

The Templars' principal teachers of alchemy were the enlightened Sufis, who during the more than one hundred years the Knights resided in the Middle East were recognized by much of the known world as the greatest alchemists. Following the expansion of the Moslem Empire, the Sufis had gathered the rarest and most valuable alchemical texts of the Egyptians, Persians, and Indians, and then stored them in monastic libraries and Islamic universities. They studied the texts and then helped evolve and modernize the ancient art. The Sufis also acquired texts from India regarding certain forms of yogic practices and sexual Tantra observances that had been practiced in that subcontinent for thousands of years previously. The Templars assimilated the Sufis' alchemy, Tantrism, and yoga, and then amalgamated it to the yogic practices they acquired from certain Middle Eastern Gnostic sects, such as the Johannites. Important adepts of the Johannite lineage, including John the Baptist, Jesus Christ and Simon Magus, are averred to have practiced forms sexual Tantra, as well as Kabbalic yoga and meditation, which was later popularized by the 13th century by the Kabbalic Master Abraham Abulafia. Simon Magus, who was a close disciple of John the Baptist, taught sexual Tantric practices to his disciples and is averred to have regularly cohabited with his consort, Helen, a prostitute he discovered in a brothel in Lebanon and immediately recognized as the embodiment of the Gnostic Goddess, Sophia. Simon's brother disciple, Jesus Christ, is rumored to have practiced Tantra with his partner, Mary Magdalene, a notion popularized by the early historian Epiphanius, who maintained that an ancient Gnostic Gospel, the *Great Questions of Mary*, outlined the sexual practices observed by Jesus and Mary and Jesus' inner circle.[4] Could the Templar monks have practiced sexual Tantra in the tradition of the Human Holy Grails of their Johannite lineage? In light of the confessions extracted from the Knights following their arrest in France during the 14th century, they did. The Knights confessed to having sexual liaisons with women, as well as each other.[5]

Much of what we currently know regarding the Templars' Tantric practices comes from later European societies that adopted their practices. One such organization was the German Templar order known as the Strict Observance, which passed the rites to many European occult groups, including the Hermetic Order of the Golden Dawn and the OTO. The OTO, or "Oriental Templar Order," is notorious for its sexual rites that the order claims came directly from the Templar Knights, as well as the Sufis and some Tantric adepts of India. The OTO, which currently supports a network of branches around the world, is historically linked to the KVMRIS, a latter-day Templar organization that was headquartered in Belgium in the late 19th century that inherited many Gnostic and sexual secrets that evolved in France during and after the time of the Templar Order. The most famous OTO Grand Master, Aliester Crowley, is alleged to have organized orgies in order to experiment with and teach the old Templar practices to his students. He is especially noted for engaging in repeated acts of sodomy with his compliant partner, the poet Victor Neuberg.

The Templar Kiss

Besides alchemy and sexual Tantra, the Templars may have had their Kundalinis awakened through the grace of Al-Khadir or St. George, the "Initiator," who could have arrived during their sacrmental rites or through special invocations. They may have also learned the secret of passing the power between themselves through practices they acquired from the Johannites, who knew the rite of transmission known as the Secret of St. John, as well as from the Sufis, who for hundreds of years had transmitted and received Baraka through the vehicle of touch, a mantra, a kiss, or by simply thinking about it. The Sufis were also known to have transferred Baraka, a Middle Eastern name for Kundalini, through the intermediary of a "Grail" vehicle, such as sacramental water or a piece of blessed bread. After their adoption by the Knights Templar, the Sufi practices of Kundalini transmission may have evolved into the infamous "Templar Kiss," which according to the Knights' own testimonies occurred between an incoming Knight and a high ranking Knight priest. The kisses, which were planted by the elder Templar on the new Knight's mouth, navel and base of the spine, may have been administered specifically to activate Kundalini, since most of these parts of the body are known by the Hindu and Buddhist mystics to be seats of the power. The most valuable transmission of Kundalini could have been induced through the Templar kiss on the mouth, however, which ostensibly involved blowing into the new initiate's mouth the breath of life, which had previously become saturated with the elder Knight's own Holy Spirit or Kundalini.

The Templar kisses were an important ceremonial adjunct mentioned in the Templars' *Secret Rules,* which was a compilation of covert Gnostic ceremonial rites that the Knights had acquired in the Middle East. Author M. Giles, an expert on the secret Templar rites of the *Rules*, compares the Templar kiss to a similar eastern rite of initiation:

"The (Templar) kisses…had nothing obscene about them, because they symbolized the transmission of the breath or Life of the Order, and Power, as was the custom in most ancient initiations. The breath which was transmitted by the mouth, and the kiss on the mouth, was certainly preferable to the custom of the Aissaouah, among whom *moqqadem* – the local chief – spits in the mouth of the received, as a magical communication, by means of the saliva, of the chief's spiritual faculties."[6]

Baphomet, the Kundalini Power

The Knights had a name for the Kundalini power transferred through their Templar Kiss. It was Baphomet, which the occult historian Gerald Massey claims is a synonym for the "Mother of Breath."[7] Much of what we know about the Templars and their relationship to Kundalini comes from their remaining images of Baphomet, which includes the three black heads that once adorned the shield of Hughes de Payen (collectively representing the universal Trinity and triune powers of the life force), and the grotesque form of the black goat-god that the 19th century self-styled Templar descendant and French occultist, Alphonse Louis Constant, a.k.a. Eliphas Levi, claimed had been a manifestation of Baphomet venerated by the Knights Templar. Levi's Baphomet, which is an androgynous black goat-god with both animal and human features, possessed a phallus in the shape of Mercury's caduceus and symbolized both the androgynous life force produced through the fire of alchemy, as well as the androgynous Kundalini at the base of the human spine. Levi claimed that his image of Baphomet was modeled after stone gargoyles of the beast that had been sculptured by Templar-trained masons and placed high upon some of the gothic cathedrals in Europe they built, such as the Church of Saint-Merri in Paris. Since Levi's time other occultists have found a links uniting Baphomet to the alchemical Kundalini, such as the 8 letters in the name and their numerological total of 8, the occult number associated with alchemy.[8] The OTO's Aliester Crowley often alluded to the magical power of Baphomet and its importance to the Templars, which is one reason he eventually chose "Baphomet" as his initiated name.

Because of their interactions with the Sufis, many of the Templars would have recognized Baphomet and the Kundalini power he personified as synonymous with Green Man Al-Khadir. Through their study of the Holy Grail Mysteries, they and their descendants would have also eventually identified Baphomet with both Kundry, a Holy Grail personification of the Kundalini, as well as Hiram or Chiram, the "Master Builder" who "rebuilds" or transforms "Solomon's Temple," an appellation for the human body. The Master Builder is a Templar personification of Kundalini that was ushered into the catechism of the Freemasonic lodges the Knights helped found in Renaissance Europe.

One manifestation of Baphomet, and perhaps its most important, was a mummified head the Knights Templars placed on their most revered altars. This form of Baphomet, the "Head of Wisdom," is believed to be the mummified head of John the Baptist, which the Knights Templar acquired in Constantinople during the Fourth Crusade. Since John had been a Kundalini master during his lifetime, his head still emanated his Holy Spirit or Serpent Power, and simply by being in proximity to it the Knights could absorb its transformative emanations. According to their own testimonies, the Knights knew that Baphomet could not only accelerate their spiritual evolution, but because it personifed the life force it even "made the trees to flourish and the earth to germinate." Even before its removal by the Knights from its reliquary in Constantinople, Baphomet's immense life force power had become renown for having healed a Roman Emperor of a fatal illness.

The Templars' Esoteric Anatomy

There are indications that the Knights may have been aware of the subtle human anatomy of chakras and meridians within which the Masters of the East maintain the Kundalini power personified as Khadir and Kundry lives and circulates. The Knights' occult wisdom regarding the *Muladhara Chakra* at the base of the spine and home of the evolutionary force appears to have been encoded as metaphor in a Welsh Holy Grail legend known as *Preiddeu Annwn*, "The Spoils of Annwn," wherein King Arthur and an entourage of his knights are depicted searching for the Holy Grail in Annwn, the underworld. Arthur and his party eventually discover their sought-after chalice in the "Four-cornered Castle in the Isle of the Closed Door," which may be a metaphor for the "four-cornered" or four "petalled" *Muladhara Chakra*, which as the first of the seven "isles" or chakras in the human body dwells within the "underworld" at the base of the spine. Moreover, the "closed door" of the Four-cornered Castle is an accurate description of the "door" within the *Muladhara Chakra* that remains closed until its owner is ready for the indwelling Kundalini to ascend the *Sushumna Nadi*, the subtle channel within the spine, and climb to the top of the head of a seeker of wisdom.

It is possible that the Knights Templar could have learned the human esoteric anatomy of chakras and energy vessels directly from their Sufi teachers, who knew them as seven power centers called *Lataif*. They could have also studied the subtle anatomy under the tutorship of Jewish Rabbis, who knew the esoteric mysteries from their study of the Kabbala. The Kabbala incorporates within it the image of the Sephiroth Tree of Life, which is a Gnostic symbol of both the Serpent on the Tree, as well as a map of the path of the Kundalini serpent up the human spine through the chakras. But if not from the Jewish Rabbis, the Templars would have acquired the Kabbalic mysteries from the Johannites and other Gnostic sects, which had inherited them from early Gnostics that had flourished in the Middle East during the first centuries of the modern era.

A Templar Knight becomes a Human Holy Grail

Once a Templar Knight had activated his Kundalini, he would have undergone a process of purification similar to that experienced by his Johannite and Sufi mentors. As Baphomet, a.k.a. the Master Builder and Al-Khadir, began its process of "rebuilding Solomon's Temple," the Knights would have experienced the acceleration of their vibratory frequency precipitated by the Kundalini, followed by the Serpent Fire's ensuing onslaught of the accumulation of toxins that had kept them from knowing their divine nature. Such toxins can accumulate through the physical toxins taken into the body through food, water and air, as well as by unresolved emotional trauma and illusory belief systems. As these toxins are interfaced with by the Holy Spirit they are brought to the surface and dispelled through physical infirmity and emotional catharsis, or they can be consumed directly within the fire of the alchemical Kundalini.

As the Kundalini ascended up the spine to the top of a Knight's head, a Templar would gradually become full of the Holy Spirit while being transformed into a Human Holy Grail. The ancient "Serpent on the Tree," the first teacher of Gnostic wisdom, would then enter the Holy of Holies, the skull of the Knight, and activate the *Ajna Chakra* or Third Eye of intuition, along with the remaining two-thirds of his brain power, to bring forth the timeless Gnostic revelation of "Be still and know that I AM GOD."

After the Kundalini serpent had completed its ascension to the top of the "tree," the Templar Knight would be full of its Holy Spirit power and a true Human Holy Grail. Then, with his abundant Serpent Power a Templar Knight could heal himself and others, and he could also transmit some of his own power into a new Knight through the vehicle of touch and/or the Templar Kiss, thus initiating a brother's process of alchemical development. A Templar full of the power of Baphomet could also use his Kundalini energy to injure and destroy an enemy, an ability demonstrated by the last Templar Grand Master Jaques de Molay, whose death curse against both King Philip V of France and Pope Clement V came to pass within a year's time of his death.

When the Templar Knights returned to Europe they brought with them the wisdom regarding Kundalini unfoldment and incorporated it into the secret societies they helped found throughout the continent. The wisdom of Hiram Abiff, the Master Builder, thus became a focus of study within the lodges of Freemasonry, followed by the experiments with yoga and alchemy enrolled in by the Rosicrucians, Europe's "Fire Philosophers." The Rosicrucians delineated the mystery of Kundalini unfoldment in their occult text *The Alchemical Wedding of Christian Rosencrutz*, which was written by the Grand Master Johann Valentin Andrea. They also promulgated some of the sexual Tantric rites of the Knights Templar in satellite branches of the sect, including the Fraternitas Rosae Crucis. One outstanding member of the Fraternitas Rosae Crucis, Pascal Beverly Randolph, a 19th century half-breed from Virginia, gained worldwide fame for his work with sexual Tantra, which he delineated in his magnum opus, *Magia sexualis*, "Sexual Magic."

In the following pages you will find descriptions and biographies of an abundance of Human Holy Grails. Chapter 8 will cover the priest kings around the globe who once governed their kingdoms with their supernatural power, and Chapter 9 will present the Johannite lineage of spiritual masters, who became Human Holy Grails or Cupbearers by ascending the Serpent up the Tree of Life and then transmitting their Kundalini power into their Gnostic heirs.

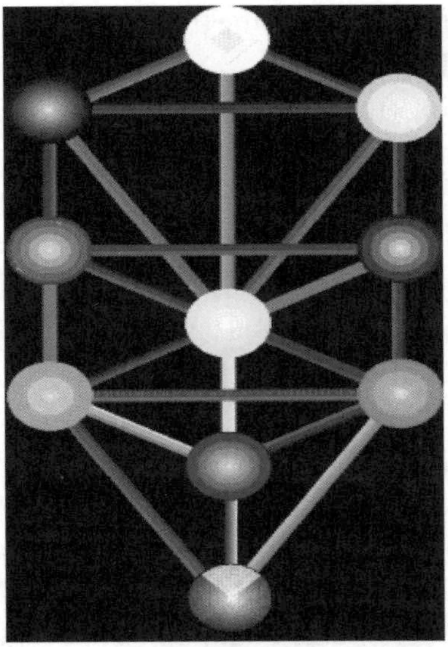

The Sephirothic Tree of Life, symbol of the path of the Kundalini.

The Tree in the Garden of Eden. Also a symbol of the path of the Kundalini.

8
The Fisher Kings
Embodiments of the Green Man

According to the Holy Grail Mysteries, the premier Gaudians of the Holy Grail and some of the most renowned Human Holy Grails to ever set foot on Earth have been the fabled monarchs who once ruled their kingdoms as enlightened priest kings. Collectively represented by the authors of the European Holy Grail legends as the archetypal Fisher Kings, these early priest kings of our planet's sacred history were renown for their supernatural power and penetrating wisdom, and their exalted status was reflected in their uniquely telling emblems, such as dragons, serpents, and lions, which are symbolic of the Kundalini life force they embodied. Their emblems also included one or more of the Holy Grail Hallows - the spear, cup, sword, and platter or stone - which are collectively referred to as the *Hallows of the Grail Castle* and known to denote the royal powers of discrimination, intuition, and the accumulation and dissemination of supernatural power. The Fisher Kings have, of course, also been identified with the symbol of a fish, which represented them as Kundalini Masters swimming within the cosmic sea of life force that surrounds and interpenetrates our universe. This chapter will cover the unique attributes of the Fisher Kings, as well as their very ancient lineages.

Whence the name "Fisher" King?

The term "Fisher" of Fisher King has created much confusion about the true identity of these monarchs among Grail scholars. Some academics have suggested that the term Fisher associates these kings with the *Synoptic Gospels*, wherein Jesus appeals to his disciples to become "Fishers of Men." But the Fisher King of Grail legend is not an evangelist seeking to "catch" and convert human "fish," he is the ruler of a kingdom. Other Grail scholars have simply associated the name Fisher King with fishing, which was the activity Percival finds the ruling Fisher King enrolled in when he first encounters him outside his castle. But by linking him to the art of fishing, scholars have succeeded in disconnecting the Fisher King from the many historical monarchs who have been affiliated with and even referred to as fishes. It should be with them that a true understanding of the name "Fisher King" is to be gleaned.

One need only to make a cursory study of history to discover an abundance of priest kings associated with the symbol of the fish. The ten pre-flood kings of Sumerian legend, for example, were represented as fishes swimming in the Apzu, the "sea of wisdom," and collectively known as the AB-GAL, the "Masters of Knowledge." Their Fisher King lineage continued after the Deluge by lineages of Babylonian priest kings who claimed descent from the bull god Marduck and his father Enki, the primal goatfish and Creator of the Universe. A little later in history, a Fisher King lineage similar to the one in Mesopotamia emerged in Medieval France as the Merovingian sorcerer kings. Merovee, the founder of the Merovingian lineage, was said to have been sired by a kind of fish, a "Quinotaur," that was half fish and half bull and mated with his mother one day as she was bathing in the Mediterranean Sea. Thus, we find that the patriarchs of the Fisher King lineages in both Mesopotamia and France were sea creatures with the "androgynous" features of a fish and bull or a fish and goat, which symbolized them to be the union of the female (fish) and male (goat and bull) principles. Such Fisher Kings were, like the Green Man, embodiments of the androgynous life force, which is generated from the union of the male and female principles.

The Hallows of the Grail Castle

Before tracing the lineages of the Fisher Kings, we will first cover the royal powers ascribed to them. These special attributes were symbolized by the Hallows of the Grail Castle - the Sword, Cup, Spear, and Platter or Stone, which the Fisher Kings stored in their Grail Castles, the regal enclosures that metaphorically symbolized their extended bodies. According to Margaret Starbird, these four Hallows are known to the world today as the four suits of the Minor Arcana of the Tarot - the wands, spears, cups and pentacles - as well as the four suits in a pack of common playing cards - diamonds, spades, hearts, and clubs. The remainder of a Tarot deck, the twenty-two cards of the Major Arcana, contain symbology depicting the unfoldment of the definitive Holy Grail legend, during which Percival, the Fool of the first card of the Major Arcana, evolves into the immortal Fisher King and Lord of World, depicted by the twenty-second card.

The Holy Grail Sword

The Fisher King's Holy Grail Sword that he stores within his Grail Castle denotes the monarch's ability to rule his kingdom with the "male" characteristics of fiery power and intellectual discrimination. Just like a sword that cuts through its target, the discrimination of a Fisher King cuts away all the extraneous mental fluctuations which hide the pure, underlying truth.

According to the Holy Grail Mysteries, as long as the Fisher King rules his kingdom justly and with both foresight and discrimination, his symbolic sword will remain strong and he will be undefeatable. But when he strays from unselfish motives and his thinking becomes clouded, his sword is liable to break. This truth is revealed in some of the Holy Grail legends, such as Chrétian's myth, wherein the degenerated Fisher King entreats the visiting Percival to rejoin the two pieces of his shattered sword. The monarch's broken sword, which reflects a weakening of both his mind and personal power, was also mirrored by his empire, which had been "broken" and transformed into an impoverished wasteland. But before Percival could mend the broken sword of the Fisher King he needed to evolve the qualities befitting the wielder of a perfect sword, and until that time, states the *Quest del Saint Graal,* only the best of knights, Sir Gallahad, could make a sword whole again. The Fisher King Arthur was apparently given his first sword, the famous Sword in the Stone, before he had developed the requisite traits needed to wield the wisdom it exemplified, which is perhaps why it was subsequently broken in battle with the wise King Pellinor, a monarch who had evolved these essential characteristics. But later, states Grail myth, after Arthur had reached a pinnacle in his royal development and matured into a righteous king, Merlin escorted him to a body of water where he was given the indomitable sword Excalibur by the Lady of the Lake.

The sword of a Fisher King with a weak mind and unsteady resolve could also be stolen or suddenly disappear. King Arthur was made to relinquish Excalibur after making a series of self-centered and vindictive decisions following the illicit affair between Lancelot and Guinevere and later during the time he was attacked by his son, Morddred. The sword that Arthur had received from the Lady of the Lake, a manifestation of the Universal Goddess, was thus returned to Her, thus symbolizing that the authority and power that supports a Fisher King's reign (or any monarch's reign) comes from the Goddess Herself.

In Europe, the sword of the king was cherished as a symbol of both power and discrimination. Beginning with their patriarch Charlemagne, the emperors of the Holy Roman Empire associated their sacred swords with the power and longevity of their reigns. Charlemagne, who referred to his sword as Joyeuse, the "Joyish One," kept his weapon shined, polished, and near him at all at all times, knowing that if it became either broken, cracked, or stolen some of his power would disappear and his empire would likely crumble around him. When he died, Charlemagne was embalmed and set upon a throne in his favorite city of Aix la Chapelle with Joyeuse placed close by his side. The royal sword of the British monarchy, which since the time of King Richard I has been divided into three swords, represents the three supreme attributes required of an incumbent English king. One sword denotes mercy and the king's merciful nature; another denotes spiritual justice and the king's defense of the Church; and the third signifies temporal justice and the king's defense of his people. The three swords are traditionally carried in procession during the time of the king's coronation by three noblemen, the Earl of Chester, the Earl of Huntington, and the Earl of Warwick, who walk together in front of the king. Of these three swords, the most important is the blunt-edged sword of mercy, known as *Curtana*, meaning "the sword cut short," which is carried directly in front of the king.

A royal sword was also a symbol of the kings of the East, including the monarchs of Japan, India, and China. In ancient Japan, a divinely empowered sword known as the *Ama-no-Murakumo-no-Tsurugi*, "the sword of heavenly gathering of clouds," was passed down within the lineage of emperors. According to legend, this heavenly sword had anciently been discovered in the tail of a slain eight-headed dragon (a symbol of the life force), and was thus infused with the tremendous life force power the beast embodied. The gods gave the sword to Ninigi, who then passed it to Jinmu, his grandson and Japan's first emperor. After this, the sacred sword, which insured prosperity for both Japan's king and his subjects, survived in the royal family for hundreds and thousands of years, but was finally lost in the 12th century. Another sword-wielding king of Asia was the ruling monarch of the Jaray, an unusual tribe of Cambodia mentioned in James Frazer's classic *The Golden Bough*. The Jaray tribe is unique for electing two monarchs to rule over them, a King of Water and a King of Fire, thus ostensibly revealing the need for a ruler or rulers who possess the attributes of both water and fire, the male and female principles. The sword was the symbol of the King of Fire, one of the two monarchs that embodied male fire and intelligence, and it was he who made most of the tribe's important decisions and led the most important rituals.[1]

Perhaps the first sword possessed by any Fisher King was that owned by the first Fisher King, Sanat Kumara or Murrugan, a monarch who ruled the world from the island of Sri Lanka when it was the Garden of Eden. Murrugan's sword is part of the motif adorning the current flag of Sri Lanka, which features a sword-wielding lion and denotes both the Fisher King's discriminating wisdom, as well as his inherent life force power. Legends maintain that the Fisher King Sanat Kumara was the fountainhead from which many lineages of Fisher Kings originated before spreading around the globe.

The Holy Grail Chalice

A second Hallows of the Grail Castle is the Holy Chalice, which is symbolic of the life force power or Water of Life that a Fisher King stores within his body and uses to uplift his kingdom. History is very instructive in revealing that as long as a monarch lives righteously and in harmony with the Divine Will, his cup "runneth over" with life force power and his kingdom is prosperous, but when he strays from the path of righteousness his cup (or body) becomes depleted of the Water of Life and his kingdom ceases to produce abundance in any form.

The most famous Fisher King of ancient times intimately associated with a chalice is the Persian King Jamshid, whose name means "Resplendent Cup," thus revealing that *he* was the cup, although he is reputed to have also possessed a physical chalice that gave him the power to see into the past, present, and future. When the Persian king strayed from righteousness and took to the path of pride and conceit, his formidable inner power abandoned him along with his cup and its attendant powers. Soon he and his subjects were conquered by invading armies.

Another tradition of Asian Fisher Kings symbolically linked to the image of a Holy Grail chalice is the ancient Scythian lineage of monarchs. According to the Greek historian Herodotus, a chalice became the symbol of the Scythian kings when a celestial cup was anciently thrown down from Heaven by Targilaos, the primal being, and then claimed on Earth by Kolaxais, one of Targilaos' sons who thereafter became the patriarch of the royal Scythian lineage. Kolaxais also received from Targilaos a plough, a yoke, and an ax, which collectively, states the French medievalist Joël H. Griswald, were the "hallows" of the Scythian king's Holy Grail Castle.[2]

In China, the Fisher Kings were vessels of life force known as *ling* and their symbol was a royal chalice in the shape of a golden cauldron. As long as the Chinese emperors remained in harmony with the Divine Will of God they and their country flourished. But when they became egotistical and self-serving, like the megalomaniac Shi Huang-ti, the monarch notorious for destroying all Chinese texts that were written before his reign so history would begin with him, then destruction, pestilence and poverty would besiege the land.

A contemporary chalice that supports a lineage of European kings is Saint Edward's Chalice, a vessel carried in the same procession as the three sacred swords during the coronation of an English king. The sacred cup is traditionally carried in royal procession by the Chancellor of England.

The Holy Grail Spear

A third Hollows of the Grail Castle is the Holy Spear or Holy Lance. Like the Holy Chalice, the Holy Spear of the Fisher King has been ascribed miraculous healing powers. In both Wagner's *Parsifal* and the Grail rendition called *Queste del Saint Graal,* the Fisher King was healed of his severe thigh wound when he was touched by the spear held by Percival and Gallahad. The spear is also related to the sword and thus denotes the royal power of discrimination, but it goes one step further than the sword and denotes a Fisher King's "higher" discrimination, his intuitive wisdom, which includes an understanding of the Divine Will and how to manifest Heaven on Earth. During ceremony, a Fisher King symbolically unites

Heaven and Earth within his own body by holding the weapon vertically, thereby making it a conduit for the life force moving up from the Earth and down from Heaven. In this way the monarch reveals himself to be the union of the Heaven/ Earth polarity.

The Holy Spear is also similar to the Grail Chalice in that it also denotes the inner power of the Fisher King. This truth was revealed in Wagner's *Parsifal* when the Fisher King's spear was stolen from his Grail Castle by the evil Klingsor and the monarch's ensuing loss of life force precipitated barrenness upon the face of his kingdom. The Holy Spear's affiliation with the life force involves the weapon's shaft, which is symbolic of Fisher King's spine and the Kundalini power that rises up it to bestow upon the ruler his supernatural powers. This occult wisdom regarding the Holy Spear has been part of the Holy Grail Mysteries since the advent of the first Fisher King, Murrugan, who for thousands of years used the power of his spear to righteously rule the Earth. Murrugan, who is also known as the "Commander of the Heavenly Host," is the archetypal spear-wielding warrior and the head of India's Kshatriya Caste, which includes all ruling kings. He is a Hindu manifestation of the spear-wielding Archangel Michael, who is both the angelic general of the Judeo-Christian tradition and the archetypal Knight Templar.

Murrugan's Holy Spear is known as his "Vel." It is symbolical of the union of Heaven and Earth and the ensuing production of *Jnana*, intuitive wisdom, that results. Murrugan, whose names include *Jnana Pandita*, the "Lord of Wisdom," is synonymous with *Jnana,* which is a component of the Kundalini life force he personifies. When held vertically, Murrugan's Vel represents both a pillar that unites Heaven and Earth, as well as the indwelling human spine within which Kundalini power rises to the head to awaken the *Ajna Chakra*, the Third Eye of Wisdom, which is symbolized by the Vel's eye-shaped blade. On the physical plane, the *Ajna Chakra* rules over the Pineal Gland, which according to Manley Palmer Hall, is also related to the Vel's blade. In this regard, he states:

"The key of the Grail Mysteries will be apparent if in the sacred spear is recognized the pineal gland and its peculiar point-like projection…"[3]

The counterpart of Murrugan's Vel in the West is the Thrysus, the spear wielded by Dionysus, who is Murrugan's counterpart and another manifestation of the Green Man. The Thrysus is a long stick surmounted by a pinecone that symbolizes the human spine and pine-al gland. When the followers of Alexander the Great marched across Asia to Sri Lanka they recognized Murrugan and his Vel to be synonymous with their beloved Dionysus and his Thrysus.

Murrugan's Vel ultimately inspired the mythology connected to the ceremonial spear wielded by Constantine the Great and the Holy Roman Emperors when the cult of Fisher King from Sri Lanka eventually moved westward across

Asia. The Holy Roman spear, which is today commonly known as the "Spear of Destiny," was built upon the legends of the symbolic Vel when Murrugan merged with the Persian Mithras and Mithras later became the patron of two important patriarchs of modern Christianity, St. Paul and King Constantine.

An example of how the power of the Holy Grail spear can be abused by a self-serving monarch was demonstrated by Adolph Hitler, who stole the Spear of Destiny from its resting place in the Hofsburg Museum in Vienna and then attempted to resurrect the lineage of Holy Roman Empires by making himself Lord of the World. Hitler, of course, was not dedicated to creating Heaven on Earth and instead proceeded to ruled his empire in accordance to his own selfishness and narrow-minded agenda, thus setting the stage for the final destruction of the Third Reich. Hitler's goal of controlling the world and purging it of all ethnic groups and races other than the Aryan white race was far from being in alignment with the Holy Spear, which is the vehicle of the Holy Spirit, the power of divine love and harmony.

The Holy Grail Stone

The fourth Hallows of the Grail Castle is the Holy Stone of the Fisher King. Also known as the Stone of Heaven and the Philosopher's Stone, the Fisher King's Holy Grail Stone denotes the monarch's affiliation to the royal tradition of the Goddess Venus, the patroness of all terrestrial kings, whose symbol the Holy Stone is. In this regard, the Holy Stone of a Fisher King supplies him with the power of the Star of Alchemy, which includes an abundance of Kundalini power.

Perhaps the most famous of all Grail Stones is the emerald that dislodged itself from Lucifer's Crown during the War of Heaven and fell to Earth to become a symbol of worldly authority. As mentioned in a previous chapter, this stone could be synonymous with the Holy Stone that legends claims is possessed by the first Fisher King, Sanat Kumara (a name for Murrugan), who keeps it interred within his throne city in Shamballa in Central Asia. Supposedly a gift from an extraterrestrial civilization that brought it to Earth from their home planet many thousands of years ago, it is believed that those who own this stone, or even a small piece of it, will rule the world.

The most famous Holy Stone of Europe is the Stone of Destiny of the Irish and British kings. When it was in Ireland, its incipient home in Great Britain, the Stone of Destiny was the "king maker." It was always present at the coronation of any Irish king and would "cry out" if the candidate to be crowned king was not the predestined heir to the Irish throne. The Stone of Destiny was eventually taken to Scotland with the Irish Clan of Scotti, where it was subsequently placed under a throne in a church in the city of Scone to become the famous Stone of Scone, the stone that determined the true heirs of the Scottish crown. After the English invaded Scotland in 1296 A.D., the Stone of Scone was confiscated by Edward I, who then placed it under the coronation seat of the English kings within Westminster Abbey. There it remained until 1996, when it was returned to Scotland and put on display in Edinburgh.

But, interestingly, many Scots today maintain that the stone that returned to Scotland - a block of yellow sandstone - is not the original stone. In fact, they assert that the true stone never left Scotland. It was replaced by a "fake" stone taken from a monastery doorway in Scotland and the original stone was secreted away before Edward I could take it to England.[4] The real stone, claim the Scots, was either composed of white marble, or it was a meteorite and therefore a true Stone of Venus. The Scots also contend that the stone came from Judea, where it had been the stone that served as the pillow of Jacob when the Biblical patriarch had his vision of "Jacob's Ladder," a great ladder upon which angels moved up and down from Heaven to Earth.

"Whom does the Grail serve?"

If a Fisher King desires to hold onto his Grail Hallows the ultimate lesson he must learn is "whom the Grail serves," otherwise he will lose his power and one or more of his Grail Hallows is likely to be destroyed, stolen, or disappear. The Holy Spirit power that moves through a Fisher King is not for himself alone, but everyone, and unless the monarch comes to this understanding he will undergo a fall and his subjects will suffer. If a Fisher King falls, only after being asked by a thoughtful visitor to his Grail Castle, "whom does the Grail serve?" can the monarch expect to be redeemed and regain his power. This question will ostensibly trigger within a fallen Fisher King some innate wisdom about the Grail and how his selfishness and pride has led to his demise.

The classic "fallen" Fisher King is Anfortas of *Parzival*, who became "crippled from his pride." The name Anfortas means "strength" or "power," a quality the Fisher King wielded in abundance before his fall. When Parzival first encounters Anfortas near his Grail Castle, the Fisher King has fallen because of his pride and forced to keep his paralyzed body in a recumbent position for most of the day.

The fallen Fisher King Anfortas of Grail legend represents the historical Fisher Kings worldwide, whose self-absorption has not allowed them to grasp "whom the Grail serves." Such kings, who consequently lost their power to rule and make their kingdoms prosperous, include Shi Huang-ti of China, whose obsession with his own glorification led to the loss of the Golden Cauldron, as well as to his own death and the extreme suffering and poverty of his subjects.

There are many historical examples of how a Fisher Kings's dishonorable conduct has negatively affected the fortunes of his people and brought a speedy conclusion to his rule. The Scythians of Central Asia, for example, were known to place their normally empowered kings in bondage whenever food became scarce, believing that the monarch's disreputable behavior was responsible for his decrease in power and their suffering.[5] A similar custom was observed in ancient Egypt, Korea, and many islands of the Pacific, where the practice extended into blaming the ruling monarch whenever the crops failed.[6] Similarly, in Sweden, the king risked becoming a sacrificial victim if the annual harvest was not bountiful, and the Chinese emperors were almost always held responsible for drought.[7]

Some cultures not only recognized a corresponding link between the prosperity of their land and the behavior of the king, but his physical appearance was often suspect as well. The Greek Spartans, for example, were careful not to choose a lame king as it could precipitate a "lame reign" and possibly defeat by an outside enemy. Among the ancient Kafir kingdoms of Sofala in Zululand, the criteria for the king's physical perfection was so important to the well-being of the tribe that even "…a slight bodily blemish, such as the loss of a tooth, was considered a sufficient cause for putting one of these god-men to death..."[8]

In addition, many of the world's theocracies not only recognized their monarch's behavior and appearance as influential to the weather and the cycles of nature, but they even acknowledged him to be an incarnation of the Lord of Nature, the ubiquitous Green Man. The Egyptian Pharaoh was acknowledged to be Osiris, the Lord of Nature, and his body was the sprawling land they walked upon. The Sumerian-Babylonian civilization venerated their monarchs as incarnations of their mythical Green Man Tammuz or Dummuzi, and thus acknowledged that the king's power must ebb and flow just as the life force annually ebbs and flows in nature. During periods associated with the decline of the Mesopotamian monarch's power, his subjects would enact a ritual "death" of their king by ceremonially slaying an actor dressed as their king. In this way they could return a reborn and reempowered king to the throne without having to slay or replace their monarch. In other cultures, the decline of the king's power corresponded to greater cycles of time, such as the 12 year cycle the monarchs of the ancient provinces of Quilacare and Calicut in southern India were allowed to rule before taking their own lives. While acknowledging that his power had waned beyond redemption, the monarch willingly sacrificed himself in front of a picture of his deity by ceremonially severing off parts of his body with sharp knives until the loss of blood was so great that he fainted and died soon afterwards. In some countries, the priest kings were not allowed to wait until the end of a fixed cycle of time to leave the throne, but instead were made to forfeit their lives just as soon as their life force began to wane. This custom was observed among the African tribes of the Congo and among the Unyoro of Central Africa, where "…as soon as the king falls seriously ill or begins to break up from age, he shall be killed by his own wives…"

In *The Golden Bough*, author James Frazer makes the interesting observation that the reason for slaying a weakened king was often not just to save his kingdom, but also to transfer the soul of the monarch to his successor. He states:

"…by killing him (the king) his worshippers could, in the first place, make sure of catching his soul as it escaped and transferring it to a suitable successor; and in the second place, by killing him before his natural force was abated, they would secure that the world should not fall into the decay of the man-god. Every purpose, therefore, was answered, and all dangers averted by thus killing the man-god and transferring his soul, while yet at its prime, to a vigorous successor."[9]

The Green Man, the First Fisher King

Thus, from the foregoing examples or the world's priest kings two conclusions can be arrived at. One, that the spirit of the priest king is the Green Man, and second, that the same royal spirit continues to reincarnate repeatedly within the same lineages of monarchs. By extension, it can be stated that the primal and first Fisher King is the Green Man and that it is the Green Man that continues to reincarnate within the lineage of kings that he himself founded. This wisdom is in complete agreement with the ancient Goddess Tradition, which has maintained for thousands of years that the first Fisher King was the Green Man and the Son of the Goddess.

As the primal King of the World, the Green Man is known by many legendary faces and names worldwide, including Murrugan, Dionysus, Osiris, Al-Khadir, Melchizedek, and Lucifer. He is the life force, so he can manifest at any time and in any form that is appropriate for that part of the world. Some of his manifestations have been benign, such as Melchizedek, and some malevolent, like Lucifer, while others, like Dionysus, have been ascribed a personna that is a combination of both qualities. This is because as the life force the Green Man is androgynous and can express a dual persona that is alternately creative and destructive, or beneficent and malevolent. He can be egotistical and self-serving, or project a self-abnegating temperament aligned with a higher will. He can be saint or demon, a Christ or a Lucifer. In the Holy Grail Mysteries the Green Man is synonymous with the Fisher King, who is beneficent at the beginning of his reign, but full of pride and self-serving midway through it. Other traits ascribed to the Fisher King in such Grail legends as *Perceval*, *Perlesvaus*, *Parzival*, and the *Quest del Saint Graal*, include a predisposition to become physically disabled and/or develop a permanent limp; a need to spend large amounts of time directly in front of a huge, blazing fire; and a sudden loss of life force making him powerless to control, protect, or uplift his kingdom. These traits are prominently associated with the Green Man in his manifestation as Lucifer, and Lucifer's counterpart, Vulcan, who are united in the Holy Grail Mysteries as the Fisher King Vulcan-Lucifer. Therefore, if the reincarnating soul of the Fisher King is most closely associated with the Green Man in his manifestation as Vulcan-Lucifer, it must be with him and his legends that we begin our journey through the lineage of historical Fisher Kings.

Vulcan-Lucifer, the first Fisher King,

The historical lineage of Fisher Kings must begin with Vulcan-Lucifer because he is the essence of them all and the personification of all the four Grail Hallows they embody. He is the formidable life force power of the Fisher Kings symbolized by the Holy Grail Chalice that supports the prosperity of their kingdoms. He is the Fisher King's discrimination, symbolized by the Holy Grail Spear. He is the power that rises up their spines to engender the intuitive wisdom of the Third Eye symbolized by the Holy Spear. And he is the fiery power of the Holy Stone, which fell from Heaven with the royal power of the Goddess.

Vulcan's unique association with the Holy Sword has been an integral part of his Roman legend, wherein he is portrayed as the patron of all smiths and sword makers. Lucifer's affiliation with swords is nearly as well known and can be found in the Jewish *Book of Enoch*, where as Azzazel, one of the Sons of God, he is known to have been humanity's first teacher in the art of smithing. One of Lucifer's titles, the Spirit of Intellectual Discrimination, firmly ties him to the royal attribute symbolized by the sword, and Vulcan's affiliation to the dispassionate intellect has recently been emphasized by esoteric astronomers who named the occult planet of intellectualism traveling inside the orb of Mercury "Vulcan," and by the later creators of the *Star Trek* television series who made the planet home to the intellectually inclined Dr. Spock. Vulcan's ancient association with the sword and the intellect was known by the students of the Holy Grail Mysteries, wherein the Fisher King's symbolic swords were a gift of Vulcan. Of Vulcan's Holy Grail swords the most famous is King Arthur's Excalibur, a sword whose name curiously links it to Vulcan. It is said that the appellation Excalibur is intimately related to *Caliburn*, the name of Arthur's sword according to Geoffrey of Monmouth, as well as *Caladbolg*, the name of the sword wielded by the Irish hero Cú Chulainn. Cú Chulainn means "Hound of Culann," and Culann is a name for the master smith, Vulcan.

Vulcan's personification as the life force is woven into his Roman legend, which from one perspective is an allegory for the arrival of the life force on Earth from the outer Heavens. Vulcan "fell" and sustained a permanent limp after being thrown out of the heaven of Mt. Olympus and onto the island of Lemnos, just as the life force "falls" from Heaven and "crash lands" upon the Earth. Vulcan made his home within the bowels of the Earth and especially within volcanoes, just as the life force lives underground within the planetary grid and is especially concentrated in volcanoes, where it builds up to become a fiery mass just before erupting onto the surface of the Earth.

Vulcan was truly understood in Egypt where he was venerated as Ptah, the smith god. Vulcan-Ptah was recognized by the Egyptian priesthood as both a personification of the life force as well as its indwelling Divine Mind, which molds the substance of the life force into its various physical forms just as a smith contours molten metal into a variety of utilitarian shapes. Because of his association to the Divine Mind, Ptah was sometimes represented in Egyptian iconography as a mummy encoiled within the sheaths of bandages, thus symbolizing that the Divine Mind is trapped within the coils of matter. Ptah, as the Divine Mind, was also conceived as a sword in a stone or an anvil, thus symbolizing the intellectual wisdom or Divine Mind (the sword) that is interred or trapped within the density of matter (the stone or anvil).

Lucifer's manifestation as the life force is revealed in *The Revelation of St John the Divine*, where as the "red dragon" - a universal symbol of the fiery life force - Lucifer is tossed out of Heaven by St. Michael. Lucifer's fall to Earth is also mentioned by the Prophet Isaiah, who states: "How art thou fallen from Heaven, O Lucifer, son of the morning!" (Isaiah 14:12). With similar contempt the Prophet Ezekiel maintained that Lucifer, the "anointed cherub," had dishonorably fallen off the "Holy Mountain of God."

Lucifer is also designated the life force and its indwelling consciousness by St. Paul in *Ephesians* when the Apostle refers to Lucifer as "the prince of the power of the air." (Eph 2:2). And seemingly in confirmation of St. Paul, the 19th century occultist Eliphas Levi referred to Lucifer in his *History of Magic* as the "Astral Light," the etheric life force that has the power and consciousness to both create and destroy.

Lucifer's role as King of the World ostensibly began following his eviction from Heaven. Once on Earth, states the 13th chapter of *The Revelation of St. John the Divine*, he assumed the form of a beast "having seven heads and ten horns, and upon his horns ten crowns." Lucifer is similarly accorded the regal status of King of the World in the *Synoptic Gospels*, which designate him the "Prince of this World," (John 12:31) a well as by St. Paul, who in *Corinthians* refers to him as "the god of this world." Lucifer is famous for proudly proclaiming his worldly dominion to Jesus in *The Gospel According to St. John*, wherein he asserts "All this power will I give to thee (the power of ruling the Earth)...for that is delivered unto me; and to whomsoever I will give it."

Vulcan and Lucifer were officially merged together as Vulcan-Lucifer during the Roman Empire. This occured when the rites of King Nemi, the principal character in James Frazer's magnum opus *The Golden Bough*, were annually observed. King of Nemi, who represented the united Vulcan-Lucifer, lived next to a lake inside a volcanic crater, i.e., Vulcan's home, and he was acknowledged to be the consort of Diana, i.e., Lucifer. Each year in Italy's Alban Hills, two freed slaves fought to the death for the honor of assuming the role of King of Nemi for the coming year. According to Frazer, the slave vying to overthrow the incumbent slave-king would break off a limb or "golden bough" from a nearby tree to sympathetically weaken the reigning monarch while simultanously revealing that the body of the King of Nemi was all nature because he was a manifestation of the Green Man. The slave that eventually won the battle would then merge with the Green Man and assume his role as King of the World.

The first Fisher King and the Garden of Eden

Lucifer was not originally considered evil. During the matriarchal era Green Man Lucifer was the Son of the Goddess, the embodiment of the life force, and the controller of the Her two powers of creation and destruction. His so-called "evil" nature was first exploited during the inception of the categorical and divisive thinking that characterized the rise of patriarchal theology. At that time the Green Man was split into two Sons of the Goddess, with Lucifer associated with Her power of destruction and his "twin" brother, who eventually became known as the Christ, the guardian of Her power of creation. Lucifer offically became evil when Patriarchy decided it was better to control and promote the status quo through its technology than let the powers of destruction run loose in the world. Lucifer thus became bad and "evil" and his brother good and beneficent.

Lucifer's early status as a beneficent support to humanity is revealed by his name Lucifer, which means "Light Bearer." As the Light Bearer, Lucifer is mentioned in the Jewish *Book of Enoch* as coming to Earth with an entourage of angels who, as the Sons of God, proceeded to mate with and teach the mundane and spiritual arts to the Daughters of Men. They entrusted their new mates with wisdom regarding astrology, gemology, herbology, smithing, and alchemy, the science that uses the fiery life force to transform base metals into gold and humans into gods and goddesses. Theses subjects have since become elements of the Goddess tradition whereever it has taken root.

When Lucifer first became the King of the World he was a righteous monarch. The Prophet Ezekiel recounts that Lucifer began his reign as the "anointed cherub" who was "perfect in (his) ways" and "set...upon the holy mountain of God." (Ezekiel 28:14-15) Ezekiel also alludes to Lucifer's early regalia by stating that he was originally "perfect in beauty" and covered with "every precious stone," including his characteristic gem, the emerald. Of special note here is Ezekiel's statement that Lucifer "walked up and down in the midst of the stones of fire" (Ezekiel 28:14), which implies that the Holy Mountain of God was a volcano, the traditional home of Vulcan-Lucifer. Eventually, state Ezekiel and all the prophets, the "anointed cherub" fell down from his volcanic Holy Mountain of God beacuse of his own egotistical pride.

The Koran is another scripture which, like the *Holy Bible*, is explicit in identifying the cause of Lucifer's infamous fall in the Garden of Eden. This holy text maintains that following God's creation of Adam, the angels that had descended to Earth from Heaven were instructed to surround the newborn son of Earth and to "Bow down to Adam." All of them complied except for the rebellious Lucifer, who as Iblis, "was haughty: He was one of those who reject faith."

Another source of information regarding Lucifer's fall comes from the Yezidhi, a sect of Kurds in northern Iraq whose ideology and rites were inspired by the Islamic Sufis. Throughout the past one thousand years Lucifer has occasionally appeared before the Yezidhi priests in his form of Melek Taus, the Peacock Angel, who as a boy with peacock feathers growing out of his tailend has explained at length the details of his fall. The Yezidhi priests have thus learned firsthand that Lucifer's fall was precipitated by his pride, especially as it relates to his own beauty, which has been especially associated with his radiant peacock plumes. Lucifer's manifestation as the Peacock Angel has been part of the Holy Grail Mysteries wherein it is reflected inthe regalia of the Fisher King Anfortas, whose hat "was of peacock feathers and lined inside."[10]

Both the Yezidhi and their Arab neighbors maintain that the fall of the Peacock Angel occurred in the fabled Garden of Eden, which they claim is Serendib, a name for the island paradise of Sri Lanka. The Peacock Angel as Al-Khadir and Murrugan is today venerated on Sri Lanka by Hindus, Buddhists, and Moslems alike, some of whom travel many thousands of miles to enter into his ancient and holy presence. At one time Sri Lanka was also a popular pilgrimage spot for Greeks, who came there to worship the Peacock Angel which they recognized as their beloved Green Man and King of the World, Dionysus.

The fallen Fisher King and the Underworld

Since they have a tradition of the fallen King of the World, Lucifer is also known among the Hopi Tribe of Arizona, who refer to the King of the World as Massaw, the planetary monarch who fell because of his pride. Massaw's fall occurred during his reign of the Third World, which is synonymous with the era of the Garden of Eden in its later stages, after which he was relegated to the underworld as its lord while also serving as patron of the Fire Clan. Massaw was, however, given another chance and now rules the world during the current Fourth World. Thus, even among certain Native Americans it is recognized that a manifestation of Lucifer is presently ruling our world.

Massaw's underworld associations are, of course, reflected by the underworld kingdom ruled over by Vulcan-Lucifer, and they are also paralleled in legends of other Green Men. Murrugan's link to the underworld can be gleaned through his name Skanda, which is related to the Greek Skandalon, a name for Lucifer meaning "obstructor" and a term used for the magical ring worn by Mandean priests in order to invoke the underworld powers of darkness. Green Man Dionysus was always feasted by his Greek devotees during the darkest times of the year, when the King of the World and wielder of the powers of destruction was said to reside in his underworld abode within the interior of our planet. King Jamshid, a legendary Persian monarch and Green Man manifestation, reveals his association to the underworld through his alternate name of Yima, which is the Persian counterpart of the Sanscrit Yama, the epithet of the Lord of Death and King of the Underworld of the Hindus.

Lucifer's underworld associations have been incorporated into traditional Grail legend as part of the Fisher King's mythos. In Robert de Borron's Grail version, for example, the Fisher King is referred to as the "Grand Black Magician of the Underworld," and in *Perlesvaus*, the Fisher King is a character known as Pelles, a name many scholars contend is derived from Pwyll, a lame Welsh lord of the Underworld.

The Fisher King Dynasties

The following are a few of the important Fisher King Dynasties that have been founded worldwide by the Green Man in his various manifestations as Vulcan-Lucifer, Murrugan, Dionysus, Enki of Sumeria, and Neptune of Atlantean fame. As you will see, the Green Man's forms as King of the World are ubiquitous. This is because as an embodiment of the ubiquitous life force, he can manifest at any time, in any country, and in any form.

Murrugan and the Fisher Kings of the pan-Pacific regions

Murrugan, or Sanat Kumara, the "Eternally Young Son of God," is the personality of the primal Fisher King and Green Man worshipped in Southeast Asia. Murrugan, the "androgynous" divine son of Shiva and Shakti, the transcendental Spirit and the universal Goddess, began his reign as King of the World when India and Sri Lanka were part of a huge continent called Kumarai Nadu that once stretched across most of the Pacific Ocean. Currently remembered by much of the world as the original Garden of Eden, most of this primeval continent eventually sank to the bottom of the ocean except for those parts of it that became islands, such as Sri Lanka, the paradise currently recognized by much of the Arab world as not only part of the primal Garden, but *the* Garden of Eden. Murrugan's main temples of worship are currently located on Sri Lanka within the shrine city of Katirgama, the Place of Karttikeya, which is one of Murrugan's names that denotes his function as a great warrior and the Commander of the Heavenly Host.

Green Man Murrugan, whose names also include Kumara, meaning "Prince" in the Singhalese language of the island, continues to reign as King of the World on Sri Lanka just as he did on ancient Kumari Nadu. As part of the "Eden" of Sri Lanka he also continues to manifest as the Serpent on the Tree, as well as the Peacock Angel, the beauteous form that led to his downfall. Murrugan, who is currently venerated by his Arab worshippers as Al-Khadir, the Initiator, is the embodiment of the transformative Kundalini. He is the Lord of the Two Rivers, the patron of alchemists, and the eternal guardian of the Water of life that is generated by the union of Sri Lanka's two sacred streams of water

Prestor John, King of the World

A name for Murrugan in his manifestation as the Kundalini serpent is *Jnana Pandita*, the "Lord of Wisdom." As *Jnana Pandita*, Murrugan bestows upon a spiritual seeker intuitive or Gnostic wisdom. Sanscrit *Jnana* has its counterpart in John, thus making Murrugan's English name "John." It is by the name of John that Murrugan's royal presence was known about in the West during the Middle Ages, when the Pope and certain heads of state received a series of letters from a Prestor John. After announcing himself as a King of the World in letters to such dignitaries as the Holy Roman Emperor Frederick II, Prestor John would often proceed to describe his paradisiacal kingdom in the East and then end with a promise to send an army to rid Christendom of the infidel Moslems. Prestor John's power and pride comes through in this letter to the rulers of the West:

"I Johannes the Presbyter, Lord of Lords, am superior in virtue, riches and power to all who walk under heaven. Seventy-two kings pay tribute to us. Our might prevails in the three Indies, and our lands extend all the way to the farthest Indies where the body of Saint Thomas the Apostle lies." [11]

Could the mysterious Prestor John, a name that means the "Elder Priest John," be Murrugan? Or perhaps Prestor John was an eastern Fisher King who had incarnated Murrugan's soul essence and reigned in his ancient lineage? Eschenbach leads us to believe in *Parzival* that Prestor John was indeed synonymous with Murrugan by naming him a Fisher King of the Holy Grail lineage. We are also led to believe they are one and the same in *A Hundred and One Nights*, which locates Prestor John's throne on Sri Lanka. While recounting the sixth voyage of Sinbad, the Arabic author of *A Hundred and One Nights* has the legendary sailor arriving on Sri Lanka and meeting the king of the island. This distinguished king, who carried "a great mace of gold, at the top of which (was) an emerald (Lucifer's stone) a span in length and of the thickness of a thumb," gave Sinbad instructions to deliver a special note to Caliph Harun al-Rashid, the introduction of which read: "Peace be with thee from the King of Al-Hind (India)." Thus, according to this classic text, the headquarters of the Prestor John, who often referred to himself in his letters as the King of India, was the island paradise of Sri Lanka, the ancient home of the primal Fisher King known as Murrugan.

Murrugan and the Lemurian Garden of Eden

According to occult legend, Murrugan initially became the Green Man and the world's first Fisher King after arriving on Earth as the leader of the Sons of God and then electing to merge his spirit with the consciousness of our planet in order to continually oversee the spiritual evolution of humanity. According to the Theosophical Society, which once had its principal headquarters near Murrugan's south Indian headquarters of Mylapur, the "Place of the Peacock," Murrugan and his Sons of God came from their native planet of Venus more than six million years ago and then proceeded to serve Earth humans as Avatars and the first teachers of yoga. It is speculated that they came in response to a clarion call from Earth's human population, which had reached a pivotal point in its development and needed the evolutionary force, the Kundalini serpent, awakened before it could evolve further. The Kumaras arrived with the wisdom of how to awaken the Kundalini power through spiritual disciplines, including alchemy and yoga, and they also assisted in the awakening of the evolutionary force by transmitting their own Kundalini into the developing human genome by mating with the "Daughters of Men." In this way Kundalini was thus awakened in much of humanity, and soon Earth humans moved to their next phase of evolution by developing the higher brain functions and the ego and intellect that accompanies them. Since the goal of human evolution is for God to identify himself/herself as dwelling within each person's heart, it was necessary for an egotistical sense of self and the intellectual capacity to discriminate to develop within the human species.

Murrugan's legend parallels that of his counterpart, the Green Man Lucifer or Azazzel, because they are synonymous. According to the Judeo-Christian tradition Lucifer is also said to have been the leader of the Sons of God who mated with and indoctrinated the Daughters of Men. Murrugan also reflects his counterpart Lucifer by having been the leader of a group of fallen angels known as the Asuras, the "No-gods." In this role Murrugan's name is Shukra, which like Lucifer is a name for Venus.

Since Murrugan's arrival six million years ago, psychics, teachers and prophets of many cultures have been blessed with his vision and history by tapping into the Akashic Records, the interdimensional records that can be accessed through the Ajna Chakra or Third Eye. These records were most recently accessed by the late Satguru Sivaya Subramuniyaswami of Hawaii under the direct guidance of Murrugan himself. Leading up to his migration to Hawaii, where he built an ashram on the island of Kauai, Subramuniyaswami had spent many years on Sri Lanka studying the mysteries of Sanat Kumara with his guru, Jnanaguru Yogaswami. After moving to Hawaii under strict instructions from Lord Murrugan, Subramuniyaswami's visions began pouring in into his Third Eye of Wisdom or *Ajna Chakra*, and the sage soon had enough information for a book, which he subsequently published under the title of *Lemurian Scrolls, Angelic Prophecies Revealing Human Origins.* This crowning achievement of Subramuniyaswami begins with the Satguru acknowledging and introducing Murrugan, the overseer of his revelations:

"This sacred text is drawn from the great inner plane library of Lord Subramaniam, also known as Skanda, Sanat Kumara, and Karttikeya.

"Lord Skanda (Sanat Kumara) came to Earth in the Sat Yuga (the Hindu Golden Age). He was one of the most highly advanced souls. He came as the leader of the first group, and will guide them all along through the next Sat Yuga. He was the celestial King of Lemuria."[12]

Subramuniyaswami continues his presentation by stating that during the Satya Yuga Murrugan helped prepare the way for souls of other "groups" to incarnate physically on Earth. He also oversaw the construction of temples for worship and meditation throughout Lemuria or Kumari Nadu, thus precipitating the creation of a highly spiritual society on the ancient Garden of Eden.

Another channel who has had access to the interdimensional records regarding Murrugan and the Sons of God is Alice Bailey, a channel for the Great White Brotherhood, which is an organization founded by Sanat Kumara and dedicated to preserving the wisdom of Kundalini he brought to Earth. Bailey received her wisdom on the inner planes from a Tibetan adept of the Great White Brotherhood named Djwhal Khul and then organized the information into over twenty esoteric tomes. Her books are currently recognized as containing some of the best information available regarding Murrugan, the Kumaras, the hierarchy of the Great White Brotherhood, Shamballa, and role of the King of the World. In regards to Sanat Kumara's arrival from Venus and his role as King of the World, Bailey writes:

"It has been stated that one hundred and four Kumaras came from Venus to Earth; literally the figure is one hundred and five, when the synthesizing Unit, the Lord of the World himself, is counted as one."

"At the head of affairs, controlling each unit and directing all evolution, stands the KING, the Lord of the World...He Who is called in the Bible "The Ancient of Days," and in the Hindu scriptures the First Kumara, He, Sanat Kumara it is, Who from his throne at Shamballa in the Gobi desert, presides over the Lodge of Masters, and holds in his hands the reigns of government..."[13]

Bailey's information was corroborated by another channel in the Theosophical Society, the famous occultist Madame Blavatsky, who claimed that references to the arrival of the Kumaras is currently inscribed on palm leaves in an underground cavern in Tibet. Blavatsky maintained that her principal book, *The Secret Doctrine*, was an English translation and commentary of the writings on these leaves, which she collectively called the *Book of Dzyan.* Having supposedly seen the pages of this book in a series of visions, Blavatsky stated that they told the story of the arrival of Sanat Kumara and his entourage of Kumaras on Earth, who are referred to in the text as the "Lords of the Flame" and "Sons of Wisdom." As the Sons of Wisdom, the Kumaras bestowed upon fledgling humankind "fire," including mental fire and the fire of Kundalini, and then taught humanity the fundamentals of many of the mundane and spiritual sciences. According to the *Book of Dzyan*, the Kumaras also established lineages of both "Holy Fathers, the Ancestors of the Arhats," as well as lines of "Divine Kings."[14]

Shamballa, the Grail Castle at the Heart of the World

Blavatsky and Bailey both concur that after arriving on Lemuria, Murrugan or Sanat Kumara built a glorious palace in the middle of an inland sea now known as the Gobi Desert. Murrugan's palace was constructed on an island esoterically known as the "White Island," which existed in the center of this huge ocean. His castle is reputed to still exist there, but on an etheric plane, and it is said that from that regal abode Sanat Kumara continues to govern our planet as the King of the World. Thus, it appears that as Murrugan or Sanat Kumara the Green Man is currently governing the world from both Shamballa and Sri Lanka.

According to M.P. Hall, who claims to have interviewed yogis that traveled there in their astral bodies, Sanat Kumara's castle is encrusted with exotic gems and ringed by a band of etheric serpents that stand guard around its perimeter. The palace exists in the center of the kingdom of Shamballa, a sacred territory that the scriptures of the Buddhist lamas of Tibet explicitly maintain has existed since the beginning of the world.[15] Shamballa, which is also known as the Heart Chakra of the Earth, is divided into eight territories, like the eight petals of the human heart chakra, and at its center is the soul and King of the World, Sanat Kumara.

It was when Sanat Kumara merged his consciousness with that of the Earth's that he officially became the Green Man and King of the World. His consciousness and presence then became ubiquitous throughout our planet, and for this reason the Jewish prophets and other mystics experienced him as the eternal "Watcher" of humanity. The eyes of Sanat Kumara have also been seen by prophets and shamans in many countries worldwide. His eyes can manifest as normal human eyes, but since he is the Peacock Angel his eyes can also appear as the "eyes" that cover the feathers of a peacock. In fact, from one perspective the world is indeed a giant peacock (see *The Truth Behind the Christ Myth: The Redemption of the Peacock Angel*)

After becoming the spirit of Earth and its etheric monarch, the will of Sanat Kumara became supreme. It was his will that determined all the activity upon our planet, including the actions of all four and two-legged creatures, including humans. He was the collective consciousness of humanity, a role that eventually led to his infamous fall. Sanat Kumara fell and became the egotistical Lucifer when that part of his will that operated within humans and determined their actions "fell" and became the will of the human ego. Ever since that pivotal time, not only has the human population become completely entrenched in their Luciferian egos, but the King of the World has reigned as Lucifer. But, say the Yezidhis of Iraq, Sanat Kumara is destined to be redeemed. He will soon move beyond his ego, reunite with his higher self, and once again become the perfected Fisher King he was on Lemuria. And when that happens, all humanity will also be redeemed and return to the legendary Garden of Eden, because we are one with Sanat Kumara.

In the past one hundred years the Russian adventurers Ferdinand Ossindowski and Nicholas Roerich have added to Sanat Kumara's lore by compiling conclusive evidence of his from their travels across Central Asia. They both discovered legends of the King of the World among many Buddhists, who claimed that their monasteries were united by a tunnel system to Shamballa, Sanat's home. In his book that chronologes his Asian journey, *Beasts, Men and Gods,* Ossendowski claims that his Buddhist mentors showed him a seat in one of their monasteries that the King of the World had once sat upon after emerging from the subterranean tunnel system and giving a private audience to the monastery's residents. The Buddhists of Mongolia also informed the Russian that the King of the World in Shamballa had anciently arrived from the planet Venus and that his name was the sound-syllable AUM, the three letters of which correspond to the three powers of the life force, creation, preservation, and destruction.[16]

Murrugan's Fisher King Lineage spreads throughout India

When much of Lemuria completed its predestined cycle of existence and sank to the bottom of the Pacific Ocean, Sanat Kumara sent his representatives around the globe to create a network of Fisher Kings. According to the Hindu *Vedas* and *Puranas,* wherein Sanat is referred to as Shukra and Bhrigu, the chief of the fallen angels, some of Sanat's missionaries arrived in India as a people known as the People of Bhrigu, or the Bhrigus. After settling in the subcontinent and founding colonies, they ruled their new subjects as Naga or "Serpent" Kings.

One of the most renowned of all Naga Kings to subsequently rule India was King Nahusha, the progenitor of the five principle tribes that eventually populated India. The name Nahusha, which denotes "serpent," is etymologically linked to the Hebrew word for serpent, Nachash, thus making this ancient monarch a relative of the primal Serpent on the Tree. Early on in his reign King Nahusha, the archetypal Fisher King, was endowed with plentiful Water of Life and righteously oversaw his thriving empire. But then, like so many other Fisher Kings before and after him, his ego became attached to his supernatural abilities and he suffered a fatal fall from pride. Consequently, he is currently spoken of as one of India's more demonic monarchs. Many of Nahusha's descendents to the throne, the monarchs of the Lunar Race, seem to have suffered a similar fate and are today collectively are referred to as the monarchs of the Asuras, the Fallen Angels.

The Chinese Fisher Kings

Sanat Kumara's missionaries also journeyed to neighboring China from Kumari Nadu and founded a lineage of Dragon Emperors there. Part of the legacy of these Dragon Kings is the legend they preserved of China's first monarch, P'an Ku, who was a dwarf and a smith god. Since P'an Ku's legend is nearly identical to that of Ptah-Vulcan, it appears that China also retains a connection to the first Fisher King.

P'an Ku successors, known as the Five Dragons, were renowned masters of the life force or Water of Life. They were succeeded by Fisher Kings known as "Fire builders," a title that ostensibly denotes their ability to control, transmit, and/or manipulate the fiery life force. Following their reign begins the historical age and the kingdoms of the five great "dragon" emperors, beginning with Fu Hsi, who is sometimes referred to as T'ai Hao, "The Great Almighty." In their enigmatic appearance these Dragon Kings were, like P'an Ku, similar to Vulcan-Lucifer, the Fisher King they descended from.

The primary goal of all Chinese Dragon Kings was to preserve their *ling,* or life force, by uniting Heaven with Earth and living in alignment with the Divine Will. If they were successful their *ling* flourished and their country was healthy and prosperous; but when they failed, their *ling* was depleted and China was overcome with chaos and plagues. The secrets of how to live in harmony with the Divine Will were discovered by the Dragon King Fu Hsi as Eight Trigrams placed around an octagon, the alchemical symbol of Heaven/Earth mediation. Fu Hsi discovered the Eight Trigrams on the back of a huge amphibious dragon he encountered one day while meditating on the banks of a river. This creature possessed the body of an eight-legged horse and was covered with fish scales. As the beast rose out of the river, Fu Hsi found the Eight Trigrams inscribed on a stone tablet that rested on its back and returned home with it to study. Sometime later in Chinese history, the Eight Trigrams evolved into the sixty-four hexagrams of the I Ching, which has arguably become the most complete system of esoteric symbols on Earth for understanding the universe and how to live in harmony with it.

The fifth Dragon King of modern history, Huang-Ti, the "Yellow Emperor," is considered the greatest emperor to ever reign in China. Leading up to his conception his mother reputedly beheld a brilliant flash of light originating from the Great Bear or Big Dipper, the Celestial Grail, which entered her womb and fertilized her ovum. Twenty-five months later Huang-Ti was born with a dragon-like countenance, and within two months of his birth he could speak fluently. During his teenage years, the precocious Huang-Ti had mastered most of the mundane and sacred sciences and was recognized as a god incarnate. Once on the throne of China, Huang-Ti revealed his affiliation to the Big Dipper by having its seven stars embroidered on his royal robes. He remained loyal to his country for the rest of his life and was never overcome by his own pride. Consequently, China prospered greatly during his lifetime.

Perhaps the most important Grail Hallows of the Chinese Fisher Kings was the Royal Cauldron, a golden pot that represented their Water of Life or *ling*. The Royal Cauldron first appeared in the court of the great Huang-Ti, and it was later passed on to the Chinese Dragon Emperors of the Hsia, Shang, Yin, and Chou Dynasties. As long as the incumbent Fisher Kings lived a life in harmony with the Divine Will, they were full of *ling* and the cauldron was safe and secure. But when they strayed from the path of righteousness their *ling* would become depleted and the cauldron would suddenly disappear and might become permanently lost. This tragedy occurred during the reign of the Black Dragon King Shih Huang-Ti, who is China's classical example of the Fisher King who fell from grace.

Shih Huang-Ti is a perfect example of the fallen Fisher King. After his ego became so enlarged that he even resolved to have history begin with him by destroying all of China's ancient histories, the country was beset with severe famine, destructive storms, and terrible floods. The Royal Cauldron quickly departed from the palace while Shih Huang-ti's *ling* was draining from his body. Knowing full well the importance of the cauldron in supporting his rule, the emperor sent out hundreds of envoys and trackers to comb the countryside for it. When it was finally located at the bottom of the River Ssu, the emperor was alerted and he rushed to the spot. He and those with him tried valiantly to recover the Royal Cauldron, but their attempts were blocked by the ferocious river-dwelling dragon that guarded it. No matter how hard he tried, the heavenly powers were not going to let Shih Huang-Ti further abuse the cauldron or its *ling* power.

After Shih Huang-ti the Royal Cauldron of the Chinese Fisher Kings remained hidden until a Fisher King worthy of its power ascended the throne. This was destined to be the Dragon King Wu of the Han Dynasty, who inaugurated a new era of prosperity and righteousness in China by observing the auspicious Sacrifice of Kiao (Kiao is a name for the Primal Dragon), and by instituting a new calendar that would begin during his reign in 104 B.C. Wu strove to align himself with the Divine Will by making his palace a reflection of the starry heavens, and also by hiring sages as his court officials and advisors. Eventually, while performing intensive austerities at the top of his nine-storied meditation tower Wu succeeded in manifesting the Royal Cauldron directly in front of him. After precipitating the elixir of immortality within it, the king became full of *ling* and prosperity returned to China.

The Peruvian Fisher Kings

Another important pan-Pacific destination for Sanat Kumara's missionaries was Peru. According to legend, Sanat Kumara had himself visited Peru, where legends currently maintain that he assisted in the construction of certain Andean megalithic temples, such as the colossal hillside temple overlooking the ancient village of Ollantaytambo.

Sanat Kumara as Murrugan may be synonymous with Aramu or Amaru Muru, the "Serpent Muru," a renowned Peruvian missionary that came to Peru from Lemuria just before the continent's destruction and brought with him the records and power objects of Mu. This identification is corroborated by the fact that Amaru Muru is identical in import to Muru-Kan, which is a Tamil rendering of Murrugan, and both names translate into English as "Serpent Muru." A connection between the two figures is also implicit in a legend that maintains that Aramu Muru brought to the Andes the Solar Disc of Mu, which was a power object that had supposedly been in the possession of Sanat Kumara, who had brought it from Venus with his entourage of the Sons of God.

Legends claim that Aramu Muru constructed the Monastery of the Seven Rays to serve as a reliquary for the Solar Disc and the sacred records of Mu. After completing his monastery, Aramu Muru is said to have traveled into the Andes and built the Inca Empire with Cuzco as its capital city. He then ruled his new empire as its first priest king, Manko, and adopted for his royal title Kapac, meaning "spiritually wealthy," thus denoting his abundance of life force and intuitive wisdom. The life force of Manko Kapac and his successors was so strong that the ruling Incas were never allowed to wear the same garment twice, otherwise the article of clothing might become dangerously charged with the Inca's prodigious power.

When Manko Kapac completed his reign as the Inca priest king he transferred his spiritual power or Water of Life to a member of his royal family, who then continued the lineage of the Inca Fisher Kings. Thereafter, through many generations of Incas, the Water of Life was passed down through a lineage of empowered priest kings, many of whom were named either Kapac, "Spiritually Wealthy" or Amaru, "Serpent." Both monikers designated their bearer to be the embodiment of the life force and the wielder of its intrinsic wisdom and power.

The Dynasty of the Fisher King Adam

The Biblical Adam was also a Fisher King and patriarch of a lineage of empowered monarchs. In fact, Adam may be synonymous with Murrugan. This notion is implicit to a curious legend on Sri Lanka, which states that God first set Adam on top of a mountain on the island called Adam's Peak, where today Christians, Buddhists and Moslems worship a five-foot footprint covered in solid gold they claim is Adam's. With spear in hand, Adam is said to have climbed down from the peak in search of a place to settle. His search led him into the jungles of Sri Lanka, and finally to grassy clearing near a river. He planted his spear in this place, which has since become known as Katirgama, the home of Murrugan.

Could Adam be synonymous with Murrugan? According to the Mandeans who originated on Sri Lanka, he definitely could be. Adam was the first Mandean prophet and teacher of Gnosticism, and in many of the Gnostic traditions of both the East and West, Murrugan (and his manifestation as the Serpent on the Tree) is venerated as the first teacher of Gnosticism and referred to as *Jnana Pandita*, the "Lord of Wisdom." But could Adam have also been a Fisher King? According to the research of Laurence Gardner, author of *Genesis of the Grail Kings*, he was. Gardner, who claims to be privy to certain records not available to the common man, makes Adam the incipient planetary monarch whose Fisher King lineage was passed down directly to the Jewish King David and his ancestor Jesus Christ.

But even if Adam was not a Fisher King, it appears that his first son Cain was. Cain, a name meaning smith, has always been associated with Lucifer through his murderous act of killing Abel. He has also been linked to Vulcan. According to the *Source of Measures,* he was affiliated with Vulcan in some of the older versions the *Holy Bible*,[17] wherein his name was written as V'elcain or V'ulcain. Cain thus appears to be a name for the first Fisher King as Vulcan-Lucifer. Gardner claims that it was Cain's infamous Mark that became the definitive symbol of the planetary lineage of Fisher Kings, so he was at least one of the founders of the lineage. Gardner explains that Cain's royal symbol, which is a cross with arms of equal length set within a circle, is identical to the lowest Sephiroth or sphere on the Tree of Life of the Kabbala known as Malkhut, which denotes "kingdom."[18]

Gardner also points out some intriguing facts regarding the Mark of Cain that not only denotes the Fisher Kings to be Human Holy Grails, but also representatives of the planet of royalty, Venus. The cross-circle of the Mark of Cain is related to the "Dew Cup or Cup of Waters" and designates its bearers to be vessels of the Water of Life. When the cross is taken out of the circle and then placed under the orb, the symbol of Venus is created, and with another slight modification this symbol becomes the sacred letter Q, the sound that begins the nouns that denote royalty, queen and king.[19]

Within the last five hundred years another version of the Mark of Cain has surfaced as an ouroboros serpent or dragon with is tail in its mouth, which repre sents "dragon kingship" and the life force power wielded by Earth's empowered monarchs.[20] This Fisher King symbol was adopted by the Holy Roman Emperor Sigismund as the emblem of an organization of princes and kings he founded called The Imperial and Royal Court of the Dragon. Sigismund also had the symbol's ouroborous serpent inscribed with the cross of St. George, who was chosen as patron of his royal order, thus revealing his order's affiliation with the Green Man and first Fisher King.

The Possessors

The Fisher King lineage founded by Cain is today known as the lineage of the "Possessors." His Fisher King descendants were the possessors of the spirit of Vulcan-Lucifer that manifested within them as both wisdom and prodigious life force. Cain, who was a Human Holy Grail, passed his Kundalini power or Water of Life to his son, Enoch, the "Initiator," who continued the transmission of energy down the line that soon culminated in reigns of the Fisher King Lamech and his son Tubal Cain, a master smith who was a full incarnation of his ancestor Vulcan-Lucifer. From Lamech the power passed to Noah, a savior of humanity regarded as an enlightened and powerful ruler by both Jews and Moslems, and Noah transmitted it to his son Ham or Khem, the founder of the Land of Khem, which later became known as Egypt. Ham's son, the Fisher King Cainan, who was another adept smith in the lineage of Cain, received a portion of his family's inherent power and carried it to Asia Minor, where he founded a Phoenician culture comprised of world renowned craftsmen, some of whom eventually assisted in the construction of Solomon's Temple. In Phoenicia, Canaan's moved down a lineage of priest kings known as the "Hiram," a title of honor that incorporates ram, a universal name for the fiery life force they embodied. The Hiram priest kings, who were also incarnations of Baal, the Phoenician Green Man, were dynamic magicians and Grand Masters of a network of Masonic lodges in Asia Minor that inculcated special alchemical disciplines to awaken the inner Kundalini fire. In these lodges the Kundalini was referred to as Chiram, the "Master Builder," in reference to the serpent fire's work of purifying and re-building the human body. Chiram is also a name for Cain, the first smith and patron of the craft, who was a personification of Kundalini.

Eventually the power of Cain's Fisher King lineage passed to the Possessor Abraham, whose original name, Ab-ram, denoted "Possessor of Fire." Abraham, a priest of Ur when called by Yahweh to father a race of "chosen ones," received much of his power from the Fisher King Melchizedek by "drinking from his chalice." King Melchizedek, whose name King of Salem (or Shalem) denotes "King of Venus," is recognized in the Arab world as a manifestation of Al-Khadir, the Green Man, who was both the Son of Venus and primal King of the World. The Water of Life Abraham received from King Melchizedek was subsequently transmitted to all the tribes if Israel, especially the Tribes of Levi and David, out of which emerged the Hebrew priests and Fisher Kings.

Enki and the Fisher Kings of the Middle East

Enki, the "Lord of the Earth," is the name for the primal Fisher King and Green Man within the Sumerian and Babylonian civilizations. Also known as Ea, the "House of Water," Enki's icons portray him as an androgynous goatfish, the Kerabu, which swims within the Apsu, which is a name for the cosmic water or life force that fills the universe. Enki was venerated by those who truly knew him as the Lord of Wisdom and the Lord of Magic, two titles that allude to his nature as the life force or Kundalini power personified. King Enki transmitted his Water of Life down a ling line of Fisher Kings that ruled over much of the Middle East.

Enki is the Middle Eastern counterpart of Murrugan, whose symbol of the Makara, a creature that is half fish and half antelope, is an eastern version of Enki's goat-fish, the Kerabu. The Makara and Kerabu are both symbols of the first sign of the Zodiac, Capricorn, so Enki-Murrugan, the primal life force that began the universe, eternally begins the astrological year. Enki and Murrugan also lead the calendar year through their joint rulership of the month of January. Enki and Murrugan's counterpart in the West is Janus, an androgynous, two-faced ruler of the year during the Roman Empire, whose name was the basis for the word January. Janus was the son and consort of Diana, thus making him a manifestation of Vulcan-Lucifer and the primal Fisher King.

Enki's rule over the Zodiacal sign of Capricorn, the sign ruled by Saturn, is instructive, because Saturn is the planet associated with governmental administration and Enki is the chief executive officer of our planet. His role as King of the World is revealed in the Sumerian poem *Enki and the World Order,* when Enki says of himself: "I am the principal among all rulers, the father of all the foreign lands." Enki's affiliation to the planet Saturn also associates him with King Saturn, his counterpart in the Greek tradition, and it also aligns him with Satan, which is a name that evolved from Saturn and became an epithet for Vulcan-Lucifer.

Like Murrugan, Enki is also said to have manifested as the Serpent on the Tree in the Garden of Eden. Enki's Garden is known as Dilman, the legendary

Eden of the Sumerians, and his tree is the Mish Tree or Gish Gana. While spiraling upon the Mish Tree, Enki moved between the three worlds he governed, Heaven, Earth and the underworld. The underworld, say the Sumerian scribes, was filled with the cosmic waters of the Apsu, which is Enki's true home. These subterranean waters emerged at the base of the Gish Gana and then divided into two physical rivers, which many historians believe became the Tigris and Euphrates Rivers. Since he rules over the two primal rivers, Enki, like his counterpart Al-Khadir, became known as the "Lord of the Two Rivers," and in this role he was portrayed in Sumerian iconography as a man with two streams of water emerging from his shoulders.

Today, the southern Iraqi city of Al-Qurna is believed to physically mark the location of Enki's primeval Garden of Eden. It is where the Tigris and Euphrates bifurcate, and the location of "Adam's Tree," the tree that supposedly marks the middle of the fabled garden. Qurna is also very near the great Sumerian city of Eridu, which became Enki's capital city.

Eridu, which means, "home built far away," was known by the Sumerian ancients as one of the first, if not *the* first city built in Mesopotamia. This important city became the location of Enki's principal temple, a towering ziggurat used for worshipping the Lord of the Earth. Eridu is, according to some ancient historians, also where Enki took physical form in order to rule his Sumerian kingdom. According to Berossus, an authoritative historian of the ancient mysteries from Babylonia, Enki took a physical form as Oannes, a culture bearer who, like his counterpart Lucifer, is said to have arrived from another land while accompanied by an entourage. After navigating up the Euphrates River to Eridu, Oannes emerged on dry land, and to the amazement of all who saw him, states Berossus, it became clear that "(Oannes's) whole body was that of a fish… under the fish's head he had another head, with feet also below, similar to that of a man, subjoined to the fish's tail." In regards to the function he played as a culture bearer, Berossus states: "This Being (Oannes) was accustomed to pass the day among men: but took no food at that season: and he gave them insight into the letters and sciences, and the arts of every kind. He taught them to construct cities, to found temples, to compile laws, and explained to them the principles of geometrical knowledge."

Berossus maintains that Oannes was accompanied by "other animals like Oannes." The Greek historian Apollodorus, who was one of the very few to read over the uncorrupted, original version of Berossus, called these strange creatures the Annedoti, the "Repulsive Ones," and claimed that they assisted their leader in educating the indigenous natives. The Annedoti have since been associated with the Annunaki, the Sumerian judges of the underworld, who were mentioned in conjunction with Enki in certain Sumerian texts. The study of the Annunaki, who were designated as "the fifty who went from Heaven to Earth,"[21] as well as "the fifty Annunaki of Eridu," have been studied in order to give insight into Enki's original homeland, which some researchers contend was another star or planet, possibly Sirius or Venus.

Enki's Fisher King Lineage

Enki founded a lineage of Fisher Kings that included ten pre-flood monarchs known both as the AB-GAL, the "Masters of Knowledge," as well as the "Seven Sages." These rulers, who were traditionally represented in Sumerian texts as fish swimming in the Apsu, were also known as Usumgal, Sumerian for "Dragon."[22]

Following the fateful deluge, the rulership of Mesopotamia was usurped by Enlil, the brother of Enki, and the Sumerian kings began to govern from Enlil's capital city of Nippur. But when Enki's son Marduk defeated his uncle Enlil and reclaimed the throne of the Fisher Kings, the seat of power later moved to Marduk's city of Babylon. From that time onwards the Fisher Kings of Babylon ruled in the lineage of Enki, annually renewing their Water of Life by grasping the principal statue of Enki's son Marduck, which was interred within the most important temple of Babylon. Each Sumerian and Babylonian king was recognized by his subjects as an incarnation of Dammuzi or Tammuz, which was a name for the Green Man and thus synonymous with Enki, while the mother and consort of every ruler was said to be the patroness of all Fisher Kings, the Goddess Venus.

King Nimrod, one of Enki's descendants, was a classic example of the fallen Fisher King of Grail legend. Nimrod, whose emblem was a fish and whose ceremonial regalia included a garment once worn by the Fisher Kings Adam, Enoch and Noah, began his rule as a righteous king but eventually suffered a disastrous fall from his pride. Previous to his fall, Nimrod was a beneficent and productive king, who rebuilt the great temple of Baalbek that had previously been constructed before the Flood by his "giant" sized ancestors, the Sons of God, which included Cain and the Nephilim. Nimrod also oversaw the construction of the famous Tower of Babylon, a Ziggurat surrounded by water that simulated the "Holy Mountain of God" and the Grail Castle of the primal Fisher King. But when King Nimrod's ego became inflated by his accomplishments and he declared himself God on Earth, his kingdom began to suffer. His inglorious reign came to its conclusion after the megalomaniac king received a prophetic vision of the Prophet Abraham reestablishing the religion of the one God in the future. In order to protect his rule, Nimrod slayed all the firstborn sons of the Babylonians just in case one of them happened to be the infant Abraham. Because he fell so far from his pride, King Nimrod is rightly regarded as having been a legitimate manifestation of the Fisher King Vulcan-Lucifer.

When Nimrod passed away, the rulership of the Middle East was placed principally in the hands of King Melchizedek and the Rephilim and Anakim, the giant descendants of the early Sons of God. These giants had assisted Nimrod in the rebuilding of Baalbek, and they also constructed the citadel of Hebron, which at 7000 feet was the highest city in Palestine. Hebron, which became the Grail Castle of the Fisher Kings of Asia Minor, may have also been the royal seat of the ancient King Thoth or Tautus, whom the Canaanite-Phoenicians remember in their historical texts as the first king of Canaan. Legend has it that Alexander the Great discovered the tomb of Thoth in one of Hebron's caves during his campaign across Asia Minor.

According to the *Book of Joshua*, under the command of the warrior Joshua the Hebrew army exterminated the giants of Asia Minor, although some of the Rephilim survived, including Goliath. Following their victorious campaign, the Hebrews laid claim to Hebron, eventually making it their capital city and the seat of power of the early Hebrew kings. King Saul built his castle in Hebron nearby the tomb of the patriarch Abraham, who had bought land in Hebron for himself and his family so they could be close to the ancient seat of the Sons of God. Saul's castle was also adjacent to temples housing statues of the Sons of God, the Anakes, who were the ancestors of the Anakim. The Anakes, who were also known as the Kaberoi, "those of fire," were depicted as twin brothers with features nearly identical to the images of the Kumara Sons of God venerated in the East. According to Blavatsky, the eastern and western twins were synonymous, and the name "Kaberoi" is simply a western evolution of the eastern "Kumara."

Hebron continued to be the home of the Hebrew kings for seven years, after which King David moved the capital city to Jerusalem, the city of the primal Fisher King Melchizedek. In Jerusalem, the "City of Venus," the Jewish kings ruled for a term of 40 years, which is the number of years of an important Venus cycle.[23]

The Fisher King Lineages of Neptune and Dionysus

King Neptune, the Lord of the Sea, is another name for the Green Man and first Fisher King. With his three-pronged trident, the symbol of the three powers of the life force he commanded, King Neptune was, like his counterpart Enki, lord of not only Earth's physical seas, but also the cosmic sea of etheric life force that surrounds and interpenetrates our planet. Although his most recognizable form is that of a man, he was, states Madame Blavatsky, originally a "dragon," the universal symbol and embodiment of the life force.[24]

Like his counterpart Enki, Neptune was principally associated with the seas although he was also known by his devotees as the Lord of the Earth. The identity of Neptune as King of the World is revealed by his Greek names, such as Enosichthon, meaning "Earth Shaker," a title that obviously links him to Vulcan-Lucifer. Two additional Greek epithets of Neptune, Phytalmios, "He who makes the plants to grow," and Poseidon, meaning "Wheat Husband," reveal that his worshippers knew him to be the Green Man and Lord of Nature.

Although he is ubiquitous throughout history as a manifestation of the Green Man, Neptune is best known for having resided on the legendary continent of Atlantis and given birth to its lineage of monarchs. Fisher King Neptune's Grail Castle was situated on top of the Atlantean "Holy Mountain of God," a mountain in the center of the island that was surrounded by water. Neptune lived in his palace with his mortal wife, Cleito, and later, during the reign of his sons and their successors, his Grail Castle became incorporated into a compound of important state buildings and temples wherein the ruling Fisher Kings of Atlantis lived and conducted their official court business.

Like his Fisher King counterparts, Neptune is also intimately associated with the planet Venus. In fact, his kingdom of Atlantis may have been known as the Land of Venus. Some researchers have identified Atlantis with the Greek Garden of the Hesperides, which is an appellation for Venus. Neptune's relationship to Venus can also be discerned through the symbology associated with his progeny with Cleito, five pairs of twin boys, because two and five are esoteric numbers specifically associated with the cycle of Venus and its manifestation as the Morning and Evening Stars. An additional link that unites Neptune to Venus is the Atlantean monarch's Venusian Crown, which displayed symbology associated with the cycles of the planet. According to L. Taylor Hansen, author of *The Ancient Atlantic*, while observing the sacred Crown Dance of the Mescalero Apaches in Arizona one hot summer's day she watched in disbelief as the lead dancer placed upon his head a version of the Venusian Crown that had once been worn by his ancestors, the kings of the Old Red Land of Atlantis. When she questioned the dancers afterwards about the symbology of the crown, Hansen learned that the original Venusian Crown of Atlantis had not only possessed a Venusian motif, but also the shape of a volcano, thus apparently affiliating Neptune and his Fisher King lineage with Vulcan, the eternal lord of volcanoes. This link became explicit during the reign of Neptune's Fisher King descendants known as the Votans, who became famous for being both expert smiths and *walking with a limp.*

According to Plato's account in the *Critias* and *Timeaus*, Neptune eventually divided up his kingdom among his ten sons by Cleito, each of whom became the ruler over one-tenth of the continent. Then, states Manly Palmer Hall, "With the trident scepter of Poseidon, the kings held sway over the inhabitants...of Atlantis."[25] But since Atlas was the oldest son of Neptune it was he who eventually became the premier Fisher King of Atlantis.

The Fisher King Dionysus and Arcadia

Following the demise of Atlantis, missionaries of the House of Votan dispersed to many pan-Atlantic regions and therein established their own kingdoms. One of their destinations was Arcadia, which has since become known as the Greek Garden of Eden. The early name of Arcadia, Gigantis, the "Land of the Giants," may be a reference to the tall Atlantean settlers the region initially harbored.

On Arcadia, the Atlantean settlers made goat-god Pan, one of the Green Man manifestations they had venerated on their motherland of Atlantis, their patron deity. Fiery Pan, whose name denotes "the All," was synonymous on Atlantis with Vulcan-Lucifer and Neptune, and he later became synonymous with Dionysus, the Green Man and first Fisher King of Greece. Dionysus' sacred animal, a black goat, was also Pan's.

Pan, who was thus in many ways synonymous with Dionysus, became part of the Fisher King's entourage and together they cavorted with a train of eternally joyful playmates. They were kept eternally young by the Arcadian Fountain of Youth known as Alpheus, meaning the "Source," a name that is curiously close to the name of Enki's home and "source" of the universe, the Apsu.

As Pan and Dionysus wandered throughout Arcadia they occasionally came into contact with one of the sacred animals associated with the Green Man, the peacock, which Greek legends claim were placed there by Hera, a name for the Goddess Venus, who was the patroness of Arcadia. The peacock was apparently also one of Dionysus', and like his counterpart Murrugan he may have even occasionally assumed the form of a peacock. This can be deduced from one of Dionysus' names, Panoptes or Pan-optic, the "all seeing," which was also a name for Argus, the multi-eyed giant who failed in his duty of guarding the white cow Io for Hera and was subsequently transformed into the prototypal peacock of Arcadia.

Another animal that was sacred to Dionysus, especially in his role as the first Fisher King of Arcadia, was the bear. The name Arcadia is derived from Arkas, which means "bear." Arkas was the name of the son of the Nymph Callisto and the nephew of Artemis, the goddess whose sacred animal was the bear. It is said that Callisto and Arkas were placed in the heavens by Zeus in the form of the Great and Little Bears, respectively. Thus, the Great Bear, the Celestial Grail, was an important part of the culture of the Eden of the West.

The Lineage of the Fisher King Danaans

The Atlantean Fisher King lineage in Arcadia was eventually passed to King Inachus, whom legends state was fathered by Oceanus, an early name for Neptune. Thus, Inachus was a blood relation of Neptune. Fisher King Inachus founded the House of Argos that ruled from Arcadia's capital city of Argos. His royal lineage eventually culminated in the reign of the Fisher King Iasos, whose best-known contribution to the history of Fisher Kings was fathering Io, the damsel that mated with Zeus and was afterwards transformed by the King of Heaven into a white cow in order to escape the wrath of Zeus' wife, Hera. Io eventually became the progenitor of a lineage of supernaturally empowered Fisher Kings known as the Danaans, the worshippers of Danu or Diana, which is a name for Artemis, whose sacred animal was the bear. The Danaans are reputed to have venerated the constellation of the Great Bear as both the seat of the celestial king, as well as "the throne of (Danu) the Queen of Heaven."[26]

Io founded the lineage of Danaans in Egypt, a country she eventually entered after wandering aimlessly throughout the Middle East in her white cow form. In Egypt, Io gave birth to Zeus's son, the Fisher King Epaphus. And then, in a very strange turn of events, Epaphus' daughter Libya somehow mated with her ancestor Neptune, thus reinvesting the Fisher King lineage with a pure infusion of blood from its original patriarch. Her progeny with Neptune was the Fisher King Belus, the king of Panopolis, who championed goat-god Pan as the city's sacred animal.

Belus fathered the warring brothers Aeguptus and Danaus, who represented patriarchy and matriarchy, respectively. Danaus, a lover of the Goddess Danu, was the antithesis of his brother Aeguptus, a warrior clearly in favor of militant control and domination. When the brothers' disagreements reached a dangerous level, Danaus fled Egypt with his fifty daughters, the Danaides, and sailed for Arcadia, the home of his ancestors. Once in the Peloponnesos, Danaus overthrew the ruling king of Argos, King Gelanor, and then reestablished the Fisher King Dynasty of Neptune in the land of his forefathers. In honor of his ancestress Io in her white cow manifestation, Fisher King Danaus then built a special temple, which then became known as the shrine of the White Goddess.[27]

During and after the reign of Danaus, the power and influence of the Danaans became so widespread throughout Greece that by the time of Homer the poet naturally referred to all Greeks as Danaans, or as the Danai. Besides their proliferation throughout mainland Greece, the Danaans also colonized many of the Aegean and Mediterranean islands, including Samothrace, Rhodes, and Cyprus, which was anciently known as the Isle of Dan. Other Danaans sailed further east, establishing settlements up and down the coast of Asia Minor, especially in its northern region, which became known as the Troad, the land of ancient Troy. One migration of Danaans that landed in Asia Minor became assimilated into the Hebrew culture and known as the Tribe of Dan, the symbol of which was both the snake or serpent, as well as a "lion's whelp," two sacred animals associated with the ancient Fisher Kings.

When Israel was eventually divided up among the twelve tribes, the Tribe of Dan received as its inheritance a stretch of land that was very unpopular with the other tribes because it bordered with the country of the inimical Philistines. The Tribe of Dan was subsequently forced to abandon this dangerous parcel and migrated north to Laish, an area where their Danaan ancestors had previously settled. Laish, which was an Asia Minor city in the foothills of the sacred Mt. Hermon, the Holy Mountain of God where the Nephilim Sons of God had once dwelt, was eventually renamed the City of Dan and later referred to in Greek literature as Paneas, the Land of Pan. This epithet alludes to the city's proximity to a cave shrine honoring the goat-god Pan that had been patronized by the early Danaans from Arcadia.

The Fisher Kings of Troy

Danaan tribes eventually founded the powerful city of Troy. The official founder of the Trojan lineage of Fisher Kings was Dardanus, a Danaan from the Greek island of Samothrace, whom legends state was a grandson of Atlas. The Fisher Kings of the House of Troy were thus in direct line to the first Fisher King, Neptune.

Following the destruction of the city of Troy, the monarchs of the House of Troy migrated to many parts of the globe, such as Rome. The Trojan Fisher King Aeneas traveled to Italy and fathered Romulus, the founder of Rome, who in turn begat an unbroken lineage of Roman Fisher Kings that continued down to the time of Julius Caesar. Ceasar became famous for proclaiming himself a descendant of the Goddess Venus and King Anchises of Troy, who together had conceived King Aeneas. In honor of Venus, his divine ancestress and eternal patroness of Fisher Kings, Ceasar had his image carried next to hers during important Roman processions, and at the time of his death the emperor's body was interred in a mausoleum resembling the Roman Temple of Venus.

Another region of Europe that the Fisher Kings of the House of Troy migrated to after the decimation of their beloved Troy was Scandinavia. In the cold climate of northern Europe they ruled over the country Denmark or Danmark, the "Land of Dan," as well as both Norway and Sweden. A definitive history of their migration was written by Snorri Sturlson in 1220 A.D., who refered to his Trojan ancestors as the Aesir, the "gods" of Asia, who were led to Scandinavia by the Fisher King Odin.

Odin founded a Norse mystery school that united many of the mysteries of the Fisher Kings. One of the esoteric icons within his school was the symbolic Tree of Yggdrasil, which had the "Holy Mountain of God," the dwelling place of the first Fisher King, resting firmly within the branches of Enki's Gish Gana or Tree of Life. The students of Odin's mystery school associated the summit of the holy mountain with the residence of Fisher King Odin, referring to it as Asgard, and they also recognized the goat near the abode of Odin (whom they also called Votan) as the goat-god Pan, the sacred patron of both the Danaans and Votan monarchs of Atlantis.

Once they had established lineages of Fisher Kings in Scandinavia, states the Irish *Book of Invasions*, the Danaans traveled further west to Ireland, where they founded a civilization of magicians known as the Tuatha de Danaan, whose emblems included four Grail Hollows: a sacred cauldron that was forever full of delectable food, a magical spear, a harp, and the Stone of Destiny. The Stone of Destiny, which was a manifestation of the alchemical stone or gem that fell to Earth from Lucifer's crown, was, according to one tradition, a meteorite.

Since the Stone of Destiny of the Tuatha de Danaan is also said to have been Jacob's "pillow," the stone that the Jewish patriarch rested his head upon during his visionary dreams, it is believed that it and the other Grail Hallows of the Tuatha may not have arrived with the Danaans from Scandinavia, but with a Danaan migration from the Middle East. A curious legend states that the Tuatha de Danaan were originally members of the Hebrew Tribe of Dan, who arrived in great ships off the coast of Ireland with a load of Jewish passengers that included the Prophet Jeremiah and Terah or Tamra, the daughter of the last Jewish monarch, King Zedekiah, who had been blinded by the Babylonian king Nebachadnesser. Tamra's escape from Palestine with the Tribe of Dan was necessary to ensure that the Jewish lineage of rulers would continue, so soon after her arrival in Ireland she married an Irish monarch. The follow-up of this intriguing story asserts that the harp of the Tuatha de Danaan was Terah's harp, and both it and her bodily remains are now buried within the mound of Ireland bearing her name, the Hill of Tara (or Terah), a sacred spot hill upon which the Irish kings were crowned.

Joining the Tuatha de Danaan and the Scandinavian Danaans in Britain was yet another migration of Danaans that had descended directly from the House of Troy. According to the 12th century English historian Geoffrey of Monmouth, Brutus, a descendant of the Trojan Aeneas, had wandered aimlessly around Europe until his beloved deity, Danu or Diana, appeared to him and advised him to travel to the British Isles where "A race of kings will be born (from Brutus) and the round circle of the whole Earth will be subject to them."[28] Diana's prophecy proved uncannily accurate; and Brutus was eventually crowned as the first king of Britain in its capital city of Troia Nova, or New Troy, which is now known as London.

The Merovingian Fisher Kings

While Brutus and the Danaans were establishing themselves in Britain, additional branches of the royal House of Troy were making a new home for themselves in the eastern lands of Asia. One such branch of Danaans is mentioned by Hugo of St. Victor, perhaps the best known of the early French chroniclers, who maintained that after the fall of Troy a branch of the royal family fled to the area of the Black Sea and founded the city of Sicambria. There, as the "Sicambrians," they coexisted and even intermarried with the native Scythians, the central Asian nomads who were devoted worshippers of the Fisher King Neptune and thus distant cousins of the Trojan refugees.[29]

The Sicambrian Fisher King was Antenor I, a direct descendant of the House of Troy. King Antenor transformed the Sicambrians into a tribe of itinerant warriors that were often combing the heartland of Asia. Then, following his death, the second Fisher King, Marcomrius, quickly grew tired of the Black Sea and moved the Sicambrians to a European territory along the Danube. Their new homeland, which was historically known as Pannonia, the Land of Pan, was at the time a Roman province although in previous ages had been a playground for the worshippers of Pan. It was in Pannonia, states both Hugo of St. Victor and Gregory of Tours, that the Sicambrian's ran afoul with the authorities of the Roman Empire and forced to migrate again. This event occurred following a great battle, during which the Sicambrians assisted the Romans in defeating the Alani, a European branch of the Scythians. The ungrateful Roman Emperor Valentinian proceeded to heavily tax the Sicambrians, who rebelled. Roman legions were then dispatched into Pannonia and the Sicambrians were forced to flee to the Rhineland.

Once settled in western Europe the Sicambrians evolved into an important branch of the Franks, which is a Germanic name meaning "Free." This occurred in the 4th century, when the Sicambrians became known as Salian (salty) Franks in order to distinguish them from another Frankish tribe, the Ripuarian (river) Franks. As the Salian Franks, the Sicambrians acquired land in the area of what is now Belgium from the Roman Emperor Julian, and from this base they gradually fanned out into the area of modern France, ultimately choosing that country rather than Belgium as the heartland of their empire. When the Salian Franks subsequently proclaimed King Pharamond their monarch, France officially had its first modern lineage of Fisher Kings. This French lineage would eventually culminate in a line of renowned magician kings founded by Pharamond's grandson, Merovee, the first Merovingian priest king.

Merovee reinfused the Fisher King lineage of France with the power of the first Fisher King, Neptune, whom legends contend was the true father of Merovee. According to the historian Priscus who documented his birth, Merovee had two fathers, Clodion, the son of Pharamond, and the *Bistea Neptunis,* the "Beast Neptune," a creature that copulated with Merovee's mother as she was bathing in the sea. Neptune, who assumed the form of a Quinotaur, a sea creature that was half fish and half bull, ravaged Merovee's mother and then proceeded to implant his divine seed within her already impregnated womb. Later, when Merovee was born he was considered to be only half human and heir to both a human line of monarchs, as well as the divine lineage of Fisher Kings engendered by Neptune.

Merovee, which means "Born from the Sea," has also been written as Merovach, meaning "Born from a Bull," as well as Merovie, meaning "Sea of Life" or "Water of Life." The name Merovee thus designates the first Fisher King of the Merovingian line to be the vessel of the Water of Life inherited from Neptune. Merovee transmitted his Water of Life down a lineage of priest kings who became known as the "People of the Bear," a designation that affiliates them with the goddess Danu or Diana, the deity of their ancestors. Their association with the Bear also affiliates the Merovingians with the Great Bear or Big Dipper, the Celestial Grail, which they were terrestrial counterparts of.

The Merovingians eventually became renown throughout Europe for their formidable powers and their abilities as magicians, healers, and wise men. It is said that just by touching the tassels hanging from their royal gowns a person could be healed of any disease. The magical practices of the Merovingians were confirmed in 1653 when the tomb of the great Merovingian King Childeric I, Merovee's son, was opened and a large crystal ball was discovered inside. Other magical talismans and power objects recovered from the tomb included a mummified horse's head and a bull's head made of solid gold, two objects which may have signified the Merovingian kings' affiliation with their ancestor Neptune. Legend has it that Neptune created the horse by striking his trident against a rock, and he later sired with Medusa the most famous of all horses, Pegasus. The golden bull's head may have symbolized for the Merovingians the head of Neptune in his manifestation as the Quinotaur, or it may have betrayed the Merovingian's link to Neptune's Atlantis, wherein sacred bulls were regularly sacrificed.

The Merovingian's dynastic emblems and titular names also ostensibly reflected their affiliation to Neptune. Their principal emblem, the fleur-de-lies, was, for example, a version of Neptune's trident. According to one tradition, the fleur-de-lies was originally given to King Clovis I, Merovee's grandson, by an angel, probably the Archangel Gabriel, during the monarch's conversion to Christianity. Gabriel, the angelic personification of the Holy Ghost and Water of Life, is the celestial patron of all Fisher Kings, beginning with Neptune.

The Merovingians also apparently revealed their affiliation to another manifestation of the primal Fisher King, that of Lucifer. The name of one of their capital cities, Satanicum, the "Place of Satan," is, of course, a common name for Vulcan-Lucifer. The Merovingian link to Vulcan-Lucifer was also implicit in a curious royal birthmark in the shape of a red cross, the ancient Mark of Cain, which a Merovingian was said to proudly display over his heart or between the shoulder blades of his back. As mentioned, this symbol also reveals a link to the Fisher King lineage founded by Cain.

In honor of their Trojan heritage, the Merovingians named one of their important French cities Troyes, and in respect for their Danaan ancestry they worshipped Diana and grew their hair long, just as their Danaan ancestor Samson had once done. The longhaired tradition of the Merovingians continued down to the time of their last incumbent monarch, Childeric, who suffered the indignity of having his head shaved by Pepin, his Prime Minister or Mayor of the Palace, who sought to destroy the king's remaining power and usurp his throne for himself. Samson's influence on the Merovingians was apparently also reflected in the kings' veneration of the honeybee, three hundred of which made out of solid gold were discovered inside the tomb of Childeric I. According to Biblical legend, Samson returned to the lion he had killed with his bare hands and found the animal's carcass full of bees and honey.

The heyday of the Merovingians, as well as the official beginning of a united Frankish empire, corresponded to the reign of Clovis I, who ascended the throne of a fledgling France and united the divergent tribes of the Salian and Repuarian Franks. According to the French historian Gregory of Tours, Clovis's royal power was then given a special dispensation of Holy Grail power in the form of a dove that flew down during his baptism and anointed him Fisher King. This occurred in the Cathedral of Reims, an honorary "Grail Castle" where a cult dedicated to the first Fisher King, Melchizedek, flourished alongside that of the Merovingians. With his enhanced Water of Life, Clovis succeeded in claiming for his Frankish kingdom the territory of Burgundy, as well as the southwestern European territories extending all the way to the Pyrenees. The pragmatic Clovis also attempted to negotiate a secure future for his Merovingian lineage by making a pact with the Catholic Pope Anastasius that stated if Clovis destroyed some of the enemies of Christendom, such as the Arian Visigoths and Lombards, the Pope would recognize both he and his successors as the emperors of the Holy Roman Empire.

Unfortunately, future Popes did not honor Clovis' pact, so the Merovingian line did not remain intact as he had hoped that it would. The first blow to the preservation of Merovingian power occurred soon after Clovis' death, when his kingdom was divided among his four bickering sons. This event was soon followed by the death knell to the Merovingian power, when the Mayor of the Palace, Pepin the Fat, had the ruling Merovingian King Dagobert II slain while he was on a hunting trip. When Pepin usurped the power of Dagobert's throne for himself, he initiated a spurious lineage of Fisher Kings that included his son Charles "the Hammer" Martel and his grandson, Pepin the Short, the father of King Charlemagne. The Pope's ancient pact with Clovis was voided during the administration of Pepin the Short, when Pope Zecharias proclaimed that Pepin and his ancestors would be the official kings of the Holy Roman Empire. This proclamation became official when Charlemagne traveled to the Vatican and was crowned Holy Roman Emperor by the Holy See.

However, even with their apparent exit from history, the lineage of Merovingian Fisher Kings did not cease to exist. According to a scenario presented in both *The Holy Blood and The Holy Grail* and *Bloodline of the Holy Grail,* the slain Merovingian Dagobert II had a son who survived him. This supposed Merovingian heir was Sigisbert IV, who under an assumed name continued the Merovingian lineage in the Languedoc area of southern France. Eventually the Languedoc became an autonomous country called Septimania and the grandson of Sigisbert IV, King Theodoric, ascended the throne as the nation's monarch. Another grandson of Sigisbert IV, Sigisbert VI, who was known in history as Prince Ursus, the "Bear Prince," organized a failed insurrection against Louis II of France in order to regain his rightful heritage. He died soon afterwards in Brittany.

The Merovingian bloodline also continued after Dagobert II via Bertha, a daughter of the Merovingian King Theuderic III, one of the sons of Clovis. Bertha continued the bloodline of the Merovingian Fisher Kings by spawning a line of rulers that culminated in the birth of Eleanor of Aquitane, the wife of Henry II and the matriarch of the Plantangenet dynasty that ruled both Britain and France in the 12th and 13th centuries. Henry's marriage to Eleanor strategically united the Merovingian line of monarchs with the Dukes of Anjou, whose wives and families were also noted for their supernatural abilities. The enlightened Fisher Kings of the House of Anjou were incorporated into the Grail legend of *Parzival* as the lineage of Fisher Kings known as Gahmuret, Gandin, Percival and his brother Feirefiz.

One of the scions of the House of Anjou remembered in history for reviving the Grail secrets of his sacred lineage was the colorful 15th century duke, Rene d'Anjou, who was an enlightened Fisher King in the true sense of the word. He was the benefactor of Holy Grail powers received from his family line, as well as lineal strength acquired from becoming a Grand Master of the Priory of Sion in 1418. Rene also procured membership in some neo- Holy Grail orders, including the Order of the Crescent, which he himself founded in order to create his own version of the Order of the Garter.[30]

For much of his life Rene worked to popularize and revive the mysteries of the Holy Grail in Europe. While doing so he traveled all over the continent in search of documented Grail history and chalices associated with the Holy Grail power. One of the most prized objects that eventually graced his altar was a red crystal goblet believed to have been used by Jesus and Mary during their wedding nuptials and later deposited by the Magdalene in Marseilles. Within his Grail Castle Rene placed many other ancient symbols of the Holy Grail, as well as some related to Arcadia, the homeland of his ancestors. In order to help revive the Golden

Age of his ancestors, Rene staged dramatizations of Arcadia, including "The Pas d'Armes of the Shepherdess," and he also breathed new life into the Arcadia theme through some of his renown paintings, including "Les Fountain des Fortune," a famous work that captures the beauty of Arcadia's River Alpheus. Rene's Arcadian enthusiasm ultimately infected Nicholas Poussin, whose "Les Shepherds d'Arcadia is currently recognize as the most famous painting related to the Arcadia theme. In this work, Poussin portrays a group of Arcadian shepherds standing around a tomb with the words "En Arcadia et ego," meaning "I am in Arcadia also," possibly referring to the fact that even in the land of immortality there is Lucifer, the Lord of Death. According to Michael Bradley, author of *Holy Grail Across the Atlantic*, Poussin's painting was also meant to reveal the "Grail Dynasty's truly ancient lineage—(was) *much* older than Jesus."

Rene d'Anjou was well versed in his family's genealogy, which apparently included some semi-playful allusions to Lucifer. His ancestor Richard the Lionhearted, for example, had exclaimed that "we (the House of Anjou) come from the Devil," and his ancestress Melusine was said to have been the daughter of Satan. Perhaps to represent his Luciferian lineage, Rene d'Anjou adopted as his personal seal the Cross of Lorraine, an alchemical symbol that denotes brimstone (a name for sulpher) and lead, both of which are elements affiliated with Lucifer.

The Spear of Destiny

One additional offshoot of the Merovingian bloodline that survived was that of Clovis's son Clotarius, who had inherited from the kingdom of Austrasia from his father. During the time of Charlemagne and the Saxon kings of the Habsburg Dynasty, Clotarius's ancestors survived as dukes and kings of their ancestral kingdom. And then, in 1273, one of their blood relatives, Prince Rudolph von Habsburg, ascended the throne of the Holy Roman Empire, thereby making the Merovingian line of Fisher Kings once again synonymous with the most powerful monarchs in Europe.

Following Rudolph was a lineage of Holy Roman Emperors whose supernatural powers rivaled those even commanded by the Merovingians. The source of their power was one of the Hollows of the Grail Castle, the Spear of Destiny, which had been an object of power for the Merovingians before it was stolen by Pepin the Fat. Pepin's son, Charles Martel, won forty-seven military campaigns with the spear by at his side, and Charles' grandson, Charlemagne, became supernaturally endowed with "phenomenal clairvoyant abilities" just be being in proximity to it. Charlemagne is reputed to have used his psychic ability to locate the tomb of St. James in Spain.[31]

After Charlemagne, forty-five Holy Roman Emperors ruled Europe for one thousand years with the power of the Spear of Destiny at their command. Many of them, including the emperors of the House of Habsburg and House of Hohenstauffen, proved to be both incredibly wise and physically powerful – at least as long as they held the spear. When the spear slipped from the grasp of the Emperor Frederick Barbarossa while crossing a rapidly moving river, the monarch fell and lost his life.

Emperor Frederick II, Incarnation of the Primal Fisher King

Barbarossa's grandson and the greatest wielder of the Spear of Destiny in the Holy Roman Empire was the Emperor Frederick II Hohenstauffen. Frederick II was hailed as the return of King Arthur, the archetypal Fisher King, and definitely reflected the lineage of Fisher Kings in all his activities. In order to appropriately care for the Spear of Longinus, Frederick II built for himself a Grail Castle based upon the alchemical eight-pointed star. Here Frederick sat daily upon his royal throne, his long, flowing ceremonial robes embroidered with both red crosses and palm trees, which were ancient symbols of Al-Khadir, the primal Fisher King of the Middle East.[32]

Leading up to Frederick II's hotly anticipated birth, legends regarding King Arthur and the Holy Grail had found fertile ground on the Mediterranean island of Sicily where his parents resided. Frederick's Norman ancestors had brought the mythology of the Grail to southern Italy and made the Holy Grail mysteries part of the Sicilian culture. And in order to firmly root the Fisher King lineage in Sicily, certain Grail Hallows were interred in the castles of Sicily, including the sword of King Arthur, which was a gift to the Sicilian King Tancred from one of the greatest of Norman monarchs and scion of the House of Anjou, King Richard the Lionhearted. The stage had thus been set for Frederick II 's auspicious birth, an event prophesied by Godfrey of Viterbo, the tutor of Henry VI, Frederick's father. According to Ernst Kantorowicz in *Frederick II*, Viterbo "in sybilline speech informed his master that the coming son (Frederick) was destined to prove the long awaited King of all the World, who should unite East and West...."

Frederick II's birth occurred the day before Christmas, 1194, so he was initially hailed not only as an incarnation of King Arthur, but also a Messiah or Christ. Since he had been born from Norman blood on his mother's side and German ancestry on his father's side, the new crown prince was also championed as the incarnating Prince of Peace who had come to unite the divergent peoples of northern and southern Europe. But Frederick would eventually do much more than this; he would also unite the spiritual traditions of the East and West.

Frederick's diverse education was strategically chosen to prepare him for his mission of unification. He grew up in a Sicilian culture that was more Moslem and Arabic than European and Christian, and he intensely studied a curriculum of the western classics prescribed to him by Pope Innocent II, who became his legal guardian following the early deaths of his parents. Pope Innocent also taught Frederick the ways of a totalitarian priest king, which was wisdom the future monarch would later heavily draw upon.

Following his coronation as Holy Roman Emperor by the Pope in 1212, Frederick proceeded to found one of the purist theocratic governments Europe had ever seen. As he gradually assumed his role as the embodiment of the archetypal Fisher King and King of the World, Frederick II was duly venerated by both his eastern and western subjects as their king and shah. He entertained sages, philosophers, mystics, Sufis, and alchemists from all over the world at his eclectic court, and he was always ready to extend his hospitality to the occasionally passing Templar Knight, such as the author of *Parzival,* Wolfram von Eschenbach, who is averred to have paid a visit to the emperor. By visiting Frederick, Wolfram had continued the tradition of his teacher, Kyot or Guyot de Provins, who is reputed to have lived for an extended period the castle of Frederick's grandfather, Frederick Barbarossa

Frederick's "Grail Castle" was the Castel del Monte, a masterpiece of sacred science and architecture, which was built in the form of a giant, octagonal alchemical crucible. Besides being designed in the form of an eight-pointed star, with towers at all of the eight points, it also incorporated the Golden Mean Proportion, the mathematical constant of the serpentine spiral, thus ensuring that the transformative life force would continue to slither through the edifice. The inner walls of the castle were painted red, the color associated with transformative fire and the red-colored Philosopher's Stone, thereby also infusing the palace with a transformative ambiance. Castel de Monte was indeed a reflection of the Grail Castle mentioned in the Grail legend of the *Vulgate Cycle,* Castle Corbenic, which is a Chaldean term meaning "The Holy Vessel."[27]

Frederick distinguished himself as one of the true scholar kings of his time. His book, *The Art of Falconry*, became an instant classic and the definitive book of his time regarding the habits and training of falcons. The brilliant king also kept up correspondence with many other kings connected to the Holy Grail mysteries, including the mysterious Prestor John. Among the special gifts Frederick received from Prestor John were an assortment of Grail Hallows that he interred in his castle, including a version of the Philosopher's Stone and a Grail chalice.

It was during a visit to Jerusalem that Frederick II would come as close as he would to proclaiming himself King of the World. After leading one of the later crusades into the holy city, Frederick II stood within the Church of the Holy Sepulcher, where, states history, "a thousand candles burned; Frederick wearing his richly embroidered imperial robes marched up to the altar, seized the crown and placed it on his own head. Thereupon Hermann of Salza read out a long speech in celebration of the event, in which God, David, Christ and Frederick were mystically united." Frederick was, at the time, excommunicated from the Catholic Church, so when news of his coronation reached the Pope, the Holy See loudly and forcefully proclaimed Frederick "A great beast (that) has come out of the sea…this scorpion spewing passion from the sting in his tail…full of the names of blasphemy…raging with the claws of the bear and the mouth of a lion, and the limbs and the likeness of the leopard, opens its mouth to blaspheme the Holy Name…behold the head and tail and body of the beast, of this Frederick, this so-called emperor…" Thus, like so many Fisher Kings before and after him that have proclaimed their dominion, Frederick had become synonymous with Lucifer.

Like King Arthur, his spiritual counterpart, Frederick II also commanded an order of knights that continually served and protected him. His order was patterned after the Knights Templar and the Teutonic Knights, and its members wore uniforms and observed secret rites that mirrored these more ancient chivalric orders. Frederick's knights are averred to have remained by his side until his death, at which time the Holy Roman Emperor had his body covered in robes of the Cistercian Order, the monastic order most closely associated with the Knights Templar. But according to an alternate legend featured in *Frederick II, A Mideaval Emperor* by David Abulafin, Frederick II never died. Instead he and his knights are reputed to have ridden together up the side of Etna and then inside the volcano's volatile mouth. "Passing through the sea (of magma), (they joined) their master in the bowel's of the Earth." Frederick's "master" was Vulcan-Lucifer, whose spirit he had incarnated.

Once inside the volcano, Frederick made it his home, and a local legend states he will remain there until the world is ready for him to reemerge and resurrect the Holy Roman Empire. One interesting postscript of this legend, which can be found in *Myths and Mythmakers* by John Fiske, maintains that in 1669 a dwarf (apparently Vulcan) led a wandering shepherd into Mt. Etna, where Frederick was found sporting a long beard and sitting at a stone table. Frederick inquired of the shepherd "Are ravens still flying around the mountain?" When the shepherd answered affirmatively, Frederick declared, "Then I must sleep for another hundred years."

King Arthur, the Bear King

Thus, Frederick II had been both an incarnation of the spirit of both Vulcan-Lucifer and King Arthur. But King Arthur, as stated earlier in this text, is an anachronism. No such king existed at the time he is supposed to have live. Instead, he is the archetypal Fisher King with a composite personality synthesized from many real and imaginary monarchs and spiritual leaders of history. When sitting at the Round Table in the 13th seat of rulership, he is the enlightened Christ. As the greatest of knights, he is a Templar Grand Master. As the vindictive monarch, he is the self-serving Lucifer. And as the monarch named Arthur, he is an incarnation of the Celestial Holy Grail, the constellation of the Great Bear. The name Arthur is derived from Arktos, "Bear," the Welsh Arth Fawr, and related to Artoius, "the Plough Man," a name for the Big Dipper. The epithet is also associated with Arcturus, meaning "Guardian of the Bear," which is the bright star in Bootes that points to the tail of the Great Bear, thus proving that the king is both the embodiment and Guardian of the Holy Grail.

Legend states that when King Arthur died he was appropriately entombed within the island of Avalon, which, with seven hills surrounding it, is a perfect reflection of the Big Dipper or Great Bear. John Michell and other sacred scientists of England believe that today Avalon is Glastonbury and the seven hills of Avalon are the seven "star-mounds" surrounding it: Beckery, Godney or God's Island, Martinsea or Marchey, Ferramere or Meare, Panborough, and Andrewsea or Nyland (Glastonbury, Maker of Myths). King Arthur's tomb was supposedly discovered by monks on the grounds of Glastonbury Abbey, which was built next to Glastonbury Tor. So King Arthur, the incarnation of the Great Bear, eternally sleeps within his true terrestrial home.

King Jamshid and the Persian Fisher King Dynasty of *Parzival*

Another Asian manifestation of the primal Fisher King and Green Man is King Jamshid of Persian legend, a king of the Golden Age who existed at least 20,000 years ago. Great King Jamshid, the "Resplendent Cup," was counterpart to Enki, Murrugan, Dionysus, Al-Khadir, and Vulcan-Lucifer, who similarly wielded an abundance of supernatural power that brought prosperity and even immortality to his subjects but later lost most of it when he let his pride obscure the truth of "whom the Grail serves."

Since the Fisher King lineage in *Parzival* is full of Persian names, it has been conjectured that King Jamshid's royal lineage might possibly be the one enthroned by Wolfram in his masterpiece. Wolfram has his Fisher King lineage begin with Mazadan, a name with Persian overtones that seems to be derived from Ahura Mazda, the high god of the Persian Zoroastrians. Ahura Mazda was physically embodied as the solar deity Mithra, whose residence is stated by the Persian *Mihr Yasht*, the "Hymn to Mithra," to be located on the legendary mountain of Mt. Albourz, which interestingly is the same place that the Persian *Bundahishn* identifies as the location of King Jamshid's castle. Thus Ahura Mazda, Mithra and Jamshid have manifold interconnections, which is perhaps why it was natural to amalgamate them together as the first Fisher King. Jamshid's alternate name of Yima, meaning "Solar Ray" and "Son of the Sun," is an epithet that has been applied to both Ahura Mazda and Mithra, and a Jamshid-Mithra link can also be perceived during the Persian New Year holiday of Noruz, when both figures are brought together as the great savior(s) of humanity who assisted in bringing immortality to the world and later ascended into the heavens. In addition, Jamshid and Mithra are jointly celebrated in the Persian-influenced Festival of Jam, the "Festival of the Cup," which is observed annually within the Middle Eastern Cult of Angels. During the Jam Festival not only are Jamshid and Mithra honored as though they are one and the same, but it is also revealed that each is synonymous with Melek Taus, the Peacock Angel and primal Fisher King of the Yezidhi. Throughout the Jam Festival all three deities are honored, one after the other, while being similarly identified with the same honored titles of "Creator," "Savior," "First Born," and "King of the World." Melek Taus' link to Mithra is even more conclusive on December 25, which is acknowledged to be their common birthday.

Albourz, the Original Holy Mountain of God?

The scriptural reference that places Jamshid's castle on Mt. Albourz may be based in fact. This is because another manifestation of the King of the World has been documented by witnesses to be living on the mountain. This planetary monarch is the Simurgh, the Fisher King and Green Man of the bird kingdom, who is reputed to possess an amalgamation of features associated with a wide variety of all the world's most beautiful and exotic birds. His most salient feature, however, is his resplendent peacock tail, a feature that affiliates him to the Fisher King manifestation known as the Peacock Angel. According to Persian myth he has appeared to humans on numerous occasions; and there is even a popular Chinese legend that maintains that the Simurgh once flew over China. The bird lost one of its plumes during this flight, which after falling to the ground was promptly taken to a gallery for display.

The Simurgh's association with the universal Green Man is revealed through his name, meaning "thirty birds," which denotes its multi-faceted form as a composite of many different species of birds. And just as the Green Man embodies the collective consciousness of humanity, the Simurgh personifies the collective bird consciousness. This truth is ilustrated in a popular Persian myth called the *Parliament of the Birds*. According to this tale, a group of thirty birds came together and resolved to fly to the holy mountain in the center of the Earth in order to have an audience with the King of Birds. After reaching the abode of the Simurgh on Mt. Albourz the birds took turns having a private audience with the King of the World. Afterwards, when they came together to share their experiences they were shocked to discover that they all had the same identical story to tell. As each of them had stood face to face with the Simurgh they realized they were looking directly at themselves! He was the Simurgh, the "thirty birds." They thus understood that the Simurgh was the collective composite of them all. He was their Green Man, their Melek Taus, and their Dionysus.

Many researchers currently contend that the mythical mountain of Albourz is the highest peak in the Albourz range, the 18,934-foot high Mount Demavend, which, interestingly, is *a volcano associated with a manifestation of Vulcan-Lucifer.* Within Mt. Demavend is the tormented body of Azhi Dahaka, the demonic conqueror who destroyed King Jamshid after the ancient monarch's fall from pride. Azhi Dahaka, who appears to be synonymous with Jamshid's egotistical lower self, and therefore one with Vulcan-Lucifer, was chained to the inside of the mountain's volcanic crater so he could undergo eternal torture. Today, the Iranians who walk the streets of Tehran daily reflect upon Demavend's visible peak towering above their city with satisfaction, knowing that its inner resident is receiving his just desserts after the way he treated their beloved King Jamshid.

Could Mt. Demavend be *the* Mt. Albourz? Perhaps, especially given that when the Mongols invaded Persia in 1216 AD Demavend was still covered with the palaces of Persian Fisher Kings who had resided upon its slopes for thousands of years. Thus, both manifestation of the Green Man, the Simurgh and King Jamshid, could be currently residing upon its slopes.

Jamshid and the Golden Age

Like his Fisher King counterparts, Jamshid is also affiliated with the symbol of the bear. The bear became the totem animal of the Persian kings during his rule and was then passed down the royal Persian lineage for many hundreds of thousands of years, finally receiving international recognition as the emblem of Persia's greatest conqueror, King Cyrus the Great. Jamshid's affiliation to the bear may have begun with the constellation of the Great Bear, which continuously rotated over the first Persian land, Airyan Vaejahi, the site of the Garden of Eden ruled over by the Fisher King Jamshid that many scholars place in the Arctic Circle.

Jamshid's Garden of Eden existed at a time anterior to the world's major ice ages, when the poles were yet to become covered with blankets of ice. The Persian *Vendidad* designates Airyan Vaejahi as having been far to the north, which Bal Gangadhar Tilak, a Hindu Brahmin and scholar of the 19th century, identified with the Arctic Circle. Tilak theorized that preceding the last Ice Age, the Arctic was warm and lush with vegetation all year round and could have supported a thriving Aryan civilization, a theory that was corroborated during his lifetime by discoveries of tropical vegetation frozen in the northern polar ice caps. According to the Persian *Vendidad*, because of the sins of King Jamshid and his Aryan subjects, the Ice Age destroyed their tropical paradise and ended their

Golden Age.

The Theosophists maintain that the first Root Race of humans on Earth were the Polarians who resided at the poles. Could these Polarians have been Jamshid's Persian subjects? It is interesting to note that Jamshid's paradise is referred to as the White Island, which is the same name used for the island that the Fisher King Sanat Kumara built his Grail Castle upon. Could Sanat Kumara's White Island originally have been at the poles and later moved to the area of the Gobi Desert during a planetary shift?

When the Ice Ages finally arrived and disturbed their paradise, King Jamshid and his subjects migrated south to their current home in Iraq. It was during that time that the Fisher King Jamshid gave way his lower passions and ego, subsequently suffering a huge fall. Before that time Jamshid had been a human Holy Grail and a vessel for the Water of Life, which in Persia was known as *Farr-e-Izadi*, or *Farr* for short, but when he gave into his selfish ways his *Farr* immediately began to be depleted, and after 23 years it had all but disappeared. Without the power to protect his kingdom, Jamshid could only watch passively as his empire was overrun and conquered by the demonic Azhi Dahaka, a prince of Syria, who picked up the Persian king and broke him into two pieces over his massive knee.

Jamshid's Royal Persian Lineage

But even after the fall of Jamshid his royal lineage somehow managed to continue, and any *Farr* he was able to retain was passed down a long line of Persian monarchs. One of Jamshid's early descendants was the legendary King Feridun, who continued Jamshid's quest to defeat Azhi Dahaka and is reputed to have allied with a blacksmith named Kawa in order to achieve his goal. The blacksmiths of Feridun's era were considered supernaturally powerful; they possessed the ability to control and manipulate fire, and some were even considered incarnations of fire gods. Kawa willingly transmitted some of his supernatural firepower into Jamshid's depleted lineage, after which the Fisher Kings in the Persian lineage of Jamshid all wore a ceremonial blacksmith apron covered with precious stones in honor of Kawa. It is interesting to note that by aligning with Kawa the Persian monarchs had essentially returned to their roots as representatives of the primal smith god and Fisher King Vulcan-Lucifer.

With the *Farr* of the Persian kings replenished, some very great and powerful kings were able to emerge within Jamshid's lineage. The greatest of these incarnated within the Kayanid Dynasty of the 19th century B.C., which was composed of Holy Grail monarchs with royal courts and knights resembling King Arthur's Camelot and the Knights of the Round Table. The Kayanid Dynasty began with the Fisher King Kei Kobad, whose court resided in a Grail Castle high upon Mt. Albourz, and he was followed by the greatest ruler of the Kayanid Dynasty, King Key-Khosrow, who is today recognized as a Persian manifestation of King Arthur. Key-Khosrow was the possessor of a Holy Grail Cup similar to the one his ancestor Jamshid once owned, and he daily surrounded himself with an order of knights similar to the Knights of the Round Table.

Because of his righteous nature Fisher King Khosrow quickly acquired a great abundance of *Farr,* which manifested within the monarch as both power and exalted spiritual wisdom. His spiritual consciousness continued to expand until his only wish was to shed his physical vehicle and ascend to the higher spiritual planes of the universe. Khosrow subsequently abdicated his throne in favor of his successor, King Key-Lohrasp, but according to popular legend Khosrow will again return to Earth on the Day of Resurrection as part of the entourage of the prophesied Persian savior, Soslyans.

Like Khosrow, King Key-Lohrasp was also a highly advanced mystic, and similar to his predecessor he eventually resolved to abdicate his throne in order to devote his life to intensive spiritual practices. Key-Lohrasp is most famous for being the ruling king during the lifetime of Persia's greatest prophet, Zoroaster, who no doubt influenced the king's decision to trade his royal status for that of a spiritual mendicant.

Following King Key-Lohrasp's departure, the lineage of Persian Fisher Kings continued to rule Persia from the slopes of Mt. Albourz for thousands of years. Their Grail Castles survived on Mt. Demavend until 1216 A. D., when hordes of Mongol invaders destroyed them. Their other palaces were at Persepolis, which was known as the Takht-e-Jamshid, the "Throne of Jamshid," and survived until their destruction by Alexander the Great. Although history maintains that the Takht-e-Jamshid was built by Cyrus the Great and the kings of the Achaemenian Dynasty, other legends assert that it was originally built and lived in by Jamshid himself.

The glorious expliots of Jamshid and Key-Khosrow and their connections to the Holy Grail Mysteries are today recounted regularly in Persian verse and song. One of these commemorative verses, the *Saghi-Nameh*, was composed by Hafiz, a Sufi adept:

Give me wine, and with the reed-flute I will sing
When was Jamshid, and when Khosrow was king

Bring me the elixir whose grace and alchemy
Bestows treasures, from bonds of time sets free

Bearer give the wine that the Holy Grail

Will make claims of sight in the void and thus fall

Give me so that I, with the help of the Grail
All secrets, like Jamshid, themselves avail

The Peacock Throne

Following the era of Khosrow and the fall of Persepolis, the Persian lineage of Fisher Kings experienced one final burst of glory during the reigns of the Shahs of Iran. These monarchs ruled Persia from their glorious Peacock Throne, which was a latter-day reflection of the throne used by the Fisher King Murrugan. The Peacock Throne arrived in Persia in 1738 with the conqurer Nadir Shah, who had captured it from its owner, Shah Jahan, the Mongol king of India famous for constructing the Taj Mahal as a tomb for his beloved wife, Mumtaz Mahal. When he constructed the Peacock Throne, Shah Jahan had, like Murrugan, his ancestor on Sri Lanka, declared his sovereignty as king of not only India, but the entire world.

The Peacock Throne was designed by Shah Jahan to be supremely empowered by the magical and priceless gems that were embedded into it. One of the throne's peacock eyes was the Koh-I-Nor, a 108.93 carat diamond that at the time of Shah Jahan was believed to have had been planted on Earth by the spirit of the Sun for use by the ruling King of the World. Other legendary diamonds decorating the Peacock Throne included the priceless "Ackbar Shah" diamond and the "Jehangir Diamond," which hung from the peacock's beak. The Koh-I-Nor diamond was eventually removed from the Peacock Throne and shipped by the East India Company to Britain, where it became one of the Crown Jewels. This massive diamond, which in 1937 was inserted into the crown of Queen Elizabeth II for her coronation, is currently in the possession of the British monarchy

The Assassin Lineage of Fisher Kings

The lineage of the Persian Fisher Kings was also resurrected briefly via the reign of Hasan-I-Sabbah, the revered chief of the mountaintop dwelling Assassins. Hasan, a Persian native, revived the tradition of the Persian Fisher Kings when he acquired one of their palaces, the castle of Alamut, which was situated high upon a precipice in the Albourz Mountains. Alamut, which is derived from Aluh amut, meaning "Eagles Teaching, " refers to both the lofty height of Alamut, as well as the castle's origins. According to legend, Alamut was constructed by a Persian prince who, when seeking to build a fortress high in the Albourz Mountains, released a trained eagle. The majestic bird flew across the landscape and finally came to rest on the rock that would provide the foundation for Alamut.

Hasan-I-Sabbah not only acquired Alamut, but he also built sixty more castles in the Albourz Mountains, thus returning splendor and wealth to the Persian Fisher King tradition. Although he never formerly proclaimed himself greater than his brethren, Hasan was given the veneration and obedience of a king and regarded by his followers, the Nazari Ishmailis, as a direct descendant of the Prophet Mohammed through his son-in-law Ali.

Under Hasan's guidance, an order of Holy Grail knights resembling the Templars came into existence at Alamut. Hasan taught his charges the Holy Grail Mysteries and instituted nine stages or degrees that the knights could ascend through as they metaphorically climbed to the top of legendary Kaf, the Holy Mountain of God, and finally merged their consciousness with that of the Green Man. One of the texts studied by the Assassins, the *Sargozast-i Sayyid-na,* explained in detail the sacred, geometrical keys that would lead an aspiring knight to the summit of Kaf.

Hasan's mystery school culminated in the Teaching of the Resurrection, which promised immortality to all Assassin initiates. The first to promulgate these teachings on a large scale was Hasan's lineal descendant, Hasan II, who in 1164 summoned all the Nazari in Persia to meet at the foot of Alamut, where he proclaimed "The Imam of our time has lifted from you the burden of obeying the ritual law and has brought you the Resurrection." Hasan's pivotal announcement was followed with new rites and teachings that were designed to rapidly accelerate human evolution and prepare his followers for their reward.

Hasan II was murdered within eighteen months of his famous declaration, but his movement survived via the work of an enlightened and supernaturally empowered Assassin known as Rashid al-din Sinan. Sinan was sent by Hasan II's son, Mohammed II, to oversee the Nazari in Syria, where he chose the Castle of Kahf in the Ansari Mountains as his hermitage, thus establishing the Persian Fisher King lineage in Asia Minor. With his limp, which was sustained by a rock that fell upon his leg during a Syrian earthquake in 1157, Sinan must have closely resembled his ancestor Vulcan-Lucifer as he moved around his Grail Castle on the Holy Mountain of Kahf.

Sinan is reputed to have proclaimed himself the incarnation of the soul that had previously incarnated as Adam, and he also maintained that he had also been the teacher of both Moses and Aaron. He thus implied that he was the soul of Al-Khadir, while also revealing that Adam was indeed synonymous with Fisher King Murrugan. In his famous declaration recorded by the French historian Guyard, Sinan formally reveals his exalted nature:

"Religion was not complete for you until I appeared to you in Rashid al-

Din…I am the master of creation...I am the witness, the dispenser of mercy at the beginning and the end. Do not be deceived by the changing of appearances. You say, So-and-so passed away, So-and-so succeeded him. But I tell you to regard all the faces as one face, for as long as the master of creation is in this world, present, existent…I am the ruler, the sovereign master of orders and of will."

Most everyone was hesitant to disprove Sinan's claims of greatness because his spiritual wisdom and power were legendary throughout the Middle East. Ascribed to Sinan was the ability to foresee past and future events as clearly as a common person perceives the present moment. He never ate or drank, and he was often found sitting alone on a rock for hours at a time while conversing with disembodied spirits. Sinan is also known to rarely open his letters, and to be able to both accurately discern their contents and appropriately respond to their queries.

Sinan was recognized by many as God's representative on Earth that was sent by the Almighty to intercede in the terrestrial affairs of both animals and humans, especially whenever karma and/or death were involved. During one incident when a butcher was about to slaughter a bull, the animal broke its restraint and ran away with the butcher's knife between his teeth. When the butcher began to pursue the distraught animal, Sinan suddenly appeared and told him that the bull had been butchered at the same place in seven previous incarnations and did not want to meet his end that way again. He then made the butcher promise not to hurt the animal and to let it die a natural death. At another time, when Sinan was watching a trained monkey perform, the sage reached over, gave the animal a coin, and it instantly died. Its confused and shaken owner then asked Sinan for an explanation of this inexplicable event and was told that the incident was related to the monkey's past life when it had been a king. The coin that Sinan had given the monkey had the face of this ancient king printed upon it, and as soon as the animal recognized the face as its own from a former existence the shock of its present degraded circumstances immediately killed it.

It was not unusual for the psychically adept Sinan to recognize the spirits of his past acquaintances reincarnated as animals. Once while watching his guards from afar who were preparing to kill a snake, Sinan psychically perceived that the spirit of an old friend had incarnated within the snake. Hurrying to the scene, Sinan quickly made the snake's identity known. Its spirit was that of a recently deceased Assassin who was undergoing purgatorial penance and he needed to be left alone. Another of Sinan's famous interactions with a transmigrated soul occurred high on a mountaintop where he was spotted talking to a green bird glowing with light. When asked about the incidence later on, Sinan remarked that he had been conversing with Hasan II, who had taken the form of the bird in order to come to him for advice.

The wounded Fisher King.

Murrugan, the Green Man and King of the World (India & Sri Lanka).

The Flower of Life, symbol of Green Man Osiris (Egypt).

Dionysus, the Green Man and King of the World (Greece).

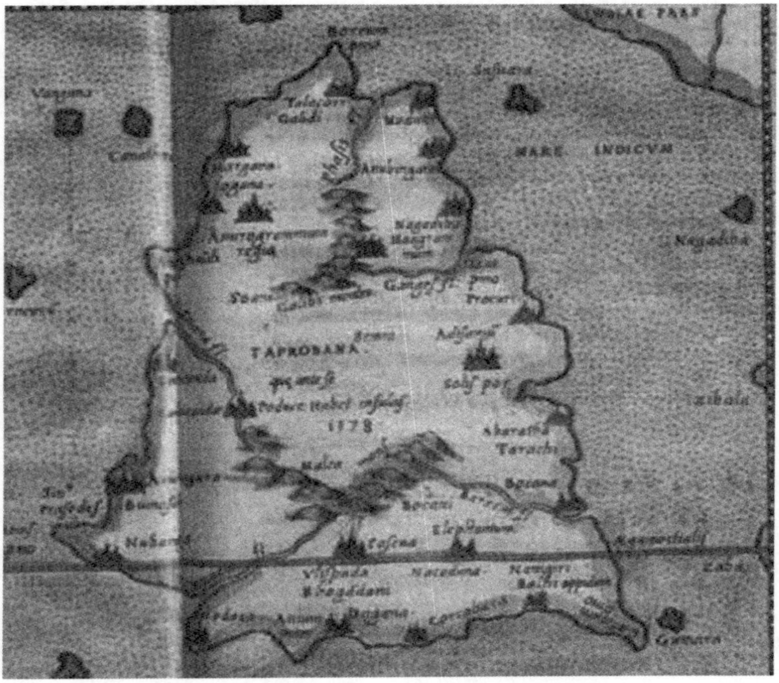

Ptolemy's map of Sri Lanka.

Ptolemy's map. His Bachi Oppidum, the "Town of Bacchus" (Dionysus), is the Hindu Kataragama, the "Place of Karttikeya" (Murrugan).

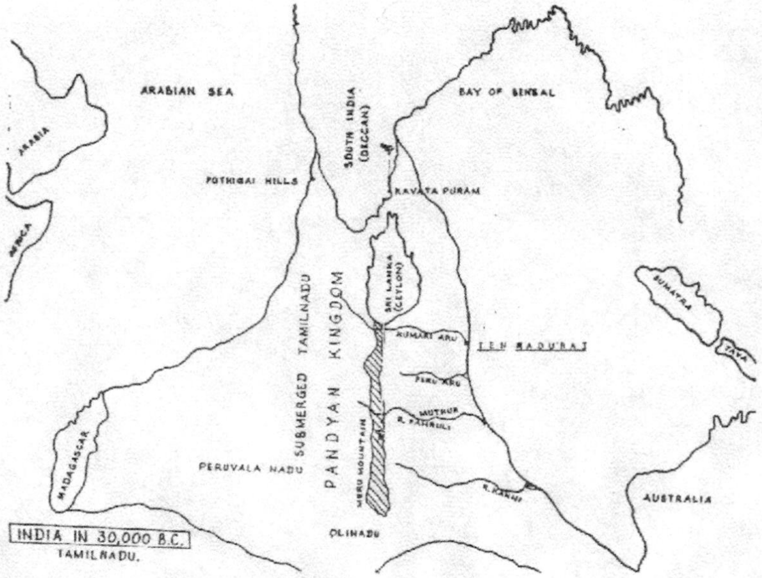

Sri Lanka, India, and Australia united as Kumari Nadu .

Adam and Eve evicted from the Garden. The Peacock Angel is on the left wall.

An image of the King of the World published in Amazing Stories magazine, May, 1946. The accompanying article states:

"He came here ages ago from the planet Venus to be the instructor and guide of our then just dawning humanity. Though he is thousands of years old, his appearance is that of an exceptaionally well developed and handsome youth of about sixteen. Some claim to have seen him...when mankind is ready for the benefits he can bring, he will emerge and establish a new civilization of peace and plenty."

Current symbol of the Imperial and Royal Court of the Dragon.

Symbol of the Imperial and Royal Court of the Dragon, 1408,
with the cross of St. George.

Castle del Monte, the octagonal Grail Castle of Frederick II.

The throne of kingship in Westminster Abbey.
Once the home of the Stone of Destiny.

King Arthur by Charles Earnest Butler, 1903.
Arthur is the archetypal Fisher King.

9
John the Baptist and the Dynastic Cupholders

Next in line as the greatest Human Holy Grails are the Cupholders, divine servants of humanity and "Fishers of Men." The Cupholders are the spiritual adepts worldwide who have produced an abundance of Holy Spirit or Kundalini power in their physical vessels through intensive disciplines, thus enabling them to serve as human cups or chalices for those thirsting for spiritual wisdom. Many Cupholders are known in India as Sat-Gurus, "True" Gurus (from gu-darkness and ru-light, the one who takes a person from darkness to light), because they have the ability to awaken others to their divine essence through the transmission of Kundalini power, whereas in other locations worldwide they have been known as white magicians, high priests, yogis, shamans, Holy Grail Masters, and the dynastic heads of various mystical traditions and lineages. At the head of most Cupholder lineages is their ubiquitous founder, the Green Man, who is the personification of Kundalini and the original Serpent on the Tree. Many Cupholder lineages descended from the Green Man in his manifestation as the Fisher King Murrugan, who sent his enlightened disciples out from Sri Lanka to establish them around the world. One of Murrugan's Kundalini lineages was taken west to the Middle East, where it culminated in the birth of one of the greatest Kundalini Masters of all time, John the Baptist, who was known by his people, the Mandeans, as the "Fisher of Souls." John was the fountainhead from which numerous Kundalini lineages eventually spread throughout the West via his foremost disciples, which included Jesus Christ and the Gnostic Master Simon Magus. One of John's most empowered lineages, the Johannite Cupholders, moved from John to Jesus, and then to John the Apostle, and was later transmitted along a line of Knights Templar Grand Masters beginning in the 12th century. The Templars carried the Johannite lineage back to their native Europe, after which they helped spawn a constellation of Kundalini-focused European secret societies that included the Freemasons, Rosicrucians, and the Illuminati.

Murrugan's first Cupbearer lineages were founded when Sri Lanka was still part of the larger continent of Kumari Nadu or Lemuria. At that time, states both Hindu legend and Madame Blavatsky's *The Secret Doctrine*, Sanat Kumara and his entourage of the Sons of God came from Venus to Lemuria, where they became known as the "Sons of Yoga," the first teachers of the *Siddha Marga*, the path that leads to enlightenment via Kundalini activation and development. To teach the mysteries of Kundalini on Kumari Nadu, the Sons of God founded lineages of adepts and special schools where disciplines for awakening Kundalini, such as yoga and alchemy, were regularly promulgated. Those that graduated as Kundalini Masters from these school were then sent out from Mu by Sanat Kumara to found lineages of Cupholders in various locations around the globe. The lineages and Kundalini Masters they created are collectively referred to today as the Great White Brotherhood.

Some of the most important of Sanat Kumara's disciples founded Cupbearer lineages after traveling north into India. One important disciple, the Cupholder Agastyar, traveled into the Indian subcontinent when Sri Lanka was still united to the southern tip of India. Once in India, Agastyar founded many lineages of Kundalini adepts through his illustrious students, who are collectively known in history as the Mahesvara Siddhas. The Maheshvara Siddhas include such spiritual stalwarts as the two thousand year old Babaji Nagaraj, the "Father Serpent;" Bogarnath, the patriarch and first teacher of Hindu Alchemy; and Goraknath and Matsyendranath, the founders of the modern Hatha Yoga tradition.

The Mandean Nasurai from Sri Lanka

One Kundalini lineage that emerged from Sri Lanka and then moved to the Middle East was the line of Mandean Cupbearers known as the Nasurai. The name Nasurai, which carries the meaning of Gnostic wisdom, is derived from the root Nass, meaning "serpent" and related to Nachash, the Hebrew word for "serpent," thus revealing that these Kundalini Masters were intimately tied to *Jnana Pandita* or Murrugan and his form as the incipient Gnostic teacher, the Serpent on the Tree of the Garden of Eden. The name Mandean, as well as its derivatives, Mandai and Madai, also denotes "wisdom," but since it also carries the meaning of "enclosure" it indicates that the Mandean Nasurai were "enclosures" of the Kundalini, or Human Holy Grails.

According to the Mandean texts, Murrugan appears to be synonymous with the first Nasurai Master and teacher of Gnosticism known as Adam. As Adam, Murrugan apparently marched down from the summit of Adam's Peak on Sri Lanka and then settled in Katirgama, the Place of Murrugan. Adam-Murrugan then founded the lineage of Nasurai Masters that was eventually taken to the

Middle East by the westward migrating Mandean people.

During the period that Mandean Nasurai Cupbearers slowly carried their lineage west and became involved in numerous cultures along the way, Murrugan's name of *Jnana* (pronounced Yana) gradually evolved into the Syrian Aramaic "Yohana," as well as the Hebrew Yochanan, the Arabic "Yahya," and finally into the English John. Yahya and Yohanna were brought together as the singular appellation of Yahya Yohana, which was Mandean name for one of their greatest Nasurai Cupbearers, John the Baptist. John was also a prophesied Messiah and an incarnation of *Jnana Pandita,* the Serpent on the Tree. This is why he was full of the Holy Spirit even from birth.

John the Baptist, Incarnation of the Holy Spirit

John the Baptist's identity as an incarnation of the Holy Spirit power was first established by the angel Gabriel even before his conception. The archangel appeared before the Baptist's parents and instructed them to name their future son the appellation John, which as an evolution of *Jnana* designated the Baptist to be an embodiment of Gnostic wisdom and power. In truth, however, Gabriel would have requested Elizabeth and Zacharias to name their son the Hebrew version of John, Yochanan, which is also instructive since it means "Yahweh has graced," or "God is a gracious giver," thus revealing that the incoming Baptist was to be a disseminator of God's Grace, which by another name is the Holy Spirit or Kundalini. Both Yochanan and John are related to the Hebrew name Jonah, which literally translates as "Dove," the avian symbol of the Holy Spirit. Since he was to be an embodiment the Holy Spirit, the special symbol of John would eventually become the turtledove.

John's identity as an incarnation of the Green Man was also revealed by Gabriel when the archangel proclaimed: "he (John) shall be filled with the Holy Ghost, even from his mother's womb…and he shall go…in the spirit and power of Elias." (Luke 1: 11-18). John's spirit, Elias or Elijah, was also known as the Tishbite, a term derived from the Hebrew Ha Tishbi, meaning "he who returns." Elijah is currently known among the Arabs as Al-Khadir, the Green Man, and Al-Khadir is a name for Murrugan. Thus, John was an incarnation of *Jnana Pandita*, the Green Man of Sri Lanka who continues to return within lineages of enlightened masters and as the Fisher Kings.

John's incarnation as the spirit of Elijah was confirmed by Jesus in the Gnostic Gospel called *Pistis Sophia,* wherein the Christ states to his disciples:

"I found the soul of the prophet Elias in the aeons (the higher levels of Creation)…and took his soul and brought it to the Virgin of Light, and she gave it over to her receivers; they brought it to the sphere of the rulers and cast it into the womb of Elizabeth. So the power of the little Iao (the power of God)...and the soul of the prophet Elias, they were bound unto the body of John the Baptizer."[2]

John, The Fish Avatar

The timing of John's pivotal birth was extremely important because it corresponded the beginning of the Age of Pisces. Every two thousand years a Zodiacal Age begins and/or ends with the appearance of an Avatar/Savior, and for the Age of Pisces, the Age of the Fish, the Avatar was John the Baptist. John was the "Messenger of God" whom the Prophets Isaiah and Malachi predicted would be incarnated into the Tribe of Levi, the tribe whose defining symbols include the fish.[3]

As the "Fish Avatar," John was especially affiliated to the Green Man in his manifestation as Enki, the primal Fish Avatar of the Sumerian pantheon. This truth was recognized by the Rosicrucian initiate Godfrey Higgins, who after deeply studying all the world's mystery traditions concluded that John had incarnated the spirit of Enki. Thus, in his magnum opus, *Anacalypsis*, Higgins formally declares:

"....And John the Baptist, or Savior of Men by means of water, was the Oannes or Avatar of Pisces, as Buddha was of Taurus, and Cristna (Krishna) of Aries...

"I suspect the Johns, or Oanneses, are like the Merus, the Buddhas, the Manwantaras, the Soleimans, etc. They are renewed incarnations, and the name was given after death, and sometimes during life, to any person whom the priests thought proper to designate as the guardian genius of the age."[4]

Could the ancient sages, like Higgins, made a conclusive identification between John and Enki, or perhaps even between John and Murrugan? Judging by the similarities between their names, it is probable that the Mandean Nasurai discerned a connection between all three figures. In the Greek language John translates into Ioannes, which is nearly identical to Enki's Greek name of Oannes, and according to the philologist Georgius, a contemporary of Higgins, Jnana, a name for Murrugan, can also be rendered as Oannes. States Higgins:

"Georgius maintains that the Tibetan word, which he renders *GNIOS* in Latin...is the same as the Gnosij of Greece, and *Agnitio* in Latin. If the Gn be written as the Hebrew letter was corrupted in Tibet, it will be O, the next letter will be Y, I or Yod, and both read from Right to Left, OI the *Deity of Wisdom.* In the same way, the Jnana for Wisdom in the Sanscrit is OANA. Here we have the Oanes."[5]

Thus, according to the circle of scholars that included Higgins and Georgius, Oannes, Ioannes, and Jnana all denote wisdom and each is a name for the Avatar of Wisdom, which has manifested on the Earth plane as Enki, John, and Murrugan.

Another name for the Avatar of Wisdom is, of course, the Green Man, whose life force power Enki, John and Murrugan personify. The aspect of the Green Man's life force power that becomes personified as the Lord of Wisdom is his preserving power, which by another name is Vishnu, the Hindu God of Preservation and the Avatar spirit that occasionally takes a physical form on Earth in order to preserve and uplift humanity. The ancient Hindu Trinity of Brahma the Creator, Vishnu the Preserver, and Shiva the Destroyer, is, in fact, essentially a division of the three powers of the life force embodied by the Green Man, which collectively are represented by his classic symbol, the trident. The middle prong of the Green Man's trident denotes the preserving power of Vishnu and *wisdom*, or *Jnana Shakti*, while the outer prongs of the weapon, which correspond to Iccha and Kriya Shaktis, denote the creative and destructive powers of Brahma and Shiva, respectively. Not surprisingly, the trident's middle prong is often rendered in the form of a geometrical "fish," a vesica pisces, thus denoting that the Lord of Wisdom and Vishnu is a fish...or a Fish Avatar.

As the Fish Avatar and Lord of Wisdom, Vishnu must be considered synonymous with Lord Enki. And, in fact, one of the incarnations of Vishnu, the Matsya or "Fish Avatar, is identical to the Sumerian Enki. The legend of the Matsya Avatar, who alerted humankind of an impending planetary deluge and chose one righteous man, Vaivasvatu Manu, the Hindu Noah, to construct a boat or ark and place within it representatives of the various species on Earth to protect them from drowning, is identical to the legend of Enki, who saved humanity from the Great Flood by instructing Ziusandra, the Sumerian Noah, to build an ark and save himself and the world's animals and plants from destruction.

It must be noted that among the Mandeans the spirit that alerted humankind of the impending flood was Hiwel Ziwa, the creator of the heavenly World of Light and *the spirit that incarnated as John the Baptist.*[6] Thus, John was the Fish Avatar and an incarnation of both Enki and Vishnu.

John, The Messiah?

If John was a manifestation of the Hindu and Sumerian Avatar, could he have also been the Hebrew Avatar, i.e., the prophesied Messiah? Some of the Hebrew tribes apparently recognized him as such. The Samarian prophets, for example, wrote in *The Samaritan Pentateuch* that the coming Messiah would be the Taheb, the "Restorer," who would be born into the Tribe of Levi and come to them from the heart of the desert. This is an obvious description of John the Baptist, the desert dwelling ascetic whose mother Elizabeth was descended from the Tribe of Levi. Other Hebrew prophets apparently identified John being *a* messiah or "anointed one," if not *the* Messiah. The prophets Isaiah and Malachi identified him as the anointed one whom God would send to His people of Israel and announce "the coming of the great and dreadful day of the Lord." He would be identified as "Elijah" and manifest as "the voice of him that crieth in the desert." (Isaiah 40:3) In the *Synoptic Gospels*, St. Mark conclusively identifies "The voice of one crying in the wilderness" as John the Baptist, and in St. Matthew we find that Jesus says of John: "Elias has come already, and they knew him not."(St. Matthew 17:12) Thus, it is irrefutably established in the New Testament that John the Baptist was indeed the expected messenger and an anointed one.

But was John simply an anointed messenger sent to herald the arrival of another more important messiah, such as Jesus? Possibly. However, John came as a messenger to warn of the "great and dreadful day of the Lord," the Lord Yahweh's "dreadful" Day of Judgment, not the coming day of the "Lord" Jesus Christ. John's message of warning and salvation was simply an echo of those who had come before him, the early Jewish prophets, who had admonished their people to take to the path of righteousness before it was too late.

There are actually some early Christian and Apocryphal texts that reveal that the disciples of John recognized their teacher as not *a* messiah but *the* Messiah, and even became enrolled in heated discussions with the disciples of Jesus on this point. The *Recognitions*, which are part of the *Pseudo-Clementine Texts*, features one such debate, during which one of John's students boasted:

"He (John) is the Christ, and not Jesus, just as Jesus himself spoke concerning him, namely that he is greater than any prophet who had ever been. If he is thus greater than Moses, it is clear that he is also greater than Jesus for Jesus arose just as did Moses. Therefore, it is right that John, who is greater than these, is the Christ."[7]

As Hugh Schonfeld rightly points out in *The Jesus Party,* many of John the Baptist's disciples had *never even heard of Jesus*, a truth St. Paul regrettably learned firsthand when he visited the Baptist's Gnostic students in the Asia Minor city of Ephesus. The Gnostics' ignorance of Jesus must be considered strange if it is submittted that the Baptist's raison d'etre was to announce the arrival of the Christ. Author A.N. Wilson makes the logical observation that had it not been for the work of St. Paul, John the Baptist might today be regarded worldwide as the Messiah. He states:

"Had Paul been a weaker personality...or had he never written his epistles, it could easily have been the case that the "Baptism of John" would have been the religion which captured the imagination of the ancient world, rather than the Baptism of Christ..."[8]

In *The Templar Revelation* authors Lynn Picknett and Clive Prince point out that not only the disciples of John, but even Jesus' own followers did not recognize him as the Messiah. In fact, it was only after being with him for sometime that even *some* of them were able to recognize him.

But if John was *the* Messiah, why did his long awaited birth not garner more widespread recognition from the Jewish community? Apparently it did. According to the apocryphal text called *The Infancy Gospel of James*, which refers to the infant John as both Messiah and future "King of the Jews," it was to destroy John and not Jesus that King Herod was compelled to murder the firstborn sons of the Jews. Fortunately for John, his parents had been alerted to Herod's carnage before it began and arranged for Elizabeth and John quick departure into the surrounding hill country. When Herod's men subsequently arrived to question Zacharias, John's father refused to tell the whereabouts of his son and he was promptly slain for his insubordination. Then, states *The Infancy Gospel of James*:

"...the agents went away and reported all this to Herod, who became angry and said, "Is his son (John) going to rule over Israel?"[9]

But even if John was not *the* Messiah, the *Dead Sea Scrolls* indicate that *he was one of two expected messiahs*. The *Dead Sea Scrolls,* which were composed by the Essenes, an austere Jewish sect living on the shores of the Dead Sea that made many prophecies regarding a coming New Age, identifies not one but two messiahs. One Messiah was to be a King Messiah born into the Tribe of David, and the other was to be a Priest Messiah born into the Tribe of Levi. The Priest Messiah appears to have incarnated as John the Baptist, and the King Messiah is believed by many to have manifested as Jesus. But while John fulfilled his destiny as Priest Messiah, Jesus never ruled as king, a truth that has convinced most Jews that the King Messiah has not arrived yet. But even if it is allowed that both John and Jesus were co-messiahs, the intensely religious Essenes would have held John, the Priest Messiah, to be the superior of the two. In this regard, Geza Vermes, author of *The Complete Dead Sea Scrolls in English* (Penguin Books, 1998), comments:

"...the Priest-Messiah comes first in the order of precedence; he is also called the "Messiah of Aaron," the "Priest," the "Interpreter of the Law." The King-Messiah was to defer to him and to the priestly authority in general in all legal matters....The "Messiah of Aaron" was to be the final Teacher, "he who shall teach righteousness at the end of days."

Perhaps Jesus, the King Messiah, was revealing his dependence on John and the superiority of the Priest Messiah when on the cross he cried out Eloi, Eloi, lama sabachthani, "My God, my God, why hast thou forsaken me." According to the *Gospels*, those around Jesus who overheard his lamentation exclaimed among themselves "Behold, he calleth Elias" (Mark 15:34-35), a name for John.

John the Nasurai Baptizer

Through the location of his residence and his aberrant behavior, John the Baptist may have been revealing to those around him his unique status as both a Mandean Nasurai, as well as an incarnation the Green Man that had previously resided within the body of the Prophet Elijah. John daily carried out the baptismal work of a Mandean priest at "Bethany beyond the Jordan" (John 1:28), which is an area that the Mosaic Map of Madaba from the 6th century A.D. locates on the Jordan near where the sacred river flows into the Dead Sea. John's settlement of Bethany is currently thought to have existed along the Wadi el-Kharrar, a river on the east side of the Jordan that was extensively excavated by the Israeli government in 1997-98. The river's excavation uncovered many intriguing sites, including the mound of Tell el-Kharrar, which is a point of intersection of four springs that unite before flowing together as one into the River Jordan. The topography of the mound is consistent with the Madaba map, and its confluence of rivers reflects the "other" name of Bethany, Bethabara, which denotes "house of the crossing."

John the Baptist may have chosen Bethany as his domicile because it was the place where he had ended his previous incarnation as Elijah. At Bethany it was natural for John to emulate Elijah in both his personality and dress, so perhaps in the body of the Baptist the spirit of Elijah simply resumed a life-style he had previously led. Like Elijah, "a hairy man, girt with a leathern girdle about his loins," (Man 234) John was an eccentric man who "wore a dress of camel's hair, with a girdle of leather fastened around his loins; and his food was locusts and wild honey." (Mark 1:6).

Perhaps by residing in Bethany John was also revealing his connection to Enki or Al-Khadir, the Lord or "Sheikh of the River." The ground plan of Bethany, where four springs unite before flowing into the River Jordan, makes it one of the planetary "Edens" sacred to both Enki and Al-Khadir. Wherever two or more rivers come together, the transformative life force is produced and the spirit of the Green Man takes up his residence. John probably chose Bethany for his baptismal rites both because he was an incarnation of the Green Man, and because the area was a natural generator of the Holy Spirit.

John's training to become a Nasurai Baptizer and transmitter of the Holy Spirit is preserved in detail within the library of Mandean holy texts, which includes the *Sidra d'Yahia*, the "Book of John;" the *Ginza Rabba*, the "Great Treasure" (also called the "Book of Adam)," and the compilation of Mandean historical records called the *Haran Gawaitha*. The *Haran Gawaitha* maintains that John, Yahya Yohanna, was conceived when his mother, Inoshwey (Elizabeth), drank some special holy water that was saturated with the dynamic life force or Holy Spirit. John's "father" was, therefore, the Water of Life or Holy Spirit itself. Following his conception, Inoshwey waited "nine months, nine weeks, nine hours, and nine minutes" to give birth to John. Then, after her child was delivered an angelic messenger named Annosh-Uthra suddenly appeared and quickly whisked John away to another world, the Frat-Ziwa, which the Mandean texts maintain is the heavenly double of the region surrounding the Euphrates River. Here John was baptized in the heavenly Waters of Life on the 31st day of his life, and then over the following twenty-one years he was taught his "ABCs," which includes the wisdom contained within the *Sidra d Nishmatha*, the "Book of Souls." Eventually, having been indoctrinated into the baptismal priesthood, John was returned to Palestine to begin his ministry in the River Jordan.[10]

The Frat-Ziwa may have been in another dimension, or it could have been on a sacred mountain where certain Mandean texts claim John spent many of his early years. This holy mountain, known as the "White Mountain" or Mount Parwan, was populated by the Mandean spiritual elite, probably Nasurai Masters. Mount Parwan may have been in the vicinity of or perhaps even synonymous with the Tura 'Madai, the "Mountain of the Madai," the most revered of all mountains inhabited by the ancient Mandeans. Since "Madai" is a name for the Persian Medes in Assyrian texts, the "Mountain of the Madai" could be either Mt. Demavend, the Holy Mountain of God of the Persian Fisher Kings, or another mountain in the Albourz Mountains of northern Iran. Because of its sanctity and remoteness, John's sojourn on Mount Parwan could have been literally comparable to an interlude in another world.

The Journey of the Mandeans

As mentioned, the long history of the Mandeans and their Nasurai Cupbearers begins on Sri Lanka with Adam, who may have been the Fisher King Sanat Kumara. Collectively, Adam and Eve are referred to in the Mandean historical texts as Adam Paghia and Hawa Paghia and identified as the physical counterparts of an etheric couple named Adam Kasya and Hawa Kasya who resided in a higher dimensional or heavenly Eden. According to the Mandeans and many other tribal groups who refer to Sri Lanka as the fabled Garden of Eden, the island was not the *original* Eden, but the place on Earth that most closely resembled the heavenly Eden. Perhaps the original Eden was Alma benhura, the "World of Goodness," which is another realm or planet that the Mandeans claim to have originally come to Earth from.

The Mandeans' terrestrial Adam and Eve were initially soulless, but the Earth's creator, Hiwel Ziwa, persuaded the universal Soul to take Her seat in their hearts. This event occurred only after an agreement was reached whereby the creator would make the earthly Eden an exact replica of the heavenly Eden, complete with the radiant flowers, trees, running water, and baptismal rites that are regularly observed in "Heaven." Once these conditions were met, the breath of life entered Adam and Eve and then the primal teacher and savior Hiwel Ziwa, which is probably a name for the Serpent on the Tree, descended from above and taught the couple the rudiments of civilization, including how to read and write. Hiwel Ziwa, the spirit that later incarnated as John the Baptist, promulgated the sacred wisdom that would eventually comprise the Mandean spiritual tradition, thereby making Adam the first Mandean prophet of Gnosticism. Adam, who thus became the first benefactor and heir to the wisdom and power flowing through Hiwel Ziwa, the Avatar of Wisdom, is said to have later traveled to Katirgama and merged with Murrugan, the *Jnana Pandita* or Lord of Wisdom, before initiating a long line of Gnostic masters. It is interesting to note that some of the later texts of Gnosticism, such as *The Pistis Sophia*, referred to Lucifer-Murrugan as Adam or Adama.

Following the era of Adam and Eve and their sons, unrighteous behavior gradually crept into the human race. The Avatar Hiwel Ziwa then alerted Noh (Noah) that the world would soon be destroyed by a deluge and that he needed to build an ark for himself, his family, and one pair of every species of animal. Then, just as in the *Holy Bible*, once the floodwaters had receded Noh and his sons left the ark to repopulate the Earth. However, it is here that the Mandean legend diverges from the Biblical story. The Mandean histories assert that Noah had not three, but four sons, the last being Sam, who became the ancestor of the Mandean people. Sam is remembered in the Mandean records as having been a righteous man who kept the sacred teachings given to Adam pure and holy. Sam was thus apparently a Nasurai Cupbearer in the lineage of Adam-Murrugan.

When the Mandean descendants of Sam eventually left Serendib, they traveled to Egypt and resided in that country for hundreds of years. They integrated themselves into the Egyptian culture to such a degree that they became completely identified with the Egyptians, a truth currently reflected in the Mandeans' annual celebration of Ashorieh, during which they sadly remember the demise of their Egyptian brethren who perished in the Red Sea at the hands of the infidel Jews. Even though they later spent many years living among the Jews in Palestine, the Mandeans remain vehemently anti-Jew. They claim that the Jewish race is of a lower order than their own and comprised of humans descended from an illicit union of Adam and Ruha, a demonic mistress perhaps synonymous with the Jewish Lilith.

According to the *Harran Gawaitha*, the Mandeans living in Jerusalem were forced to flee Palestine around 37 A.D. One of their principal adversaries at that time was St. Paul, who was actively persecuting many sects connected to John the Baptist and Jesus. But the fleeing Mandeans had no problem finding refuge in the progressive and sympathetic city of Harran, which at the time was an Asian haven for those searching for religious and political freedom. The religious leaders of Harran espoused the philosophy of the "The Way," which promoted a life-style devoid of mortal masters and only governed by God.[11] The philosophy of Harran was in direct alignment with the Mandeans' long-held ideology, which included the wisdom that "man is not ruler of man, man is not leader of society, man is not king of man, and man is just friend and helper of man." It is because of their purely democratic ideals that for most of their history the Mandeans have not had any formal, elected government to rule over them.

It was during their time in ancient Harran that the Mandeans also resided within their settlements on Mount Parwan and the "Mountain of the Madai." The holy Mountain of the Madai and its obscure location have been the theme of continual speculation since it was first alluded to in the writings of Lady E.S. Drower, an intrepid anthropologist from Britain who in the 1930's and 1940's spent many years studying the Mandean people and their ancient texts in their villages in Iraq. Lady Drower's own fascination with the mythical mountain compelled her to painstakingly translate the Mandean histories alluding to it and to interview many of the Mandean elders who preserved oral legends of it. Although the information she acquired was somewhat inconclusive and ambiguous, the clues to its location gathered by Ms. Drower led her to deduce that the Mountain of the Madai must have been in Persia or Iran. One Mandean man she interviewed stated "It is, I think, in Iran, for Madai is in Iran," while another man asserted "The Subba (a name for the Mandeans meaning "immersers") of old time were with the Persians in a place where there were springs which were hot in the winter and cold in the summer."[12] These two references, if taken together, could point to the Mountain of the Madai as being synonymous with Mt. Demavend in the Albourz range of northern Iran, which is a volcanic peak renown for its many hot and cold springs that cover its lower elevations.

A Mandean link to Mt. Demavend is corroborated by a study of their name "Madai," which is also an Assyrian name for the ancient Persian tribe of Medes. As the Madai, the Medes who inhabited the region in and around Mt. Demavend, thus indicating that the mountain was indeed the "Mountain of the Madai." The ancient Medes are mentioned in Assyrian texts as having had their land subjected by the conqueror Sargon II, who controlled the territories of the Medes all the way to the distant mountain of "Bikni," which is an ancient Median name for Mt. Demavend.

The Powers of the Nasurai

The ancient holy residents on the Mountain of the Madia, the Nasurai Masters, are currently remembered by the Mandeans as the *Bnia d bnia d Ardban*, the exalted sages who were "skilled in religious matters and white magic." They are alluded to in *The Story of Qiqel and the Death of Yahya*, which recounts a meeting between the Nasurai and a conquering chieftain. At the beginning of this legend the Nasurai are portrayed as living together peacefully when their village is invaded by an inimical tribe of warriors. The impetuous leader of the intruding warriors promptly questioned the Nasurai about what work they did and is told that they simply prayed and talked to the stars. Another Nasurai further explained: "all the stars talk in Mandean…a pure soul can hear the prayers of the Sun and the prayers of the stars…like the singing of birds." When the chieftain then demanded that the Nasurai teach himself and his warriors their unique knowledge he was refused, as it was very clear to the Mandean adepts that neither he nor his troops were ready for such knowledge. This infuriated the chief, who then built a huge fire while commanding his cohorts to "Bring them here (the Nasurai), and throw them on the fire!" But when the Nasurai were pushed into the fire they didn't burn; instead, they walked on top of the fire! A white light descended from the sky and enclosed each Nasurai in an envelope of divine, protective radiance. When the frustrated chief loudly lamented "Can you not prevail against them?" One Nasurai unhesitatingly answered "Never! For (we) do not use magic, but knowledge. (Our) power, it is of God."[13]

According to the Mandean texts, when John the Baptist lived in Jerusalem he resided among his brother Nasurai that had come down from the Mountain of the Madai. Their cohabitation in the holy city is alluded to in one Mandean scripture, which states: "Anush Uthra brought (John) and came with him to the city of Jerusalem amongst the community founded by Ruha. All of them (in Jerusalem) belonged to her and her sons *except those from the Mountain of the Madai.*"[14]

Since John was a Nasurai, the Mandean texts ascribe him the same powers as those possessed by the Nasurai Masters who resided on the Mountain of Madia. According to the *Haran Gawaitha*, while in Jerusalem the Nasurai John "opened the eyes of the blind, cured the sick, and made the lame to walk." But, like his brethren on the Mountain of Madia, John was also coerced into revealing his divine abilities in order to protect himself from those less spiritually gifted or enlightened. After one long day of healings and baptisms, for example, the *Hara Gawaitha* states: "The (Jewish) priests were angry and came to Yahya (John) and ordered him to leave Urshalam (Jerusalem) immediately. Yahya refused to go and defied them saying, "Bring swords and cut me, bring fire and burn me, or water and drown me!" And the priests replied, "Yahya, we know that swords will not cut thee, nor fire burn thee, nor water drown thee." Then, when his detractors had left, "Yahya began to read in his *Ginza Rabba* (and) the birds of the air spoke, praising God, and the fishes opened their mouths and glorified the Life."[14]

Some contemporary Mandeans believe that both John the Baptist and his Nasurai brothers and sisters from the Mountain of Madai were synonymous with the ancient Essenes, who like the Mandeans also observed a strict regimen of spiritual rites that included regular baptisms. John's abode at Bethany was well within walking distance of the Essene settlements on the Dead Sea, so there is no question that he could have come into contact with members of the group quite often, and the name of his Order, the Nasurai, could easily have been a variation of Nazaria, an Essene sect that the ancient historians Pliny and Josephus claimed existed along the River Jordan in the vicinity of where John baptized. It is also possible that the Essenes and Mandeans may have also united as the Elchasaites, an historical sect of baptizers who lived close to both John and the Essenes while observing water purification rites in strict accordance to the mandates of the Essene-Mandean law. In *The Secret Adam,* Lady Drower maintains that a connection between the Elchasaites and the Mandeans is revealed in the name of the founder of the Elchasaites, Elchasai, which she claims is a synthesis of El and Kasia, with El meaning God and Kasia being a name for the Mandean Adam. Elchasai could have thus been a Mandean-Essene prophet in the lineage of Adam, the first great Mandean prophet.

The Mandeans of Southern Iraq

When the Mandeans left Harran they began what would be their last migration, into southern Iraq, a territory that some contemporary Mandeans contend was once populated by an earlier migration of Mandeans from Sri Lanka. In southern Iraq, the Mandeans founded settlements along the Tigris and Euphrates Rivers in order to observe their regular baptismal rites. Their communities became especially concentrated in such locales as Basra, Nassuaya, and Al-Qeda, which are towns adjacent to the confluence point of the two mighty rivers and also near the region associated with the Biblical Garden of Eden. Some of their southern Iraqi colonies were also built nearly on top of ancient Eridu, the capital city of Enki, the Avatar spirit that incarnated as John the Baptist.

The Mandean priesthood of southern Iraq quickly assimilated many of the deities and rites of the ancient Ashipu priests of Enki. The Mandean priesthood adopted white outfits identical to those worn by the priests of Enki, and replicas of Enki's ancient temple huts were copied by the Mandeans, who found blueprints of them in the Sumerian texts.[15] The Mandeans designed their temples with adjoining sacred pools, and like the ancient Ashipu probably considered them manifestations of the Apsu, the legendary home of Enki.

Today, the Mandeans are referred to by their Middle Eastern neighbors as "Mughtasilah," meaning "Those who wash themselves," in reference to their continual immersions within their temple pools. Just as they were during the days of Enki's priesthood, these pools have become infused with an abundance of the Water of Life, a term used by both the ancient Ashipu and the Mandean priesthood to denote the transformative life force that moves within physical water. The

Water of Life is defined as water's "heavenly part," as opposed to its dense, "earthly part." It is also acknowledged to be synonymous with the Holy Spirit and reputed to wash away sins while transmitting a portion of itself into, around, and throughout the body of the Mandean getting baptized. The mantras of the Mandean priests are chanted during immersions to activate this Water of Life, which tends to remain at least partially dormant when mantras are not used for its activation.

Ritual baptism among the Mandeans is of three kinds. It can take the form of daily immersion, which is a cleansing each person administers to his or herself, or it can be "triple immersion," wherein a person is immersed three times in succession to wash away some specific impurities, such as those that attach to a women during menstruation. But the most important form of baptism is "full baptism," when a Mandean becomes not only cleansed, but also full of the Holy Spirit. During this rite, the Holy Spirit is transmitted to the worshipper through the activated Water of Life, as well as through efficacious ceremonial gestures of the presiding priest, which include a special handshake and a kiss, which is traditionally referred to as "giving Kushta." These rites are followed by the "final blessing," when a priest places his right hand on the head of the person being baptized, and their completion is often accompanied by an anointing of oil, which is sometimes administered to the forehead of the baptized Mandean in the shape of a cross, the symbol of alchemical transformation and spiritual immortality.

All of Mandean life and philosophy is in some way related to their baptismal rites, including the Mandean concept of God. God, the Supreme Being, is known among the Madai as Malka d Nhura, the King of Light, whose first emanation and power is the Water of Life. State the Mandean texts: "first (comes) Water (the Water of Life); from Water, Radiance; from Radiance, Light; and from Light, *uthri,* the spirits whose function it is to govern natural phenomena." The Mandeans thus regard the Water of Life to be even closer to pure God consciousness than Light itself, which is why when it manifests within bodies of flowing water on Earth it is considered a precious link to Malka d Hura.

John the Baptist's lineage of Cupbearers

The Two Cupbearer Lineages

John the Baptist, the fountainhead of the Holy Spirit in the Middle East, eventually spawned two divergent lineages of Cupbearers: one that was Gnostic in ideology and practice, and a second line that became "Christian" and "Catholic" in its theology. The Gnostic lineage of the Nasurai passed from John to his disciples Simon Magus and Jesus Christ, and from Jesus it was transmitted to the "Beloved Disciple," John the Apostle, and then down a line of Johannite adepts. The Nasurai Jesus also conveyed a portion of his spiritual power to Saint Peter, the founder of the Catholic line of Cupbearers, which has since become passed down the long line of Holy Roman Popes.

The Cupbearer Jesus Christ

It is thus apparent that the link between John's two principal Cupbearer lineages was his most famous disciple, Jeshua ben Joseph or Jesus the Christ, who according to the Mandeans was also a great Nasurai possessing power and wisdom equal to his teacher. According to the Holy Grail Mysteries, Jesus was, like John, also a messiah. He was a prophesied and "anointed one," whose birth was predicted 1200 years earlier by the Holy Grail astrologer Flegetanis:

"One night in the stars he (Flegetanis) found
How after the lapse of twelve hundred years,
Into the world would be born a child
In honor surpassing all the Jews."[16]

Author Trevor Ravenscroft quotes Flegetanis' above prophecy in *The Cup of Destiny* while additionally maintaining that his birth was known about by the Holy Grail Masters because "Jesus is the Grail." This notion, that Jesus was a Grail vessel and a Cupbearer, was eventually confirmed by the Messiah himself, when, state the *Gospels,* he proclaimed to some of his disciples: "Of my cup shall you indeed drink." Jesus also alluded to his own indwelling Water of Life in a passage in *The Gospel of St. John*, when he states:

" Whosoever drinketh of this (physical) water shall thirst again: But whosoever drinketh of the water that I shall give him shall never thirst; but the water that I shall give him shall be in him a well of water springing up into everlasting life." (John 4:13-14)

Those that drank deepest from the water of Jesus' cup were, of course, his own twelve Apostles. While the Messiah walked the Earth they were blessed with regular infusions of his Water of Life, although the greatest portion of the Messiah's power was received by them during the Day of Pentecost that followed Christ's Ascension. This momentous event is dramatically recounted in *The Acts of the Apostles*:

"And when the day of Pentecost was fully come they were all with one accord in one place.

"And suddenly there came a sound from heaven as of a rushing mighty wind, and it filled the house where they were sitting.

"And there appeared unto them cloven tongues like as of fire, and it sat upon each of them.

"And they were all filled with the Holy Ghost, and began to speak with other tongues, as the Spirit gave them utterance."

After they had received an abundance of Jesus' power on the Day of Pentecost, the Apostles moved to a nearby river and proceeded to transfer the Holy Spirit to many spiritual seekers through the ancient Mandean rite of Baptism. Just as the Nasurai priests had done for centuries before them, the Apostles cleansed and awakened worthy seekers with the Water of Life moving within a river of pure, flowing water. Some time later, the new Cupbearers John and Thomas took the Holy Grail power they had received north and east, while the Apostle Peter journeyed west with it, eventually reaching Rome where he became the premier bishop of the Catholic Church.

Jesus, the Gnostic Heretic

Although not normally spoken of as a Gnostic Cupbearer, Jesus received the power of the Gnostic lineage from John the Baptist. And like his master, he was at heart a Gnostic, a truth revealed within certain Nag Hammadi scrolls, such as *The Gospel of Thomas* and *The Pistis Sophia,* wherein numerous conversations between Jesus and his disciples are recounted that contain a decidedly Gnostic tenor. In the *Gospel of Thomas*, for example, Jesus makes the characteristically Gnostic statement – and one that is extremely radical and heretical in relation to traditional Christian Catholic theology - that God's Kingdom of Heaven, and therefore God Himself, exists inside of every human being. While discoursing to his Apostles, Jesus states:

"Let him who seeks continue seeking until he finds. When he finds, he will become troubled. When he becomes troubled, he will be astonished, and he will rule over the All.

"If those who lead you say to you, "See, the Kingdom is in the sky," then the birds of the sky will precede you. If they say to you, "It is in the sea," then the fish will precede you. Rather, the Kingdom is inside of you, and it is outside of you…"

Jesus also speaks the Gnostic vernacular in *The Pistis Sophia,* which is a conversation alleged to have taken place between Jesus and his disciples eleven years after the Messiah's crucifixion. Using cryptic Gnostic terms such as the First Mystery, the 12 Aeons, Barbelo, the Goddess, and the Plethora, Jesus describes the evolution of the universe and the creation of humanity in the strictest of Gnostic nomenclatures.

The Gnostic dialogues between Jesus and his disciples have only recently been studied because they were either hidden of outlawed by the Catholic Church for most of the past two-thousand years. The Messiah's Gnostic message has, however, still managed to shine through in the *Synoptic Gospels*, wherein he states to his students "the Kingdom of Heaven dwells within."

But even with his obvious Gnostic heritage and leaning, Jesus is not currently recognized as one of the Mandean prophets. This is because Christ and his students, especially St. Paul and St. Peter, took liberties and made crucial omissions while practicing and teaching the Jewish and Mandean Law. Because of his omissions, Jesus, who is today regarded by the Mandeans as a perverter of their ancient rites, was, according to the Mandean *Book of John*, even initially denied baptism from John. The Baptist severely chastised Jesus for even requesting baptism from him, and then declared:

"You have deceived the Jews and lied to the priests. You have caused the seed to stop from men and childbearing and pregnancy from women. In Jerusalem you deconsecrated the Sabbath, which Moses enjoined. You lied with horns, and you proclaimed disgrace with the trumpet."

John, of course, eventually acquiesced to the Messiah's request, but, states the *Book of John,* he did so only after receiving a communiqué from a Mandean colleague name Abathat, who was probably a Nasurai Master like himself. The letter instructed John thus:

"Yahya (John), baptize the liar in the Jordan. Go down in the Jordan, baptize him, ascend to its bank, and confirm him."[17]

One of the greatest transgressions that was ascribed to Jesus and his disciples – and perhaps the most unforgiving – concerned the sacred Mandean rite of baptism. Under the guidance of these earliest of Christians, baptism was not practiced regularly as it should have been, nor were the ancient Mandean mantras recited during the rite. And what is worse, baptism eventually came to be administered in pools of *stagnant water.* This is strictly anathema according to Mandean Law. If water is not flowing it cannot purify the one receiving the baptism, and dark, toxic energies will eventually enter into it. The Holy Spirit moving through the water will also become depleted, corrupted and unclean.

Jesus and his Church also strayed from the Mandean Law when celibacy was eventually introduced into the Catholic priesthood and within the orders of monastery-dwelling monks and nuns. From the Mandean perspective, marriage and child rearing are such an important part of life that by refraining from them one potentially loses his or her chance to ascend to the higher heavenly worlds at death. It must, however, be noted that Mandean history reveals that some Nasurai lived within communities of only men, and that the *New Testament* makes it clear that John was a Nazarite and a lifelong celibate. Thus, the Mandean injunctions for marriage and parenthood may have applied to the common Mandeans, but not to their more spiritually evolved Nasurai.

But even though John and his Mandean contemporaries had their reservations towards Jesus and his followers, they knew that nascent Christianity was not destined to operate within the confines of Mandean Law and that certain facets of Mandeanism needed to flow into the world through it. So they succumbed to the requests of the early followers of Jesus and transmitted the ancient Mandean wisdom to them even while knowing it would eventually be transgressed and distorted.

The Gnostic Lineage of Cupbearers

Although it moved through Jesus to John the Apostle, John the Baptist's Gnostic lineage of Cupbearers is traditionally said to begin with Jesus' brother disciple, Simon Magus, who founded an alternate lineage of Gnostic Cupholders. Simon was, however, not the immediate Cupholder to succeed John the Baptist in this Gnostic lineage, that distinction goes to Dositheos, another close disciple of the Baptist. The name of Dositheos, which translates as "God has given" or "God is a gracious giver," carries the same meaning as John or Yohannan, thus apparently revealing that Dositheos was the "John" Cupbearer in the Baptist's Gnostic lineage. While some critics contend that John placed his mantle upon Dositheos because Simon Magus was away tending to the Baptist's Gnostic flocks in Alexandria, Egypt, mistakes are never made in lineal transmissions, which are predestined. Dositheos had more than earned his predestined right of succession by being arguably the best of the Baptist's Gnostic teachers in Samaria.

Following John's murder by King Herod, Dositheos took the Gnostic lineage north to Damascus. There, according to the Christian historian Origen, he proclaimed himself "the prophesied Christ," a declaration that was to become commonplace among future Gnostic Cupbearers who ascended their consciousness until it was one with the Christ. Legends assert that Dositheos also acquired the clairvoyant ability to read from the Akashic Records, wherein he discovered some ancient Atlantean wisdom that had been recorded on three stele before the Great Flood. His Atlantean visions are recorded in the Naga Hammadi text called *The Three Steles of Seth.*

Dositheos was always vigilant about giving due homage to the Baptist, whom he described as the true Messiah, the "righteous teacher...of the Last Days."[18] Dositheos also apparently took great pains to make his Gnostic school a pure reflection of ancient Mandean ideology and the sacred rites taught by John. This seems certain because the Syrian theologian Theodore bar Konai concluded from his in-depth research that Mandean culture must have been derived from the Dositheans, the students of Dositheos, rather than the other way around.[19]

Following Dositheos as Cupbearer of the Gnostic line was Simon Magus, who either received the lineal succession directly from Dositheos or somehow managed to usurp it from the Cupbearer. Simon could have also received a special designation and dispensation from John the Baptist before he left on his journey to Alexandria. History is sketchy on this point. But one thing is certain, a contest of sorts took place between Simon and Dositheos for the control of the Gnostic school and Simon emerged the victor. The incident was recorded by Bishop Clementine in the *Pseudo-Clementine* texts:

"… on one occasion when Simon arrived for the ordinary meeting, Dositheos struck out at him with indignation. The stick seemed to go through Simon's body as if it were smoke. Dositheos shouted to him out of fear, "If thou be the Standing One, I also shall pay homage to you." As Simon answered in the affirmative Dositheos, knowing that he himself was not the Standing One, fell down and did homage to Simon and, associating himself with the twenty-nine others, set Simon in his own place. Then Dositheos died a few days after Simon had attained the leadership but he himself had suffered a downfall."

Following Simon's recognition as Cupbearer, he gained complete control over most of the Gnostic congregations throughout Asia Minor. His unique brand of Gnostic theology soon became much more widespread and popular than that of Dositheos or even John the Baptist, which is why he is today recognized as the seminal teacher and the "Father of Gnosticism." Simon's Gnostic school, the Simonians, also achieved widespread recognition and became the model for many of the later Gnostic schools that followed it.

To reconstruct an accurate history of Simon Magus' life requires piecing together a multitude of references to him from a variety of dubious sources, many of which were composed by Church historians who harbored an obvious bias towards the Magus. These works include the Samarian history of Justinian, the *Apocryphal Acts of Peter,* and Irenaeus' works on the early heretics. Collectively, such documents maintain that Simon was born in Gitthae in Samaria before embarking upon his prodigious missionary work abroad. Later in his life, states Justinian, "(Simon) worked magic spells in the time of Emperor Claudius, was considered a god in (the) Imperial Capital, Rome, and (was) honored like a god ...with a statue erected in the Tiber between the two bridges…" Irenaeus, who often dwelled upon Simon's inflated ego, added that the Roman statues erected in the Magus's honor were in the "likeness of Jupiter (Zeus)."[20]

In most accounts of Simon's life it is maintained that he was revered by his disciples and followers as an "embodiment of the supreme power."[21] The "supreme power" embodied by Simon was a reference to both the Almighty, as well as to the power that flowed from the Almighty, i.e., the Holy Spirit or Water of

Life, which the Magus himself defined in his *Megale Apophasis,* a textbook of the Simonians, as the cosmic fire that creates and sustains the universe. Hippolytus, who wrote a commentary on Simon's *Megale Apophasis,* maintained that Simon's cosmic fire was twofold, both hidden and manifest. In its hidden aspect it is the ethereal life force, and in its manifest form it is physical fire. Simon is known to have also specified that his power was the Water of Life transmitted along the Cupbearers of John's Gnostic line when he stated that it dwells within a "man bred of the same line."[22]

Simon also recognized that the supreme power was synonymous with the Gnostic Sophia, which he venerated within his school as the Universal Goddess. While visiting a brothel in the city of Tyre on the Asia Minor coast, Simon discovered Sophia incarnated in the body of a prostitute named Helena, whom he made his lifelong companion and consort. According to Simon, Sophia had assumed the body of Helena after wandering aimlessly throughout the universe created by Her after it was confiscated by Her megalomaniac son, Ildaboath. As Simon and Helena, the Almighty and His power were reunited on Earth

It is because Simon Magus was a Gnostic and believed himself God incarnate in a human form that the early Christian references to him are very derogatory. In order to downplay the immense supernatural powers he had accrued through his Kundalini path, Simon was accused of stealing power from God and the Christ and making it his own. With his profound abilities Simon could hack himself to pieces with a large knife and then quickly rejoin his scattered body parts back together. He is also reputed to have raised the dead, flown through the air, and to have shape-shifted into a various wild animals.

According to one of the biased treatises written against him, the *Apocryphal Acts of Peter*, Simon supposedly met his death during a magical contest with St. Peter while flying over Rome. When Peter saw the soaring Magus he called upon the power of Jesus Christ for assistance and thus brought Simon crashing to the ground, breaking both of the Magus' thighs in the process. This dubious tale is obviously based upon the legend of the fallen Lucifer-Vulcan, who is renowned to have fallen to Earth from the realm of the Gods and broken both his thighs.

Before Simon's supposed death scenario in Rome, the Magus was, however, able to transmit his spiritual power and wisdom into his designated successor, Menander, who thereafter reigned as the Cupbearer of John the Baptist's Gnostic lineage. Menander, who was another extreme Gnostic heretic in the opinion of most Catholic historians, similarly proclaimed himself an incarnation of the supreme power as his master had, but, states the historian Irenaeus, in addition he also referred to himself as "the man sent down as Redeemer by the invisible (Spirit) for the salvation of men." Many miracles were attributed to the supernaturally empowered Menander, but the most important of the powers ascribed to him was his ability to make a disciple immortal through transmitting into them the power of the Holy Spirit. In reference to this greatest of services, Irenaeus states: "Through their baptism by him (Menander), his disciples receive the gift of resurrection, and therefore can no longer die; and do not age, but remain immortal." One interesting legend states that Menander traveled into Persia to teach Gnosticism to the students of Zoroastrianism, thus returning to one of the ancient homelands of his Nasurai and Mandean predecessors.

After Menander, the Gnostic lineage divided into two branches. The Gnostic adept Saturnius of Antioch became Cupbearer of the Gnostic line in Asia Minor, and the Master Basilides of Alexandria served as Cupbearer for the Gnostic sects that flourished in Egypt. Saturnius, who was probably the principal successor of Menander, began his Gnostic reign in Menander's home of Antioch. But Basilides had the biggest impact on Gnosticism by uniting it with fledgling Christianity, thus founding the incipient order of Christian Gnostics. Both Basilides and Saturnius were similar in championing the harsh asceticism of their patriarch John the Baptist, and they encouraged their students to spend long, solitary hours in dank caves while seeking the inner stillness from which emerges the true Gnostic wisdom. While in their desert retreats, the Gnostic seekers would daily invoke the power of Chnouphis, a Gnostic name for the Kundalini serpent, while also observing the alchemical practices of Kabbalic Yoga, some of which had come from India, the home of the first planetary teacher of Gnosticism, Murrugan, the Serpent on the Tree. Some Gnostic seekers would also soar in their astral bodies to the upper aeons or heaven realms like their spiritual cousins from Qumran, the ancient Essenes, had once done. According to the Gnostic text known as *Zostrianos*, when the Gnostics traveled through the levels of the universe they would pause in each aeon long enough to undergo its corresponding baptism, which involved using increasingly refined forms of the Water of Life.

In the wake of the pioneering work of Basilides, Gnosticism reached its greatest flowering in Alexandria, where it was amalgamated to many compatible ideologies promulgated within the Egyptian city. Alexandria's brilliant philosophers, who had come to Egypt's melting pot from all over the world, amalgamated Gnosticism to the sacred knowledge of Hermeticism, the precepts of Buddhism, the esoteric cosmology of Greek Neoplatonism, and the doctrine of the Christian Son of God, thus producing a unique collection of planetary religions. Perhaps the greatest Gnostic contributor that helped drive the Alexandrian religion machine was Basilides' successor, the Gnostic Cupbearer Valentinus, who regularly exchanged his ideas in spiritual forums organized through the Museum, the Alexandrian University. One of the eclectic treatises of Valentinus, *The Tripartite Tractate*, succeeded in clarifying and unifying the previously conflicting Christian and Gnostic perspectives on the Holy

Trinity and clearly reflects the synthesizing movement the Gnostic adept was a part of. Valentinus eventually took his *Tripartite Tractate* with him to Rome where he established an Italian school of Gnosticism with its own Gnostic lineage of Cupbearers. The heirs of this Gnostic line eventually moved north on missionary expeditions that took them deep into the heartland of Europe.

The Cupbearer John the Apostle

With Valentinus' Gnostic Cupbearers streaming into Europe, it was only a matter of time before a Gnostic reunion of sorts would take place. This is because another Gnostic movement with origins in the Middle East arrived in Europe at about the same time, although it had followed a road through the portal of Turkey. This second Gnostic movement, which was influenced by the eastern Gnostic sects known as the Bogomils, Paulicans, and the Gnostic religion of Manicheism, united with Valentinus' Cupbearers in southern France to produce the Cathars, a sect that advocated direct personal experience of the Divine, as well as the veneration of the Gnostic Cupbearer John the Apostle, just as its parent sects had. John had become the patron saint of almost all the Gnostic orders at that time, and he was recognized as the glue that finally brought them altogether. His two scriptural works, *The Gospel of John* and *The Revelation of St. John the Divine*, had become compulsory reading for Gnostics everywhere, and he was rightly venerated as the Father of European Gnosticism.

John's exceptionally important status among the European Gnostics was set forth in one important version of *The Gospel of St. John* known as the *Evangelicon.* This text stated that the Apostle John had received esoteric wisdom and an abundance of the Holy Spirit power through Jesus that the other Apostles did not. He was thus identified as Jesus' true successor and a Cupbearer in the Gnostic lineage of John the Baptist, a truth conveyed by his name of "John," which was the titular name of all true Gnostic Cupbearers. But John was, apparently, more than just a titualr Gnostic Cupbearer; he had fully incarnated the spirit of John the Baptist. According to the esotericist Rudolph Stiener of Theosophical fame, John the Baptist returned to life on Earth as the Cupbearer John the Apostle. Thus, the power and wisdom of the Green Man, the *Jnana Pandita*, that had once entered John the Baptist later entered the Cupbearer John the Apostle.

Cupbearer John the Apostle chose as his symbol a golden chalice with a spiraling snake emerging from it. This emblem, which was immortalized in a painting by the great Spanish artist El Greco, denoted the Cup of Immortality or Holy Grail and its indwelling serpentine Kundalini or Water of Life. John's chalice also represented the Apostle's inheritance from his Master Jesus that the Messiah had promised when he stated to him: *"Of my cup you shall indeed drink."* The snake or serpent symbol of John, when combined with the eagle, another of the Apostle's symbolic animals, comprises the symbol of the Zodiacal sign of Scorpio, which not surprisingly is the sign associated with the transformative Holy Spirit or Kundalini.

From his earliest years it was obvious that John the Apostle was destined to be a Cupbearer. He met his first Kundalini Master, John the Baptist, when he was very young and then completed his spiritual training with John's principal disciple, the Kundalini adept Jesus Christ. John and Jesus were, therefore, spiritual brothers and co-disciples of John the Baptist, which is perhaps why from the moment John entered Jesus' inner circle he was both disciple and close friend of the Messiah. John was followed into Jesus' circle by some brother disciples of John the Baptist, including his brother James, and his friends Andrew and Peter, each of whom been born in Bethsaida on the east side of the River Jordan near the Sea of Galilee and grew up together.

The training and transmission of the Holy Spirit that John and James (and perhaps Andrew and Peter, as well) had received under John the Baptist before coming over to the Christ also set them apart from the other disciples of Jesus. The Messiah officially acknowledged the abundance of Holy Spirit power wielded by the brothers when he nicknamed them *Boanerges*, meaning "Sons of Thunder." This designation had previously been merited by the receivers and transmitters of Kundalini power around the Mediterranean Sea, such as the "Sons of Thunder," who were the initiates of the Cretan mystery school known as the Thunders of Nocturnal Zeus.

Jesus revealed Apostle John to be his heir apparent in his Cupbearer lineage twice; once when he had the Apostle sit at his right hand during the Last Supper, and later when he placed his mother Mary in John's care. Such honors are extremely rare and only bestowed upon disciples who have shown such special devotion that they are considered part of the Master's family.

The modern order of Johannites, the latter-day Cupholders of John the Apostle's lineage, maintain that Jesus' official transmission to John of the Kundalini power within his Gnostic lineage occurred during the final moments of the Messiah's crucifixion, when all the other Apostles had scattered and only John and Mary Magdalene stood at the base of the cross. Jesus' transmission to John ostensibly occurred when Jesus "gave up the Ghost," or took his final breath. This was a common practice among the Jewish prophets, as demonstrated by Elijah when he placed his mantle on his successor Elisha just before leaving the Earth and ascending into the heavens.

After the Ascension of his Master, John is said to have left Jerusalem in order to begin spreading the Gospel with his brother Apostles throughout Asia. John proceeded to run into difficulties with the authorities in most of the places he subsequently visited, most notably Rome, where legends state the Emperor Domitian forced him to consume poison for proselytizing his Christian wisdom.

But John not only did not die from the poison, and it is reputed that he even brought back to life another condemned prisoner who had drunken the same fatal liquid. This frustrated Domitian to such a degree that he had John thrown into a cauldron of boiling-hot oil, but again the Apostle survived. Finally resolving to rid himself of the pesky Apostle, the Roman Emperor had John sent into exile on the Island of Patmos so he could work himself to death in the emperor's mines. But Domitian passed away a year or two later and John was set free. It was at that time that John journeyed to his final resting place, Ephesus, the Turkish city of the Gnostics where St. Paul had previously discovered the disciples of John the Baptist living peacefully within a Gnostic community.

It was in Ephesus that John is recorded as having manifested his greatest miracles, including healing the terminally ill and even raising the dead. One legend states that after a fire suddenly consumed Ephesus' famous Temple of Diana and killed 200 of its worshippers, John demonstrated his supernatural power by bringing the congregation back to life under the condition that they would accept being baptized. Later, after John had denounced idol worship to an assembly in front of the temple, a frenzied crowd of worshippers gathered to stone him to death. But instead of reaching John, the rocks boomeranged and squarely struck all those who had tossed them.

Before his death, John appears to have passed the power of the Gnostic Cupbearers to a close disciple, who then became the dynastic "John." The existence of the Apostle's successor may have been alluded to by both Dionysius and Eusebius, a couple of early historians who recorded the existence of both the Apostle John and another renowned Gnostic teacher named John in the Asia Minor city. Both St. John and the second John, known as Presbyter John, had both been acquaintances of Papias, the Bishop of the Asia Minor city of Hierapolis, and each was eventually entombed in Ephesus.

Like other Gnostic Cupbearers, John's spiritual power continued to impact the world even after his death. All prayers directed to the deceased Apostle bore fruit, and the dust rising around his tomb, which became the most sacred place of worship in Ephesus, was collected for its miraculous healing power. One popular legend of Ephesus sought to explain the power surrounding John's tomb by asserting that the Apostle had never truly died. Instead, he had become immortal and simply slept soundly in his tomb. This intriguing notion was later corroborated by St. Augustine, who maintained that the earth under John's tomb would rise and fall in rhythm to the sleeping Apostle's breathing patterns. Eventually John and his tomb were enclosed by the Emperor Justinian, who built over them the huge Basilica of St. John, a citadel that was 380 feet long and rose 90 feet upwards. The church was later captured by Seljuk Turks and a mosque arose in its place.

St. John's feast day is currently celebrated on December 27, when his chalice, the symbol of his power and Water of Life, is held high while each participant declares to the person next to him or her, "I drink you the love of St. John."

The Cupbearer Mary Magdalene

Besides the Apostle John, the Kundalini power of Jesus' Cupbearer lineage appears to have also been received by the other close disciple at the foot of his cross, Mary Magdalene. This truth is corroborated by the Gnostics' *Pistis Sophia*, which refers to Mary as the "one who is the inheritor of the Light."[23] It is because of the divine wisdom she achieved after acquiring Jesus' power that Mary eventually became known by all Gnostics as the "woman who knew the All."[24]

Although not normally spoken of in the same breath as the 12 Apostles, Mary was a special disciple who received certain honors and privileges the Messiah withheld from his other disciples, such as the task of anointing his head and feet, which in the East are considered the two most sacred and powerfully charged body parts of a Kundalini Master. It is possible that Mary is mentioned in the *Synoptic Gospels* as being no more than a prostitute because of the intense jealousy the Apostles harbored for her regarding the special attention she received from the Messiah. Their envy is born out in the Gnostic *Gospel of Philip*, which states:

"…(Christ) loved her more than all the disciples, and used to kiss her often on her mouth. The rest of the disciples…said to him 'Why do you love her more than all of us?'"

The original 12 Apostles no doubt sensed the obvious; Mary was in many ways Jesus' closest disciple. She was certainly the Messiah's premier female student who, according to the *Acts of Philip*, merited the title "chosen of women." She was also the first disciple to preach the gospel of Christ's resurrection, the news of which she was told to pass to her brother disciples after encountering the risen Messiah in the familiar scene recorded in the *Gospel of St. John*:

"(Mary) turned herself back, and saw Jesus standing, and knew not that it was Jesus. Jesus saith unto her, Woman, why weepest thou? Whom seekest thou? She, supposing him to be the gardener, saith unto him, Sir, if thou have borne him hence, tell me where thou hast laid him, and I will take him away. Jesus saith unto her, Mary. She turned herself, and saith unto him Rabboni; which is to say, Master. Jesus saith unto her, Touch me not; for I am not yet ascended to my Father: but go to my brethren, and say unto them, I ascend unto my Father, and your Father; and *to* my God, and your God." (John 20:14-17)

Mary has recently been specially linked to John the Apostle because both were present at the crucifixion, each was a "beloved disciple" of the Christ, and both have been identified as the loving apostle resting his or her head on Jesus' shoulder in Leonardo da Vinci's famous painting of the Last Supper. What truly links them together is their affiliation with the Gnostic path, a tradition that made them so closely intertwined that early authors even referred to them as married. They are also jointly linked to the ancient Goddess tradition, which is the tradition that Gnosticism originally emerged out of. It is because of this link that in some circles John the Apostle has, since his death, been called an incarnation of the Holy Spirit power of the Green Man, and Mary Magdalene has been designated an incarnation of the Goddesses Venus and Sophia. Susan Haskins, author of *Mary Magdalene: Myth and Metaphor*, calls Mary the "*alter ego* to the symbol of divine Wisdom herself."[25]

Mary was a Cupholder and a Holy Grail Chalice twice over since she received the Messiah's Kundalini power through direct transmission, as well as through being the vessel of his holy seed. As previously mentioned, history convincingly proves that Mary and Jesus conceived a child together who was later born in either Egypt or southern France. Some historians, such as Margaret Starbird, identify their child with the black servant girl called Sarah who accompanied Mary to the coast of France. Sarah, who is currently venerated by her gypsy worshippers as Sarah-Kali, the Black Queen, could have been an actual physical child, but it is more likely that she represents the power of the dark Goddess, Kundry or Kundalini, that had been transmitted to Mary from the Christ when she became a Cupbearer. This seems more than apparent in light of the fact that Sarah-Kali's disembarkation at the French seaport of Saintes-Maries-de-la-Mer corresponded to a heavy proliferation of Black Madonnas in southern France that were associated with the Dark Goddess and the transformative Holy Spirit or Kundalini. These images were regularly patronized by the practitioners of Hermetic Alchemy, the venerators of John the Baptist, and the lodges of the Knights Templar in the Languedoc region of France.[26]

Jesus' special love for Mary Magdalene may have been the result of the Messiah's deep love and reverence for the Universal Goddess. A profound love for the Goddess had no doubt been nurtured within Jesus by his Goddess-loving teacher, John the Baptist, and it was also shared by his brother disciple Simon Magus, who chose as his companion the prostitute Helena because he believed her to be the incarnation of the Gnostic Goddess Sophia. Jesus apparently harbored the same feelings for Mary as Simon had for Helen, because we know that Mary was eventually worshipped within the later Gnostic sects as the "Savior's terrestrial companion, the counterpart of the celestial Sophia."[27]

It is not conclusively known what happened to Mary in France, however iconographic images of her in France suggest that she became a teacher and healer during the remaining years of her life. Her prodigious spiritual power is revealed through the legends of the miracles she produced, such as blessing couples with children and bringing the dead back to life. One of the more famous women Mary blessed with a son was the Princess of Marseille, who unfortunately drowned soon after giving birth to her progeny from falling off a ship bound for Rome. Resolving to complete the journey, her steadfast husband left both the princess and her son on a sheltered rock. Upon his return two years later, the Prince miraculously found his boy still alive from having continually suckled the beast of his dead mother, which had apparently been made ever-plentiful through the grace of the Magdalene. The joy of the reunion with his son was so overwhelming that the prince immediately sunk to his knees and between sobs of joy thanked the Magdalene. Hearing his prayer, the compassionate St. Mary bestowed yet another blessing on the couple and brought the princess back to life. As an interesting postscript to this unusual story, when the prince recounted to his wife his two-years of adventures he discovered that she was oblivious to the fact that she had even been dead. On the contrary, she remembered having been on a two-year pilgrimage with Mary to Jerusalem!

Other indigenous legends of southern France claim that for forty years Mary lived the life of a hermit in a desolate cave high up on a cliff face in Sainte Baume. While deep in meditative trance she is said to have sometimes levitated for many hours, and if she ever needed any material sustenance she simply manifested it. Some legends even contend she subsisted on pure life force. When Mary died her body was entombed by St. Maximin in a chapel in southern France and was later transported to the small town of Vézelay to become the treasure of the Abbey Church of Saint Marie-Madeleine. The Magdalene continues to produce miracles in the lives of those who pray to her; and because of the immense spiritual power that still surrounds her relics, people from all parts of the world regularly receive profound healing at Vézelay.

But while Mary's body was being worshipped by pilgrims in southern France, a second body reputed to also be that of the Magdalene was being paid homage to in Ephesus. It was said by the people of Ephesus that following Christ's Ascension Mary had reunited in the Asia Minor city with her brother disciple of the Gnostic lineage, St. John, and then finished her life in the city of the Gnostics. This was later chronicled by the historian Gregory of Tours and by Modestus, a patriarch of Jerusalem, who states:

"After the death of Our Lord, the mother of God and Mary Magdalene joined John, the well-beloved disciple, at Ephesus. It is there that the myrrhophone ended her apostolic career through her martyrdom, not wishing to the very end to be separated from John the Apostle and the Virgin."

Incarnations of John the Baptist, the Paraclete

Following the passing of John the Apostle and Mary Magdalene, their Gnostic Cupholder lineage took a number of twists and turns as it moved deeper into the minds and hearts of the population of Asia and Europe. Over the ensuing two millenniums, the Holy Spirit power and wisdom that had once dwelt within the body of John the Baptist was passed to worthy Cupholders in a variety of secret sects and brotherhoods, including the Knights Templar and the Priory of Sion, two related orders that anointed their Grand Masters with the honorary Cupholder title of "John." Some leaders of these later Gnostic sects proclaimed themselves to be direct physical incarnations of the spirit and soul that had once walked the Earth as both the Prophet Elijah and John the Baptist, while other Gnostic leaders only claimed to occasionally channel the power and wisdom of John, which they referred to as the "Paraclete."

The Paraclete, which is the name of the Holy Spirit mentioned in *The Gospel of St. John,* translates as "Comforter" or "Counselor" and is derived from the Greek Paracletos, meaning "one who gives support." The Paraclete, which also has the meaning of "messenger," is said to occasionally take a male form to uplift the world as it did as the prophets Elijah and John the Baptist. The Paraclete is thus the messenger that is occasionally sent to Earth to give support by helping humans prepare for God's coming judgment.

Montanism and the Paraclete Channelers

The first historical Grand Master of a Gnostic sect to proclaim himself the vehicle of John the Baptist's power and wisdom was Montanus, the founder of Montanism. Montanus, a native of Phrygia, claimed that he had been chosen by the Paraclete to be its vehicle and he often performed this service in a room full of Gnostic students. Once the Paraclete entered the body of Montanus, the individualized ego of the prophet would, essentially, disappear, and the Holy Spirit would shine through his physical body long enough to speak some profound truth or predict a future event. Didymus, the historian of Montanism, stated that once it had occupied the body of Montanus the Paraclete would introduce itself to those present with "I am the Father, the Word, and the Paraclete." Or, claims Epiphanius, a second recorder of the event, the Paraclete might also identify itself as "…the Lord God omnipotent, who (has) descended into a man." If confusion and fear enveloped the audience after witnessing this enigmatic spectacle, the Paraclete might explain the unusual phenomenon of channeling by stating: "…the man (Montanus) is like a lyre, and I dart like the plectrum. The man sleeps, and I am awake." Montanus' channeling eventually became commonplace to his students;

in fact, a similar form of it even continues today within certain charismatic Christian sects, such as the Pentecostal Church, which seeks to embody the Holy Spirit within its congregation and "speak in tongues" and perform healings. The Pentecostal Church currently refers to Montanus as one of the early forefathers of the sect.

Montanus eventually allied himself with two female companions, Maximilla and Priscilla, who also claimed to have been chosen as vehicles by the Paraclete. The three of them first united for two short sermons in the small villages of Ardabau and Peuza in Phrygia in 156 A.D, however they were quickly forced to expand their mission when hundreds of Phrygian natives applied to join the Order. Losing one's individuality through channeling was natural to most Phyrgians, especially those who were members of the orgiastic cult of Cybele and regularly experienced the dissolution of the ego through communion with the Phrygian goddess. Eventually the Paraclete instructed Montanus to expand his congregation all the way to Rome, where a cult of Cybele had flourished since being brought to the city by soldiers returning to Rome from Asia Minor. While in Rome, Montanus also found converts to his path among Christians who had been followers of the Goddess Isis, and he also attracted the interest of the cadre of intellectuals that followed the famous scholar Proclus, who eventually became the most outspoken philosopher and advocate of Montanism.

After Montanism had established roots in many areas from Phrygia to Rome, the Paraclete chose additional human vehicles to speak through, and it quickly became apparent that the Paraclete was not one individual soul, but the universal power and divine wisdom of the Holy Spirit that can find a foci of expression within any human vessel. The Paraclete is the power and consciousness attendant upon the Kundalini or Water of Life. It is the spirit of the first Fisher King, and it is the power and wisdom personified as the Green Man.

From the start of their mission the three founders of Montanism allied with other Gnostic sects by promulgating the eternal wisdom in *The Gospel of St. John* and *The Revelation of St. John the Divine.* Like their cousins in other Gnostic orders, the initiates of Montanism acknowledged that the Paraclete had been embodied as the Apostle John and that part of the reason for the Paraclete's return within the sect of Montanism was to finish the work it had begun while in the body of the Apostle. This it did by both completing and disseminating a new interpretation of St. John's *Revelation*.

The Paraclete's revised rendition of *The Revelation of St. John the Divine* had the effect of placing Montanism squarely in the spotlight and under the scrutiny of the Catholic Church. The new dispensation of the Paraclete maintained that the "New Jerusalem" was destined to manifest in Phrygia, thus encouraging Montanus' followers to purchase land in their teacher's native country. The Catholic

Church, which, of course, did not approve of tampering with St. John's *Revelation*, quickly moved into action after learning of the Paraclete's revisions and some members of the sect of Montanism were soon excommunicated. The Church followed up this action with a thorough investigation of the sect, eventually concluding that when the three heads of the sect went into trance their aberrant behavior was no doubt the work of their Devil. This spelled the beginning of the end for the Paraclete-inspired sect of Montanism.

Mani, an Avatar of the Paraclete

Following the demise of Montanism, the Paraclete found a worthy vehicle in Mani, the prophet of Manicheism, who eventually spread Gnosticism throughout most of the known world. Under the guidance of the Paraclete, Mani became both an inspired messiah and a reformer, who transformed the ancient path of Gnosticism into a religion that was more appealing and relevant to the era he was born into.

Mani's family was of combined Persian and Mandean descent, so Gnosticism flowed through his veins from birth. Mani, whose mother was of Persian royalty and whose father was Mandean, spent his early years living in a Mandean community in Iraq. His ideology and spiritual beliefs eventually departed from the ancient tradition of the Madai, however, when he received a vision of his "twin double" who introduced itself as the Paraclete. Mani was informed by his double that he was an Avatar of the Paraclete, and that the spirit that had moved through John the Baptist was destined to inspire his actions while he reformed and spread the ancient Gnostic teachings.

Mani initially attempted to orchestrate a reformation within his own Mandean community. Tampering with the fixtures of Mandeanism eventually got the young prophet in trouble, however, and the ruling Mandean Nasurai priesthood soon had him expelled. This did not deter Mani, because, like the Nasurai Jesus Christ before him, he was destined to become a world teacher and mold the ancient Gnostic teachings to the needs and sensibilities of people all over the globe. Because of his uncanny ability to relate to all nationalities, Mani and his missionaries eventually founded a Gnostic empire that extended all the way from China to Spain.

But sadly, like his Jewish counterpart, Mani eventually met his end at the hands of intolerant authorities who sought to preserve the religious status quo rather than reform it. Mani's demise came at the hands of the Magi of his Persian bloodline who didn't agree with his tampering with their ancient Gnostic wisdom. After placing the prophet in a prison cell where he eventually died, the Magi had his body flayed, which was the accepted treatment accorded heretics at the time.

The Cathars

Mani's work survived his death, and his reformed Gnostic theology found fertile ground both within the Paulicans, a Gnostic sect that had thrived in Syria since the 7th century A.D., as well as within the later Gnostic sect of the Bogomils in Bulgaria. The Bogomils brought their brand of Gnosticism to southern France where it co-mingled with the Gnostic catechism that had been carried north by the Valentinus Gnostics of Egypt. The resultant Gnostic synthesis produced the sect of the French Cathars, the "Pure Ones," who were also known as "Manicheans" in honor of their parent sect.[28] The Cathars thrived throughout southern France, and especially within the Languedoc region, down to the time of the Albigensian Crusade, when the Catholic Church sent its Inquisition to exterminate them.

Like most other Gnostic sects that have come before and after them, the Cathars similarly adopted John the Apostle as their patron saint and designated *The Gospel of St. John* as one of their principal texts. They also chose the white dove, symbol of the Holy Spirit and Paraclete, as their emblem, and during one of their initiations, the *Consolamentum*, a Cathari priest, known as a Parfait or "Perfect," would place his hands on the head of an aspiring Cathar seeker while channeling into them the power and wisdom of the Holy Spirit, which would ultimately assist them in merging with the transcendental light of God. The Cathars knowledge of the Paraclete also extended into their understanding of Rex Mundi, a prominent figure of Gnosticism whom they recognized to be a manifestation of the King of the World. Rex Mundi, whose name literally means "King of the World, was a personification of the transformative Kundalini and Green Man.

Many of the Cathar Parfaits were Cupbearers full of the Holy Spirit who governed their Cathari flocks from the hilltop edifice of Montsegur, which some authors have proclaimed the true Montsalavant, the Holy Mountain of God and Grail Castle of the Holy Grail Mysteries. It is said that the Cathars once kept some of their Grail Hallows within Montseguer, including a Grail chalice and possibly the Shroud of Turin. These were removed from the castle on the night preceding the Inquisition's raid on Montsegur and then hidden someplace in the surrounding countryside. Or perhaps they ended up in the possession of the neighboring Knights Templar.

Although many Cathars were silenced by being burned to death or slaughtered by the sword, their Gnostic flame of wisdom was not extinguished and continued to illuminate several underground movements in Europe for hundreds of years to come. Their sudden revival in France during the 19th century as the Universal Gnostic Church is testimony to this truth.

Eugene Michel Vintras, Incarnation of Elijah

France's 19th century Gnostic revival was spearheaded by a series of new incarnations of the Paraclete, whose mission it was to unite the wisdom of the Cathars and the Middle Eastern Gnostics with contemporary Gnostic thought. One such incarnation was Eugene Michel Vintras, a mystic who proclaimed himself to be a full manifestation of the Paraclete and a reincarnation of the Prophet Elijah. Vintras' mission began after a series of visions wherein Archangel Michael, Joseph, and Mary all appeared to him and prophesied the return of the Paraclete. He then proceeded to found the Oeuvre de la Misericorde, the "Work of Mercy" or Church or Carmel, as a vehicle to spread the wisdom of the Paraclete.

Vintras became famous for conducting public performances during which the latter-day prophet would go into a trance and bring forth the wisdom and power of the Paraclete for all those in attendance. As the Paraclete spoke, Vintras' body would sometimes convulse and become covered with a bloody sweat, and at other times empty cups and chalices in the room would simultaneously become filled with a red liquid that tasted like wine but created bloodstains when spilled on fabric.

When Vintras finally completed his worldly mission the mantle of his Gnostic lineage was passed to his successor, the Cupbearer Abbé Joseph-Antoine Boullan, who followed in Vintras' footsteps by immediately proclaiming himself an incarnation of John the Baptist, and by also bringing forth the wisdom and power of the Paraclete in trance. Boullan had previously served as a Catholic priest and the head of the Society for the Reparation of Souls, an organization he co-founded with an ex-nun that contained many Gnostic practices, including Tantric sexual rites. Thus, with Boullan, the Church of Carmel took on a Tantric veneer.

The "Era of the Paraclete"

Another Gnostic lineage in 19th Century France that paralleled Vintras' was founded by Joseph Rene Vilatte, an aspiring Roman Catholic priest who sought to infiltrate the Church with pure, Gnostic wisdom. Vilatte never succeeded in acquiring Holy Orders within the Catholic Church, which may have been cause of much regret, but he did manage to become initiated as a Cupbearer within the Apostolic Succession of Antioch, a tradition of Gnostic Cupbearers that had been founded by the descendants of John the Baptist and Simon Magus in the Middle East. Cupbearer Vilatte also garnered consecration into the Independent Catholic Church of Sri Lanka and India, a progressive church that united Gnostic and Christian theology. His consecration took place on May 29, 1892 on the island of Sri Lanka, the ancient home of *Sri Jnana Pandita* or Murrugan, the Father of Gnosticism. Thus, through the initiations of Vilatte the earliest Cupbearer lineages of Gnostics from Sri Lanka were united within a latter day church of Gnosticism.

When Vilatte returned home from the Far East he was ready to actively participate in the 19th century French revival of Gnosticism, but the fledgling Gnostic sects of France were not yet prepared to unite under the singular banner of a Universal Gnostic Church. An event would soon transpire to trigger this synthesis, however. This was the creation of the *L'Eglise Gnostique*, a Gnostic church founded by the visionary Jules Doinel.

Doinel's important influence on the evolution of French Gnosticism began during a series of nighttime visions, when Jesus Christ and two Bogomil Bishops appeared to him and consecrated him as the first Patriarch of a revived Gnostic Church. Following these visions, Doinel, a librarian, discovered an ancient Cathar charter in the Library of Orleans written by Stephon d'Orleans and dated 1022. This gave Doinel an authentic Gnostic document he could use to infuse credibility and authority into his new church.

Doinel was eventually guided by the Holy Spirit to organize a series of séances, during which he summoned and spoke directly to many Cathar priests of the past. One of his séances produced the spirits of 40 Cathar bishops, who after introducing themselves as the "Very High Synod of Bishops of the Paraclete" proceeded to instruct Doinel on how to organize an "Assembly of the Paraclete. " Another pivotal séance soon afterwards summoned the Holy Spirit as the Gnostic Goddess Sophia, who proceeded to address Doinel's Gnostic congregation thus:

"I address myself to you because you are my friend, my servant, and the prelate of my Albigensian Church. I am exiled from the Pleroma, and it is I whom Valentinus named Sophia-Achamôth. It is I whom Simon Magus called Helene-Ennoia; for I am the Eternal Androgyne. Jesus is the Word of God; I am the Thought of God. One day I shall remount to my Father, but I require aid in this; it requires the supplication of my Brother Jesus to intercede for me. Only the Infinite is able to redeem the Infinite, and only God is able to redeem God. Listen well: The One has brought forth One, then One. And the Three are but One: the Father, the Word, and the Thought. Establish my Gnostic Church. The Demiurge will be powerless against it. Receive the Paraclete."

The result of Doinel's numerous séances was the creation of *L'Eglise Gnostique* in 1890, a year that Doinel promptly declared to be the beginning of the "Era of the Paraclete." As head of the revived Gnostic Church, Doinel assumed the dynastic name of Valentin II, thereby designating himself to be part of the same Gnostic lineage as Valentinus, the last Gnostic Cupbearer of Alexandria.

The theology and curriculum in Doinel's church were base upon the mandates dictated to him by the 40 Cathar Bishops. He was told his church was to include the ancient Gnostic wisdom of Simon Magus, as well as the works of the Gnostic scholar Valentinus of Alexandria. The Cathar Bishops also mandated that the church was to have equal consecration of both men and women, who were to be the church's Bishops and "Sophias." From among these priests and priestesses eight were to be chosen high bishops known as Tau (a name for the Egyptian Ank), thus designating them Cupbearers in the Gnostic line of Valentinus that had previously flourished in ancient Egypt.

When Doinel eventually retired from *L'Eglise Gnostique*, one of his students, Jean Bricaud, set out to complete the mission of his teacher by uniting all the assorted Gnostic sects in France into the Catholic or *Universal Gnostic Church*. Some of the sects that Bricaud succeeded in amalgamating into his worldwide church included *L'Église Gnostique,* Vintras' *Church of Carmel*, and the *Église Johannites des Chretiens Primitif*, which was the Gnostic Church of Johannites founded by Bernard-Raymond Fabré-Palaprat, a French doctor who had revived the Gnostic tradition of the ancient Knights Templar. Thus, with Bricaud the many divergent branches of Gnostic Cupbearers that had anciently flowed from John the Baptist were reunited into the *Universal Gnostic Church.* In order to give himself authority to govern this panoply of Gnostic sects, Bricaud, whose titular name of Tau Johannes denoted him the dynastic "John," procured initiation into each of them. His last, and perhaps most important induction, was administered by Bishop Louis-Marie-François Giraud, an ex-Trappist monk, who initiated Bricaud into the Gnostic lineage of Joseph René Vilatte, the apostolic line that extended back to Antioch and the Sri Lankan residence of *Sri Jnana Pandita.*

The Johannites and Knights Templar

As fate would have it, Bricaud's united Gnostic church was short lived because Fabré-Palaprat's Knights Templar Order soon broke away from it. At least the military elements of Palaprat's Templarism separated from the *Universal Gnostic Church*, while its Gnostic and Johannite elements remained. This was a crucial turn in the history of Templarism because it meant that from the 19th century onwards the Gnostic elements that had once been part of Templarism through its affiliation with the Johannite lineage in Palestine were expunged from the Order.

When Fabré-Palaprat initially founded his Gnostic Templar Order in 1804 with his friend and colleague, Ledru de Chevillon de Saintot, he named it *Église Johannites des Chretiens Primitif,* meaning the "Johannite Church of Primitive Christians." Palaprat asserted that his authority for reviving Templarism came via the Larmenius Charter of Transmission of 1324, which supposedly had been passed from Jacques De Molay, the last historical Grand Master of the Templars, to his successor, Johannes Marcus Larmenius, in order to perpetuate the Order. This document, which ostensibly proved that the Templars had survived their attempted extermination by the French authorities in 1307, had been purchased along with The Statutes and Election Charter and other important Templar documents by Ledru from the estate of Duc du Cosse-Brissac, a former Grand Master of the Societe d'Aloya, which was founded in 1705 by the Duke of Orleans under the authority of the Larmenius Charter. Previous to this time, the Duke of Orleans, who later became Regent of France, had maintained that he was the representative of an unbroken line of Templar Grand Masters that stretched back to Larmenius.

Another important document that lent authority to Fabré-Palaprat's Templars was the *Levitikon,* a document discovered by the French doctor in a used bookstore in central Paris that he purchased for only 25 francs. Written by a Greek monk of Athens named Necephorus, the *Levitikon* was an introduction to the *Evangelicon*, a rendition of the Gospel of St. John that listed an unbroken lineage of Templar Grand Masters that ruled before and after Molay and Larmenius. It also maintained that the Johannite lineage was intimately connected to the Egyptian priesthood through Jesus, who had been initiated into the Egyptian Mysteries of Osiris and afterwards passed this Gnostic wisdom to John the Apostle. Thus, through their affiliation with the Johannites, the Knights Templar apparently aligned themselves with two divergent manifestations of the Green Man, the Hindu Murrugan and the Egyptian Osiris.

Ledru and Fabré-Palaprat also presented to the world a paper supposedly written in 1154 that designated the Templars to be the true lineal successors of the Johannite line of Gnostic Cupbearers, which had moved from John the Baptist to St. John the Apostle, and then along a line of titular Johns. According to this document, when the Knights Templar were living on the Temple Mount in Jerusalem, Theoclete, the Patriarch of the Johannite Church, was presiding over the nearby Church of John. The Patriarch Theoclete, who at the time claimed lineal descent from John the Apostle and referred to himself as the titular "John," sensed a remarkable spiritual development in Hughes de Payen, the first Grand Master of the Templars, and resolved to pass the apostolic succession of the Johannite lineage to him. The Templars thus became married to the Johannites and remained so until the 19th century.

When Fabré-Palaprat revived the Templars he proclaimed himself the 45th Grand Master of the Order in direct line from Hughes de Payen. He then mass-produced copies of both the *Gospel of St. John*, which was to be studied within his Gnostic Order, as well as a Templar handbook for his Knights that was entitled *Manuel des Chevaliers de L'Order du Temple.* He also revived some mystical rites that he maintained had been observed since the time of St. John the Apostle, some of which he learned from a manuscript acquired in the same Parisian secondhand bookstall where he purchased the *Levitikon.* This additional document included specific protocols to be performed for each of the nine levels that the initiated Knights were required to ascend through.

Once Fabré-Palaprat had made his dramatic announcement that the Knights Templar had never ceased to exist as most people had previously believed, the documentation he disseminated in support of his claim was so persuasive that many occultists and academics of Europe fully embraced his assertions. In 1828, for example, Fabré-Palaprat's notions became the definitive theory regarding Templar history in Abbe Gregoire's *Histoire des Sectes Religieuses*, "The History of Religious Sects," which was considered the most authoritative historical text on religious sects of its time. Then another respected religious authority, the world famous occultist Madame Blavatsky, stepped forward to proclaim that Fabre-Palaprat's revelations were consistent with the prodigious research she had compiled from her many years of travel around the globe. In *Isis Unveiled*, she thus affirms:

"The true version of the history of Jesus, and the early Christianity was supposedly imparted to Hugh de Payens, by the Grand-Pontiff of the Order of the Temple (of the Nazarene or Johannite sect), one named Theocletes, after which it was learned by some Knights in Palestine, from the higher and more intellectual members of the St. John sect, who were initiated into its mysteries. Freedom of intellectual thought and the restoration of one universal religion was their secret object. Sworn to the vow of obedience, poverty, and chastity, they were at first the true Knights of John the Baptist, crying in the wilderness and living on wild honey and locusts. Such is the tradition and the true kabalistic version."[29]

Following *Isis Unveiled*, the Frenchman Eliphas Levi published another occult milestone, *The History of Magic: Including a Clear and Precise Exposition of Its Procedure, Its Rites, and Its Mysteries,* wherein he also agreed in content with Fabre-Palaprat's assertions regarding the early history of the Knights Templar. Levi, who was one of the greatest French occultists of the 19th Century, was intimately involved with covert information passed between the European secret societies of his time, so his acceptance of Fabré-Palaprat proved that the French doctor had been accurate in his information. After synthesizing Fabré-Palaprat's wisdom with his own, Levi proclaimed:

"The secret thought of Hughes de Payens, in founding his Order, was not exactly to serve the ambitions of the Patriarchs of Constantinople. There existed at that period in the East a sect of **Johannite Christians**, *who claimed to be the only true initiates into the real mysteries of the religion of the Savior...*

"The tendencies and tenets of the (Templar) Order were enveloped in profound mystery, and it externally professed the most perfect orthodoxy. The Chiefs alone knew the aim of the Order; the Subalterns followed them without distrust."[30]

And finally, there is the famous address of no less an authority than Pope Puis IX, who publicly stated:

"The Johannites ascribed to Saint John the foundation of their Secret Church, and the Grand Pontiffs of the Sect assumed the title of Christos, Anointed, or Consecrated, and claimed to have succeeded one another from Saint John by an uninterrupted succession of pontifical powers. He who, at the period of the foundation of the Order of the Temple, claimed these imaginary prerogatives, was named Theoclete; he knew Hughes de Payens, he initiated him into the Mysteries and hopes of his pretended church; he seduced him by the notions of Sovereign Priesthood and Supreme royalty, and finally designated him as his successor.

"Then the Order of the Knights of the Temple was at its very origin devoted to the cause of opposition to the Tiara of Rome and the crown of Kings, and the Apostolate of Kabalistic Gnosticism was vested in its chiefs. For Saint John was the Father of the Gnostics…

"The Templars, like all other Secret Orders and Associations, had two doctrines, one concealed and reserved for the Masters, which was Johannism; the other public, which was the Roman Catholic. Thus they deceived the adversaries whom they sought to supplant."

The Order of Sion and the lineage of Johns

Some of the hidden information regarding Templar history possessed by Eliphas Levi and the European secret societies has recently emerged into the public arena with the publications of *The Holy Blood and The Holy Grail* and *The Templar Revelation*, two works that disclose the existence of a French organization founded in Palestine named the *Prieure de Sion*, the "Priory of Sion" or Priory of John. "Sion" denotes "John" in the Welsh language, a language with confirmed links to Hebrew.[31]

The Priory of Sion or John was intimately connected to the Knights Templar and the Johannites. Founded in 1099 by Godefroi de Bouillon, the commander general of the First Crusade, the Priory of Sion was modeled after the Church of John, which had conceivably existed in the Holy Land since the time of John the Apostle. From the Priory emerged the Knights Templar, which served as the military arm of the Order, thus establishing a bond between the Church of John, the Templars and the Priory of Sion. This important triangle was recently alluded to in *Rennes-le-Château: capitale scrète de lihistoire de France*, a book published in the 1980's by Jean-Pierre Deloux and Jaques Bréigny, two students of Pierre Plantard de Saint-Claire, the modern Grand Master of the Priory of Sion. It explicitly designates the Knights Templar as being "the sword bearers of the Church of John and the standard-bearers of the premier dynasty, the arms that obeyed the spirit of Sion."[32]

Apparently Godefroi founded the Priory of Sion to serve the interests of the Church of John as well as the sacred bloodline of Jesus. According to their in-depth research, the authors of *The Holy Blood and The Holy Grail* discovered that Godefroi de Bouillon had created the Order for the purpose of protecting and further researching the family and descendants of Jesus Christ and Mary Magdalene. Christ's divine bloodline was Godefroi's own ancestral line, and he knew it. The Messiah's lineage had engendered the French lineage of monarchs that included the legendary Merovingian Kings and Godefroi's own family and relatives.

It must be allowed, however, that Godefroi may not have founded the Priory of Sion, but simply adopted its cause. *The Holy Blood and The Holy Grail* reveals that the Priory of Sion might have been founded hundreds of years previously by the Gnostic sage Ormus, a descendant of John the Baptist who lived in Alexandria, Egypt during the 1st century. Ormus, whose name appears to be an anagram for words associated with "bear" and "light," was not only a Gnostic Master of Alexandria, but also a priest of Serapis and a follower of St. Mark, the Apostle who administered a small Christian Church in the city while Ormus resided there. Ormus synthesized the various traditions he had been initiated into in Alexandria to found the amalgamated Order of the Rose Cross. When Godefroi arrived in Palestine, Ormus' order had apparently merged with the Church of John, because the commander chose the red or rose cross of the Order of the Rose Cross as the symbol of the Priory of Sion. An even more compelling link between the two orders came later, in 1188, when the Priory of Sion became alternately known as L'Order de la Rose-Croix Veritas, or simply as ORMUS.[33]

Through its alignment with the Priory of Sion and Church of John, the Order of the Knights Templar also acquired a special affiliation with the ancient Order of the Rose Cross. The Templars' association to Ormus' Order eventually became evidenced by the red cross that the Knights wore over their white mantles, as well as by the later 18th degree of the Scottish Rite Freemasonry, the Knight of the Rose Croix, which the Templars helped to create in Europe. The founding of Scottish Freemasonry by the Templars and their affiliation to the Order f the Rose Corss was alluded to by the Templar historian Baron de Westrode, who in 1789 wrote:

"The disciples of the Rose Croix (the Knights Templar) came, in 1188, from the East into Europe... Three of them founded in Scotland the Order of the Masons of the East (Knights of the East,) to serve as a seminary for instruction in the most sublime sciences."

The date of 1188 is significant as it marks the year that the Priory of Sion officially split from the Knights Templar. The cause for this schism is unclear, but a number of theories exist, including one from the *Dossier secrets*, a document discovered by the authors *The Holy Blood and The Holy Grail*, which implies that the split occurred over an act of "treason" instigated by the reigning Grand Master Templar of that time, Gérard de Ridefort. But the schism might also have had something to do with the need to protect the dual manifestations of the Holy Grail, i.e., the lineage of John the Baptist and the holy bloodline of Jesus Christ. The Knights Templar may have chosen to devote themselves more exclusively to the Gnostic rites and lineage of John the Baptist, while their brethren in the Priory of Sion could have resolved to continue making the preservation of the bloodline of Jesus their raison d'etre. A third scenario makes the split utilitarian. The Templar Knights, the "disciples of the Rose Cross," may have simply needed to separate from the Priory in order to devote their time and energy to the development of Freemasonry in Europe.

When the 1188 schism was complete, two Cupholder lineages of Grand Masters, each of with the dynastic name of John (or Jean), had been formed. The Cupbearer lineage of the Templars has already been mentioned and their "Johns" are listed below. Within the Priory of Sion, the first Grand Master after the 1188 split was Jean de Gisors, and after a succession of Jeans had ruled the Order, the famous Renaissance Man, Leonardo da Vinci, was installed as Grand Master Jean IX. Leonardo is reputed to have given special attention and honor to the first Cupbearer of his Gnostic lineage, John the Baptist, who became one of artist's favorite subjects. John's dominating presence is reflected in the last statue sculpted by Leonardo, and the Baptist's preeminent position in the Gnostic lineage appears to be revealed in Leonardo's *Virgin and Child with St. Anne*, wherein the artist has the Baptist's upraised finger surmounting that of the baby Jesus, thus denoting a level of supremacy over his disciple.[34] Leonardo's understanding of John as the embodiment of the Green Man is reflected in one of his paintings wherein he portrays the Baptist as the Greek Green Man, Dionysus. Perhaps in order to surround himself with the presence of the Baptist, Leonardo da Vinci chose as his place of domicile Florence, Italy, a city dedicated to John.

Thus, the Knights Templar were on their own when they reentered Europe. They arrived with a collection of Gnostic rites they had acquired from the Church of John and the Sufi sects they had interacted with in the Middle East. Their foreign rites, which became perceived as heretical in the eyes of the Catholic Church, eventually precipitated a scandal within the Templar Order and led to the dramatic fall of the Knights.

Grand Masters of the united Priory of Sion and the Knights Templar to 1188

1118-1136 Huge de Payens
1136-1146 Robert de Craon
1146-1149 Everard des Barres
1149-1153 Bernard de Trmelai
1153-1156 Andre de Montbard
1156-1169 Bertrand de Blanchefort
1169-1171 Philip de Milly
1171-1179 Odo de St. Amand
1179-1184 Arnold de Toroga
1185-1189 Gerard de Ridfort

Grand Masters of the Priory of Sion after 1188

1188-1220 Jean de Gisors
1220-1266 Marie de Saint-Clair
1266-1307 Guillaume de Gisors
1307-1336 Edouard de Bar
1351-1366 Jean de Saint-Clair
1366-1398 Blanche d'Evreux
1398-1418 Nicolas Flamel
1418-1480 René d'Anjou
1480-1483 Iolande de Bar
1483-1510 Sandro Filipepi
1510-1519 Leonardo de Vinci
1519-1527 Connétable de Bourbon
1527-1575 Ferdinand de Gonzague
1575-1595 Louis de Nevers
1595-1637 Robert Fludd
1637-1654 J. Valentin Andrea
1654-1691 Robert Boyle
1691-1727 Isaac Newton
1727-1746 Charles Radclyffe
1746-1780 Charles de Lorraine
1780-1801 Maximilian de Lorraine
1801-1844 Charles Nodier
1844-1885 Victor Hugo
1885-1918 Claude Debussy
1918- Jean Cocteau

Grand Masters of the Knights Templar after 1188

1191-1193	Robert de Sable
1193-1200	Gilbert Erail
1201-1208	Philip de Plessiez
1209-1219	William de Chartres
1219-1230	Pedro de Montaigu
(?) -1244	Armond de Perigord
1245-1247	Richard de Bures
1247-1250	William de Sonnac
1250-1256	Reynald de Vichiers
1256-1273	Thomas Berard
1273-1291	William de Beaujeu
1291-1293	Tibald de Gaudin
1293-1314	Jacques de Molay
1314-1324	Johannes Larmenius
1324-1340	Franciscus Theobaldus
1340-1349	Arnold de Braque
1349-1357	John de Clermont
1357-1380	Bertrand de Guesclin
1380-1381	John de l'Armagnac
1381-1392	Bertrand de l'Armagnac
1392-1418	John de l'Armagnac
1418-1451	John de Croy
1478-1497	Robert de Lenoncourd
1498-	Galeas Salazar
1516-1543	Philippe de Chabot
1544-	Gaspard de Chobane
1574-1614	Henri, Duke of Montorency
1615-	Chales de Valois
1651-	James de Grancey
1681-	Jacques de Durfort
1705-1723	Phillipe, Duke of Orleans
1724-1737	Louis Auguste de Bourbon
1737-1741	Louis Henri de Bourbon
1741-1746	Louis Francois de Bourbon
1776-1792	Louis Timoleon
1804-1839	Bernard Fabre-Palaprat

St. John the Baptist.
The last painting by Leonardo da Vinci.

John the Baptist by Diego Valazquez.
The Holy Spirit fire burns brightly around his head.

Leonardo da Vinci's *John the Baptist* as Green Man *Dionysus.*

The Lineage of Gnostic Cupbearers
Virgin and Child enthroned between St. John the Baptist and St. John the Evangelist
by Alessandro Botticelli

Cupbearer John the Apostle
Evangelist John by Anthony van Dyck

El Greco's *John the Evangelist*

The Black Madonna of Montserrat.
A personification of Mary Magdalene's Kundalini power?

The middle prong of the trident is the vesica pisces "fish."

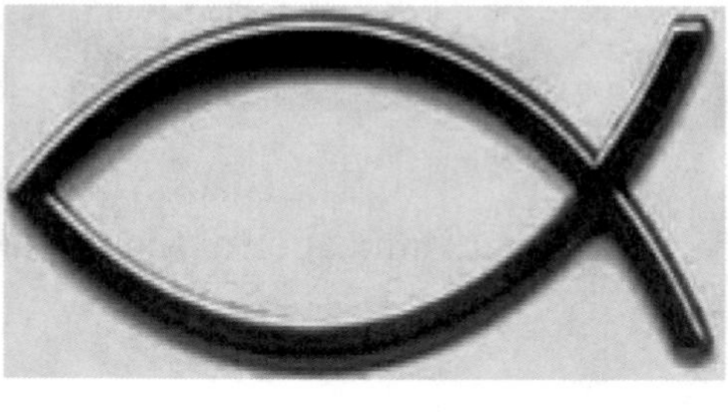

The symbol of the Fish Avatar and Lord of Wisdom.

10

Baphomet, the Head of John

The most fateful day in the history of the Knights Templar, Friday the 13th, October 1307, is the historical origin of the ominous superstition surrounding any Friday that falls on the 13th of a month. On that pivotal day King Philip the Fair of France ordered the arrest of all French Knights for the observance of their Gnostic rites, an action that was supported by Pope Clement V, whose bull *Pastoralis Praeeminentiae* had sanctioned the mass arrests. Many of the five thousand Templars in France were duly imprisoned as the darkest hour of Templar history set in. Extreme torture of the Knights at the hands of the Inquisition, as well as permanent dissolution of the Order, were imminent.

King Philip's allegations against the Templars, which had been compiled from reports from the monarch's spies that had infiltrated the Order, were soon circulated within the French courts and read to the downcast Knights during their individual arraignments by the Catholic Inquisition. Most Knights confessed to many of the 87 articles of heresy brought against them, although only 4 of the allegations were consistently avowed to by a majority of the Templars. These four "articles," which thus acquired more weight as being true and accurate, are as follows:

1. *Article*: The Templar initiation ceremony included denying Christ as Savior and Son of God, and defiling the Cross by spitting or urinating upon it.
2. *Article*: The Knights worshipped an idol in the form a bearded human head.
3. *Article*: At their initiation the Knights received a sacred cord to wear around their waist that had first been bound around the idolized head.
4. *Article*: During initiation the Knights kissed each other on the mouth, the navel, the base of spine, and the penis.

Each of these articles refer to Gnostic observances whose origins can be traced back to the Gnostic mystery schools of the Middle East and/or European secret societies. The first, that of denying Christ and defiling the Cross, was a common practice of the Gnostic Cathars of southern France, who considered it an offense not against Christ, but the Catholic authorities that had crucified him. According to the records of the contemporary Johannites, the Knights Templar interpreted their own "heretical" defilement of the cross from an identical perspective. And as for their supposed denial of Christ, the Templars also understood this act from a different perspective than their critics perceived it. It was not Christ they were denying, but the notion that Jesus was *their only Savior.* John the Baptist was also a Savior of the Knights, and he superseded the Christ by being first in the lineage of Johannite Cupbearers.

It is interesting to note that the alleged denial of Christ among the Cathars has since been found to be erroneous. These Gnostics of southern France are now recognized as having been great lovers of Jesus. But if even Saint Bernard, the original patron of the Templars, could not understand the Cathars' true motivations behind their supposed denial of Christ, what hope did the Templars themselves have of being understood? In regards to the Cathars, St. Bernard laments:

"The (Cathars) deny Christ and their temples resemble synagogues. The sacred character of God's sanctuaries is ignored, and the sacraments are not accounted holy. Feast days are not observed with due solemnity. Men die in their sins and their souls are carried off, alas, before the awesome Judgment Seat without being reconciled with the Lord and provided with the holy sacraments. Children do not learn to know Christ and the grace of baptism is not conferred on them."[1]

The Crusade of King Philip the Fair

In order to insure that the Knights Templar were adequately prosecuted for their heretical crimes, King Philip hired a stable of expert legal advisors, including the "first lawyer of the realm," the conniving Guillaume de Nogaret, who had made his reputation as a former legal counsel to the King of Majorca, and as the vicious prosecutor determined to bring down the progressive-minded Pope Boniface VIII. King Philip and his legal henchmen moved forward with their case against the Templars only when they were sure their damaging accusations against the Knights would stick. They knew they had all the evidence they needed after King Philip infiltrated the Order with twelve specially chosen spies and when Esquin de Floyran, a former Templar Knight who had separated himself from the Order in 1305, stepped forward with first-hand incriminating evidence against the Order.

The events that led up to King Philip's extreme antipathy towards the Templar Order has been the subject of endless debate. If the Knights' testimonies were authentic and not extracted under duress, then perhaps it can be argued that the king's dislike of the Templars came from a sense of moral and civil duty. But if, as some historians contend, the testimonies were forced out of the Knights while undergoing extreme torture, then perhaps Philip's motivations lied elsewhere.

Conspiracy theorists currently contend that King Philip's motivations in prosecuting the Templars went well beyond his puritanical Christian indignation. The king had inherited an empire that had taken a financial beating while funding the Crusade led by his father, and while trying to get his kingdom back on its feet Philip had gotten himself into severe debt with the Templar Knights. And a huge sum borrowed from the Knights for the dowry of Philip's daughter, Princess Isabella, had only compounded the issue. But Philip's antipathy towards the Templars went far beyond their roles as his bankers. He had a long standing resentment against the Templars for not paying the ransom of his grandfather, Louis IX, after the monarch had been captured by the Saracens while fighting in Outremer.

Simple logic would also say that Philip must have been motivated by a vendetta against the Templars when he seemingly "stacked the deck" against them by replacing the ruling Pope, Boniface VIII, with one of his own uncles, Bertrand de Got, archbishop of Bordeaux, who was thenceforth known as Pope Clement V. Philip even had the Holy See's seat of operations moved from Rome to Poitiers in France so that the Church leader could be more completely under his control.

But there was also another side to King Philip's ambiguous personality. He was grandson of King Louis IX, popularly known as St. Louis, whose saintly nature many believed Philip had fully inherited. In many parts of Europe Philip acquired a reputation as "the most Christian King of France," and many of his admirers even accorded him a "semi divine" status.[2] Those researchers who have emphasized Philip's saintly nature have repeatedly pointed out that the king could not have been motivated by avarice or vindictiveness in his treatment of the Templars because whatever the king received from the Order was promptly given over to the Catholic Church or to the Order of the Knights Hospitallers. Clement V is himself on record as explicitly stating that the king was "not prompted by avarice since he desired to keep or appropriate for himself no part of the property of the Templars, but liberally and devotedly left them to the Church to be administered."[3] In truth, asserts the 19th century Templar historian Eliphas Levi, it was not King Philip's motives that were impure, but those of the Knights. He affirmatively states:

"The Templars, whose history is understood so little, were the terrible conspirators in question, and it is time at length to reveal the secret of their fall, so absolving the memory of Clement V and Philip the Fair."[4]

It also appears strange that King Philip would so vehemently desire to persecute the Templars when over the years he had apparently cultivated a symbiotic friendship with them. Protection was mutually extended between Philip and the Templars, and for their part the Knights are noted for having offered the king refuge in their Paris headquarters when public opinion had turned against him for debasing the French monetary system.[5] King Philip extended his friendship towards the Templars when he asked the Templar Grand Master Jacques de Molay to be the godfather of his son Robert, and when he later sought to become the Grand Master of a united Templar-Hospitaller Order.

But regardless of his motivations for bringing down the Templars, Philip's game plan went awry almost from the start. He immediately found his plans obstructed by a pawn he had underestimated, Pope Clement V, who like his predecessor Popes considered the Knights Templar to be the Church's Holy Cow. They had been the Popes' bodyguard and subject to his will exclusively. It was, therefore, an abomination in Clement's estimation that the king could have ever even considered trying to arrest the Knights Templar without first getting full approval from him, and he let Philip know his feelings regarding this issue through an official Church communiqué. Clement also took steps to get to the truth behind the Templar allegations by summoning into his holy presence "a certain Knight of the Order, of great nobility and held by the said Order in no slight esteem."[6] The outcome of the meeting with the high ranking Knight backfired, however, as the esteemed Templar confessed to many of the most disreputable allegations that had been leveled at the Templars by Philip, including defining the cross and sexually illicit behavior among his fellow knights.

Clement soon found himself in a hole to deep to climb out of. On October 25, only two weeks after the Templars' mass imprisonment, Jacques de Molay publicly admitted to the allegations against the Order in front of a forum of scholars at the University of Paris. The following day, thirty more leaders confessed to "spitting on the cross, obscene kisses, and the worship of a hideous idol in the form of a human head."[7] With so many confessions coming at once, Clement V was forced to reevaluate his position regarding the innocence of the Templars.

But losing the Knights Templar, the defenders of the Catholic faith, was going to be a big setback for the Pope, especially if he decided to rally another crusade or annihilate another heretical culture like the Cathars. Therefore, in February 1308, Clement decided to momentarily abolish the French Inquisition and invite a group of knights to Poitiers, where they could speak openly to the Holy See without fear of torture. Seventy-two knights were thus transported to the Pope's residence and given all the amenities necessary to make them feel comfortable and at-ease. But to the Pope's surprise and dismay, even with their safety assured the Templars still confessed to their alleged crimes. "The full and pure truth" of the Templars' crimes was presented to the Pope, and afterwards the Knights' confessions were "committed to writing in their presence, and these being afterwards read aloud to them, they expressly and willingly approved them."[8]

Clement was now cornered. He had to take a stand either for or against the Knights Templar. Deciding to give the Order one last opportunity for vindication, the Pope summoned a Papal Commission to completely investigate the Templar allegations and report their findings two years hence at a scheduled Council of Vienna. Unfortunately for the Pope, it was during this two-year hiatus that some of the most damning testimony of all was extracted from the Templars, even though much of it was acquired under extreme torture from the Inquisition. One of the most persuasive torture machines used by the Inquisition at this time was the strappado, which involved tying a victims arms behind his back with one end of a rope while the other end was tossed over a high ceiling beam. The offending victim would then be suddenly dropped and raised off the floor like a puppet on a string, while all his joints and bones were simultaneously dislocated.

The Templars' "last stand" was February 3, 1310, a day when Philip relaxed his iron grip on the Knights' legal proceedings long enough for 15 Templars to come forward and officially retract their confessions to the Papal Commission. More Templars followed suit, until 597 had summarily recanted their transgressions against the Church. But Philip had made too much progress acquiring a body of damning testimonies against the Templars for the Knights to suddenly recant now. An emergency meeting of the Inquisition was, therefore, convened by the Archbishop of Sens, Phillipe de Marigny, a Church official loyal to Philip, with the result that 54 of the Knights who had professed innocence were declared "relapsed heretics" and sentenced to be burned alive. And to drive home the point even further, within just days afterwards a total of 120 Templars were consumed in lapping flames. Fear had returned to the Templar brethren, who now realized that the time for retracting their confessions had long passed them by. With great apprehension, all they could do was silently and passively await their inevitable destruction.

The Confessions of the Templars

The Templar confessions were initially recorded by Papal Commission scribes and later published by numerous authors in Latin. However, it was not until 1955 that these Latin editions were translated into French so that laypersons could study them. But once in French, the confessions quickly found their way into most of the Templar histories written in the 1950's and 1960's. Perhaps the most popular and authoritative Latin book on the Templar trial that was translated and used as a reference guide at this time was *Proces des Templiers,* which had been written in 1813 by Jules Michelet, a researcher that, according to the modern Templar historian Peter Partner, had become thoroughly convinced of the Knights' guilt after studying the their early, unaltered testimonies. States Partner:

"(Michelet's) judgment on the evidence given by the Templars at the trials was that so much of it was consistent from one Templar to another…that some of the charges…must have been well founded."[10]

The authors of other popular Latin texts regarding the Templar confessions that were translated at this time similarly echoed Michelet in their conclusions, including Raymond Oursel, who after studying the Templar testimonies became so convinced of their crimes that he wrote in his book's commentary:

"Too numerous and too much in accord in all their essentials, to precise in their evocations, and too detailed do these confessions appear, on reading them, for the accusations brought against the Templars not to repose here on some foundation. It was in full knowledge (of these transgressions) that the accusers struck; they knew beforehand that they would not be gainsaid (denied)."[11]

Once many of the Latin translations were complete, Templar researchers sought confirmation for them by comparing the testimonies of the French Templar Knights with those of Templars from other countries, including Britain, Spain and Germany. What they found was that even though they may have been hundreds and thousands of miles away from each other, the testimonies of the divergent European Knights were often identical. Nesta Webster, an author who studied the transcripts of Templar trials from all over Europe, has this to say about what he discovered:

"It is certainly difficult to believe that the accounts of the ceremony of initiation given in detail by men in different countries, all closely resembling each other, yet related in different phraseology, could be pure inventions. Had the victims been driven to invent they would surely have contradicted each other, have cried out in their agony that all kinds of wild and fantastic rites had taken place to satisfy the demands of their interlocutors. But no, each appears to be describing the same ceremony more or less completely, with characteristic touches that indicate the personality of the speaker, and in the main all the stories tally."[12]

Webster and others have since tabulated the numbers of Knights throughout Europe who confessed to the most severe allegations against their Order. One cross-section of 138 Templars, for example, revealed that 111 Knights had confessed to renouncing Christ as his Savior; 121 had admitted to spitting on the cross; 109 confessed to inappropriate kissing of fellow knights; 99 maintained that they had been given license to indulge in carnal behavior with their fellow monks; and only 6 Templars pleaded innocent to all charges. These numbers are, apparently, in alignment with those originally tallied by the Papal Commission, thus giving them added credibility. The Papal Commission recorded that of the Knights brought before them 183 confessed to renouncing Christ; 180 admitted to spitting on the cross; 96 confessed to inappropriate kissing; 78 admitted to sexual license, and only 17 claimed ignorance of all charges.[13]

Contemporary Templar researchers who have since taken the side of early Latin authors regarding the Knights' guilt to their most serious crimes currently propose their own corroborating evidence for the guilt of the Templars. They point out that if the Templars confessed to the charges against them only to relieve themselves of the extreme torture they were under, then why did they not confess to many of the lesser charges they were accused of, such as "Negligence or restriction of alms" and "Secrecy concerning admissions?"[14] Admission to these charges would have carried a much milder sentence, but out of 231 Knights studied only five confessed to being forced to swear secrecy regarding their initiations and only four confessed to being negligent in collecting and disseminating alms.

Templar researchers striving to champion the work of the Latin authors have also point out that the most convincing evidence of Templar guilt can be found in the incriminating testimonies extracted from the heads of the order, including the Grand Master Jacques de Molay, Templar Visitor-General Hughes de Peraud, the Receiver (Initiator) of the Province of Champagne, Raoul de Gizy, and Godfrey de Gonneville. These "Grand Dignitaries" summarily confessed to the most heretical allegations against the Knights within two months of the Orders' mass arrest. Moreover, their confessions were corroborated by their attendants. Jacques de Molay's long-standing attendant William de Giac, for example, testified to having had numerous sexual encounters with the Grand Master, including three in one night on the island if Cyprus.[15]

The first incriminating interview extracted from one of the Grand Dignitaries occurred between the Inquisition and Hughes de Peraud. Presented below, it alluded to both denying Christ and sexual license among the Templar brethren.

Inquisitor: Have you yourself received other brothers (for initiation)?

Brother Hughes: Yes, many times.

Inquisitor: How?

Brother Hughes: First, they promised to observe the rules and secrets of the order; then the mantle was placed on them. After which I took them aside and made them give me a kiss at the base of the spine, on the navel, and on the mouth. Then I had a Cross brought, and told them that, according to the rules of the order, they would have to deny the Crucified (Christ) and the Cross three times, and spit on them; but those orders I didn't give with my heart at all.

Inquisitor: And were there any who refused?

Brother Hughes: Yes, but in the end they always agreed to deny and to spit. And then I would tell them that if they felt any natural (sexual) heat that pushed them toward incontinence (ejaculation), they had permission to cool it with the other brothers. All that I didn't say with my heart, but only my lips.

Inquisitor: Then why did you say it?
Brother Hughes: It was the rule that we followed.
Inquisitor: Those whom you had received (that had been initiated) by others, were they received in the same way?
Brother Hughes: I know nothing about that, because what happened at the chapters was not allowed to be revealed to those who had not participated: they were to nothing about it. So I don't know.
Inquisitor: But do you believe that all the brothers of the order were received in the same fashion?
Brother Hughes: No, I don't think so…
Brother Hughes (Later): (*At a second appearance the same day Hughes declared straight off that he had misunderstood and had answered wrongly.*) To the contrary, I think that everyone was received in that manner and no other. I here rectify my deposition in order not to perjure myself.

The deposition of Raoul de Gizy directly followed that of Hughes. Gizy, who was also a Templar initiator, confessed that he omitted the licentious kissing part of the ritual, but not the other parts of it.
Inquisitor: How many brothers have you yourself received?
Brother Raoul: Ten or twelve.
Inquisitor: In the same fashion as you were received?
Bother Raoul: Yes, except that certain of them I refused to kiss on the repellant part, because of the horror I had of it. For the rest- denial, spitting, and all- I didn't proceed any differently.

The interview of Grand Dignitary Godfrey de Gonneville that followed was a little different in tenor because he had been admitted into the Templar Order in England and not France. Godfrey claimed that he was initially afraid to denounce Christ, but he was persuaded to by his initiator, Robert de Tortaville, Master of the Temple in London, who instructed him: "Do it boldly, I (Robert) swear on peril of my soul that it will never prejudice you in soul or conscience; it is the custom of the Order…"[15] Godfrey's coerced initiation was representative of other inductions performed in Europe, during which the candidate was even threatened into swearing his Templar vows. One Templar Knight known as John de Puvino, for example, testified that he only consented to renounce Christ and spit on the cross after he initially refused, and was then forcefully imprisoned for eight days and fed a diet of bread and water.[16]

Apparently many Knights were not even informed why they were being forced into their heretical vows. Only the upper echelon of the Order was privy to this information. States Eliphas Levi:

"These tendencies (the rites and initiations) were enveloped in profound secrecy and the Order made an outward profession of the most perfect orthodoxy. The Chiefs alone knew whither they were going; the rest followed unsuspectingly."[17]

The Head Called Baphomet

Thus, it appears that most or all the Templar allegations were based on some measure of fact. This includes the worship of an idolized head called Baphomet, which the Knights commonly referred to as the "Savior and Maker of the Order."[18] Some Knights confessed to having seen Baphomet, while others simply professed to having received at their initiations sacred "Little Cords" that had been bound around the head, thus eternally connecting them to Baphomet. Since only 8 of the 231 Knights interviewed by the Papal Commission professed to have had any direct contact with Baphomet, and of these most were of the upper echelon of the Order, it appears that interaction with and knowledge of Baphomet was reserved principally for the Grand Dignitaries and the Templar hierarchy.

The first mention of Baphomet during a Templar testimony came from Raynier de Larchant, who was interviewed by the Inquisition on October 20, 1307, just one week after the Orders' mass arrest. Larchant was apparently not one of the Templar chieftains because although he had seen the head, he appeared to be ignorant as to what it truly represented.

Brother Raynier: I was received at Beavais-en-Gatinais (the diocese of Sens) by Brother Jean du Tour, who was Treasurer of the Temple at the time: about twenty-six years ago…

Inquisitor: Have you seen the head that the brothers worshiped at the chapters-general, according to what has been said?

Brother Raynier: Yes, a dozen times, at the chapters. In particular at Paris, the Tuesday last St. Peter and St. Paul (a holiday dedicated to the two Apostles).

Inquisitor: What was it like?

Brother Raynier: It was a head, with a beard. They worshipped it, and kissed it and called it their Savior.

Inquisitor: Where is it?

Brother Raynier: I don't know anything about that; I don't know where they keep it. I have the impression that it's the Grand Master, or whoever presides at the chapter, who keeps it in his possession…

When one of the Grand Dignitaries was interviewed about Baphomet, it quickly became clear that he, and perhaps the other Dignitaries, knew much more about the head than Raynier did. His damning testimony implicated the Grand Dignitary Hughes de Peraud, the second-in-command under Jacques de Molay, as one of the Templars in charge of Baphomet.

Inquisitor: Now tell us about the head.

Brother Raoul: Well, this head, I've seen it at seven chapters held by Brother Hugues de Pairaud and others.

Inquisitor: What did one do to worship it?

Brother Raoul: Well, it's like this: it was presented, and everyone threw himself on the ground, pushed back his cowl, and worshipped it.

Inquisitor: What was its face like?

Brother Raoul: Terrible! It seemed to me that it was the face of a demon, of an evil spirit. Every time I saw it I was filled with such terror that I could hardly look at it, trembling in all my members.

Another Knight whose testimony firmly linked Hughes de Peraud with Baphomet was Stephon de Troyes. Stephon had been initiated into the Order by Hughes and given a shirt and a "Little Cord" that had been wound around Baphomet. Stephon maintained that Baphomet was a human head that was annually taken by the Knights in a grand procession and then laid upon a sacred altar for all to see. He claimed that the head was "very pale and discolored, with a grizzled beard like a Templar's," but that it had been made regal in appearance by having its neck covered with gold, silver, and precious stones."[19] "

Hughes de Peraud was eventually called before the tribunal to give his own account of Baphomet. Although his testimony is short, he does confirm his connection with the head.

Inquisitor: And this human head, of which there was some question in our inquiry?

Brother Hughes: Well, yes. I have seen it, held it, and handled it, during a chapter meeting at Montpellier, and I worshipped it like all the brothers present. But it was only with my mouth, and in pretense; not with my heart. As for the other brothers, I don't know if they worshipped it from the bottom of their hearts.

Inquisitor: Where is it now?

Brother Hughes: I left it with Brother Pierre Alemandin, Preceptor of the Temple at Montpellier, but I don't know if the King's men have found it. This head had four feet, two in front, and two in back…

Hughes' testimony thus added features to Baphomet not previously alluded to in other testimonies. Other Knights that followed Hughes were equally forthcoming, claiming that the head possessed a reddish color and a "fierce-looking face and beard." For some it had two faces, one in the front and one in back. Such unusual features might lead one to conclude that the head was not real; but that was certainly not the conclusion of Guillame de Paradin, one of the first historians to collate and study the Templar depositions. After pouring over hundreds of Templar confessions, Paradin concluded that Baphomet was definitely human shaped and possessed "carbuncles" for eyes and "the skin of a human body. " The head was human and mummified, a conclusion corroborated by a very old Templar document called *The Chronicles of St. Denis,* which describes the head as "..an old piece of skin, as though all embalmed and like polished cloth."

The Head of John the Baptist

If Baphomet was the mummified head of a man, then that man must have been very dear and powerful in the estimation of the Templars since the Knights honored him as the Maker and Savior of the Order. Some historians have conjectured the head must have belonged to Hughes de Payens, the first Templar Grand Master. However, nowhere in Templar literature is Hughes referred to as the Knights' Savior. Nor does it appear that the revered head once belonged to Jesus Christ, since numerous Knights confessed to having renounced the Messiah as their Savior during their inductions into the Order. The most likely owner of the head was, therefore, John the Baptist, who is the only other physical Master honored by the Templars to have merited the distinction of "Savior." John was also the "Maker" of the Templars by being the Father of Gnosticism and patron of both the Church of John and the Priory of Sion, the organizations that the Knights had emerged out of.

So the question remains: could the head of John the Baptist have somehow come into the possession of the Knights Templar? We know that following John's decapitation at the hands of King Herod, the Baptist's head could not have been buried with the rest of his body because many writers during the centuries that followed claimed to have seen it or heard of its whereabouts. According to some authoritative Middle Eastern writers, King Herod transported the head to the city of Damascus in order to convince the Romans that John was indeed dead. Later, in 330 A.D., the Roman Emperor Theodosius enclosed the head within a cathedral in Damascus that he dedicated to John the Baptist, and in 636 A.D. this cathedral was converted into a mosque. The current Islamic worshippers of the Damascus mosque claim that the head is still there. An alternate Middle Eastern accounting of John's head maintains that it was first interred in

Eliseus in Samaria and later given over to St. Athanasius, who hid it in a wall of his church. The head eventually found its final resting place in a church built over the ancient temple of Serapis in Alexandria, Egypt.

Additional meritorious accounts of John's head maintain that it ended up in Constantinople. Of these accounts, one asserts that the head was first taken by St. Luke to Antioch or Ceasarea and then carried by Christian worshippers to Constantinople, while a second account based on records preserved by the Greek Orthodox Church maintains that the head found its way to Constantinople after first being kept by Herod and then residing for a time in the city of Emmesia in Phoenicia. In order to commemorate the capricious journey of John's head, the Greek Orthodox Church currently observes two important festivals each year. On February 24 the Church faithful come together to honor the day when the head was discovered by two monks in the home of King Herod and then taken to Emmesia. And later, on May 25, the Christians celebrate the day in 823 A.D. when John's head was taken to Constantinople.

The Baptist's head was eventually discovered by the Knights Templars in Constantinople during the Fourth Crusade, which began as a misguided campaign instigated by avaricious Venetian traders seeking to plunder the treasures of the world's richest city. Robert de Clari, one of the Crusaders who plundered Constantinople's Boukoleon Palace, left behind a documented account of finding John's head there:

"When the city was captured...they found in the palaces riches more than a great deal. Within this palace (Boukoleon) …there were fully five hundred halls, all connected with one another and all made with gold mosaic. And in it were fully thirty chapels, great and small, and there was one of them which was the Holy Chapel, which was so rich and noble that there was not a hinge nor a band nor any other part such as is usually made of iron that was not all of silver, and there was no column that was not jasper or porphyry or some other precious stone. And the pavement of this chapel was of a white marble so smooth and dear that it seemed to be of crystal, and this chapel was so rich and so noble that no one could ever tell you its beauty and nobility. Within this chapel were found many rich relics. One found there two pieces of the True Cross, as large as the leg of a man and as long as half a *toise*, and one found there also the iron of the lance with which Our Lord had his side pierced and two of the nails which were driven through His hands and feet, and one found there in a crystal phial quite a little of his blood, and one found there the tunic which He wore and which was taken from Him when they led Him to the Mount of Calvary, and one found there the blessed crown with which He was crowned, which was made of reeds with thorns as sharp as points of daggers. And one found there a part of the robe of Our Lady, and **the head of my lord St. John the Baptist** (bolded by the author) and so many rich relics that I could not recount them to you or tell you…"

De Clari goes on to say that one of the "many rich relics" discovered in the chapel was a golden vessel hanging from the ceiling of the Holy Chapel. Within the vessel was a sacred cloth, which today is known as the Shroud of Turin. This holy relic also became a prized possession of the Templars.

Following the discovery of John the Baptist's head in the Boukoleon Palace, history throws up a smokescreen as to where it was taken. Complicating this search are numerous allusions to the Baptist's skull or pieces of it that appear simultaneously in cathedrals all over Europe. One account holds that after leaving Constantinople the head was taken to the city of Amiens, France, by the Crusader Walter de Sarton, while an alternate record claims that only half the head went to Amiens while a second portion was taken to the Church of St. Sylvester in Rome.[20] Templar scholar Guy Jordan currently claims that the Amiens' head, which is today embellished with precious and semiprecious stones and annually displayed to the public on June 24, John the Baptist's Day, is "nothing less than "la vrai tete Baphometique Templiere – the true Baphometic head of the Templars."[21]

Other cathedrals and churches that claim to possess John's head, or a portion of it, as one of their holy relics include Saint Mark's Cathedral of Venice, Sainte Chapelle in Paris, Sainte Chaumont in Lyonnais, and the Abbey of Tyron, France. It is thus very difficult to ascertain which, if any, of these religious institutions might be the true owner of John's head. Perhaps none of them. In 1839, a list of European holy relics circulated around the continent maintaining that two complete heads of John were then in existence, along with at least two complete bodies of Mary Magdalene. This news was probably not received with great consternation since at the time 28 thumbs and fingers of Saint Dominic and 150 nails of the True Cross had been accounted for. The famous relic collector Henry VI of England was known to have gathered so many teeth of the female Saint Apollonia that historian Thomas Fuller was later compelled to observe: "Were her stomach proportionate to her teeth, a country could scarcely afford her a meal."[22]

It thus appears that because of the existence of the endemic spread of the Cult of Relics in Europe during the Middle Ages it would now be nearly impossible to accurately determine the final resting place of any saint's body parts or bones, including John the Baptist's. However, many contemporary Templars contend that John's head eventually ended up in one of their commandaries and that it is indeed the relic referred to in the Knights' testimonies as Baphomet.

The Templar Savior and Embodiment of Kundalini

It stands to reason that if John's head did indeed end up on a Templar high altar, then the salutations of the Knights, such as "Savior" and the "Maker of the Order," were terms of endearment directed at the Baptist. Such salutations are easily accounted for considering John's premier position in the Johannite lineage. But there are other salutations that were reputedly directed at Baphomet that are ostensibly more difficult to reconcile, such as *"Yah Allah"* or *"Yallah,"* an exhortation many historians have speculated to be none other than the Saracen cry of "Hail Allah." But this Saracen cry could not have been directed at Baphomet as believed because Allah has never been worshipped in the form of an idol. It is thus more probable that the Templar cry of *Yallah* was a version of *Jahla Sidna,* a name meaning "O God, our Lord," that the German researcher Baron Von Hammer-Purgstall found incorporated into alchemical icons discovered in some Templar commanderies in France. *Jahla,* which is pronounced Yahlah or Yahya, is obviously related to *Yahya,* the Mandean name for John the Baptist. Thus, *Yallah* could have been *Yahya*, meaning John, and *Jahla Sidna* was perhaps synonymous with *Yahya Sidna,* a salutation denoting "Yahya, our Lord," or "John, our Savior."

The name *Jahla Sidna* was discovered by Hammer-Purgstall engraved upon the lid of a ritual coffer that was found among Templar sacred relics in the Orders' Burgundy Temple. The symbols on the lid with the inscription *Jahla Sidna* included a solitary head, which was probably that of John the Baptist, as well as Gnostic motifs identical to those ascribed to the first century A.D. In the center of the lid was an alchemical figure with the head and beard of a man and the breasts and genitals of a woman. In each hand this androgynous figure grasped a pole surmounted with one of the polar opposite symbols of the Sun and Moon, thus making the image a classical motif related to the alchemical union of the opposites. Taken as a whole, the coffer lid may have revealed secret links between Baphomet, the head of John the Baptist, and the transformative process of alchemy.

Besides the Gnostic icons adorning the Templar relics, Hammer-Purgstall looked elsewhere to discover evidence linking John the Baptist to Baphomet. In his book *The Mystery of Baphomet Revealed*, for example, Hammer-Purgstall reveals that he found the sought-after evidence incorporated within the name Baphomet, which is a version of the Greek Baphe Meteos, meaning "Baptism of Wisdom."

The study of the name Baphomet was later taken up by author Hugh Schonfield, who asserts in *The Essene Odyssey* that when Baphomet is translated via the Atbash Cipher, a code used by the ancient Gnostics and Essenes, it becomes "Sophia," meaning "wisdom." Sophia is the Gnostic name for both the power and wisdom of the Holy Spirit or Kundalini, which is the power that John the Baptist incarnated. Baphomet is, therefore, a name for John.

While studying the name Baphomet, some Sufi and Arab researchers have also alluded to its Gnostic overtones. They maintain that Baphomet is an evolution of the Arabic *abufihamat*, meaning "father of wisdom." Their perspective, interestingly enough, affiliates Baphomet with Murrugan, the *Jnana Pandita,* the Lord of Wisdom. Murrugan, whose essence incarnated as John the Baptist, is an embodiment of Kundalini and the father of Gnosticism in the East.

If Baphomet is indeed synonymous with the Kundalini, then it should have been represented by forms other than just a human head. It was, at least according to the 19th century Freemason and self-proclaimed Templar descendant Eliphas Levi, who popularized an ancient Templar image of Baphomet that the Knights had supposedly made into a gargoyle and placed high upon a cathedral in Paris, France. The foundation of the Templars' image, states Levi, was the black Goat of Mendes, the Egyptian symbol of the Philosophers Stone, to which the Knights attached the breasts of a female and the phallus of a male. The image was a classic alchemical motif that betrayed a profound knowledge of the transformative Kundalini.

The alchemical nature and inherent androgyny of Baphomet was also emphasized by von Hammer-Purgstall, who found evidence of it after examining 24 engravings that were apparently symbolic representations of the Knights' idolized head. Some of the etched heads he studied possessed faces in both their fronts and backs, thus making them reminiscent of the two-faced Roman god of wisdom Janus and androgynous manifestations of the Kundalini. Janus, who was the consort of Diana, was a manifestation of Lucifer and a southern European personification of the Green Man and Kundalini.

Stemming from Hammer-Purgstall's research and the Templar testimonies, it appears that the Knights worshipped the Baptist's dried-up, grizzled head while associating it with the creative and transformative power of the Holy Spirit or Kundalini. The power of the head, stated the Knights at their trail, was so full of the Holy Spirit that it "made the trees to flourish and the earth to germinate." The head's healing and transformative power was recognized in Constantinople even before the Templars discovered it there. In fact, states Dr. Karl Simrock in *The Parzival of Wolfram von Eschenbach,* the head had kept an eleventh century emperor of the Eastern Roman Empire vibrant and alive through daily passes near his body. Thus, John's Holy Spirit power had remained intact within his body even after his murder, a phenomenon that is well understood and documented in the East, where saints are traditionally entombed rather than cremated so that their residual Kundalini power can continue to bless and uplift the world long after their deaths.

The Holy Spirit power emanating from Baphomet would have given the head powerful alchemical properties. This would explain why John's head was present during the ceremonies and Templar initiations reserved for the Order's hierarchy. Perhaps only the most advanced Templars were ready for the rapid-fire transformation that followed the descent of the "dove" (the symbol of John's power) or Holy Spirit upon them.

But even those Templars that did not come into direct contact with John the Baptist's head were able to benefit from the Baptist's power via their "Little Cords." These were cords that had been wound around Baphomet to saturate them with the Holy Spirit power of the head and then presented to the Knights during their induction ceremonies.

John the Baptist and The Holy Shroud

An additional source of John the Baptist's Holy Spirit power could have flowed into the rites and initiations of the Templars through the Holy Shroud, another sacred relic the Knights are reputed to have acquired from Constantinople's Boukoleon Palace. Although popularly regarded as the cloth that covered the body of Jesus after he was taken down from the cross, the Holy Shroud may instead have been the funerary wrap of John the Baptist, especially considering that the telling human image upon it depicts a person with his head severed from the rest of his body. The man in the Shroud's image is also apparently wearing a myrtle wreath and a *Padan,* a rectangular cloth of the Mandeans, which are traditional accouterments placed upon a deceased Mandean priest for his burial rite. Such accoutrements would, of course, have been absolutely essential for John, a Nasurai priest, but may not have suited Jesus, who had at the time of his death had strayed far from the Mandean fold.

John's Head is *the* Holy Grail of the Templars

If John's head was the principal power object used within Templar initiation ceremonies, could it have been not *a* Grail, but *the* Holy Grail of the Knights? Certain Grail legends, such as *Peredur*, where the Holy Grail is synonymous with a severed head, indicate that it must have been at least considered one of the Knights' most valuable Grail manifestations. The Grail in *Peredur*, which is brought by the Grail bearer to the presence of the Fisher King, is a platter upon which is "…a man's head…and blood in profusion around the head."[23]

Although some historians have equated the severed head in *Peredur* with the Welsh deity Bran the Blessed, there is no doubt that the Welsh version of the Grail legend was influenced by renditions of the Grail myth that had migrated to Britain from mainland Europe. And the fact that the head in *Peredur* belongs to *a cousin* of Peredur, the future Fisher King, indicates that this head may be related to the legend of the head of John, who was the cousin of Jesus, the future "King of the Jews."

Severed heads serving as manifestations of the Holy Grail can also be found in the Grail renditions known as *Perlesvaus* and the *First Continuation. Perlesvaus*, which is believed to have been authored by an anonymous Templar

Knight, has two Grail maidens presenting three versions of the Holy Grail to the Fisher King, including a chalice, a Holy Lance, and a severed head dripping with blood. Later in *Perlesvaus,* more heads appears as a Grail maiden leads a cart containing the heads of 150 knights that have been sealed in jeweled boxes of gold, silver and lead and thus given the honor of Holy Grails. One can also find an alchemical association with the *Perlesvaus* heads. In one scene, Percival is instructed to collect and bind together the severed heads of a king and queen, which is an obvious reference to the male and female principles and their unification during the process of alchemy.

Perhaps the best evidence we have that the Templars regarded Baphomet as *the* Holy Grail is found within the initiation ritual of the Knights Templar degree in York Rite Freemasonry. During this esoteric degree, which is believed to have been anciently observed by the Knights Templar themselves, the initiate pledges loyalty to the order while toasting John the Baptist and drinking sacramental wine *out of a human skull.*

L'Apparition of Gustave Moreau.
Salome and the Radiant Head of John the Baptist.

Eliphas Levi's Baphomet.

The Templar's Baphomet. From a Paris cathedral.

The Androgynous Alchemical Man of the Templars.

The torture of a Templar Knight.

Templars being burned alive.

11

Rosslyn Chapel: The Home of John

Legends imply that when the Knights Templar were summarily arrested in 1307 many or most of the Knights fled from France with an assortment of the Order's sacred relics and priceless scrolls. Since King Philip of France had ordered the arrest of the Templars two weeks before the fateful day of October 13th, the Order's efficient intelligence network in Europe would have given the Knights ample time to prepare for their ensuing destiny, thereby supporting them in drawing up a plan of escape. But if the Templars fled, where did they go? What happened to the Templar treasures, including the head of John the Baptist? These questions and others have, for hundreds of years, haunted Templar researchers and ultimately led them to Rosslyn Chapel, a small chapel in Scotland, the country many of the Knights are known to have fled to after leaving France. According to many contemporary Templar scholars, Rosslyn Chapel, which currently exists about 20 miles south of Edinburgh, might possibly have become home to not only the head of John but a variety of Holy Grail manifestations, including the Cup of Christ and possibly even the Ark of the Covenant. The Chapel may have, in fact, been built to serve as the last bastion of Templar glory.

Escape from France

What made the Templar escape possible from France was the Order's formidable fleet of merchant and warships it had produced over a one hundred year period, the majority of which were moored off the coast of France and along the Seine River. According to the testimony of one of the arrested Knights, Jean de Chalon, the Templars had anticipated their arrest by Philip the Fair and during the night of October 12th clandestinely marched a convoy of coaches full of Knights and holy treasures to their ships moored at the Orders' principal port of La Rochelle, which they had used for years to sail between France and their castles in Italy, England, Denmark, the Orkneys, Spain, Scotland, and throughout the Mediterranean Sea. Once the Templars had arrived at La Rochelle they and their treasure entered 18 galleys and silently set sail upon the open sea. Exactly where they went is open to debate, but most clues point to them having sailed to friendly countries which were not under the control or influence of either King Philip or Pope Clement V.

After steering their ships into the enveloping darkness during the night of October 12, some of the fleeing Knights may have sailed south to Malta, Spain and Portugal, where they became assimilated into Templar branches or sister organizations that had prospered within those neighboring countries. The Knights who found refuge in Portugal are reputed to have become assimilated into a Templar order that had thrived in the Portuguese city of Tomar since 1169. This Templar branch absorbed many of the fleeing Templar Knights, and under a mandate from the reigning monarch of Portugal, King Dinis, had its name changed to the Order of the Knights of Christ. As members of the Knights of Christ, the Templars were to later gain distinction for producing many world-renowned naval explorers, including Vasco de Gama and Christopher Columbus. Other Templars who disembarked at ports on the coast of Spain found refuge in the Knights of St. James of the Cross, a chivalrous order that had been founded in 1158 to protect pilgrims traveling to and from the shrine of Santiago de Compostela, an important religious center for the Templars. From Spain, many Knights traveled to the neighboring land of Aragon, a country where, in 1134 A.D., the Templars had inherited six castles from the estate of the deceased Aragonese king, Alfonso I, a monarch whose love for the Templars and the Holy Grail merited him the nickname of "Anfortas, the Grail King."[1] Additional Spanish orders that assimilated the fleeing French Knights include the Knights of Alcantara, the Knights of San Julian, and the Knights of Nuestra Senora de Montjoie.

Some Templar Knights may have sailed directly westward from France in the direction of the New World. This is not an unreasonable notion considering that Templar relics have been found in North America dating to the late 1300's. According to the testimony of Walter de Clifton, a later Grand Preceptor of the Scottish Templars who was captured by the English authorities, many Templars did indeed flee "across the sea" just before the Order's arrest.

Those refugee Knights that did not find safe haven in either Europe or the New World simply embraced the life of nomadic sailors. For years they crisscrossed the Mediterranean Sea while surviving on whatever bounty they could gather as roving pirates. Their plundering vessels flew flags painted with the ancient Templar skull and crossbones motif, an alchemical symbol of the early Knights that became nicknamed "Jolly Roger" after Roger II, a Templar king of Sicily.[2] Ever since that time, the Jolly Roger has been the symbol of pirates the world over.

The Knights Templar Arrive in Scotland

Those Templars who sailed north after fleeing France found refuge in Scotland, a country that had been a northern European headquarters of the Knights since 1128, when Hughes de Payen founded a temple for the Order at Balantrodoch, a place now known as Temple. Scotland was one of the most attractive of all countries to the refugee Templars because it was free of papal authority and ruled over by the sympathetic Robert the Bruce, a maverick king who had been excommunicated for slaying John Comyn, a close friend of the Pope's.

It has been conjectured that the Knights Templar first found refuge in Britain when they sailed into Solway Firth, a channel that is now in England but was then part of Scotland. Other researchers assert that the Knights first sailed around the north coast of Ireland before landing at Bruce's ancestral property in Argyll, Kintyre, and the Sound of Jura.[3] But regardless of where they first moored in Scotland, remaining Templar artifacts and tombs in the northern part of the country reveal that the Knights did indeed find the safe haven they sought. Templar tombs have been discovered on the Isle of Skye, and at Noss Head on Sinclair Bay, a Templar castle built in 13th century still stands. Currently known as Sinclair-Girnigoe Castle, the ancient edifice is believed to be a repository of some ancient Templar artifacts.

Following the first wave of Templar colonists from France, states a legend first published in *Freemasons' Quarterly Review*, (London, 1843) another small group of Knights were led to Scotland by the Templar Peter d' Aumont, a Grand Dignitary of France who had previously served as the Provincial Grand Master of Auvergne. This small group of Knights, which consisted of two "Commanders" and five Knights disguised as stone masons, landed on the Scottish Island of Mull, which was at the time the residence of several Templars, including the Grand Commander George Harris. The two Templar migrations joined forces on Mull and created a new Scottish order of Templar Knights, and then on St. John the Baptist's Day, 1313, Peter d'Aumont was made its first Grand Master. Later, in 1361, the Order was moved to its official Scottish headquarters in Aberdeen, from where it eventually spread throughout much of Europe. Supposedly it was Peter d'Aumont and the knights of his Order who eventually devised many of the degrees of Scottish Rite Freemasonry from the ancient Templar rites.

Once the various waves of French Templars had settled in Scotland, the Knights proceeded to create a long and inter-supportive relationship with their new country. Their support to the crown was first evident in 1303 when they joined the Scots in defeating 30,000 English soldiers. Then, in 1314, the Templars are reputed to have fought beside Robert the Bruce at the Battle of Bannockburn, thus playing a major role in the emancipation of Scotland. This later battle, which took place on June 24th, the feast day of John the Baptist, had all but officially been lost when reinforcements dressed as Templar Knights rode onto the battlefield and completely routed the English forces of King Edward II. Listed among the Templar reinforcements are four Knights of the St Clair or Sinclair Clan, as well as the Templar Knights Sir Adam Gordon and Alexander Seton. The Knights' timely assistance ensured that Scotland would not only achieve independence, but that the country would remain distant from papal authority and continue to be a safe haven for the Knights. The victory at Bannockburn is currently commemorated annually at Bannockburn by the Scottish Knights Templar on the sacred day of its occurrence, St. John the Baptist's Day.

Robert showed his appreciation for the Templars' participation at Bannockburn by granting a charter of lands to Walter de Clifton, the Grand Preceptor of the Templars in Scotland. His support was also evident when he founded a Masonic order for the Templar Knights, known as the Order of St. Andrew of the Thistle, "to which was afterwards added that of Heredom, for the sake of the Scottish Masons, who had made part of the thirty thousand men who had fought against an hundred thousand soldiers (during the Battle of Bannockburn)."[4] Robert the Bruce made himself Grand Master of the Order of St. Andrew and then saw to it that its initiations were based upon the rites of the early Templars.[5]

The Knights Templar in Scotland eventually crystallized into three or four Templar Knight organizations, including the Militi Templi Scotia, wherein they have quietly and often covertly conducted their activities for many centuries. Occasionally they have revealed their continued Scottish presence, such as in 1689 at the Battle of Killiecrankie, when one of the slain soldiers was identified as John Grahame, a.k.a. the Viscount of Dundee, a Grand Master Templar who wore on his person the Grand Cross of the Order of the Temple.[6]

The Templars and The Sinclairs

One reason for the Templars' continued survival in Scotland is the support it has received from the St. Clair or Sinclair Clan (the French and Scottish version of the same name), who are the builders Rosslyn Chapel. The St. Clairs, who are descended from the Merovingian and Norman kings, first came to Scotland from Normandy as part of the entourage of their cousin, William the Conqueror, and quickly achieved prominence as a royal family of wealthy Scottish landowners. Included in their vast holdings was the land in and around Roslin, which they received in 1057 as "life rent" from the Scottish King Malcolm III, who hoped at the time that the St. Clairs would reciprocate his generosity with their continued resistance against the English. A portion of Roslin was later selected to be the site of Rosslyn Chapel, while another section, known as Ballantrodoch, was bequeathed to Hughes de Payen and the Knights Templar as the site of the Order's first Scottish headquarters.

The intimate relationship between the St. Clair Clan and the Knights Templar began with one Henri de St. Clair, who fought in Palestine in 1096 alongside Godefroi de Boullion and the soldiers that eventually became the first Templar Knights. When the Knights Templar Order was made official soon afterwards in 1118, the Knights chose as their first Grand Master Hughes de Payen, a French noble who had married Catherine de St. Clair. Thus from its inception, the Templar Order was intimately allied with the St. Clairs and their bloodlines were permanently united.

When the Templars later moved into northern Europe, many St. Clairs distinguished themselves as Grand Masters and high-ranking knights of the Order. One St. Clair, Henry de St. Clair, both administered the Knights as their Grand Master and assisted King Robert the Bruce in ruling Scotland, while another distinguished St. Clair, William St. Clair, was appointed by Robert the Bruce to be hereditary Grand Master of the Crafts and Guilds and Orders of Scotland. This appointment, which ostensibly included rulership over both the various Templar Orders in Scotland as well as the country's lodges of Freemasonry, was passed down for many years through the St. Clair line until a later William St. Clair relinquished the post, believing that it should not be hereditary but earned through merit. His pious denial eventuated in his election as first Grand Master of the Scottish Grand Lodge of Speculative Masons, which was founded upon the ancient rites and teachings of the Knights Templar.

The tomb of one outstanding Templar Knight of the St. Clair family is currently located in Rosslyn Chapel and contains the inscription "WILLIAM DE St. CLAIR, KNIGHT TEMPLAR." This St. Clair Knight is renowned for having been part of a pilgrimage to the Holy Land to deposit the heart of Robert the Bruce at the Church of the Holy Sepulcher. Although he and his party never reached the Holy Land – they became sidetracked by a battle against the Moors in Spain - William de St. Clair showed such great valor as a warrior that when he lost his life in Spain the victorious Moslems allowed a fellow Templar, Sir William Keith, to escort his body back to Scotland for interment. Today, William's three-foot tombstone in Rosslyn Chapel is distinguished by the etchings of a sword and eight-pointed star within a circle, an esoteric symbol that relates to the Holy Grail Chalice and the Order of Templar Knights. A chalice on the tombstone of a knight such as William de St. Clair is, states *The Rosicrucians: Their Rites and Mysteries*, "a sign of the Knights Templar, of whom St. John the Evangelist was the Patron Saint."[7]

Prince Henry St. Clair

The St. Clairs reached the height of their power and prestige during the lifetime of arguably the greatest St. Clair, Henry St. Clair. During his distinguished lifetime Henry was honored with titles of nobility by the kings of Scotland, Norway, Denmark and Sweden. His nicknames, which included "Prince Henry" and "the Holy," referred both to the kingdom he ruled in northern Scotland, as well as to the lofty spiritual ideals that compelled him to participate in a crusade to the Holy Land in the tradition of his ancestors. When only 24 years of age, Prince Henry was granted the titles of both Jarl of Orkney and Lord of Shetland by King Hakon VI of Norway. He then built Kirkwall Castle of Orkney as a base for his semi-autonomous rule of northern Scotland.

Prince Henry fit the description of a Holy Grail King in the truest sense of the epithet. Besides inhabiting a "Grail Castle" in the Orkneys, Henry also wore a crown and possessed a version of the Holy Grail. And perhaps most importantly, through his St. Clair bloodline that extended back to the Merovingians, Prince Henry was aligned with the Neptunian Fisher King lineage.

Prince Henry became both a Grand Master Templar and the hereditary head of the Crafts and Guilds and Orders of Scotland. From his castle at Roslin and the nearby Templar headquarters at Balantrodoch, Henry applied himself to important affairs of the St. Clair lands, as well as to the activities of the Scottish Templars and Freemasons. Henry's most significant function as a Templar was, however, his exploration and colonization of the New World for the Order. His Neptunian calling to embrace the life of the sea was reflected in the coat of arms he designed for himself, which included a Neptunian sea-dragon surmounting the engrailed cross of the St. Clairs.

Prince Henry St. Clair set sail for America in 1398, nearly one hundred years before the pivotal voyage of Christopher Columbus. Accompanying him were more than two hundred sailors and passengers, including Templar Knights, farmers, craftsmen, and his captain, the Venetian Antonio Zeno. The scant information that remains regarding Prince Henry's journey and what led up to it comes from letters passed between Antonio Zeno and his brothers, Nicolo and Carlos that are currently preserved in the *Zeno Narrative*.

The *Zeno Narrative*, which refers to Prince Henry as Zichmni, claims that Henry was first introduced to the Zeno family in 1380 when Nicolo Zeno and his Venetian expedition crash-landed on the "Island of Frislanda," which is currently believed to be one of the Faroe Islands. The native occupants of island viciously attacked Nicolo and his party and would have certainly murdered them all had not Prince Henry intervened and saved them. Nicolo was, of course, deeply indebted to Prince Henry for his assistance and a close friendship ensued. For the rest his life Nicolo would live in or near Scotland while continuously remaining in the service of Prince Henry.

At one point during their long relationship, Prince Henry sent Nicolo on an expedition to Greenland in hopes of expanding his northern empire and creating a midway layover stop for his later voyages westward. While in Greenland, Nicolo discovered a preexisting Catholic monastery, as well as the vestiges of Norse settlements that had survived on the landmass for the previous two hundred years. He also spent many hours charting the coastline of Greenland. When Nicolo eventually returned to Scotland, he arrived fatally ill from the harsh cold he had endured in Greenland and died soon afterwards. Prince Henry then called upon Nicolo's brother, Antonio, to help him conduct his further expeditions westward.

In the *Zeno Narrative*, Antonio writes to his brother Carlos about the events that led up to Prince Henry's voyage to North America. Apparently in Scotland both Antonio and Henry overheard an account regarding an expedition that had sailed to the New World *twenty-six years earlier* and had visited Estotiland (Nova Scotia) as well as some other America ports, including some in Mexico. Prince Henry immediately sought out and hired the sailor who had captained the earlier expedition, but his new crew chief died soon afterwards. It was thus left to Antonio to serve as both captain and navigator for the pan-Atlantic voyage, which he accomplished by memorizing some old Venetian maps, including charts drawn up by his brother Nicolo, which accurately revealed the islands of the northern Atlantic and coastline of the North America landmass.

Antonio plotted a course to North America via the Orkneys, the Shetlands, the Faroes, and a series of islands referred to in the *Zeno Narrative* as Ledovo, Ilofe, and Icari. The expedition encountered tumultuous seas along the way and Henry's fleet of 12 ships was nearly destroyed. But after approximately one month the party finally landed in Estotiland and docked their vessels at Guysborough Harbor in Chedabucto Bay. While commenting on his party's first moments in the New World, Antonio Zeno writes in the *Zeno Narrative* :

"...we brought our barks and our boats in to land, and we entered an excellent harbor, and we saw in the distance a great mountain that poured out smoke. .... there were great multitudes of people, half-wild and living in caves. These were very small of stature and very timid; for when they saw our people, they fled into their holes. .... When Zichmni (Prince Henry) heard this and noticed that the place had a wholesome and pure atmosphere, a fertile soil and good rivers and so many other attractions, he conceived the idea of staying there and founding a city."

Prince Henry immediately sent most of his fleet back to Scotland with Antonio Zeno while he remained in the land that would soon become known as

Nova Scotia, "New Scotland." With only a skeleton crew to assist him and two oar-powered boats, Henry worked tirelessly for the next two years to establish colonies in the northeastern territories of the New World. Some scholars claim that one of Henry's accomplishments during this time was the creation of a "Grail Castle" at the Cross on Cadbury Hill, which served as a temple for a Holy Grail chalice in his possession. Henry's mysterious chalice was later supposedly taken to Montreal, which was then known as Ville Marie, the City of Mary, by a secret society known as the Compagnie du Saint-Sacrement, and remains there still.[8]

During their first winter in Nova Scotia, Prince Henry and his crew lived among the Micmac Indians, who today remember Prince Henry in their legends as Kuloskap, the "White God" who arrived among them in a granite boat and then taught the tribe many things, including how to catch fish using nets. The Micmac, who have since received the Sword of Peace from the Sinclairs in commemoration of their alliance with Prince Henry, remember Kuloskap in this poem:

"Kuloskap was the first,
First and greatest,
To come into our land -
Into Nova Scotia, Canada,
Into Maine, into Wabanaki,
The land of sunrise, or Light.
Thus it was Kuloskap the Great
Made man: He took his arrows
And shot a tree, the ash,
Known as the basket-tree.
From the hole made by the arrow
Came forth new forms, and these
Were the first of human kind.
And so the Lord gave them a name
Meaning "those born from trees".
Kuloskap the Lord of Light
Made all the animals.
First he created
All of giant size;
Such was the beginning."

Besides the Micmac records, other evidence of Henry's visit to Nova Scotia currently exist as a Venetian cannon from the 14th century and the famous "Money Pit." The 14th century Venetian cannon was discovered in 1849 in the Nova Scotia port of Louisbourg, which is one of the colonies founded by Henry. It is identical to one now on display in the Naval Historical Museum in

Venice and believed to have once been owned and used by Carlo Zeno, the "Dragon of Venice," in the Battle of Chioggia, before being brought over to the New World by his brother Antonio. The "Money Pit," which exists on Oak Island, a small island in Mahone Bay that is just a short jaunt from where Henry's expedition landed on Nova Scotia, has been found to contain numerous metallic artifacts, including an ancient watch chain, as well as some coconut fiber that has been dated to the 14th century.

When Henry left Nova Scotia, he and his party traveled to Massachusetts and explored the Merrimack River up to Stony Brook. They then moved south through virgin forestland to the area of Westford, where Henry's "right-hand" man, Sir James Gunn, died unexpectedly while exploring the surrounding woods. Sir Gunn was buried in Westford near the area of Prospect Hill and a stone was set upon his grave with an etching containing the Gunn family insignia, a ship, and a Scottish Templar carrying his sword and shield. Another granite stone was since been erected near Sir Gunn's tomb by Allister MacDougall, the Town Historian, with the following inscription:

"Prince Henry, First Sinclair of Orkney, born in Scotland, made a voyage of discovery to North America in 1398. After wintering in Nova Scotia he sailed to Massachusetts and on an inland expedition in 1399 to Prospect Hill to view the surrounding countryside, one of the party died. The punch-hole armorial effigy that adorns this ledge is a Memorial to this Knight."

After completing their tour of Massachusetts, Prince Henry and his crew visited the territory around Newport, Rhode Island, where they built a stone tower to serve as a lookout station. Currently known as the Newport Tower, this enigmatic circular, stone edifice was recently studied by the late James Whittal, who came to the conclusion that it is more than probable it was built in the early 1400s by Prince Henry's expedition. Whittal found the architecture uniquely different from any other New England building. Its octagonal and circular design mirrored the layered slate buildings of Prince Henry's Orkneys, and its base measurement, the Scottish "ell" of 37 inches, was consistent with the medieval buildings constructed all over Scotland. After Whittal completed his work on the Newport Tower, the structure was studied by other scholars who dated the structure to between 1150 and 1400.[9]

Prince Henry left the New World more than two years after his arrival and returned to Scotland. His triumphant return to his native country was marred by his sudden death, either by natural causes or at the hands of an English raiding party. The memory of Henry's expedition lives on, however, in the *Zeno Narrative*, as well as within Rosslyn Chapel, which contains images of the New World plants that Prince Henry returned home with: aloe, cactus and corn. Henry's voyage is also commemorated by a plaque in the crypt below Rosslyn Chapel, which has a motif containing the St. Clair or Sinclair "Engrailed Cross" situated directly under the image of a twin-sailed ship identical to the one inscribed upon Sir Gunn's shield on his Westford tombstone.[10]

William Sinclair and Rosslyn Chapel

Prince Henry's grandson, Sir William Sinclair, designed Rosslyn Chapel to be both a monument to Prince Henry's journey to the New World, as well as a reliquary within which could be interred the mystic esoteric symbols and priceless artifacts and scrolls that the Knights Templar had brought back from the Holy Land. Sir William began the construction of his chapel in 1446, just six months after a fatal fire had broken out in nearby Roslin Castle, which had for many years served as a warehouse for five cases of priceless artifacts brought from Palestine by Hughes de Payen during his early visits to Scotland. Thus it appears certain that Rosslyn was built as a new vault to protect these five cases of Templar treasure.

William, who was not only a Scottish Knights Templar but also an initiated knight of The Knights of Santiago and a member of the Order of the Golden Fleece, also wanted Rosslyn Chapel to a monument to the Holy Grail. So he adorned the Chapel with icons associated with the Holy Grail Mysteries, and he designed the structure so that it would generate the Holy Spirit power ascribed to a true manifestation of the Holy Grail. According to Niven Sinclair, one of the current elders of Scotland's Clan Sinclair, William succeeded in creating the alchemical power he sought, which was then used for both healings and initiations.

The work on Sir William's Rosslyn Chapel, which also came to be known as the Collegiate Chapel of St. Matthew, was completed in 1486, forty years after the first corner stone was laid. 1446 may have, at least in part, been chosen as the starting point for Rosslyn's creation because during that year on St. John the Baptist's Day a special planetary alignment occurred involving the planets Mars, Saturn and Jupiter, as well as three stars considered sacred in Freemasonry, Spica, Regulus, and Asellus Austrailus.[11]

Sir William sent out a clarion call to the most skilled master masons in Europe for assistance in constructing Rosslyn Chapel. In order to house all the visiting masons that he thus summoned, Sir William built homes for them in the nearby town of Roslin, which had, since the 2nd century A.D., marked the end of the Romans' Great North Road.[12] Sir William did not spare any expense where Roslin and Rosslyn Chapel were concerned, and he could afford to pay his masons top dollar for their work. Since the arrival of the Templars from France, the St. Clair treasury, which apparently benifited greatly by the refugee Knights, had overflowed with Templar wealth. While commenting on the Sinclairs' vast wealth, Tim Wallace-Murphy in *Rosslyn, Guardian Of The Secrets Of The Holy Grail* states: "the Lords of St. Clair of Roslin were escorted by 400 mounted knights when they rode abroad, their ladies were attended by 80 ladies-in-waiting, and they were reputed to have dined off gold plate."[13]

The secret treasure of the Knights Templar has always been interwoven into the history of both the Sinclairs and Rosslyn Chapel, and it is this treasure that endows them with their persistent air of mystery. After seeing some of the Chapel's treasure firsthand during her tour of Rosslyn, Mary of Guise, the Queen Regent of Scotland, was compelled to make her now famous remark that there was "a great secret within Rosslyn." And it was perhaps the knowledge of this treasure that prevented Freemason Lord Cromwell from destroying the chapel during the English Civil War, even though he had already decimated nearby Roslin Castle and counted the St Clairs among his most virulent opponents. According to the authors of *The Hiram Key*, the existence of a treasure in Rosslyn is not just a legend; in fact, its existence is even encoded into the structure of the building as the 8 columns strategically placed in the formation of a "Triple Tau," which according to Freemasonic interpretation denotes "A place where a precious thing is concealed."[14]

The treasure of Rosslyn has become synonymous with what the Knights Templar are rumored to have discovered in the Holy Land. This includes everything from the Ark of the Covenant, to the Cup of Christ, to the heads of both Jesus Christ and John the Baptist. Ancient texts and hidden scrolls have also long been designated part of the Templar wealth in Rosslyn. While commenting on these scrolls and the Templar mission to return with them from the Holy Land, French historian Gaetan Delaforge states in *The Templar Tradition in the Age of Aquarius*:

"The real task of the nine knights was to carry out research in the area (the Holy Land), in order to obtain certain relics and manuscripts which contain the essence of the secret traditions of Judaism and ancient Egypt, some of which probably went back to the days of Moses"[15]

Christopher Knight and Robert Lomas, the authors of *The Hiram Key* and researchers of Freemasonic history, believe that the Templars succeeded in their quest of discovering numerous ancient manuscripts in Palestine. Some of these scrolls, which were found while excavating the ruins of Herod's Temple, apparently revealed the lost history of Freemasonry and its connection to both the Knights Templars and the Jewish Essenes, while others included references to Jesus' bloodline and information regarding the family he sired with Mary Magdalene. One of the scrolls that the Templars seem to have discovered, the *Copper Scroll,* was recently brought to light as part of the *Dead Sea Scrolls* and shown to reveal the exact location of many relics that had been hidden by the Jewish priesthood in the Holy Land. Could the Templars have followed clues in the *Copper Scroll* and discovered the buried treasure encoded within? By all accounts, they did. Signs of Templar excavations have been found at the locations indicated by the scroll, but the treasured relics supposedly hidden at these remote places are gone!

One proven location of treasure in Rosslyn Chapel is its underground vault, which has been sealed up since the burial of William Sinclair's son, Earl William Sinclair, who was killed at the Battle of Dunbar after completing his father's temple. Modern investigators believe that they have located a number of relics in the subterranean crypt, including 20 deceased Templar Knights of the Sinclair Clan clothed in full armor. Bowls and human skulls have also been located in the crypt, and Niven Sinclair believes a Black Madonna that once graced the central altar of Rosslyn and been "sacred to both the gypsies and the Templars," will also be discovered there in the future. In the early years of Rosslyn's existence, Gypsy descendants of the Middle Eastern Gnostics who had a common ancestor with the Templars and Sinclairs in John the Baptist, were protected and supported by the Sinclair Clan and allowed to reside in Roslin Glen next to the Chapel.

The Apprentice Pillar and The Cup of Christ

Another Templar relic whose supposed existence in Rosslyn is currently given some merit is the Cup of Christ, the Holy Grail Chalice that the Apostles drank out of during the Last Supper and the vessel that Prince Henry may have once had in his possession. It is interesting to note that beginning with the first St. Clairs of Roslin, the family has been consistently associated with chalices, cups and Grails, a trend that began with William "the Seemly" St. Clair, who was bequeathed the St. Clair land in Roslin in 1057 while serving as the honored Cupbearer to Queen Margaret.

Since 1962, when an Edinburgh schoolteacher proclaimed that the Apprentice Pillar of Rosslyn Chapel contained within it the Cup of Christ, the ornate pillar has been under continual scrutiny because of its supposed treasure. Metal detectors have located a large metallic object inside the pillar that may be Christ's chalice, but a radar scan undertaken via the urging of the wife of the late author Trevor Ravenscroft was inconclusive. But even if a metal cup is eventually found in the pillar, can it be identified as the chalice that Jesus and the Apostles drank out of at the Last Supper? It is a known fact that the common household drinking vessels of Jesus' era were either made of wood or clay, but not metal.

The shape of the column and the carved symbols adorning the Apprentice Pillar have also been studied for clues regarding its potential indwelling chalice. The shape of the pillar appears to be that of an axis mundi or Heaven/Earth mediator, and may be a representation of the Norse Tree of Life, the Yggdrasil, thus making it a monument to the Norse heritage of the St. Clairs. The alchemical number of Heaven/Earth mediation, 8, is prominently manifest as the octagonal base of the pillar and its ring of 8 winged-serpents. A spiraling motif that connects the base to the top of the pillar appears to be symbolic of the spiraling serpentine life force that continuously moves between Heaven and Earth. And the top of the column, which is encircled with symbols describing the twelve signs of the Zodiac, appears to be an obvious representation of the upper heavens.

The Head of John the Baptist in Rosslyn Chapel

Author Keith Laidler recently outlined his theory that not only does the Apprentice Pillar hold a cup, it is also the site of a severed human head. In *The Head of God,* Laidler presents his assertion that the symbols lining the Apprentice Pillar collectively convey the message: "Here, beneath this column, lies the Head of God."[16] Although Laidler concludes that the head is the mummified head of Jesus Christ, it must be acknowledged that the head of John the Baptist is much more a part of Templar history than is Jesus', so if there is a head in Rosslyn Chapel it is probably that of the Baptist's. This notion becomes more probable in light of the fact that the Apprentice Pillar corresponds to Boaz, one of the two main pillars of Solomon's Temples. Boaz is associated with the position of the Sun at the summer solstice, the time traditionally associated with the holy day of John the Baptist.[17]

Could the venerated head of the Baptist be in Rosslyn Chapel today? Could it be in the area of the Apprentice Pillar? The carved head of the "apprentice," which looks down from above the west door of the Chapel, may give an answer. According to Rosslyn researcher Keith Laidler, the head was originally longhaired and bearded like John, and its owner was supposedly murdered.

But even if the mummified head of John the Baptist is not interred in Rosslyn Chapel, his head is manifest as the 103 Green Man heads that adorn the interior of the Chapel. Rosslyn's Green Man heads have been identified by scholars as those of the Celtic Green Man, who is synonymous with Green George or St. George. Since St. George is a name for the Arabic Khadir, the spirit that incarnated as John the Baptist, the Green Man heads in Rosslyn Chapel belong to John's spirit.

The Green Man heads of Rosslyn Chapel appear to be a synthesis of Green Men from both Europe and the Middle East. They resemble the Middle Eastern heads of Al-Khadir, whose Asian images appear to have been the model for the Green Man heads attached to the walls and ceilings of Chartres Cathedral, which was built under the guidance of the Knights Templar. Chartres, which possesses a distinctive Islamic architectural influence, is adorned with two sets of triple Green Man heads, one of which contains a head nearly identical in expression to a nearby image of John the Baptist, thus implying that John *is* the Green Man.[18] The trinity of heads at Chartres ostensibly represent the three powers of the life force wielded by the Green Man, creation, preservation, and destruction, and may be synonymous with the three black heads that once graced the shield of the first Templar Grand Master, Hughes de Payen.

Human skulls possibly venerated as those of the Green Man have recently been discovered in the crypt underneath Rosslyn Chapel. According to Ian Sinclair, two human skulls were recently discovered under the Chapel's floor, examined, and then sealed back up in the crypt. Both skulls had trepanation holes in locations that correspond to the horns emanating out of some Green Man heads. Could these skulls have been worshipped as manifestations of Baphomet? This appears probable in light of the fact that at least one confession extracted from the French Templars indicated that the venerated head of Baphomet possessed horns.[19] If these skulls were indeed meant to be replicas of Baphomet, then they must be recognized as both manifestations of the Green Man and signs of the presence of John the Baptist in Rosslyn Chapel.

In *The Spear of Destiny,* author Trevor Ravenscroft provides compelling evidence that Rosslyn Chapel and the surrounding area of Roslin has, for hundreds and perhaps thousands of years, been associated with a head. It has always been the location of the "head" that surmounts the "spine" of the continent of Europe.

The basis of Ravenscroft's theory is an ancient pilgrimage route through Europe that is punctuated with churches built over the continent's seven chakras, the power centers that line Europe's "spine." He reveals that Rosslyn Chapel is situated at the end of this pilgrimage route and corresponds to the European crown chakra, the uppermost chakra that lies within the continent's "head." Thus, from Ravenscroft's perspective, Rosslyn Chapel is the "head" of Europe and must therefore be considered a natural reliquary for the interment of a sacred head or heads.

The churches that dot Europe's ancient pilgrimage route are fully delineated by Ravenscroft's protégé Tim Wallace-Murphy in *Rosslyn, Guardian Of The Secrets Of The Holy Grail.* Wallace-Murphy maintains that the chakra points along the European spine were first utilized by the Celtic Druids, who built shrines and temples over them. Later in history, Catholic Churches and Cathedrals, such as Notre Dame in Paris and Chartres Cathedral, were erected upon the foundations of these Druidic "chakra" shrines, and the pagan mythology and rites that had become attached to each shrine for hundreds of years were summarily Christianized. But some traces of pagan and esoteric symbology have remained.

Following the construction of Rosslyn Chapel, thousands of Catholic pilgrims traveled from one "chakra" cathedral to the next along the European spine. They began their journey at Santiago de Compostella, the cathedral built over Europe's root chakra, which was dedicated to Jesus' brother James, whose skull is interred there. They then progressed to Toulose, Orleans, Chartres, Paris, Amiens, and finally to Rosslyn. Before leaving Santiago, they were given a symbolic scallop shell that they were instructed to keep with them throughout their ensuing pilgrimage. Like most scallop shells, these shells had a series of naturally occurring parallel lines on their backside that originated at a common point at the shells base, thus symbolically tracing the subtle energy lines that stream out of Europe's root chakra.

The purpose and meaning of the shells was irrefutably revealed to the pilgrims at their third stop, the Cathedral of Orleans, wherein they were greeted by a statue of John the Baptist holding a scallop shell in his right hand and bent over in a posture of baptizing. Following John's lead, the pilgrims filled their shells with holy water from the cathedral's fountain to baptize themselves and each other. Although this water was physical, it acted as a vehicle for John's Holy Spirit or "Water of Life."

It is interesting to note that Ravenscroft corresponds each European chakra to a ruling planet and symbol. To the Cathedral of Orleans he assigns the planet Venus, the planet of the Goddess and Holy Spirit, and the symbol of a knight. Apparently, the Holy Spirit presence was so strong at Orleans that initiations into knighthood occurred there under the etherial guidance of the Goddess Venus and John the Baptist. Such initiations were Johannite in nature, a point alluded to by Tim Wallace-Murphy, who maintained that the entire pilgrimage up the European spine was intimately connected to the "Johannite heresy."[20]

To complete his planetary schematic, Ravenscroft associates the planet Saturn and the symbol of a crown to Rosslyn Chapel. The crown is, or course, associated with kingship, and Saturn rules the "head" of all human civilization, i.e., all its governing and parliamentary bodies. Rosslyn Chapel is thus the abode of the etheric king of Europe.

Rosslyn's etheric king is King Saturn, who is synonymous with the spirit of the Green Man and John the Baptist. In Greek mythology, King Saturn, is said to have ruled the world during the Golden Age; so he is synonymous with Al-Khadir or Murrugan, the Green Man and first Fisher King. King Saturn's Golden Age comes alive in Rosslyn Chapel as the Garden of Eden motif that covers the interior of the structure. Every kind of vegetation is represented here, including cedar and date-palm trees, figs, pomegranates, olives, almonds, hazel, corn, chestnuts, apples and walnuts – in fact, every plant that is averred to have been cultivated in the famous Garden of Solomon is represented.[21] There are also an abundance of animals represented, including an elephant, a camel, a fox, and geese.

King Saturn manifests at Rosslyn Chapel as the Green Man, who can be found peaking through the Chapel's lush foliage and surveying all the various life forms. Saturn, in his manifestation as the fallen Fisher King, can also been seen as the inverted image of Lucifer/Azazzel attached to a wall of the Chapel, as well as the demonic Baphomet that decorates the outer north wall of the chapel. Thus, in Rosslyn Chapel, the past and the present come together in the various manifestations of the ubiquitous Green Man.

According to Niven Sinclair, by building Rosslyn Chapel William Sinclair hoped to revive the "pagan" religion of the Goddess tradition, which he believed was the true path of the Knights Templar. William referred to his "pagan" temple of Rosslyn as his "Chapel in the Woods," and, states Niven, "He even built seats into the Eastern wall of the Chapel so that worshippers could identify God and Nature." William represented the Goddess in Rosslyn with the five-pointed stars and the eight-petalled roses of Venus that adorn the roof of the Chapel, as well as with the striking Black Madonna that once graced the central altar. Niven maintains that Sir William would have spoken out against Christianity and how the Romans had "hijacked" religion and made it their own if he had not been concerned about being hanged for heresy. Instead, states Niven, he "wrote his book in stone."

In order to generate the presence of the Goddess and Green Man within Rosslyn Chapel, William Sinclair designed his temple so that it would capture the life force that flowed through it from the Earth's leyline grid. According to author Andrew Collins, the Sinclairs were experts in sacred geometry and geomancy, sciences that teach how to design physical structures so that they harmonize, capture, and amplify the natural currents of energy that flow under and upon the surface of the Earth. In order to harmonize with and capture the Earth's natural energy at Rosslyn, William Sinclair based the Chapel's dimensions on the Golden Mean, the proportion that determines the geometric spiral, which is synonymous with the path of the serpentine life force. It also appears that William was inspired to have the Chapel generate the presence of the Green Man through the use of the 7x2 pillars that line the interior of the structure. In Egyptian legend, Green Man Osiris is always represented by numbers that are a multiples of seven; and according to the Scottish Templar Robert Brydon, the number seven is also related to St. Matthew, one of Rosslyn's patron saints who may be a Christianized Green Man.[22] St. Matthew's day is September 21, the autumn equinox, a day that corresponds to the annual celebration of the Persian Mithra, a Green Man who was patron of the "pagan" temple upon whose foundations Rosslyn Chapel was built.

In order to adequately generate the presence of the Green Man, Rosslyn Chapel and the "pagan" temple that preceded it were situated upon the confluence of important ley lines that united it with sacred landmarks throughout Britain. One of its intersecting leys comes from the direction of Bore Stane Hill, where, according to Niven Sinclair, "five powerful ley-lines radiate." But apparently the life force moving into Rosslyn Chapel was blocked at some time in its storied history, perhaps intentionally. This was the conclusion of Niven Sinclair, who invited Professor Lin Yun, a master Feng Shui practitioner, to Rosslyn to measure the energy flow in the Chapel. Professor Yun was impressed by the "earth energy" moving within Rosslyn, saying that it was different from anyplace else he had investigated on Earth. Yun maintained that the Chapel was destined to be a Centre of World Peace, but this might not occur until an important change is made at Rosslyn. The professor found that the energy flowing into the temple from the nearby glen was obstructed by the east wall, and a full activation of the Chapel will necessitate tearing down the wall.

Even though the energy of Rosslyn may currently be blocked, it still generates the healing and alchemical power William intended it to, a truth that has been experienced by anyone who has undergone a healing or initiation within the Chapel. Rosslyn Chapel became a natural alchemical cauldron and initiation chamber for the union of the polarity when William incorporated into its design both the octagon and the Star of David. He also made the Chapel a place for the divine union of the male/female principles by investing it with the symbols of Jesus Christ and his consort Mary Magdalene. In doing so, states Niven Sinclair, William made the momentous union of two very important and powerful tribes of Israel, the Tribe of David and the Tribe of Benjamin.

The discovery of the Templar treasure in Rosslyn and the complete reactivation of the Chapel may be near. Its renewal corresponds with the current revival of the "pagan" or nature religion of the Goddess and Her Son, for whom the Chapel was originally built. This truth is conveyed in a prophecy alluded to by Wallace-Murphy that states that within Rosslyn is an "enormous treasure whose hiding place will not be revealed until the day when a trumpet blast will awaken from her long sleep a certain lady of the ancient house of St. Clair."[23] The ancient "lady of St. Clair" is the Goddess herself and the Sinclairs are Her ministers on Earth via their chapel known as Rosslyn.

The French Templar Port of LaRochelle

The Templar Jolly Roger

A Templar ship

Prince Henry St. Clair's Coat of Arms

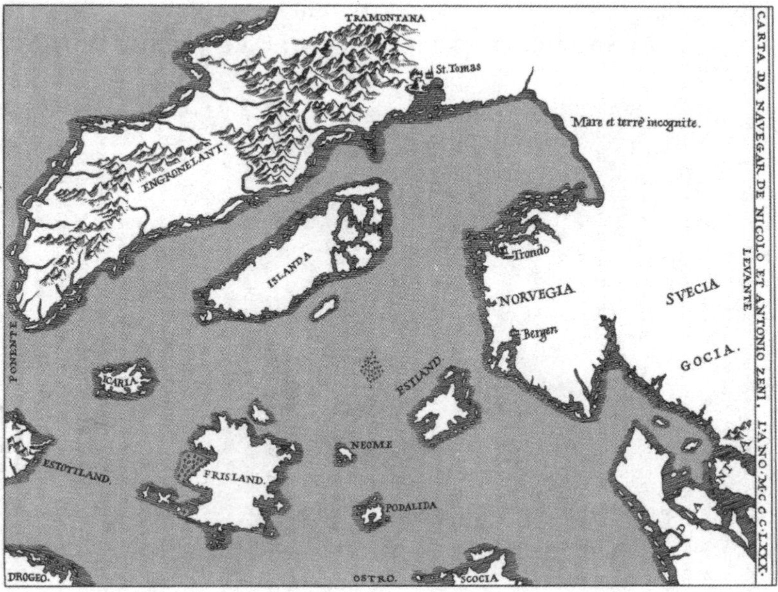

One of the Zeno Sea Charts

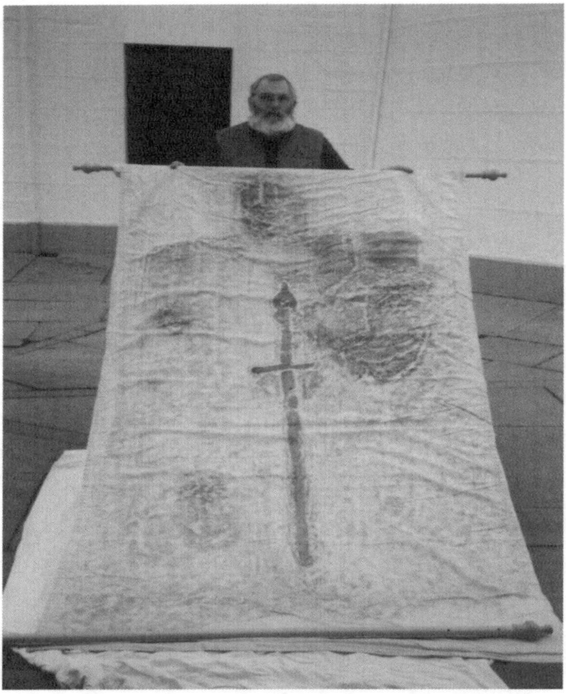

Ian Sinclair holds an image of the knight found on the gravemarker of Sir James Gunn in Westford, Massachusetts.

William St. Clair, the builder of Rosslyn Chapel.

Rosslyn Chapel

The west entrance into Rosslyn Chapel.

An angel holds the Engrailed Cross, symbol of the Sinclairs.

The tomb of William de St. Clair.

The Fallen Lucifer in Rosslyn Chapel.

The 8-pointed Star of the Goddess at Rosslyn Chapel

The Apprentice Pillar

Roslin Castle

12
The Lodges of St. John

"How many (Templars) survived Philip the Fair's onslaught? The answer must be most of them. Thousands. Retellings of the legend often give the impression that *all* members of the Order of the Temple died between 1307 and 1312, or were at least imprisoned for life. The truth is quite different…Ironically, there is no need to fabricate stories of dramatic escapes or local survivals to sustain continuation myths. There really were a lot of ex-Templars around: some repentant, some camouflaged, and some still proud of their own and the Order's past – like many old soldiers."[1]

The above passage is an accurate description of the state of the Knights Templar following the Order's mass arrest at the hands of King Philip the Fair of France and the circulation of Pope Clement V's papal bull *Vox in excelso,* which effectively dissolved most of the Templar commanderies in Europe. As previously stated, many Knights found a way to survive by fleeing to countries sympathetic to the Order, such as Portugal and Scotland, as well as by becoming assimilated into the Teutonic Knights, the Knights of Christ, and a multitude of neo-Templar orders. But many remained in France and somehow managed to survive in that inhospitable country by disappearing into the King's Guard or some of the protected French knighted orders, such as the Order of the Star, the Order of the Golden Fleece, and the Order of St. Michael.[2] Some Templars also went "underground" and became members of France's masonry guild. This was an expected move considering the Templar Order was at the time of its arrest overflowing with French masons aspiring to become Knights.[3] An ensuing transformation took place as an abundance of Templars became initiated French Freemasons and helped engender the founding of Freemasonic lodges in not only France, but throughout all continental Europe and Great Britain. The beginning of this turn of events is alluded to by the Freemasonic historian Albert Pike in *Morals and Dogma*:

"…the Sword and the Trowel (became) the insignia of the Templars, who…concealed themselves under the name of Brethren Masons. (This name,

Freres Macons in the French, adopted by way of secret reference to the Builders of the Second Temple, was corrupted in English into Freemasons.)"

The Templars had, of course, already established a long term relationship with the European masons during the Knights' nearly two hundred years of existence. The Templars, however, placed more emphasis on their relationship with the masons when it appeared eminent that their Order would require their lodges for camouflage in order to survive. With this in mind, Jacques de Molay, the last Templar Grand Master, applied himself while in his French prison cell to the task by securing a future for his Knights by formulating the rites and degrees of the branches of Freemasonry they would unite with and/or found. States Levi:

"The end of the drama is well known, and how Jacques de Molay and his fellows perished in the flames. But before his execution, the Chief of the doomed Order organized and instituted what afterwards came to be called the **Occult, Hermetic, or Scottish (Free) Masonry**."[4]

Following de Molay's death, Templar-influenced Freemasonic lodges rapidly spread throughout Scotland, England, France, Spain, and Germany. Like their parent Order of the Knights Templar, these lodges chose as their patron saints John the Baptist and St. John the Apostle instead of the more likely candidate, St. Thomas, who was the patron saint of builders and architecture. John the Baptist would have been chosen as their principal and perhaps sole patron saint, state Eliphas Levi and Albert Pike, a Scottish Rite Grand Master, but Freemasonry "did not want to arouse the suspicions of Rome…(by) proclaiming itself the child of the Kabbalah and Essenism together."[5]

Once a European network of the Lodges of Saint John was in place, the Masonic hierarchy proceeded with formulating a calendar and canon of rites that reflected those of their ancestral Templars. They divided up the Masonic year into two parts, with one half of the year beginning December 27, St. John the Apostle's Day, and the other half following June 24, St. John the Baptist's Day. These two important holidays, which corresponded to the summer and winter solstices, divided up the year into the progressively longer and shorter days. The Baptist, who acquired complete rulership over June 24 and the summer solstice when he replaced a pagan solar deity, thus became celebrated when the Sun's ascended to the highest point in the midday sky, an event that ostensibly represented John's preeminence in the Masonic tradition. June 24 acquired the most honored overtones when the Grand Lodge of England publicly revealed its previously hidden network of Freemasonic Lodges on St. John the Baptist's Day, 1717. On that day, the Grand Lodge elected its first Grand Master and officially became known to the world as the Ancient Order of Free and Accepted Masons.

The holidays of the two Johns were so important to fledgling Freemasonry that the most important councils and initiations were annually scheduled either during or around them. During their holidays, Masonic initiations were administered within lodges composed of floors laid out in a black and white "alchemical" motif, which reflected the two polar opposite Johns, as well as the Knight Templars' black and white flag, the *Beasant*, and the union of the universal polarity. The floor design of the Freemasonic lodges also featured the "Masonic Circle," which was a circle with two parallel lines attached to it representing the "staffs" of the two Johns. While standing upon or near this alchemical motif, a Freemasonic candidate for initiation acknowledged fealty to both his lodge and the two patron Johns while receiving induction into the three "Blue Degrees" of Freemasonry: Entered Apprentice, Fellow Craft, and Master Mason, which are collectively known as the "Blue Lodge" or as "St. John's Lodge." The new initiate also received the holy Word of St. John and learned the sacred history of the Craft, which maintained that "the first lodge was in the holy chapel of St. John."[6] And, finally, as a symbol of their connection to the early Templars, each Freemason received a ceremonial sheepskin apron modeled after the sheepskin wrap of the monkish Knights.[7]

Chevalier Ramsay and the Templar Revival

The Knights Templar remained hidden within their network of Freemasonic lodges for hundreds of years. Then, on December 26, 1736, a day chosen because it fell just before St. John the Apostle's Day, the Scottish Knight Michael Ramsay of the Order of St. Lazarus and a high ranking Freemason of the Grand Lodge of France, delivered his now famous oration to a forum of his brother Freemasons in Paris during which he revealed the debt that Freemasonry owed to the Knights Templar and its sister order of the Knights of St. John. Ramsay, who was born and raised near Kilwinning, the Scottish birthplace of Freemasonry, had learned firsthand the true history of his tradition. In Gould's annotated version of Ramsay's speech in *A Concise History of Freemasonry,* the Scottish Knight begins his oration thus:

"At the time of the Crusades in Palestine many princes, lords and citizens associated themselves...They agreed upon several ancient signs and symbolic words...Sometimes afterwards our order (the Knights Templar Order) formed an intimate union with the Knights of St. John of Jerusalem. From that time our Lodges (Freemasonry Lodges) took the name of the Lodges of St. John."[8]

The Knights of St. John of Jerusalem referred to by Ramsay have been mentioned earlier in this text, although their connection with the Templars has not been fully presented. Known popularly as the Knights of Malta or Knights Hospitallers, the Knights of St. John were connected to the Knights Templar and the Holy Grail Mysteries from their very inception, when they chose John the Baptist as their official patron saint. At that time, which was previous to the First Crusade, they were known as the Hospitallers of St. John and operated as a service organization funded by merchant mariners from Amalfi, Italy, who had obtained permission from the ruling Moslem Caliph Monstaser Billah to built a hospital for sick and injured Christian pilgrims visiting the Holy Land. Within their allocated plot of land in Jerusalem, the merchants from Amalfi constructed a hospital and a church in honor of St. John the Baptist over the spot where the angel Gabriel had once announced his conception to John's mother Elizabeth. Contiguous with the church was built a Benedictine Monastery dedicated to St. Mary.[9]

After many years of vigilant service in Jerusalem, the Hospitallers of St. John evolved into the Knights of St. John under the guidance of their second chief, Raymond du Puy, a French knight who proceeded to infuse the militant practices of French chivalry into the service organization. The Order of the Knights of St. John quickly prospered thereafter, and it subsequently acquired a multitude of forts and castles along the Asia Minor coast. From these fortresses the Knights of St. John were able to patrol the Holy Land while establishing a nearly autonomous kingdom of knights like their brother Templars.

In 1291 the Knights of St. John were forced to flee the Holy Land because of encroaching Moslems. Then, for nearly five hundred years they resided on a series of islands in the Mediterranean that included Cyprus, Rhodes, and Malta. On Rhodes, where they lived for 213 years, the Knights of St. John constructed huge fortresses and shrines, some of which still exist. And on Malta, where the Knights officially became the Knights of Malta, they resided for 268 years while helping to restore and preserve an abundance of megalithic temples that had existed on the island since their construction by ancient worshippers of the Universal Goddess. Eventually forced out of Malta by Napoleon, the Templars undertook a long and determined migration north, subsequently finding safe haven in St. Petersburg, Russia, where they existed under the protection of the Russian kings until the time of the Russian Revolution. Today, the Knights of Malta are again known as the Knights of St. John and have their headquarters in many of the major cities of Europe and America.

Since becoming a knighted order, the Knights of St. John have shared more with their brother Templars than just their connection to John the Baptist. Their initial attire consisted of the alchemical combination of black robes with a white version of the knighted Cross Pattee, which according to the early Freemason historian Elias Ashmole in *The History of the most Noble Order of the Garter: And the several Orders of Knighthood extant in Europe,* was the same cross that the Knights Templar initially adopted for their robes. Both knighted orders eventually adorned themselves with a red-colored Cross Pattee, which had become the symbol of John the Baptist when the Baptist absorbed the fiery solar tradition of the pagan deity of the summer solstice.

Besides its association with John the Baptist, the eight-pointed Cross Pattee of the Templars and Hospitallers also affiliated the knights with the ancient tradition of the Goddess, whose symbol in the Middle East for thousands of years had been an eight-pointed star. The eight-pointed Cross Pattee, which is an alchemical and Gnostic symbol associated with the Goddess Venus, the Patroness of Alchemy, was influential in the octagonal design of the Dome of the Rock, an image of which comprised the original seal of the Knights Templar. In reference to the alchemical and Gnostic import of the eight pointed cross or star, Ecclesia Tau Iohannes CXXVII, Primate and Patriarch of the Apostolic Johannite Church in Canada, states in a correspondence to the author:

"The eight-pointed star is the symbol of our spiritual ideal. The eight points represent the Western Esoteric system of Initiatory evolution and Self-Advancement. Seven are the steps, and the eighth begins again on a higher scale.

"It also contains within itself a great deal of Gnostic Symbolism as well. The Eight points representing the Seven Planetary Spheres and Sophia, which resides above them, as well as the eight Emanations from the True God, which were emanated in pairs…"

Like their Templar brothers, the Knights of St. John probably acquired their wisdom of alchemy from their neighboring Sufis and the Assassins in Outremer. It is a well-known fact that the Order had many interactions with the Islamic sects, even signing treaties of mutual support with them. One such pact, which was signed jointly by the Assassins and Knights of St. John in 1230 A.D., stipulated that the two orders would join together against their mutual nemesis, Bohemond IV, a Christian King of Antioch. But this was an abominable alliance in the eyes of the Antioch king's successor, Bohemond V, who wrote a letter to Pope Gregory IX disparaging the Knights' complicity with the heretical Assassins.

The Templars and Freemasons in Scotland

Following the Templar escape to Scotland in the early 1300's, the Knights Templar and the Knights of St. John were ostensibly united into one amalgamated order under the guidance of the Scottish King Robert the Bruce, who in 1314 founded the "Order of the Knights of St. John and the Temple" to protect and preserve his beloved Templar Knights. Uniting the two Johannite orders of Knights was a sensible move since the Templars' prodigious real estate holdings all over Europe had been summarily transferred to the Knights of St. John through the papal bull *Ad proviendan.* But a wedge of distrust still existed between the two orders of knights, and in Scotland the Templars' real estate continued to remain in Templar control.

The united Order of the Knights of St. John and the Temple was the engine that fueled many of the lodges of Freemasonry in Scotland. It drove the Freemasonry protocol emerging from Kilwinning, the Mother Lodge of all the Scottish lodges, and it supported the Grand Masters of Scotland, the Stewards. The Steward association with Scottish Freemasonry was alluded to by Ramsay, who stated:

"At the time of the last Crusades many lodges were already in Germany, Italy, Spain, France and thence in Scotland, because of the close alliance between the French and the Scotch. James, Lord Steward of Scotland, was the Grand Master of a Lodge established at Kilwinning, in the West of Scotland, 1236, shortly after the death of Alexander III., King of France, and one year before John Baliol mounted the throne."[10]

Knight Ramsay was an expert on Kilwinning history, having been born and raised in the nearby Scottish town of Ayr. From his countrymen Ramsay learned the legends of Kilwinning, beginning with the Mother Lodge's founding in 1107 A.D. and its continued relationship with the Knights Templar. He also learned that the Templar-Freemasonry marriage at Kilwinning had produced the three Masonry Blue Degrees of Entered Apprentice, Fellow Craft and Master Mason. The elements of these degrees had been acquired by the Templars in the Middle East from the Johannites, the Jewish Gnostics, and the Sufis. According to Idries Shaw in *The Sufis*, an important influence on the Templars was the Al-bana, an order of Moslem Freemasons in the Middle East that they studied directly under.

The Templars also assisted in the creation of the many higher degrees that eventually evolved in Freemasonry. In order to accommodate these higher degrees, two national Freemasonic orders, one in Scotland and one in England, were founded. The York Rite of England instituted 10 higher degrees and the Scottish Rite of Scotland added 30 more levels to the initial three. In some respects the higher degrees of the York and Scottish Rites overlapped and/or ran parallel to each other, but there were also many divergences between the two systems. Most importantly to this study, however, is that both systems included knighted degrees that allowed aspiring Freemasons to imbibe the esoteric wisdom of the early Knights Templar.

Scottish Rite Freemasonry

The first historical figure to either introduce and/or make public the higher degrees of the Scottish Rite was Templar Knight Michael Ramsay, who began to popularize them while residing in Paris. Ramsay probably acquired the higher degrees from Kilwinning; however it is acknowledged that he embellished them with the pro-Jacobite politics he subscribed to while in France. Like many supporters of King James Stuart II, Ramsay had taken refuge in France when his beloved monarch went into exile and then became involved in the French Jacobite movement that was dedicated to returning King James to the throne of Great Britain. Since the Stuarts or Stewards were the Grand Masters of the Kilwinning Lodge, Knight Ramsay and all the members of Scottish Rite Freemasonry were intimately connected to their destinies.

In France, Ramsay initially began popularizing 6 degrees above the initial three Blue degrees of Scottish Rite Freemasonry. These higher degrees, which were quickly adopted in 1754 by the Chapter of Clermont, the senior Freemasonic lodge of France, reflected Freemasonry's Templar and Johannite heritage. They included the degree of St. John's Masonry, the Knight of the Eagle and Pelican, the Illustrious Knight or Templar, and the Sublime Illustrious Knight. The 6 degrees were soon absorbed into the 25 degrees of the Rite of Heredom, the Rite of Perfection, which the descendant of King James II and heir to the British throne, Charles Edward Stuart, presided over as Grand Master. According to one legend, Prince Charles Edward Stuart brought the Rite of Heredom to France from his native Scotland after assisting in its formulation. Heredom is named after a mythical mountain located near Kilwinning, thus revealing the Rite's affiliation to the Mother Lodge of Scotland.

Through the Rite of Heredom, which was in some respects is an elaboration of Ramsay's Knight of the Eagle and Pelican degree, an initiate of Scottish Freemasonry was given the opportunity to align with the ancient lineage of the Knights Templar and Johannites. The power of the Baptist's lineage flowed freely through the Grand Masters of Heredom, and Prince Charles Stuart – in fact all the Stuarts - were technically Cupholders of John the Baptist's Holy Grail, a tradition they had inherited from the Grand Masters of the Knights Templar.

The Scottish degrees were again embellished upon in 1762 to become 30 degrees, which with the original 3 Blue Degrees equaled 33, the number of Christhood, the culmination and completion of the spiritual journey. Scottish Rite Freemasonry had thus reached the end of its evolution.

The Knighted Rose Croix Degrees

Today, as a Freemason ascends the Scottish Rite's 30 higher degrees he moves into the realm of the ancient Templars as he passes through the 16 chivalric or knighted degrees, beginning with the 15th degree of the Knight of the East or Sword. This important degree is the first of four Rose Croix (Cross) degrees, which includes the Prince of Jerusalem, the Knight of the East and West, and Knight of the Rose Croix. Collectively, the Rose Croix degrees align a rising Freemason to both the Johannite Church that existed in Palestine during the time of the First Crusade, as well as its Alexandrian ancestor, the Brotherhood of the Rose Cross founded by the Gnostic master Ormus.

The most important Rose Croix degrees are the last two, the 17th and 18th degrees of Scottish Rite Freemasonry. Known as the Knight of the East and West and the Knight of the Rose Croix, these degrees are called "Historical Degrees" because they recount some of the early events in the formation of Freemasonry, including the initial incorporation of the Knights Templar under King Baldwin II and the Order's early affiliation with the Johannite Church. The patron saints of this degree are the founders of the Johannite lineage, John the Baptist and John the Apostle, and the most important scripture of the degree is the *The Revelation of St. John the Divine.*

Of all the 33 degrees, the 18th degree of the Knight of the Rose Croix is considered one of the most treasured and sought after because it aligns the Freemason with his earliest Templar and Gnostic roots. Legend has it that the early Knights Templar were themselves initiated into it, so the degree possesses an authenticity that some of the other degrees are missing.

When the Freemason rises to the 18th degree he becomes a Knight of the Rose Croix and Knight of the Eagle and Pelican, which was the degree's name when it was the highest degree of the Rite of Heredom. During his induction into the Knight of the Rose Croix degree, a Freemason becomes a Gnostic and receives special alchemical emblems that are to be worn ceremonially, including a special pendant and a double "cordon" or dual sash to be worn over the shoulder. The pendant, which is half gold and half silver, as well as the cordon, which is half white and half black, denote the alchemical union of the polarity and the production of the Gnostic essence, the Holy Spirit or Kundalini. On the back of the seven-sided pendant (seven is a number of transformation) are two united swords, again denoting polarity union, and on the front is the image of a lamb resting upon a copy of John's *Book of Revelation*. The lamb, which is often ascribed to Christ, was for the Knights Templar also symbolic of John the Baptist.[11]

As an initiate of the Knight of the Rose Croix degree, a Scottish Rite Freemason technically becomes a fledgling chalice and Human Holy Grail.

This truth is implicit to the name "Rose Croix," which according to Laurence Gardner in *Genesis of the Grail Kings*, was anciently rendered as Rosi-crucis, meaning of "Dew Cup" or "Cup of the Waters," an epithet for the Holy Grail.

Once a Freemason becomes a Human Holy Grail initiate of the Rose Croix degree, he inherits the motif of the 18th degree, a pelican feeding its chicks with blood picked out of its own self-inflicted wound. The pelican is the archetypal Christed being, who sacrifices himself to the world by "feeding" his brethren with his own wisdom and power. According to Manley Palmer Hall, a 33 degree Mason and referred to in *Scottish Rite Journal* as "Masonry's Greatest Philosopher," the pelican is synonymous with the Holy Grail, and its blood is analogous the power and wisdom of the Water of Life. In this regard, he states:

"As the Rose Croix degree is based upon Rosicrucian and Hermetic symbolism, it follows that the pelican represents one of the vessels in which the experiments of alchemy are performed and its blood that mysterious tincture by which base metals are transmuted into spiritual gold."[12]

When a Freemason is ready to ascend even higher in Scottish Rite Freemasonry he becomes one of the "Holy Ones" and enters the Council of Kadosh, the "Council of the Holy." He then progresses through 12 "Chivalric" degrees that fine-tune his mind and body into a perfected Knight. Then, upon reaching the final degrees of the Scottish Rite, the Freemason Knight enters the "Consistory" of the three "Inspector General degrees," wherein he assumes responsibility over all his brothers in the order. He also learns secrets regarding Templar history and rites not previously available to him.

The final degree of the Scottish Rite, the Sovereign Grand Inspector General, is given to very few, as it makes its owner a member of the order's Supreme Council and heir to its most treasured secrets. This degree, which, states M.P. Hall, "represents the human head atop the thirty-three vertebrae of the back," theoretically bestows both intellectual and intuitive or Gnostic wisdom, which was the divine inheritance passed to the ancient Templars from the lineage of Johannites. This supreme knowledge awakens when the Kundalini power completes its ascent up the spine and reaches the "head atop the thirty-three vertebrae," which is symbolic of the decapitated head of the Baptist.

Scottish Rite Freemasonry was brought to the United States in 1761 by one Stephen Morin, who founded lodges of it in the Caribbean Islands and within many cities of North America. In 1801, a Supreme Council of Scottish Rite Freemasonry was founded in Charleston, South Carolina, and in 1804, this council standardized the name of the Scottish Rite worldwide by officially proclaiming it the Ancient and Accepted Scottish Rite. Since 1867, when a second Supreme Council was established in Massachusetts, the states of the U.S.A. have been divided by the Mason Dixon and co-governed by two Supreme Councils.

The Brethren of John the Baptist

An important offshoot of the Scottish Freemasonry that was founded under the guidance of Templar Knights and Grand Masters of the Scottish Rite is the Brethren of John the Baptist, also known as the Order of the Strict Observance. This order was founded following Ramsay's Paris oration by the Templar Knight Baron Karl Gottlieb von Hund, who claims to have received initiation into the highest levels of the Knights Templar in Paris by the Scottish Rite chiefs.

Baron von Hund received his initiations between 1742 and 1743 at the senior Lodge of Clermont in Paris, France. His initiators were Prince Charles Edward Stuart, Grand Master of the Rite of Heredom, and a mysterious "Knight of the Red Feather," who according to authors Baigent and Leigh in *The Temple and the Lodge* was one Alexander Seton, a high ranking Templar whose family had been allied with the Templars since the Order's earliest days in Scotland. One of the Setons, the Templar Grand Master David Seton, was renowned for having orchestrated the split that turned the Templars and the Order of the Knights of St. John back into separate orders again. This action was taken when the Grand Master of the amalgamated Order of the Knights of St. John and the Temple, Sir James Sandilands, sold off Templar lands for a great profit to both himself and the Knights of St. John.

After his Templar initiations Baron von Hund left Paris with authorization from "Unknown Superiors" to found a branch of the Knights Templar in his native Germany. His Brethren of John the Baptist subsequently became the principal form of Freemasonry throughout all of Germany, including within its membership the likes of such luminaries as Adam Weishaupt, the founder of the ill-fated Order of the Illuminati, as well as the famous healer Cagliostro and the immortal Comte de Saint Germain, who eventually served as its Grand Master. Weishaupt's affiliation to the Brethren of John the Baptist and its Mandean heritage was made clear when he adopted the Persian calendar for his Illuminati, and Weishaupt's Templar heritage was evident when he had his initiates achieve a level of illumination through the consumption of marijuana, the plant used in making hashish, the Flesh of Al-Khadir. It is Interesting to note that with their slogan, *Ewige Blumenkraft*, meaning "Eternal Flower Power," the Illuminati foreshadowed the drug-consuming hippies of the 1960's.[13]

Baron von Lund eventually revealed that his Unknown Superiors were Templars and that the Strict Observance was directly descended from the ancient Knights. Although Alexander Seton and Prince Charles Edward Stuart were definitely two of von Hund's Unknown Superiors, the Baron implied that his other Superiors were descended from the Templar missionaries sent to Europe by the legendary Pierre d'Aumont, the Templar Knight who is reputed to have brought Templarism directly from France to Scotland at the time of Order's 14th century arrest. Thus, the legend of the Scottish Grand Master Templar Pierre d'Aumont finds its fulfillment in Baron von Lund's Brethren of John the Baptist .

The York Rite

Although the York Rite was deeply influenced by the Knights Templar, scholars of the Rite claim that its roots go back much earlier in history. Collectively, such scholars concur that the York Rite was officially founded in 929 A.D., but previous to that date their histories diverge. Some of their histories begin Masonry in Egypt, some in Rome, and others in the Holy Land. The most ancient Masonic histories, however, regress back to the earliest Biblical patriarchs and even to the Garden of Eden itself.

According to the antiquarian Masonic history revealed by the York Rite initiate Dr. Anderson, Masonry began in Eden when Adam acquired a "knowledge of Geometry" (The "G" in the current Freemasonic symbol denotes Geometry, the foundation of Masonry) that he passed to his first son, Cain, who thus became history's second "mason." Cain used his architectural genius to design and build the City of Enoch, which many occultists equate with the "city" of the pyramids of Giza in Egypt, and he then passed the Craft to Lamech and his Masonic sons, including Tubal Cain, "an instructor of every artificer in brass and iron." Another of Lamech's sons, Noah, the famous builder of the Ark, disseminated the Masonic wisdom following the Great Flood, and thus became the first post-diluvian teacher of the Craft. It is for this reason that Anderson refers to every subsequent mason in Masonic history as a "true Noachida," or "Noachite."

Through Noah's grandson Cush, the Craft eventually passed to King Nimrod, the famous builder of the Tower of Babel, whose kingdom encompassed much of Asia Minor. Nimrod spread his wisdom to that part of his empire that was later known as Lebanon, a land wherein the monarch had overseen the reconstruction of the temple of Baalbek immediately following the Flood. In Lebanon, the wisdom of the Craft flourished greatly and eventually engendered a network of lodges in Tyre and Sidon that were overseen by a lineage of Grand Masters and priest kings known as Hiram, a title evolved from Chiram, the Master Builder or Kundalini. Within these lodges it became the cherished goal to awaken the Master Builder and "Rebuild Solomon's Temple," which is a metaphor for transmuting the human body into an immortal temple of God through the power of the Kundalini.

The era of Grand Master priest kings continued well into the time of the Roman Empire, when King Numa presided over a Masonic lodge and school of the Craft known as the Roman Collegia. When the Roman Legions went on campaigns around Europe they always took with them graduates of the Collegia, who not only built forts for the legions but also founded lodges that were auxiliary to Numa's Grand Lodge of Rome.

One initiate of Numa's Roman lodge, St. Alban, is remembered for having brought Masonry north to Great Britain, wherein he assisted in the founding of the York Rite while helping to establish the lodges of English Freemasonry. St. Alban had originally arrived in Rome after leaving his home in Hertfordshire, England, in the 3rd century A.D. in order to study the Craft in one of its resident lands.

After serving seven years as a soldier for the Emperor Diocletian, St. Alban returned to England where he was given the position of mason for the ruling King Carausius. The English monarch was so pleased with his work that St. Alban was soon promoted to the office of Master Builder of England, a position that gave him the power and freedom to set up a network of fully functioning Masonic lodges in the country. St. Alban then "assisted in making Masons, and framed for them a constitution-for such is the meaning of the phrase, "gave them charges."[14]

But although English Freemasonry technically begins with St. Alban, contemporary Lodges of the York Rite currently trace their beginnings to 929 A.D., when a meeting of masons sanctioned by the Norman King Athelstan, a grandson of Alfred the Great, was convened in the city of York in order to revive the Craft and endow it with a reformed set of laws and rites. King Edwin, who is described as either Athelstan's brother or son, emerged from this meeting as the first Grand Master of the York Rite.

Another very important event in the evolution of York Rite Freemasonry was the assimilation of the rites and degrees of the Knights Templar. According to *Illustrations of Masonry,* the Templars were in England in 1135 during the reign of Henry II and employed many members of the Craft living in the area of London to help them build their London Temple. This alliance led to many elements of Templarism infiltrating the English version of the Craft, a trend that would continue for the next hundred years. The 10 degrees of the York Rite were formulated during this era, or perhaps later, when according to Ramsay a "colony" of Templars existed in England under the auspices of the future King Edward I. States Ramsay:

"...during the eighth and ninth Crusades, the great Prince Edward, son of Henry III, King of England, seeing that there would be no security for the brethren in the Holy Land when the Christians should have retired, led them away, and thus a colony of the Fraternity (the Templars) was established in England. As this prince was endowed with all the qualities of mind and heart which constitute the hero, he loved the fine arts and declared himself the protector of our Order. He granted it several privileges and franchises, and ever since the members of the confraternity have assumed the name of *Freemasons*."

The York Rite Mason becomes a Knight Templar

The Templar influence on the 10 degrees of the York Rite is especially noticeable in its final three degrees of knighthood. Of these three degrees, which include the Order of the Red Cross, the Order of Malta, and the Order of the Temple, the last is said to make a York Rite Freemason a bonafide Templar Knight. During initiation into this final degree, which is believed to resemble an initiation ritual facilitated by the Templars in the presence of Baphomet, the Freemason stands before an open Masonic text that has a human skull resting upon it. While several swords are aimed at the candidate's throat he takes five symbolic drinks of wine, with the most important being the last. As he drinks wine directly out of the human skull (sometimes a seashell is used in place of a skull, but has the same meaning), the candidate declares his allegiance to St. John the Baptist and the Order of the Knights Templar with the following words:

"...may the soul that once inhabited this skull, as the representative of St. John the Baptist, appear against me in the day of judgment: so help me God and keep me steadfast in this my solemn obligation of a Knights Templar."

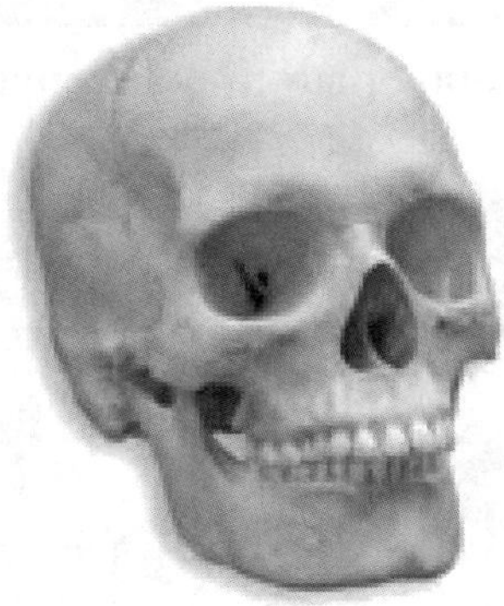

The two Johns, patrons of Freemasonry

A Masonic Lodge

British Masons apron with the Knights Templar skull and crossbones

Medallion of the 18th degree of Scottish Rite Freemasonry

Symbol of the 33rd degree of the Scottish Rite

George Washington, Master Mason

13
The Templars, Freemasons, Johannites, and Mandeans Today

Today, in this 21st century, the Lodges of St. John, especially the Scottish and York Rites of Freemasonry, continue to initiate Templar Knights, while the Knights of St. John, which is now known universally as the *Sovereign Military and Hospitaller Order of Saint-John of Jerusalem, Rhodes and Malta*, still initiates knights and also attracts a steady flow of new members to help staff their network of outreach and service programs around the globe. The principal Templar organizations worldwide are currently known as the SMOTJ, *The Sovereign Military Order of the Temple of Jerusalem*, the OSMTH, *Ordo Supremus Militaris Templi Hierosolymitani*, the CMOTJ, the *Chivalric Military Order of the Temple of Jerusalem*, and the *Commandery of the Knights Templar*. The Johannites have become a global organization and currently have branches in both the East and West, although their main headquarters still resides in Ephesus. Meanwhile, the Johannites' ancient brother and sisters, the Mandeans, still observe their rites in the Middle East just a they have for thousands of years, but they also meet together for ritual in the various countries around the world that groups of them have migrated to, including Sweden, Holland, New Zealand, Australia, Great Britain, and the USA.

Unfortunately, both the Johannites and most of the various Knights Templar orders have lost much or most of their original gnosticism and are now predominantly patriarchal and fundamentalist Christian in their ideology and rites. Most Templar organizations function primarily as charitable organizations or men's clubs, and the initiations that occur within them are often perfunctory, with neither the initiated or initiator being cognizant of the true import behind the symbology involved. But, on a positive note, things could be favorably changing in the near future. The Johannites maintain that the location of some hidden Gnostic secrets and relics, including the head of John the Baptist, may be revealed in 2005, and the Sinclairs of Scotland are looking forward to a restoration and reactivation of their sacred temple, Rosslyn Chapel, which was built in dedication to the union of Christianity with Goddess or nature religion. The Sinclairs are also excited at the possibility of soon rediscovering the secret Templar artifacts hidden in the crypt under the Chapel. It is also very encouraging to see women currently gaining inroads within Templarism. The SMOTJ and OSMTH, the main Knights Templar organizations in the USA and forty other countries worldwide, began inducting women into their orders in the 1960's and currently have them placed in even the highest ranking positions. The Militi Templi Scotia and the Association of Scottish Knights Templar also currently accepts women into their ranks and similarly elevates them to the highest positions of authority. In these orders women even have the opportunity to become full-fledged Templar Knights.

The following interviews were conducted between the author and important members of the current Templar and Templar-related organizations, including the Johannites and Mandeans. The questions asked during these interviews were designed to gain information about the present activities of each organization, as well as clarity regarding their past histories.

The SMOTJ, the Sovereign Military Order the Temple of Jerusalem

The SMOTJ is one of the principal Knights Templar organizations in the USA. This order traces its origin back to 1804, when Fabre-Palaprat revived the Knights Templars under the auspices of Napoleon Bonapart. As mentioned in Chapter 9, Fabre-Palaprat was responsible for reviving an ancient form of Gnostic Templarism that had descended through the lineage of Gnostic Johannites. Following Fabre-Palaprat's death, the Johannite elements were removed from his Order, and what had formally been an organization of Gnostic Templarism became exclusively military and driven by Catholic Christian rites and ideology.

In 1892, the leadership of the new purely military Templar Order passed to one Joséphin Péladan, who was proclaimed the Grand Master Templar. Following Péladan's death in 1918, his Order in France, *Ordre de la Rose-Croix Catholique et Esthetique du Temple et du Graal,* merged with the KVMRIS, a Martinist lodge in Belgium, whose legitimacy came via its supposed earlier link to Fabre-Palaprat's Gnostic Templars. An international Order of Templars was thus born with its headquarters in Brussels. Then, in 1932, this amalgamted international order of Templars officially became known as The Sovereign and Military Order of the Temple of Jerusalem, the SMOTJ. Finally, in 1995 the SMOTJ merged with the OSMTH, the Ordo Supremus Militaris Templi Hierosolymitani, which is Latin for "The Sovereign Military Order of the Temple of Jerusalem." Today, the names SMOTJ and OSMTH are used interchangeably as names for the same worldwide Templar organization.

The SMOTJ is a fundamentally a charitable organization and only accepts members of the Christian faith. Its membership of approximately 2350 is comprised mostly of military and ex-military personnel. Growing steadily, just 10 years ago the SMOTJ had less than 700 members. There are currently approximately 250 members inducted per year.

The 5 Goals of the SMOTJ

- 1. To assist Christians at risk, in danger and in Holy Land.
- 2. To build a bridge between Christian Churches of East and West
- 3. Be first to respond to crises worldwide. Send money, clothing, etc.
- 4. Advance understanding to the Sons of Abraham, i.e., the Jews, Moslems, and Christians.
- 5. To contribute understanding between people anywhere in the world.

Interview with Grand Prior Patrick Rhea

The current Grand Prior of the SMOTJ and the subject of this interview is former Brigadier General Pat Rhea, who currently resides in Tinley Park, Illinois.

MAP: You are a former brigadier general and now a Knights Templar Grand Prior. Apparently, you have advanced quite far in both the military and the SMOTJ…

PR: Yes, we (the SMOTJ) are heavily military in the United States.

MAP: Are you saying that many of the officers in the SMOTJ are former officers of the US military?

PR: Yes. Of our officers, roughly half have prior military experience. And of that number over two hundred of our members were either generals or admirals.

MAP: Do you attempt to recruit for the SMOTJ out of the ranks of the military?

PR: Yes, It is part of the recruiting process. But only a part.

MAP: Besides retired military, are some of your members currently active in the military?

PR: Yes. Many of them.

MAP: Are there new priories being created?

PR: Yes, About five a year. Both new Commandaries, which are 10 or more members, and new Priories, which are 25 or more members, are being created.

MAP: Are the founders of the new Priories normally ex-military?

PR: Yes, about 60%, although our membership is about 50-50, 50% ex-military and 50% civilians.

MAP: What is a Grand Prior and what are your duties in that role?

PR: The Grand Prior moves to his position through a system of chairs in the organization. They include the Inspector, the Chancellor, and then the Grand Prior. You are earning your "spurs" over a four-year period. Then, once you become Grand Prior, your term is for two years and you can only serve once in that position.

MAP: When was the SMOTJ founded?

PR: The SMOTJ in the USA goes back to the 1940's, right after WWII, but its incorporation only goes back to early 1960's.

MAP: Who founded the SMOTJ in the USA, was it one person or a group?

PR: A group founded it and some of the founding members are still alive today.

MAP: Were the founding members affiliated with another order or perhaps a secret society before they founded the SMOTJ?

PR: No. The founders had not been part of a secret society, nor did they intend for this to be one. They were sponsored by the autonomous Grand Priory of Switzerland.

MAP: When was the OSMTH, the larger, international order that the SMOTJ is part of, founded?
PR: 1995. It grew out of the Templar Order that traces itself back to Napoleon. A schism occurred along the way when the International Grand

Prior (of the SMOTJ), a man name DeFontes, decided that he was the hereditary head of the order and developed the title of Prince Regent for himself. That did not sit well with the American Templars or a significant number or European Templars, so they left his command and established their own order. That is the OSMTH.

MAP: Was the Order democratic before the war?

PR: Yes. But when the International Grand Priorship was passed from Vandenburg in Belgium to DeFontes after WWII, Defontes decided to make the rulership hereditary. At that time the Americans, the Brits, the Finns, and other Templars decided to succeed. A 21st Century order needs to be a democratic order if it is really going to be vibrant.

MAP: Does DeFontes's order still exist?

PR: Yes, but not in the United States.

MAP: How many degrees are currently in the SMOTJ?

PR: We don't have degrees per se. We do, however, have four ranks. Knight, Knight Commander, Knight Grand Officer, and Knight Grand Cross. The women in the order also have a set of ranks: Dame, Dame Commander, Dame Grand Officer and Dame Grand Cross.

MAP: Have women been accepted into the order from its inception?

PR: No, it was originally men. Women have been a part of the order since its incorporation in the 1960's. The first initiated Dame, Dr. Martha Conan, is still alive.

MAP: Are the women allowed to serve in the same high offices as the men?

PR: Yes. The highest offices include the Grand Prior and eight Deputy Grand Priors. One of the Deputy Grand Priors is currently a woman who has half the state of California under her. She just represented us in Russia at the dedication of a shrine there. You will find women leadership at every rank in our organization.

MAP: Is there only one Grand Prior in the US?

PR: Yes, every country where SMOTJ is established has one Grand Prior.

MAP: Is there a Grand Master Prior that is the head of all the world's Priors?

PR: Yes, and right now it is an American Admiral named James Carey. He is the Grand Commander of OSMTH. There is also a titular head of the order called the International Grand Prior, who is now a Brit named Sir Roy Redgrave. He is a Knight of the British Empire. He and Lady Redgrave are our two most senior members.

MAP: How is the SMOTJ connected to the medieval Knights Templar Order?

PR: We are in possession of the protocols of induction into the Templar Order that existed in the year 1200. But our induction ceremony is closer to that of the chevalric Christian orders that existed in the Middle Ages or were founded after the dissolution of the Templars, such as the Order of the Garter, which is the most senior order of knights of the British Queen.

MAP: How does one come into the possession of the original protocols of the Templars?

PR: They exist in the French and Papal archives. It is not hard to get a copy.

MAP: In what other ways does the SMOTJ mirror the early Templars?

PR: You have to keep in mind that the first Templars were monks on horseback, so it is difficult to completely model our order after them. The first Knights went through a series of tests to prove that they were combatants. They also went through intensive religious training, similar to what one would undergo to become a deacon today. We do not require those high standards in the SMOTJ. So, although we are dedicated to helping Christians at risk in the Holy Land and other places like the old Templars were, we do not have the same requirements in order to execute that mission. In today's world one executes this mission through diplomacy, reason, leadership skills, networks and some financial investment to achieve the same goal of the early Templars. We also try to bring other like-minded organizations, Christian or not, to our side.
You also have to keep in mind that the Templar Order itself was not always the same. Its inductions started to become reformed in the 1200's

and at that time they began to look more like that of the later knightly orders of Europe, such as Order of the Garter.

MAP: I suppose that there were many orders of knights after the Templars…

PR: Yes. Every single court in Europe did, and still does, have knightly orders, as does many Church leaders, such as the Papacy and the Patriarch of Jerusalem.

MAP: Do you have a patron saints for your order, such as John the Apostle or Mary Magdalene?

PR: No. We have a very alive royal patron in Princess Elizabeth, and we have a religious patron in Theodosius, the head of the Orthodox Church of America.

MAP: One of the symbols of the SMOTJ is the Cross of Lorraine. What does it symbolize for the order?

PR: Our cross, with two crossbars, could be considered the Cross of Lorraine, but we call it the Patriarchal Cross. It was the cross of the patriarchs, and since we were initially supported by the Patriarch of Jerusalem, we took that as our cross.

MAP: Do you recognize the list of ancient Templar Grandmasters that is currently being advertised on the Internet?

PR: We believe that the grandmasters up to DeMolay is legitimate. But we don't generally acknowledge any of the grandmasters after that time until 1804.

MAP: What happened in 1804?

PR: Napoleon revived the Order.

MAP: Did Napoleon have any office in the revived order?

PR: If he did we have no record of it. A French Duke became Grandmaster at that time.

MAP: 1804 corresponds to the revival of Fabre-Palaprat, does it not?

PR: He was part of the revival. He was a little bazaar in his thinking.

MAP: Do you consider him a past Grand Master?

PR: We consider him one of the leaders that reorganized the Templar Order. But in the reorganization he was much more liberal than the others in what he believed, and his documentation is not too solid. But in his defence, throughout history since the death of Christ there have been all kinds of documents, including some that the Roman Church used to justify and support some of their positions and doctrines, which may or may not be authentic. For, example, one such document was supposedly given to Rome by the Emperor Constantine and hundreds of years later it was found to be a fraud. So it is often nearly impossible to prove whether an old document is true or false.

MAP: Besides the ancient protocols of the Templars and protecting Christians, are you consciously modeling the SMOTJ on the old Templar Order in any other way?

PR: You need to understand that we are far more directed to carrying out good works than we are to looking over our shoulders to fossilized thoughts.

MAP: So rather than focus on the controversies of the past you would rather focus on the present?

PR: Absolutely. We do know that the original mission of the Order was to protect Christians at risk, especially pilgrims, and during the early years of the Knights Templar it took soldiers and a lot money and time to do it. Today, we believe we still need to focus on Christians at risk, most specifically in the Holy Land but not exclusively.

MAP: How are you currently protecting pilgrims in the Holy Land?

PR: A series of ways. We bring the interests of the American Grand Priory to the highest levels of our government and to other governments, including the Israeli government, Jordanian government, Palestinian government, etc. And because the majority of our Order are successful leaders from every walk of life in the US, the legitimacy of their word and the

thoughtfulness of their ideas in the international market of free ideas, carry weight. We use networks that each one of us has created to assist in creating the Orders' goals. We use our capacity to bring financing to key areas at the right moment. We are also involved with United Nations and we belong to the International Peace Bureau, as well. Through each of these channels, we are heard again and again and again. But we also send pilgrimages ourself to the Holy Land to meet with the Christians there. We extend a hand of support to them financially, morally and through prayer.

MAP: How often do you send pilgrimages to the Holy Land?

PR: We try to do it every year. This time last year we were there. As you know, the environment over there is not always safe. Those of us that choose to go usually have had more experience in having been shot at.

But even when we are not in the Holy Land we continue to remain connected to it. For example, we welcome the Christian leaders of the Holy Land to America. Two weeks ago I hosted a reception in Milwaukee for the Primate of the Lutheran Church of Jordan, and five months ago in Los Angeles we hosted a reception for a Bishop Rhea, the Anglican Bishop of the Holy Land. We make sure their message is heard not just in our Order, but throughout the USA.

MAP: When you visit the Holy Land are their specific pilgrimage sites that you visit which are related to the old Templar Knights?

PR: Like all Christians, we visit the Holy Sepulchre and the churches in Bethlehem. We also make sure we visit with the three senior patriarchs and bishops of Jerusalem. And when we visit them we stay with them not just for moments, but for extended periods of time.

MAP: Do you make a point of visiting the Temple Mount, home of your Templar beginnings?

PR: We didn't last year. I think you are struggling to find an order latched to the past. We are an order with respect for the past but looking towards the future.

MAP: In your Five Goals (*see above*) you state that you seek to "advance understanding to the Sons of Abraham, including the Jews, Moslems and Christians.

How do you go about accomplishing this?

PR: We try to bring them together in understanding and mutual respect and love. To that end we work very well with the Israelis and Palestinians. When we were in Israel last year we were extremely well treated and brought to key locations with the active participation of the Israeli foreign office.

MAP: Do you donate money to your causes in the Holy Land?

PR: Not a lot. Our annual support for the Holy Land is about 30,00 dollars. It is directed into the hands of the bishops and patriarchs so they can use it for the preservation of the holy sites.

MAP: Are all the members of the SMOTJ Christians?

PR: Yes and no. We have some members of the Order who are not full members of the Order. They are part of what we call the National Order of Merit. This Order includes both Jews and Moslems. They do not have voting rights and they can not hold office in the SMOTJ. But they are honored by us because they have helped to bring the Sons of Abraham together.

MAP: Do the rites and ceremonies in the Order have Christian overtones?

PR: Yes, one hundred percent. We use the Nicene Creed a lot. Probably one third of our investitures have the Eucharist in them. The investiture is a heavily influenced Christian ceremony. It is full of prayers and hymns. And a chaplain is always part of it.

MAP: What is a normal SMOTJ meeting like and how often do you meet?

PR: The Priories and Commandaries meet three to five times a year. There is usually always a business meeting during which are discussed the charities, the recruiting of new members, and the policies of the national order. There is also at least one investiture a year in which you bring new members into your priory.

MAP: Other than being Christian, what are the requirements to becoming a Templar in the SMOTJ?

PR: Candidates have to be sponsored by three current members. And regardless of age, we look for proven leadership abilities or leadership potential.

MAP: What is the current average age of a Templar in the SMOTJ?

PR: Probably between 40 and 45.

MAP: What is the youngest age allowed to become a Templar?

PR: 21 is the youngest age, and right now we have a number of recruits that age.

MAP: How long have you been a Templar?

PR: About 12 years.

MAP: How long would you say it takes to progress through the ranks of the Order?

PR: About eight years.

MAP: If there are no Priories in a person's town can they start their own, or must they travel to where there is one?

PR: They can start their own. It happens all the time. The new Commandary of Abraham Lincoln just sprung up in Springfield Illinois. There's a couple of new Commadaries that have sprung up in New York State even though there are three Priories there, one in New York, one in West Point, and in New Jersey just outside New York City.

MAP: Do you and your knights visit Priories in other parts of the world?

PR: Yes, when we can. And they visit here, also. The French Grand Prior is here quite often. He has a special relationship with our Priory in New Orleans. The Austrian Grand Prior visits and sometimes the Finnish officers visit, as well. And we do have international meetings where we meet and collaborate.

MAP: Is Rosslyn Chapel one of your important pilgrimage places?

PR: That is a spot of a high degree of interest to us. It has very interesting Templar lore. And, personally, I think that every third American thinks he is a Scotsman. So anytime you have a Scottish attraction, such as the beautiful and historic Rosslyn Chapel and Castle, you are going to have a lot of interest. We just had some of our Templar candidates go over there for an investiture two weeks ago. They were knighted in Rosslyn Castle. And in November of this year in Bottingin, Germany, which is just outside of Frankfurt, where we have a large American and international meeting at the castles of our royal patron, Princess Elizabeth, we will be bringing the Earl of Caithness, the Lord of Sinclair, the head of the Clan of Sinclair (Malcolm Sinclair), who is the lord over Rosslyn (not true, the Lord of Rosslyn is currently Peter Sinclair Erskin)**, into the Grand Priory of the United States.**

MAP: Who performed the induction at Rosslyn Castle?

PR: The Deputy Grand Prior for the United States, Brigadier General Shellfont.

MAP: Do your inductions happen regularly at Rosslyn?

PR: Yes, every couple of years…

MAP: Are they planned to occur on a particular day of the year?

PR: No.

MAP: Do you have any other special pilgrimage places in Europe?

PR: The Priory of St. Patrick, the priory of Westpoint Academy, tries to have a pilgrimage to Ireland every few years and visit the important sites there that are associated with St. Patrick.

MAP: Is the SMOTJ aligned at all with the Order of the Garter?

PR: Only that we measure the quality of what we do against their protocol to make sure that we are not doing something substantially different. We don't want to breach knightly protocol, so we double check our procedures against those of the Order of the Garter.

MAP: Do other branches of the SMOTJ around the world model themselves on the Order of the Garter?

PR: Not necessarily. The French have their own unique investiture. The German Grand Priory uses the protocols of the Order of St. John. We in America will use the protocols of the United Kingdom because they are most familiar to us...and we are able to read through them without any problem.

MAP: What would you say is currently your most important charitable project?

PR: We probably give more assistance now to church maintenance and construction, children's education and orphanages, and hospitals.

MAP: Are your projects mainly in America or all over the world?

PR: Throughout the world.

MAP: Are you expected to pay dues as a member of the SMOTJ?

PR: Yes, annual dues are required.

THE COMMANDERY OF KNIGHTS TEMPLAR

The Commandery of Knights Templar is comprised of those Knights who have ascended the ladder of the York Rite of Freemasonry and become Knights Templars. To gain entrance into the Commandery, a candidate must first be a Freemason who has risen to at least the degree of Royal Arch in the York Rite. Then, once they are accepted for membership, they are eligible to move through the three Knights Templar degrees of the Commandery: the Order of the Red Cross, the Order of Malta, and the Order of the Temple. Although it is only necessary to have a belief in a higher power to progress through the lower degrees of the York Rite, the Commandery of the Knights Templar recommend that inductee have a Christian affiliation.

The following interview was conducted with Jacob Baird, who is an officer in the Grand Encampment of the United States, the governing body of all the Commanderies (lodges) that comprise the Commandery of Knights Templar in the US. There are nearly 1,600 Commanderies residing within the towns and cities of the United States, Germany, Italy and Mexico, and altogether there are approximately 260,000 practicing members of the Order worldwide.

Jacob lives in Norwood, Missouri, and is currently presiding over the Committee on Knights Templar History for the Grand Encampment, for which he has written a book on the history of the Knights Templar during the twentieth century. Jacob, who is now 82 years old, has been a Freemason for nearly thirty years and during that time has been initiated into the higher degrees of both the York and Scottish Rites.

Interview with Jacob Baird, Templar Knight

MAP: What is the official name of your Templar organization?

JB: I am a member of the Mountain Grove Commandery no. 66 in Missouri. The next step up is Grand Commandery of the state of Missouri, which charters all the Commanderies in the state of Missouri. The final step is the Grand Encampment of the USA. It charters all the Grand Commanderies.

The only way you can become a member of the Grand encampment of the USA is to be a Grand Commander or past Grand Commander of one of the Grand Commanderies. All states have a Grand Commandery. Some states are just getting Grand Commanderies, like Delaware, which got one four years ago.

There is nothing secret about Freemasonry. But if I was standing in front of you now I could tell if you were or were not a Freemason. We have ways to tell this. This idea of secrecy in Templarism is a misconception.

MAP: To become a Templar in your organization, you must first become a Freemason?

JB: Yes. You have to be a mason to become a York Rite Mason. And to be a York Rite Mason you must be a member of the chapter Royal Arch Masons. Then you become a member of the council of Crypt Masons. After that you can become a Templar.

MAP: How long did it take for you to become a Templar?

JB: It took me three months to become a Master Mason. It took me one month for each degree. At that point I branched out to become a York Mason and a Scottish Rite Mason.

MAP: How many degrees did you pass through in York Rite Masonry to become a Templar?

JB: To become a Royal Arch Mason you must go through four degrees. Then you have to go through three degrees to become a member of the Council. Then there are three degrees to become a Templar. There are ten degrees altogether.

MAP: How long does it take to go through this process?

.

JB: You can take all four degrees of Royal Arch in one day. One right after the other. They take about one hour to go through. We have a system set up so that you can go through all the degrees of the York Rite in one weekend and become a Templar. Friday night you go through the Royal Arch degrees. Saturday morning we give the three degrees of the Council, and in the afternoon we give the three Orders of the Temple.

MAP: How often do you meet outside of the weekend initiations?

JB: In general, it depends on the state you are in and the size of the organization. In Missouri, we normally have one meeting every month for each level. There is one for the Master Masons, one for the Arch Masons, one for the Council, and one for the Templars. That's four a month. I am a member of an organization now that has one meeting a month for all ten degrees of the York Rite.

MAP: The Templar rites that you observe...did they come directly from the Knights Templar?

JB: That depends on who you talk to. I became a Mason in 1975. I have studied quite a bit. At the moment I am a member of 34 different Masonic organizations. Each believes a little bit different. I would say yes to your question, but 95% of the Templars I know believe otherwise. The things we do to become Masons are all part of the old Knights Templar code that has survived for hundreds of years.

When the Templars were arrested by De Molay many fled to England and Scotland and disappeared. There is plenty of evidence that they went underground. But the proof of their continued existence are their gravestones in Britain that have Masonic and Templar emblems. They

laid low until 1717, the date when Masonry began. But I am convinced that the Templar tradition continued on in Freemasonry, which was founded by the Templars who went underground. The Freemasons are the progeny of the Knights Templar.

A book I am familiar with that came out about ten or fifteen years ago, *Born in Blood* by John J. Robinson, proves the connection between the Templars and Freemasons. The author was not a Templar when he wrote the book, but when he eventually became one later in life he was even more certain of the Templar/Freemason connection.

MAP: Tell me about the current activities in your Templar organization.

JB: There are three or four major charities we support. As a whole, Freemasons contribute at least one and one-half million dollars each year to charity. The Templars lend money to those who want to further their education. They lend it at 5% interest. The Templars also have an eye foundation for persons going blind or have some eye disease that can be cured. If a person cannot afford the surgery they need, the Knights Templar eye foundation will pay for them. We also have 22 hospitals across the USA for those who are lacking funds for medical care.

MAP: Is it possible to become a Knights Templar through the Scottish Rite?

JB: No, not technically. There is not a Knight Templar degree in the Scottish Rite, but there is a degree that is very similar. Like the York Rite, they have the same first three degrees, but the other 29 of the 32 are a little different. In truth, however, they give similar degrees in just slightly different ways.

MAP: But the Scottish Rite has Knight degrees does it not?

JB: Yes, and it has just about as many as the York Rite.

MAP: How many degrees in the York Rite?

JB: There are the three Blue degrees, as well as the four Royal Arch Mason, three for the Council, and three for Templar. There are thirteen altogether. Scottish Rite has 32. The 33rd degree is given to only a select few.

MAP: Can you move through the 32 degrees of Scottish Rite in a weekend?

JB: They have a system. When I took mine it was after I had gone through the York Rite and finished my year as Grand Commander of the Grand Encampment of the State of Missouri. The first weekend I received seven degrees, and got the rest later on. Usually they have only a few degrees you can get in a weekend, and they are usually not in order. You might, for example, attend one weekend that gives the 6th, 11th, 14th, and 27th degrees. The next weekend might give the 19th , 23rd, 16th. So you have to go to a series of weekends.

MAP: How does one become a Freemason?

JB: There is one extremely important qualification, all Freemasons are supposed to be good men. They should not be criminals, and they should never have spent time on jail. The only other qualification is that you must not be an atheist. You must have a belief in a Supreme Power. You can call it the Maker, the Holy One, God, Allah, or whatever you want. No one cares what sect or denomination you are part of. You are encouraged to go to church or a temple for learning. But there are plenty of people like me, also. I don't belong to any church, never have and don't ever intend to. But even though you are encouraged to attend a church you never discuss church or religion in a Masonic meeting. It's just not done. During one meeting a member began to bring up religion and I pointedly told him "Get off that subject right now or leave." We don't discuss religion of politics.

MAP: What do you discuss during your meetings?

JB: We talk about people in the surrounding area and how to help them. If a woman recently lost her husband and she has a family to take care of, we might spend the entire meeting discussing how to help her.

MAP: Are there any special rituals you observe during your meetings?

JB: Yes, there is a special ritual for running the meeting which all the officers take part in. We have certain rituals but they are not secretive rituals. These rituals help you to conduct a good meeting.

MAP: What is your opinion of the international order of Templars known as OSMTH?

JB: I've never heard of them. I can't tell you anything about them.

Symbol of the Knights Templar degree of the York Rite.

The Knights Templar in Scotland

The Militi Templi Scotia

The Militi Templi Scotia is one of the largest remaining organizations of the Knights Templar Order in Scotland. Along with its sister sects, the Militi Templi Scotia is what remains if the Scottish Templar Order founded by refugee Knights who settled in Scotland following their departure from France in the 13th century. The Militi Templi Scotia operates out of Preceptories run by Preceptors, wherein regular meetings and initiations are held. The degrees of the order include Squire and Knight, and it is open to equal participation of both men and women. Religious affiliation is not of special concern, although most members are Christian. Governing the organization is a Grand Council that meets periodically to discuss important issues in the M.T.S., and at its head is a Grand Prior, a chair currently held by Graham Grant of the Isle of Sky.

The Militi Templi Scotia was, until recently, a member of the SMOTJ, but because of difficulties with its administration, the M.T.S. has decided to withdraw its membership. There are certain members in the Order that are not in favor of this decision, such as Ian Sinclair, because they feel that the M.T.S. needs to expand and become progressively more international. They would like to see persons of other nationalities inducted into the M.T.S.

Ian and Niven Sinclair

Templar Interview with Ian Sinclair, KCTpl
Preceptor of the Militi Templi Scotia

Ian Sinclair was born in northern Scotland and lived his early years there before moving to Manchester, England, where he worked as both a teacher and hotel owner. After retirement, Ian returned to the homeland of his family and ancestors in Caithness, northern Scotland, where he purchased a compound of buildings around a lighthouse at Noss Head, near Wick. Here Ian, a Templar Knight and Preceptor in the Militi Templi Scotia, currently operates the Prince Henry Sinclair Preceptory and Study Centre. The compound includes lodging for visitors, as well as the Niven Sinclair Library, which was donated to the Study Center by Ian's cousin, Niven Sinclair, who currently runs a chauffeur business in London. The titular head of the Sinclair Clan, Earl Malcolm Sinclair, also currently resides in the area of Caithness.

One of the principal reasons that Ian moved to Noss Head was to be near Sinclair-Girnigoe Castle, which stands just a quarter-mile away from his Preceptory. First built in the 13th century by Sinclairs affiliated with the Knights Templar, it was later added onto to become a fort. Recent ground scans have revealed underground vaults at the castle which the Sinclairs plan to open in 2004-5 in hopes of finding some hidden relics and holy treasures dating back to the time of the Knights Templar.

MAP: Hello Ian. Is it alright to call you Ian or should I be calling you baron or some other royal title?

IS: I am not a baron but a laird, which is a person in Scotland who owns land above a certain size. You can call me Ian.

MAP: You live in Caithness (a northern Scotland territory). Are the Sinclairs still the Earls of Caithness that they once were?

IS: Yes. The present earl, Earl Malcolm Sinclair, is the twentieth Sinclair Earl of Caithness.

MAP: I understand that the Sinclairs were also once the Jarls of Orkney. Do the Orkneys continue to remain in the Sinclair possession?

IS: No. The first Earl of Caithness, before he became Earl of Caithness, was William Sinclair, the third and last Jarl of Orkney. He lost that title when the king accepted Orkney from him, but then the king gave William the Earldom of Caithness.

MAP: The title Jarl of Orkney came from the King of Norway, did it not?

IS: Yes. And had there been a slight twist of fate there is a great probability that a Sinclair would have become a king of Norway.

MAP: Your family line is very intriguing. How far back can you trace your ancestry?

IS: Back to William the Conqueror, and before that the Vikings. The Sinclairs arrived as assistants to William the Conqueror. They were knights that accompanied him to the Battle of Hastings. That is how the Sinclairs gained their notoriety in the north of Scotland.

MAP: Has your family always been associated with warriors and warrior societies?

IS: Yes, even down to today. We still have many crusades to fight even though we don't fight with swords anymore. We fight with pens and education. The raison d'etre of our present organization, the Militi Templi Scotia, is to serve both God and Scotland. That includes any way that we can be of help in preserving Scottish history, Scottish buildings, etc.

MAP: So the present crusade is to preserve Scottish history….

IS: Yes, and to get as many people involved under the banner of the Scottish Knights Templar, the Militi Templi Scotia.

MAP: Is it true that you recently opened a preceptory for preserving Scottish and Templar history?

IS: Yes. It is a meeting place. It is for meetings between Knights and Squires and anyone else who wants to see what we are doing here. Our principal objective here at the preceptory is preservation and education, including the history of not only the Knights Templar but of all Scotland. Unfortunately, in schools today they are not teaching children the history of Scotland. The only thing they teach them about is the new parliament, which is only four years old.

MAP: Obviously you are trying to change that…

IS: Not change, but enhance. Here we have a study center with many books with the history of the Knights Templar, Freemasonry, etc. The theme of all the books are interconnected. We have authors coming from all over the world to do their research here as we have books here that have no seconds anywhere. We have three authors from Bulgaria staying with us right now.

MAP: And what are you doing in regards to the old Scottish buildings?

IS: If there are any Scottish buildings that need preserving we attempt to get hold of stone masons and architects and raise funds for their preservation.

MAP: Do you have anything other than books at your preceptory?

IS: We have artifacts in the preceptory itself. Actually, the study center is in a building separate from the preceptory. You see, on our property we have a lighthouse. Next to it we have a building comprised of two cottages converted into one; that is where we have our study center and library. Then across a courtyard is another building, which was the old stable; that is the one that has been converted into the Templar preceptory. That is where Squires are made, Knights are knighted, and where both Squires and Knights meet to discuss their business.

MAP: What artifacts do you have in the preceptory?

IS: We have a few artifacts, such as the hilt of an old Templar sword and a small Templar cross. These were found during the excavations of King Solomon's Temple. They were left there by the original Templars who excavated the ruins of Solomon's Temple. Hughes de Payen and his original eight knights excavated for eight to nine years in the ruins. In 1887 a British army company was sent to Jerusalem to study the structure of the Wailing Wall and found the artifacts.

MAP: Does the Militi Templi Scotia have a record of what Hughes de Payen and the first knights found while excavating Solomon's Temple?

IS: The Dead Sea Scrolls tell us exactly what was buried in the ruins. Whether Hughes de Payen actually found all that was buried we are not entirely sure. But we do know that he brought back with him five cases. Those five cases came through Kilwinning and stayed there for a period of time before being transferred to Roslin Castle.

MAP: Are the five cases still at Rosslyn Castle?

IS: They are probably in Rosslyn Chapel, where they would have been transferred to after Roslin Castle. There was a huge fire in Roslin Castle and everyone thought that the deeds and the documents that had been brought to Scotland by the Templars had been destroyed. But it was discovered that the priest to the Sinclairs and some of his monks actually rescued the five cases and many of the manuscripts. Many years ago we did a ground scan and we know that there are five containers down in the crypt under Rosslyn Chapel.

MAP: I assume they were placed there by your ancestor William, the builder of Rosslyn Chapel?

IS: That is the supposition. The five cases were interred by him next to five knights in full suits of armor. What stops us from investigating further is that the whole of the crypt is backfilled with silica sand. So there are thousands of tons of sand covering all these artifacts. One has to ask the question: why go to all the trouble of filling the crypt with sand?

MAP: Who is historically responsible for filling the crypt with sand?

IS: No one is completely sure. The last person that was interred in the crypt was William Sinclair himself. It must have been either his second son by his second marriage, William, who become the second Earl of Caithness, or his first son by his second marriage, Oliver, who became the Baron of Roslin. Oliver continued to complete his father's work and added to the Chapel. We know he built the Lady Chapel section and that he stopped building after two years.

MAP: Do you have any plans for future excavations under Rosslyn Chapel?

IS: We would love to. It's a case of diplomacy now. Too many people have had a hand at doing things with the Chapel in the past and everyone is now very cautious, particularly Historic Scotland.

MAP: Don't the Sinclairs have an important say as to what happens with the Chapel?

IS: They do have an important say but the most important person is the owner of the Chapel, Peter Sinclair Rosslyn, also known as Peter Erskin. The Erskins married into the Sinclair family five generations ago. One of the Erskins married one of the female Sinclairs who owned the deeds to the Chapel at the time. She had acquired them because there was no male apparent to receive them. And because of this, when the Erskins married into the Sinclair Clan they obtained the Barony of Rosslyn and it has been in their possession ever since. To date, the Erskin descendant, Peter Rosslyn, has not done much with the Chapel, and in fact he's probably done the least of anybody in history.

MAP: Can you tell me the original reason that Rosslyn Chapel was built?

IS: The Templar group that I belong to are in no doubt whatsoever that Rosslyn Chapel was built as a receptory for the items that were brought back from the Holy Land with the Templars, and not as a place of worship. This seems clear since within six months of the fire at Rosslyn Castle in 1445 William Sinclair began the creation of Rosslyn Chapel. He began building in 1446.

MAP: How did the fire start?

IS: It was started by a chambermaid going under a bed with a candle to

rescue a cat. At least that is the story. It was certainly an accidental fire.

MAP: Was there something special about the area chosen for Rosslyn Chapel?

IS: We believe that there was a structure there, possibly a castle or keep that preceded the construction of Rosslyn. The structure had a crypt under it, which we believe Rosslyn Chapel was built over and then utilized as a repository. I believe the lower chapel was built a long time before the structure we see now. The lower crypt connects with cave structures. There could have been a cave formation where the crypt is now and used by the early people of Scotland.

MAP: Many legends maintain that when the Templars were run out of France they traveled to Scotland with their sacred relics and documents. Could those have also ended up in Rosslyn Chapel?

IS: There is no doubt at all that when the Templars were expelled from France in 1307 a number of ships left the Port of New Rochelle with the Templars and their treasures. We know that they were pre-warned of their imminent arrest. We know that some of them went round to Portugal and Malta, and the rest came round to the western isles of Scotland. What they had to do was sail out into the Atlantic because they could not cross the Irish Sea since it was serving the monarch of England at the time. So they went way out into the Atlantic and the first place they came to was Solway Firth, a huge estuary in what is now Cumberland. At that time it was part of Scotland. And we know from the discoveries we have made that there were a number of Templar activities occurring in and around Solway Firth. Apparently they harbored there for many years.

MAP: And where did they go after Solway Firth?

IS: After that they made their way to the western Scottish isles and stopped at many of them. Eventually they made their way around to Pentland Firth. From there it is presumed that one of the first places they reached was Sinclair Bay, which is where the Sinclairs went on to build Sinclair-Girnigoe Castle. There is definitely a Templar influence in the building of the castle. It has an Islamic influence, and the Templars, of course, obtained their building skills from the Moslems. Right now we are very involved in the restoration of Sinclair-Girnigoe Castle because this played a major role in what happened to the Templars and what happened to them after they

joined Robert the Bruce at Bannockburn. Robert the Bruce changed their name from Knights Templar to the Royal Order of Scotland. That was the banner they fought under.

MAP: What do you think the Templars may have brought with them to Scotland after leaving France that might be in Rosslyn Chapel today?

IS: I am not completely sure. Certainly it would include the great wealth that they had taken out of France. King Philip conspired to steal the wealth of the Templars but failed in his attempt and most of it left France. I feel certain that they also brought with them certain documentation plus holy relics and artifacts.

MAP: Is there anything else you can tell me about Rosslyn Chapel?

IS: There are five tunnels leading between the chapel and Roslin Castle. They go towards the castle, but they don't reach the castle because the ground in-between has been disturbed.

MAP: Could the tunnels hold some treasures?

IS: Possibly. There must be a reason why the land that the tunnels run through was purchased by the Friends of Rosslyn (a trust run by the Sinclairs) and not the Rosslyn Trust, which is overseen by the Erskins.

MAP: Have you discovered anything in the tunnels or anything unusual in the crypt that they are joined to?

IS: We found one or two strange objects which in our minds shouldn't have been there. I am not in a position to talk too much about them now, but there have certainly been objects found that have got us puzzled. But we are talking to people, things are being unveiled, and we believe one day we will have an answer as to why we found what we did. Two skulls were found – and I don't want to go into great detail regarding where they were found – are a mystery. We photographed them and replaced them. We didn't have a great deal of difficulty finding them, so they seem to have been placed so that they would be easily discovered. I also believe that there is also a lot of things within the crypt that have not been discovered yet and lie waiting to be discovered. Many psychics have said as much. Some say we will eventually find something that we had no idea was even

there.

MAP: Speaking of skulls, one of the Templar relics was a head or skull known as the Baphomet…what was Baphomet, really?

IS: I believe, as do many Templar historians, that Baphomet was the head of John the Baptist.

MAP: Could that have ended up at Rosslyn?

IS: There are two schools of thought. One has it that it is somewhere on the continent of Europe, and the other has it that it is somewhere here in Scotland. It could be in Rosslyn Chapel, and it could be in other areas in Scotland renowned for their Templar influence. One of the most important is a little Scottish village called Durlot. Durlot has a Templar cemetery in it. The cemetery is right in the middle of seven thousand acres of moorland. From where it is you can see for miles and miles around. There was a castle there, probably not a castle but a keep, and in that keep a secret was kept closely guarded. This could have been a location of the head of John the Baptist. The head apparently came to Durlot from an island near one of the Orkneys called Eynhallow, where there are the ruins of a Cistercian monastery. The Pope sent a man named Abbot Lauren Sinclair to the island of Eynhallow to guard a secret for two years. The secret was very precious. No one knew what it was, but every Scottish Knight who went on the Crusades first visited Eynhallow. Robert the Bruce once spent eighteen months on Eynhallow. Then…all of a sudden Eynhallow became insignificant and Durlot became prominent. It is possible that whatever was on Eynhallow was transferred to Durlot. Could it have been the head of John the Baptist? We are not sure yet. It certainly seems that it was a very holy relic of some sort.

IS: Right now we have a lot of information that we have waited twenty years to gather that we are piecing together. The Templar movement and I are doing that work here at the preceptory, and anyone from around the world who would like to be an associate member is welcome to help and we will share the research with them. Right now we have a lot of interest in the Middle East, where the Templars gained their knowledge.

MAP: As I am sure you are aware, Fabre-Palprat claimed that a lot of the Templar knowledge was passed to them through the Johannites. Do you think there is truth is this?

IS: It is feasible, but proof is lacking. We have evidence for certain theories like this one, but we also have massive gaps within our system. So one has to piece this together to see what kind of pattern in produces. And we have to stay true to our research. A lot of Templar books written over the past thirty years have been published simply to make money.

MAP: Apparently Fabre-Palaprat used the Charter of John Mark Larmenius to give authority to his theory. Do you think the charter is real or a fake?

IS: There are a number of historians who say it is a fake, but I know of a lot of good historians who say there is a good probability that it is true. I have an open mind about it myself. If you study the charter the words and the structure fits in and it seems valid.

MAP: My own research has lead me from Fabre-Palaprat's theory to the Mandeans and the notion that John the Baptist was the true Messiah. What do you think of this?

IS: It could be. There is also the theory that James the Just, the brother of Jesus, was far more important than Jesus himself. In my opinion Jesus Christ was a great politician. He would have to have been at that time to make the changes he was trying to make. The actual prophet and Messiah I have no doubt at all could have been John the Baptist. He was the true inspirational person around at that time. He inspired not only Jesus, but also the disciples of Jesus.

MAP: Do you think that the Templars' supposed predilection for gnosticism and alchemy might itself point to their alignment to the tradition of John the Baptist?

IS: It could very well be. In fact, during the last 25 years there have been a number of reputable doctors and others who have joined the Templar organization and have carried on alchemical experiments that can be done now. I have been alarmed – not surprised – but alarmed at the supernatural power these people have achieved. They could be reviving the tradition begun by John the Baptist.

MAP: Do you invite those persons involved in any kind of Templar research and experiments around the world to come to your preceptory?

IS: Yes, I do! We have some accommodations here that they can stay in if they want. Or, if they want to stay in their own countries and communicate that way, that is fine also. If they want to become an associate member that can be done without them going through any rituals. They just pay a fee that covers the cost of documents and the postage for them.

MAP: Where did the name of your Scottish Templar organization, the Militi Templi Scotia, originate?

IS: To my knowledge no one has been able to find the origin of it. It was supposed to be the original bloodline of the Templars, although I don't know if there is any proof of that.

MAP: Do you know how old the Militi Templi Scotia is?

IS: It may have evolved out of the Holy Royal Order founded by Robert the Bruce. This could also be true of the other orders of Templars in Scotland. One is fronted by the Laird of Belgonie Castle, where the Templars wear cloaks of green, and other, the Knights of Scotland, which have a similar ritual to the Militi Templi Scotia.

MAP: So all these orders may have roots that go back to the original Templars?

IS: Yes. The ancient Templars are still with us today. The experts say that if you get three hundred Scottish persons in an audience at least one-third of those people will have genetic connections to someone in the past who was connected to the Templars. The person could have been a provider, an armorer, an assistant, a land manager or a Knight.

MAP: Were there preceptories of the Holy Royal Order around Scotland at the time of Robert the Bruce?

IS: Yes, there were preceptories but they were not just used for Templar activities.

MAP: Is it true that to become a member of the Militi Templi Scotia today you must be Scottish?

IS: No, but I am not a spokesperson for the Militi Templi Scotia. I am but

a member of the organization. To be a member of M.T.S. you must be made a squire first and then after 12 months you may receive the Accolade and become a Knight. During the 12 months as a Squire, you work on a special project. If the Grand Council members decide that you have put enough time into your project, you are given the Accolade of a Knight at Rosslyn Chapel or at the Prince Henry St. Clair Preceptory.

MAP: So, if I wanted I could become a knight of the Militi Templi Scotia?

IS: Yes, you can certainly apply, and if accepted you would need to have a physical presence here for the initiation ceremonies. We have people coming all the time who want to be members, but we try to be a bit selective. We are not just people who dress up in a white mantle with a red cross. We are people who pursue knowledge. When I put on the white mantle I am very proud, but I am also very concerned. It gives me a good feeling to know that I belong to an organization that I have helped to create and that it has got a future, but only if the people within the structure work towards its objective of wisdom and preservation.

MAP: You do the initiating?

IS: Yes. I am the Preceptor.

MAP: There are probably a lot of persons in the US who would be interested in either becoming a Templar or an Associate Member of your preceptory. I often encounter people with vivid dreams or what they believe is past-life recall of being a Templar. Some would like to realign with the Templar organization this lifetime, but for one reason or another are not interested in becoming members of the US based Templar groups.

IS: I know of a number of people within the Militi Templar Scotia who similarly believe that they are reincarnated Templars.

MAP: Interesting...That probably includes members of the Sinclair Clan. How big is the Clan these days?

IS: The clan system still exists in Scotland, but it exists more in the mind than in the body. The clan system is now spreads around the entire world. There are probably as many Scotsmen living in America as in Scotland.
MAP: Do you still have Sinclair Clan meetings or conclaves?

IS: Yes. The present Earl of Caithness recently held a clan gathering in the year 2000 for Sinclairs from Scotland, Canada, New Zealand, Australia – we had a total of about 250 who gathered here in Caithness.

MAP: Were any special Sinclair issues addressed during the gathering?

IS: Yes, many things came up, many decisions were made. It was the first time in many years the whole of the Clan was together. Rosslyn Chapel, for example, was talked about because, as you know, Rosslyn Chapel is the cradle of the Sinclairs, although Sinclair-Girnigoe Castle is an extension of that cradle. Our ideas and philosophy were generated at Rosslyn. The politics of Rosslyn Chapel were not discussed because they are not within our boundaries at this time. Concern for what is happening at Rosslyn was voiced, as well as how Rosslyn would affect the future of Clan Sinclair.

MAP: What about Roslin Castle? Was that discussed?

IS: The Castle and the Chapel are in the hands of the current Earl of Roslin, Peter Sinclair Erskin. The castle can currently be rented from the Rosslyn Trust. You could book it for a week, if you wanted. I think the Sinclairs would really love to be back at home in Roslin Castle and the guardians of Rosslyn Chapel. We have done more for Roslin Castle than anyone, and Rosslyn Chapel is our Holy Grail.

MAP: Are there many Sinclairs currently involved with Templarism and Freemasonry?

IS: Yes, a lot, both Masonic and non Masonic. I have been surprised over the years to find out how many Sinclairs around the world are involved with these organizations. There are, for example, many Sinclairs involved with Freemasonry in America. Some came to the gathering from Canada, Australia and other places.

MAP: Do you feel that the Sinclairs are truly united and working as one united clan?

IS: There is a form of unity between all of us, a body, but we are all free spirits. Everybody seems to be doing there own thing, but somewhere along the way it all comes together. But even though we are not all united geneti-

cally, we all consider each other cousins.

MAP: The better known Sinclairs, Andrew and Niven, do they help to hold the clan together?

IS: Yes, even though the chief of the clan, Malcolm Sinclair, holds remarkable power and influence within the clan, Niven, I would say is the most inspirational. He is a kind of mover. Andrew is a free spirit. He comes back to the fold in search of knowledge.

MAP: Do you think that the Clan Sinclair has inherited a certain power or magic from the early Sinclairs and Templars?

IS: We certainly question many things; unusual things happen to us. We are certainly the prime movers in areas where others fear to tread. Most of the time things work. They may not turn out just the way they were planned, but they do have a way of turning out right. We often seem to be at the right place at the right time. If you want to call that power, then I suppose it could be considered as such.

MAP: Money is also power. Your clan was once very wealthy, was it not?

IS: Yes. William Sinclair, the First Earl of Caithness was alleged to have dined on plates of gold. The whole of Roslin Castle was at that time full of gold and silver. The wealth continued until the Third Earl of Caithness, and then there was a major decline. The decline seems to have begun with the Fourth Earl of Caithness, who got heavily involved with castle building. At one point there were seven castles under construction at the same time and this caused a massive draining of capital. Later, the Sixth Earth of Caithness borrowed massive amounts of money from the Campbells. After he passed away and the money had not been repaid, the Campbells came and took over, for a time, the Earldom of Caithness.

MAP: In other words, the Sinclair money has been spent…

IS: It has been spent or secreted away. There is also the legend of Henry Sinclair – he could have taken the vast majority of Sinclair wealth to the New World, possibly depositing it in certain places, like the Oak Island Money Pit or perhaps Massachusetts.

MAP: What do you see as the future of the Sinclairs and Rosslyn Chapel?

IS: I think the restoration of Rosslyn Chapel is going along okay. I had real concern a couple of years ago when the scaffolding was put over the top of the chapel. It caused major problems – the water leaving the tin roof was going into the ground and making the entire area twice as wet as normal. Overall, the present caretakers have done a reasonable job, but I think that it is time it came back to the Sinclair ownership.

I firmly believe that 2005 will be a year of revelation. For people who are now searching for things, 2005 will be a pivotal year. 2004 will be a searching year, a testing year, a preparation year. We will plant the seeds in 2004 and reap the harvest in 2005. I believe the area around Sinclair-Girnigoe Castle, in fact all of Noss Head, will come alive again. For the next couple of years the Castle needs to be the center of attention for the Sinclairs, even more than the Chapel. I think the Castle is going to reveal some secrets that are hidden away within it.

MAP: What specific plans do you have for Sinclair-Girnigoe Castle?

IS: Ground scans have shown that there is a six foot cubed room cut into the rock directly below the kitchen area. In 2004, we will be investigating what might be there…

Postscript

Since this interview was conducted Ian Sinclair has officially resigned from the Militi Templi Scotia because the organization was not moving in the direction he desired it to. He is now a Preceptor of the reformed Order of the Scottish Knights Templar and its Gnostic branch known as the International Order of Gnostic Templars, both of which are dedicated to inducting into its fold seekers from all over the world, without regard for race, nationality or religion. Ian, like many Templar Knights, believes that the agenda of the original Knights was to exist without boundaries. It was their intention to be an international organization that would ultimately unite the spiritual traditions of the East with those of the West. When the Knights Templar were not able to complete their mission, their goal of international unification was later taken up by the European secret societies they helped to found, including the Freemasons, Illuminati, and Rosicrucians. Ian has also commited himself to completing this most important work of the first Templar Knights.

Sinclair-Girnigoe Castle at Noss Head.

Women Knights Templar

Women have been initiated as Knights almost as long as the Knights Templar Order has been in existence. During the past one-hundred years they have been either associated directly with the Templars, or with some of the other knighted orders, including the Teutonic Knights and the Order of the Garter. The Knights of St. John or Knights Hospitallers are known to have founded nunneries for its sisters in England, Aragon, Spain, and France. Women have also have been part of knightly orders that have an exclusively female membership, including The Order of the Hatchet, founded in Catalonia in 1149, as well as The Order of the Glorious Saint Mary, which was founded in Bologna in 1233. Today, women are currently members of certain international organizations of Templars, including the SMOTJ and OSMTH. They are also members in the English knightly orders of the Garter, the Royal Victorian Order, and the Order of Bath and of St. Michael and St. George. Women can currently become fully initiated Knights Templar in all the Scottish Templar Orders.

The following is part of a letter to the author from Dr. H. J. Nicholson, Professor of History and Archaeology at Cardiff University in England, which solely addresses women's participation in the Knights Templar Order. Dr. Nicholson has written numerous articles and books on the Knights Templar, including *The Knights Templar: A New History.* States Dr. Nicholson:

" They (women) were not knights or sergeants. When they appear in the records they are called sorores, sisters, and their function was to pray (like the chaplains in the order). They did not fight. So far as I can ascertain, there were no sisters in the East. I have found references to sisters in the Iberian Peninsula, France and the Low Countries, Italy and Germany. The only reference in England is to an associate sister rather than a full sister.

"Most of the references to sisters appear in charters of donation to the order; the sisters appear among the Templar as witnesses to a gift, or are giving a gift themselves. Scholars who study the order argue whether these are full sisters who had made the three religious vows of poverty, chastity and obedience or whether they were only associate members who had made a vow of obedience. However, we know that the order had a nunnery in Germany which it was given mid-thirteenth century by the local bishop. After the dissolution of therder the nuns refused to become Hospitallers, and the pope was asked to rule on the matter."

"The earliest reference to a woman being associated with the order is one Acalaidis in Rousillon who gave herself to the order under a vow of obedience in

1133 — so scholars see her as an associate rather than a full sister. There are a few references in the sources to individual women being sisters of the order in the twelfth century, but the first group reference comes from the house of Rourell in the kingdom of Aragon at the end of the twelfth century."

Interview with Joan Campbell, Scottish Knight Templar

Joan Campbell is one of the few high-ranking female Templar Knights in Scotland. She is head of the Association of Scottish Knight Templars and also the official Scottish Templar spokesperson for the OSMTH.

MAP: What Templar order or orders are you currently a member of?

JC: I am a member of three Templar organizations: The Chivalric Military Order of the Temple of Jerusalem known as CMOTJ; The Association of Scottish Knight Templars known as SKT; and OSMTH, the international Templar group.

MAP: Are you married and do you have a family?

JC: I am married and I have 5 children and 14 grandchildren.

MAP: How long have you been a Templar?

JC: I have been a member of the Templars since 1987.

MAP: What motivated you to become a member?

JC: I was and still am fascinated by anything to do with the Crusades and the Templars. In the early nineteen eighties I met some interesting people at a clan gathering and became friends with them. I was asked to join the Templars by one of them, who happened to be the Clan Chief. At that time I was too busy and just ignored the request. Then, the following year I again was asked to join, and again I ignored the request. When I was asked a third time it was made clear that you only got asked three times and if you did not join then you were never asked again. By this time I had more time to spare so I decided join the CMOTJ.

MAP: What were the prerequisites for you becoming a member? Are women allowed to become members of all the Templar organizations in Scotland, or are there some that they are not?

JC: The only prerequisites was that I had to be a practising Christian; Women are allowed in all of the groups in Scotland

MAP: What is your position in the organization and what are your duties?

JC: My position at the beginning was as ordinary member [Dame of the order] I became Preceptor of our area within three years and Secretary to the order 4 years later. Then I became Grand Prior in 1997. I was the first woman to do this in SCOTLAND. I was voted in by a large majority of voting members.

At this time I have retired as Grand Prior of the CMOTJ, but am currently head of the Association of Scottish Knight Templars. In this position I am the Scottish spokesperson within the international organization of Templars, the OSMTJ. My time of office ends at the end of this year (2003). In my own small group of Templars (her preceptory) I am now the membership secretary, a position I am happy with as I am now retired.

MAP: How many women are currently members of your order, and what is the women to men Templar ratio throughout Scotland?

JC: We have in my group roughly 50% female, but the ratio throughout the other groups in Scotland is definitely smaller.

MAP: Do you feel that you are given equal rights and opportunities as the men in your order?

JC: Because of my strong character, yes. But remember, not everyone wants to be deeply involved with high positions

MAP: Is your Templar order principally patriarchal, and would you like to see it become more matriarchal?

JC: The order is definitely Patriarchal. There are times when it would be nice to have more women in the International group.

MAP: Do women have the same levels or degrees as men in the order?

JC: We do have the same levels and degrees as men.

MAP: Can you hold the same positions as men in the order?

JC: Yes, we can hold the same positions as men. I have done so and still do.

MAP: Do you attend the same meetings as men? Do you attend the same ceremonies?

JC: Yes, we attend the same meetings and attend the same ceremonies.

MAP: How far back in history have women been initiated into Templar orders?

JC: There is research being done on this question. I will send you some literature on this. (The information above on women knights was based on the literature she sent).

MAP: Do you believe as some do that the Templars may have at sometime been worshippers of some form of the Goddess and therefore aligned with the path of female spirituality? Could their sexual tantric activities have evolved out of their affiliation to an eastern Goddess related tradition?

JC: I have never heard of this theory so I can only say that I do not believe this nor do I know of anyone else within any of the (Templar) groups who even thinks like this.

MAP: Have there been any Templar related orders you know of founded solely for women?

JC: Only in the past a long time ago.

MAP: Could a woman found a branch or priory of your order by herself?

JC: The answer is yes to this question if that person is not very clever. I have found during my time as a Templar it is mostly men who want to start things up, especially when there is already any number of groups already available. It is usually men who think they are more important than anyone else. This has been the bugbear of the modern day. There are numerous men who have done this (continually founding organiza-

tions) and they have caused many problems throughout the world.

MAP: Could an American woman be initiated into your order and/or possibly found a branch of it within the USA?

JC: Yes, but under the new rules in our International group, OSMTH, we are trying to discourage this as we believe that prospective members should be encouraged to join their own national group. Of course, we can affiliate to any other country once we are full members within our own country.

MAP: Do women play as big a part as men in the international meetings of Templar orders?

JC: At the moment we have very few women within the International group. We keep trying to get more woman to attend these functions, but without much success. I personally think this is because women in general think Templarism is for men only. I have found only respect for my position within the International Group. But that is not to say I have found it easy. In fact, I would say it has become very hard to climb any ladder within the international order and it may be because I am a woman, although I have never let it get me down.

MAP: According to the philosophy of reincarnation, do you think that some women who are attracted to Templarism may have been male knights in another lifetime and this is the reason they are attracted to the order now?

JC: I think that some people do believe this as there are times when in conversation with both men and women things are said that relates to this. But I have only found a few who think like that

MAP: Are there any public assistance programs run exclusively by female Templars?

JC: We do not run any public assistance programs specifically for women or by women. We equally help (men and women) at all times.

Interview with Margo Daru Elliot of Militi Templi Scotia

MAP: You are currently a Squire, are you not, of the Militi Templi Scotia?

MDE: Yes. I am a Squire preparing to become a knight, which I will do sometime next year, probably next March (2004). People will decide if I am ready…the order is still pretty hierarchal. I am part of a preceptory located in Edinborough.

MAP: Are there many women in your preceptory?

MDE: We have one woman who is a knight. She is the only woman besides myself. I am currently squire to her.

MAP: Would you describe your preceptory as predominantly patriarchal?

MDE: Yes. But I have to be fair and say that even though most of the members are men I have not received any noticeable discrimination from them. I am acutely aware of the patriarchal element, having encountered it quite a lot in my life, through the financial world and other areas.

MAP: But you have even deeper roots with the Goddess Tradition than the MTS?

MDE: Yes. I have traveled quite extensively while working to bring back the Goddess Principle rather than the worship of any specific goddess.

MAP: Are you currently involved with any goddess circles or goddess organizations?

MDE: Yes, I am a member of a number of women's circle. I participate in Grandmother Circles and circles where we observe Celtic mysteries and shamanic rites. But I am currently most involved with my own personal "Morganna Speaks" (a dramatic production) because I have a particular connection to Cornwall through one side of my family. So I have been very connected to the Arthurian legend for quite awhile.

MAP: Can you explain what Morganna Speaks is about?

MDE: It is a presentation I do during which I take on the part of Morganna. Morgan le Fay was the half sister of Arthur. She was closely connected to Merlin and possessed magical powers. She had nine sisters, not actual blood sisters. They were called the Sisters of the Ladies of Avalon and possessed the ancient magical rites. She was also related to the high priestesses of Brittany.

MAP: I know that you have done a lot of research on the Templars, including traveling to the places in southern France where they resided. What have learned regarding the Templars and their connection to the Goddess Tradition?

MDE: I have done quite a lot of investigative work, as have many people connected to the Goddess Tradition, with Mary Magdalene, as well as the influence of the feminine on those who have been connected to the Templar Order. I am certain that there is much more that needs to be discovered about this. When I was in Istanbul I met a number of men of eminent standing, including Islamic diplomats from Jordan, Iraq and Kuwait. One day a group of them invited me to their table to tell me explicitly that they were not against women. They know that we in the West consider them antagonistic to women, but they have great respect for the female principle. I believe that this is an attitude that the Templars learned from the Moslems while they were in the Middle East.

MAP: The research you have done on the French Cathars…does that tell you anymore about the Templar/Goddess connection?

MDE: I am sixty years old now and have been constantly visiting southern France since I was 18 years old. What I know about the Cathars comes from both academic research as well as personal revelation, because I have had past-life recall of being one of them. Before I came across any books on the Cathars, I was down in the south of France visiting all the chateaus and staying with different people who were giving snippets of information about the Cathars. From one family I stayed with I learned that the head of Montsequr had been a woman, a priestess and an initiate. Among the Cathars there had been a perfect balance of male and female priests and priestesses. The Parfait or Perfecti were the ones who held the priestly roles. The Perfecti were celibate, but previous to taking on their priestly positions they had been married because they needed those experiences of life. This woman priestess of Montsequr had been married and bore eight children, but at some point decided she would pursue the Perfecti path. She then went through the last Cathar initiation that taught one how to transcend death.

MAP: Did you visit Montsequr at that time?

MDE: Yes. I was told that I needed to go to Montsequr, but I at first

hesitated. I didn't want to go because I knew that I would find something there. But the man I was staying with gave me a basket of fruit and cheese and some water for the journey. So I went on my own to Montsequr.

MAP: Were you on your way to someplace else at the time?

MDE: Yes, Rennes le Chateau. But I knew I had to go to Montsequr. So I drove to there, parked my car and began walking. In those days there were no huts charging money. I was all alone.

I climbed up to the castle of Montsequr and sat right at the top of it, on the chateau walls. I had a very large book with me, my journal, wherein I wrote the guidance I received. I began writing and drawing in the book and quickly became completely unaware of the time. It felt like I shapeshifted into another reality. Then, when I did become more aware of my surroundings I realized that most of the day had passed and I better climb back down.

I began to walk down but soon realized that I had lost my way, and there was nobody there to get directions from. I returned back to the castle where I found a French man and his son. They told me to go in another direction, but again I got lost. Returning one more time to the castle I realized that everyone had disappeared and there was no one left to get directions from. I started climbing down another route but I was on the opposite side that the main trail was on. It was steep, and I quickly became terrified. Carrying my big book, and with only a light dress and sandals on, I came to place that was a shear drop-off and I knew I would never be able to make it down it. I told myself "this is it, this is the end of the line." Then a voice, who said it was a Cathar spirit, said "Don't panic, you were here before. You've done this before and you can do it again." Then the voice said "Put your feet where I tell you, put your hands where I tell you." I started obeying, but the last thing I can remember is that I could not step over the next large gap in front of me. I simply leaned against a rock and can not remember anything else…except that I found myself at the bottom of Montsequr.

MAP: How far had you come that you aren't aware of?

MDE: Three-quarters of the way down the mountain. I had only been one-quarter of the way down.

MAP: So you just closed your eyes and then you were at the bottom…

MDE: Yes, but the most extraordinary thing was that I must have climbed down, perhaps in a trance, because my fingers were all bloody and my sandals were ripped.

MAP: You must have been pretty shaken up…

MDE: Yes. I immediately got into my car and drove to the village of Montsequr as fast as I could. Getting out of my car while in the town, I hid against a wall. Then the voice again spoke up saying "Yes, you were a Parfait and this is how you had to hide."

MAP: The entire experience was apparently calculated to awaken you to who you had been…

MDE: Yes. In retrospect, I believe the whole experience was an initiation. It occurred to wake me up to what I had been, a Cathar Parfait, as well as my connection to Montsequr. I do believe that the Cathars had transcended pain and fear, otherwise how could they have thrown themselves, laughing, into the flames? I experienced their transcendence on my climb back down the mountain of Montsequr.

MAP: Do you think that the Cathars may have developed magical abilities through their rites?

MDE: Yes, and I believe that it was the Cathar women who safeguarded the magical tradition. In the rites of this tradition and in their alchemy- which I know that the Templars had knowledge of and practiced- it was necessary to work with women and the female principle to get the best results.

MAP: So, do you believe that the Templars also once worked with women?

MDE" Either that or they were able to contact the sacred feminine within themselves. Some famous alchemists, such as Nicholas Flamel, who succeeded in transmuting a base metal into gold, worked with women in their experiments. Although you never hear of her, the Lady Paranel assisted Flamel in his experiments. The patriarchy has suppressed this information.

MAP: Is there any evidence of the Templars as having been married and/or observing their Tantric rites with women?

MDE: Not that I have discovered, but lay Templar Knights existed who were definitely married and most probably practiced Tantra.

MAP: What other rites, besides alchemy and possibly Tantra, were practiced by both Cathars and Templars?

MDE: Well, the Templars were accused of working with black cats, and the Cathars or Cathi were known as the "People of the Cat." The cat was a sacred among them and part of the Cathar rites. Another common symbol for both Templars and Cathars was the rose, which is the symbol of the heart and alchemy. As the Cathars died on the flames, roses were thrown in along with them to symbolize their final alchemical merger into the love of Spirit.

Like the Templars, the Cathars practiced transcending fear and pain, and both orders were very austere. As you know, the Templars were always the first on the battlefield and the last ones to leave. So perhaps there were common Gnostic practices both sects observed for transcending human emotions. One reason that the Cathars practiced transcending fear is to prepare themselves for the next incarnation. They did not want to end life without honor and dignity. During the two weeks they were kept imprisoned on Montsequr before being massacred, the Cathars practiced these rites to prepare for their own deaths.

The Johannites

As mentioned in Chapter 9, during the year 1907 aspects of the Johannite Church that had been revived by Fabre-Palaprat merged into the *L'Eglise Catholique Gnostique* founded by Jean Bricaud, a student of Jules Dionel, one of the 19th century revivers of Gnosticism in France. Bricaud attempted to bring all the divergent sects of Gnostic Christianity into one united organization, even going so far as to procure initiation from the lineal heads of each sect to do so, but many Gnostic sects refrained from becoming part of his synthesis. A number of these fringe Gnostic sects even became more alienated from each other by becoming infiltrated with Haitian Voodoo and the sexual and occult rites of the OTO. So the formation of a universal Gnostic synthesis had to wait for a more conducive time. This was to finally occur in the 21st century, when all the various Gnostic sects worldwide united under the common banner of the Johannite Church.

Following World War II, Gnosticism spread throughout Europe as well as in the Americas. At that time Bricaud's Universal Gnostic Church was renamed *Eglise Gnostic Apostolic*, the Apostolic Gnostic Church, and became headquartered in Brazil. Its highest official at the time was the Primate and Patriarch, Pedro Freire, who was given the honorary title of Johannes XIII. Freire designated as Primate of North America an American named Roger Saint Victor Herard, who then contributed to the spread of Gnosticism by founding churches in many major cities around the USA. But Herard eventually died without leaving a successor, and the preservation of the Apostolic Gnostic Church appeared threatened until Jorge Rodriquez Villa and Michael P. Bertiaux, two lineal holders of Gnostic sects from Europe and the Americas, took it over. The cross-pollination these Cupholders engendered was fortuitous and caused the apostolic lines that Bricaud was not able to synthesize himself to finally unite under one umbrella, that of the Johannite Church. Then, in 2002, an American named James Foster was chosen as Patriarchal Primate of the unified Johannite Church and given the honored title of Tau Johannes III.

Primate James Foster currently lives in Cleveland Ohio where he gives weekly sermons of the Johannite Church. The following is an interview with him from his office:

MAP: How did you get involved with the Johannites?

Primate: I think it was just a matter of being in the right place at the right time. I met my consecrator in Toronto. We were at a convention for an organization we both belonged to. We were sitting around drinking coffee and struck up a conversation. We both realized that we had a lot of common interests. He slowly began revealing more about himself and the Church. He lived in San Francisco. Our dialogue was to last for many years, continuing later as both on-line and phone correspondence.

During our initial conversation, I heard myself say "This sounds like what I have been doing all along, how do I get involved?" The next thing I know the years have whizzed by and someone is saying why don't we put you in charge?

MAP: Why did they choose you to be Primate? What were your special qualifications?

Primate: When I was consecrated, I was consecrated with right to succession. I was an auxiliary bishop, which means I was an assistant bishop with right to succession. When my predecessor retired, I was moved up. The

way we use primate is not like the way pope I used. We have another primate in Canada, for example. The primate is simply the senior ranking bishop in a geographical region. It doesn't necessarily make me any more important than any other bishop. It just means I speak more to the public than the other bishops do.

MAP: Are there primates all over the world?

Primate: There are three primates in Brazil. There is one in America, one in Canada, and one in Turkey.

MAP: The one in Turkey, is he the only one outside the Americas?

Primate: Yes. But he is the Head Primate. If we used the term of pope or patriarch, he would be that for our Church.

MAP: Where is he located in Turkey?

Primate: He is located in a little town just outside of Ephesus.

MAP: Ephesus…Do you mean the ancient town of John the Apostle?

Primate: Yes. It is one of the two main towns. Ephesus and Smyrna were the two earliest Johannite centers.

MAP: Has the Head Primate been located in one of those areas for the past two thousand years?

Primate: We were mainly grouped around Smyrna right up until about 120 A.D. That is when there was a split in the Johannite community. One faction broke off to follow the more Gnostic teachings of the movement. We are part of that group. The other group became a more mainstream body of Johannites. After the split, we stayed around Smyrna for many years - up to the seventh century - when we were run out by the Moslems. We spent many years in Jerusalem after that - right up until the time of the Crusades, actually. Then, with the consecration of Hughes de Payen, the Johannite Church really took of. It found fertile soil in southern France.

MAP: So you consider Theoclete, the initiator of Hughes de Payen, to be part of your lineage?

Primate: He was, at that time, the "John." He was the sovereign patriarch.

MAP: John is the dynastic title of your patriarchs?

Primate: Yes. Traditionally we have four primary bishops or primates that take the title of one of the four Evangelists, Matthew, Mark, Luke, and John. The highest ranking primate holds the title of the "John."

MAP: So even though historically he is known as Theoclete, his title was John?

Primate: Yes. He was referred to as John. He signed epistles as "John."

MAP: Where are the records of your lineage? Are there records that document the Johannite lineage following John the Apostle?

Primate: Yes, we have sheets of apostolic succession. We are one of the few churches that can trace our lineage directly back to an apostle. Our lines of succession are more complete and better documented than those of the popes. This has been important for us, especially during the last century, since we are so often challenged by the mainstream churches. We have about fifty pages which are nothing but lists of names and dates of consecration.

MAP: Is there a lineal transmission of some kind that takes place when one becomes a Primate?

Primate: There is, and it is given with a specific purpose. The Johannite Church has what we refer to as the Secret of Saint John. The Secret of St. John is held by the four Evangelist primates. It is passed verbally. As far as I know, it has never been written down. The transmission at ordination is based upon the Valentinian cosmology. It gives the ability to transcend the authority of the seven archons, which have traditionally been represented by the seven planets, in order to maintain the Secret of St. John. We also have an internal organization referred to as the Knights of St. John. Their function is to support the four offices in the keeping of the Secret. You can get an idea about the rite when you read through the consecration of the bishop when the Secret is being passed. There is an anointing of the hands with specific Greek letters and Greek vowels and these

are intoned. This creates an attunement through vibration. Both the symbol and the anointing oil and the intoning of the vowels over the new bishop comes from another bishop who has previously received this transmission.

MAP: Where did St. John himself receive the Secret?

Primate: He received it by virtue of location, by being the beloved disciple at the foot of the cross.

MAP: Are you saying that there was at that time a transmission from Jesus to John and that was the Secret?

Primate: It was a combination of transmission and information. John gained special knowledge by being a witness at that time.

MAP: Do you include John the Baptist as part of the Johannite tradition?

Primate. Yes. According to out tradition, both John the Baptist and Jesus were initiates of various Egyptian mysteries. As far we can best put together, John was the mentor to Jesus and/or the head of the local community to which Jesus belonged.

MAP: The Tau title that consecrated bishops receive – is this related to the Egyptian influence in your lineage?

Primate. Yes it is.

MAP: Do you agree with the Mandean history of John and Jesus?

Primate: Yes and no. We are not as upset with Jesus as are the Mandeans. Historically, the way that the Johannite Church explains the last three years of Jesus's life is that at that time there was going to be an overshadowing of someone by the logos. There were several contenders who were eligible to serve this function. John the Baptist was the frontrunner and it appeared that he would be the one chosen. Jesus, to use a modern metaphor, threw his hat in at the last minute because the appropriate qualities manifested in him at a late stage. His personality and qualities distinguished him and he was the one chosen. There was a little rivalry between Jesus and John because of this. How much is hard to say, because John was

murdered relatively soon after this. It may have been extensive since there was a lot of hostility between the group led by Jesus and the one led by John's primary disciple, Simon Magus. It was felt that Jesus usurped John's place.

MAP: What do you think about the historical records indicating that the Knights Templar renounced Jesus as their savior, defiled the cross, and then aligned themselves with some other savior, perhaps John the Baptist?

Primate: This is very much directed to what we call the Secret of St. John. One of the interpretations of Baphomet is that it is a corruption of Baphe Metis, which translates as baptism into wisdom or understanding. Baphe is a Greek dyers term. When a clothe was completely soaked in a dye, that was baphe. We interpret Baphomet as being saturated by wisdom – which is based on the Secret of Saint John. The Templar initiation was not a process of rejecting or disparaging the figure of the Christ or the person of Jesus. Instead, is was a method of overcoming centuries of mainstream Roman Catholic indoctrination.

MAP: Do you believe that there was a mummified head called Baphomet?

Primate: Yes. It was the head of John the Baptist.

MAP: According to records, the Templars considered the head to belong to their true savior. Through their ritual of initiation did they mean to indicate that John the Baptist and not Jesus was their true savior?

Primate: It is true that the head was referred to as the head of the savior, but more often it was referred to as the Christ or the Anointed. But these terms do not negate Jesus as also the savior of the Templars. Historically, even primates in the Johannite Church have been referred to as the Christ or the Christos.

MAP: So John and Jesus were both saviors of the Templars? Could this be related to the Dead Sea Scrolls, which prophesy the coming of two messiah's, a Messiah of David and a Messiah of Aaron?

Primate: This is correct. There were indeed two messiahs. And a lot of the anger projected to Jesus by the disciples of John manifested because at the death of John, rather than giving due regard to John, Jesus repre-

sented himself as the Messiah of both David and Aaron.

MAP: But before the death of John the Baptist there were officially two Messiah's?

Primate. Yes, That is correct. The lineage, knowledge and transmission of John continued, but his function of messiah was not passed on. The role played by these messiahs was one caused by an aeonic overshadowing. Beings from the plueroma, from the fullness, who had a vibratory affinity with these individuals because of the training they had undergone, assisted them in this function.

MAP: Do you think head of John the Baptist still exists and is hidden away someplace?

Primate: Yes.

MAP: Are you able to say where?

Primate: No.

MAP: Within your Johannite logo is a cup with a snake curled around it. I have seen this symbol associated with John the Apostle. Is this the ancient symbol of the Johannites?

Primate: Yes. The cup with the snake curled around it is synonymous with a flame emerging from the cup.

MAP: What do the cup and flame represent?

Primate: The cup is representative of both the Holy Grail and the human vehicle which possesses the sacred flame within.

MAP: Would you then call the Johannites Guardians of the Holy Grail?

Primate: In a sense. For a time the actual (physical) Holy Grail was in our possession.

MAP: Does it still exist?

Primate: Yes. I have been told where it exists, but I am not at liberty to say

MAP: Do you foresee that the head of John the Baptist and the Holy Grail will be rediscovered or re-revealed to the world?

Primate: Yes. The Johannite Church has a plan that is referred to as the Plan of Five. These are stages of revealing that will occur as our church becomes public again. The tentative date for everything becoming public is May 5, 2005.

MAP: Isn't it public now?

Primate: Yes, to a degree. It became public again in the year 2000. The last time the church was public was under the restoration of Fabre-Palaprat in France.

MAP: In the Johannite literature there is reference to a Synod that occurred in 1973 when Gnostic groups from all over world met. Supposedly a representative of the Peruvian Monastery of the Seven Rays attended. Is there a connection between the Johannites and this monastery? (This question was asked because the Seven Ray Brotherhood is intimately related to Sanat Kumara, the ancient master of Sri Lanka who founded the Holy Grail lineage of John the Baptist).

Primates: Yes. The connection is derived from the mid-sixties, when a large number of monks of the monastery left and moved to Spain. When in Spain, one of our bishops, Jean-Maine, was initiated into their lineage and received from them several teachings related to St. John and our Gnostic cosmology. These teachings were transmitted by Jean-Maine to his successors.

MAP: Do you continue to communicate with members of the Seven Ray Brotherhood?

Primate: Yes. That is handled by our Bishop Tau Orphaeo IV, who resides in the mid-west.

MAP: I have read that at some point Catholic rites were assimilated into the Johannite Church. Is there currently much Catholic influence in your rites and ideology?

Primate: Yes and no. A Roman Catholic showing up at our service would

see much that is familiar, just as he would if he showed up at an Episcopal service. There are differences, however. We have a more pronounced epiclesus than you would normally find in the more western influenced liturgies. And we are generally more intimate with the congregation.

MAP: What is the current Gnostic influence in the Church mass?

Primate: There are addresses to the Archons, to Sophia, and to the Holy Logos. In fact, there are more references to the Holy Logos than there is to Jesus. During the mass, the participants are really operating within the sphere of their own sacred flames and the priest is not considered the intermediary between them and the Divine. He is simply the one wearing the robes and certainly not any more sacred or divine than anyone else. During the consecration you often find the congregation passing the cup between themselves rather than each receiving it only from the priest as it is done in Roman Catholic mass. They thus honor what they receive from each other.

MAP: Between masses are their Gnostic practices that those in the church daily observe?

Primate: Yes. There are a lot of similarities between Buddhism and Gnostic Christianity in its Johannite expression. Some form of regular chanting and meditation is usually observed.

MAP: There are some legends that maintain that John went to the East and founded some sects there. Are there any records of this in the Johannite Church?

Primate: John, like all the other apostles, did a lot of traveling. He did travel to the East and there are several legitimate branches of Johannite expression there, although they are not affiliated with the larger Johannite church. We do, however, recognize them as being legitimate.

MAP: When you perform your spiritual rites do you invoke St. John or just Jesus to assist you?

Primate: There are two masses. There is a private mass that is performed by the priest alone and there is the public mass. In the public mass there is section at the beginning called the Institutional Narrative which is a retelling of the Johannite story. This is followed by an invocation to all the sov-

ereign patriarchs, including John. This is, however, more pronounced in the private mass.

MAP: When does the private mass take place?

Primate: The private mass is said daily.

MAP: If someone wanted to become part of the Johannite Church, what could they do?

Primate: We have several study groups composed of persons who want to be part of the church, but they are not near one of the cities where we have churches. If someone one wants to start a study group where they are, they can contact us and we will help them by providing Johannite literature and getting them in contact with members of the clergy that are relatively close to them. Perhaps from this study group will emerge someone who wants to pursue ordination and the eventual establishment of a Johannite Church.

MAP: As part of your Johannite emblem there is a banner that reads in Latin "Order of the Sacred Flame." What is the Sacred Flame ?

Primate: The Agathodeamon, the Good Spirit, the Holy Angel, the Higher Self, the Divine Spark of an individual.

MAP: This is the same flame that emerges from the cup?

Primate: Yes. It is the personal manifestation and indwelling of the Holy Spirit.

MAP: The flame is related to the snake coiled around the cup?

Primate: They are one and the same.

MAP: I have traditionally associated the snake with power, or Kundalini…

Primate: Yes. We generally equate the flame with the eastern expression of the Kundalini.

MAP: Would you say that this is the power that is exchanged during the primate transmission?

Primate: No. The ability to arouse that and control the Kundalini comes through the transmission.

MAP: Are you saying, then, that the Kundalini is already awakened when the primate transmission occurs and what is received is the ability to control that power?

Primate: Yes.

MAP: How is the power initially awakened?

Primate: All the initiatory sacraments are designed to awaken this energy.

MAP: Did the practices to awaken Kundalini begin with John the Apostle?

Primate: Yes. The common story that associates John with the serpent encoiled cup - that he was given poison wine and when he prayed over it a snake came out - is an invention. Traditionally, what that has represented is that it was John was the Apostle who taught the uncoiling of the snake or the rising of this power.

MAP: Was this the special wisdom John received from Jesus that the others did not?

Primate: Yes.

Author: In your public relations material you are called the Dean of the College of Seven. Can you explain to me what the College of Seven is?

Primate: The College of Seven is the administrative board of the Order of the Sacred Flame. There are seven directors.

Interview with Mandean Matriarch, Lamea Abbas Amara

Lamea Abbas Amara is an elderly Mandean woman from Iraq currently living in San Diego. Of pure Mandean blood, Lamea has contributed to the Mandean movement in the USA by publishing a monthly magazine, and by being the caretaker of some priceless Mandean texts inherited from her family. Being very concerned with the current plight of the Mandean people around the globe, she is currently working to create a universal Mandean community in Florida. This interview was taken from her home in San Diego.

MAP: How long have you been in America?

LAA: I came eighteen years ago. I left Iraq in 1979. I went to Lebanon and Morocco. My son was studying in San Diego so I decided to come to America. I liked it and have been here ever since.

MAP: Your name is interesting. Is it Mandean? (This question was asked because the name is similar to the author's name of Amaru, which is from the Peruvian Quechuan language, a sister tongue to Sanscrit.)

LAA: It is from a language that came before Arabic. Amara is the name of the place of my family in Iraq.

MAP: Do you have relatives living in Iraq now?

LAA: Most of my relatives have left there.

MAP: Those that remain…are they having problems with the unrest in Iraq now?

LAA: They have always had problems. This is not new to them. As it has been in the past, they have no protection from any government. But many have left for their safety. They have gone to Iran, Sweden, Holland, New Zealand, Australia, Great Britain, America, Belgium, Denmark, and a small number are now in Arab countries.

MAP: Are you able to observe your Mandean sacred rites in America?

LAA: Yes, I try to, with my sister and son. We are also publishing a Mandean magazine. It is the first Mandean magazine in 5000 years.

MAP: Do you meet with other Mandeans for special rites where you live?

LAA: Yes, we have about 100 Mandeans in San Diego. We try to make opportunities to meet together on weekends and holidays. We stay home on Sundays, the most important day, and perform our sacred rituals with

our families. We also get out in nature that day because Mandeans worship nature, especially water. It is for us a major sin to urinate in or pollute water.

MAP: Is there a river in San Diego that you go to for your baptismal rites?

LAA: No, that is why we want to find and purchase a place with a river flowing through it. I have thought of Florida because it is nearby Europe and many Mandeans can come who are living in Europe.

MAP: Have you found a place in Florida yet?

LAA: No. And we have no money to buy land right now.

MAP: Are you doing anything to raise the money you need?

LAA: No, because I don't know how to raise money. We had some money for the magazine but the money has gone and the magazine has stopped. The Mandeans are poor and many are without work now. I have nobody to help me.

MAP: Do you plan to resume the publication of the magazine again?

LAA: Yes, if I can find the money I need for it.

MAP: What is your circulation?

LAA: We make photocopies and send it everywhere, to many people. It is free. I write almost all the articles for it myself.

MAP: Can I get some issues for study?

LAA: Yes, but the magazine is in Arabic.

MAP: Are you currently able to perform regular baptisms as prescribed by your tradition?

LAA: We do, but we make it easy for ourselves. Instead of going to the river we use our showers or our sinks. There are many baptisms we observe. If a person has sex on a given night they must take a shower to

purify before touching anything. Every month during their periods the girls must take special showers to purify themselves from head to toe. After going to the toilet we must purify ourselves with water. Before eating, also.

MAP: I would like to ask you a few questions now about your prophet John the Baptist.

LAA: You might want to know that one of the books I have in Arabic is the Book or Study of Yahya Yohana, the Mandai name for John the Baptist. Yahya denotes one who lives and does not die. Yohana means "live life." His mother called him this name because she did not want him to die. She was very protective of John. She hid him when the Jews tried to circumcise him because in the Mandai tradition a human is born perfect. They don't need anything cut away.

MAP: And John means the same as Yohana?

LAA: Yes, life, to live life.

MAP: Do you believe that John was the Messiah?

LAA: We don't use the word "Messiah." We believe that John was the last prophet of the Mandeans. We existed before John for many thousands of years. We are a very ancient people and we have had many prophets.

MAP: Do the Mandeans believe that there will be other prophets among their people in the future?

LAA: No. Everybody is a prophet of himself. But wise women and wise men will continue to come forth from the Mandai and do something good in the world. They are our future prophets. They will be like Thomas Edison, the inventor of the light bulb.

MAP: Do you count as your prophets the ones in the Bible?

LAA: Some were our prophets. Abraham was from us…he was a Mandai. We believe that Moses was also Mandai. Mandai is the Gnostic tradition. Gnostic and Mandai both mean "knowledge." The Mandai always seek

to learn knowledge. For example, a Mandai must learn reading and writing when they are seven years old. This is the Mandai law. Teach your child the alphabet and reading and writing. Then do something for the Earth and for the Earth's people. Practice law, medicine, goldsmithing, etc.

MAP: What about the prophet Jesus? The Mandeans apparently believe he distorted the teachings of John.

LAA: We believe that Jesus was one of us. He was a Mandai. He was a relative of John the Baptist. His cousin. They came from the same religion and shared the same knowledge. In the Bible John was giving Jesus his second baptism. In Mandai tradition there are two important baptisms; you get one when you are young , when you officially become Mandai, and later you get one to become a Mandai priest in order to baptize others. John gave Jesus the second baptism because Jesus wanted to become a Mandai priest. After that baptism, those who were not Mandai made Jesus a messiah or a god.

MAP: So Jesus was a Mandai priest?

LAA: Yes, but he was one for a very short time. And he didn't baptize Mandai. He baptized other people.

MAP: Did all the people John baptized become Mandai?

LAA: Yes.

MAP: Did Jesus transgress the Mandai teachings?

LAA: Jesus wanted to make the Mandai religion easier. He tried to change some things. He ate with non-Mandai people, and he ate without washing his hands. This is against the Mandai law. Also, he did not forbid eating some food and Mandai people are forbidden to eat some kinds of food. Jesus was easier to follow than John the Baptist. John was very strict about following the law.

MAP: Is Jesus considered a Mandean prophet?

LAA: No. Mandai is its own religion. Jesus became separated from it and created his own religion. We are different from Christians. We believe the world is heaven and we don't have to wait until we die to go to heaven. We must live good lives; we must make money; we must have enjoyment. This is the life the Mandai try to live, not just a life of prayer and hoping for a better world afterwards.

MAP: So you are constantly seeking to make Earth paradise?

LAA: Yes. The Mandai are very practical people. In this way they are similar to the Jews, which they were a part of until Moses died.

MAP: Before Moses the history says your people came from Sri Lanka. Is this right?

LAA: Yes, some Mandai wrote about this…and later on when the Portuguese army came to Basra they sent some of the Mandai to Sri Lanka. This was after the Portuguese came to our shops and asked who we were. We told them we are the "People of John the Baptist." So they put some of the young Mandai boys in ships and took them to Sri Lanka. But we have lost contact with those boys…

MAP: I understand that today your people living in Al Qurna in southern Iraq are calling it the Garden of Eden.

LAA: There are many places they are calling the Garden of Eden. There is a place in Yemen they are calling the Garden of Eden. It seems that many people have different ideas about this.

MAP: Why did the Mandai people go to southern Iraq. Was it because they wanted to be near the Garden of Eden there?

LAA: No. They went there because there are many, many rivers they could use for their baptisms. I think, according to my study, that the Mandai are the remains of the Sumerian people. Some people say that the Sumerians came from India and Sri Lanka, so the Sumerians may have been the original Mandai. In Iraq, they mixed with the Aramaic people who came from the north from Syria and Lebanon. The Aramaic came to Iraq and mixed with the remains of the Sumerians to produce the Mandai.

MAP: Do the Mandai today worship some of the old Sumerian gods?

LAA: Perhaps, but they are called something else in Mandai.

MAP: John was supposedly taught by Mandean adepts on a place called Mount Parwan. Do you know where that mountain is located?

LAA: I believe it is in Palestine or Lebanon. John said they "took me and taught me." They took him and sent him back at 21 years of age.

MAP: Do you believe that John was also an Essene?

LAA: I feel sure of it.

MAP: Were the Essenes and the Mandai one and the same?

LAA: Yes. The Essene rites were very similar to what the Mandai today practice. They also wore white like the Mandai priests. Like the Mandai, the Essenes didn't use the meat or skin of an animal, only the wool. And they also practiced baptism and studied very hard like the Mandai priests. John the Baptist was a priest trained by the Mandai and Essenes on Mt. Carmel.

MAP: Your tradition teaches that John was a special kind of adept called a Nasurai.

LAA: Nasurai means the same as Mandai. They both mean "knowledge." A Nasurai is a special Mandai, one who studies the religious books and baptizes.

MAP: Are their Nasurai in your tradition today?

LAA: Yes, but very few. Today the Nasurai are the great Mandai scientists, writers, and poets. They give a lot to the country of Iraq.

MAP: According to Mandai tradition, what happened to the body of John?

LAA: He is in a tomb built by the Mandai in Lebanon. This place is very holy for the Mandai, and many visit it. It was later taken over by the Christians, and now it is a mosque. A similar thing happened in Bethlehem, which was also a Mandai place. The Mandai built a special temple there.

Then the Jews came and took it over, and they were followed by the Christians who made a church there. The same thing happened in Mecca, which was also originally a Mandai holy place. It was anciently known as the "Home of God." Then the Moslems came and took it over and now it is forbidden for Mandai to go there.

MAP: What do the Mandai say about the stone in the Kaaba. Where did it come from?

LAA: The histories say that it came from the heavens. The Mandai used to put olive oil on the rock and pray next to it. They also used to go to the Great Pyramid every year and burned candles inside while praying. But the Turks killed them when they occupied Egypt, and the Mandai stopped going there.

MAP: It sounds as though the Mandai have resided in many places on Earth...

LAA: Yes, and before that the history says that we came from another planet called Alma benhura. It means the "World of Goodness." The original Mandai came and married the women of Earth and taught mankind.

MAP: Did the first Mandai go to Sri Lanka? Your history books say that the Mandai came from Sri Lanka...

LAA: Yes, as I have said we came from Sri Lanka as the Sumerians. The Mandai of today are the remains of the ancient Sumerians. Many of us look like Indians from India. Even my father looked Indian. I myself could pass for an Indian.

MAP: So, would it be right to say that the Mandai have lived in Mesopotamia for thousands of years, ever since the founding of the Sumerian civilization?

LAA: Yes. Especially in southern Iraq. There was originally very many of us, but we have been killed off by Jews, by Christians, by Moslems. We have been forced to change our religion. Now, there are very few of us left. There are in the world now less than 100,000 Mandai.

MAP: Are the Mandai still getting persecuted today?

LAA: No. Now the Moslems are fighting each other and the Americans.

They have no time to fight the Mandai. They don't care about the Mandai because the Mandai do not want power. They do not want to rule the countries they are in.

MAP: Thank you for taking the time to answer my questions today. You have been very helpful. I hope I can raise some money for your cause.

LAA: Thank you. I admire your interest in John the Baptist. He was a great prophet.

FOOTNOTES

Chapter 1

1. *The Templars and the Assassins: The Militia of Heaven*, James Wasserman, Inner Traditions, Rochester, Vermont, 2001
2. *The Woman's Dictionary of Symbols and Sacred Objects*, Barbara Walker, HarperSanFrancisco, CA, 1988
3. *Arab Historians of the Crusades*, Franceso Gabrieli, University of California Press, Berkeley, CA, 1984
4. *An Encyclopedic Outline of Masonic, Hermetic, Qabbalistic, and Rosicrucian Philosophy*, Manly P Hall, Philosophical Research Society
5. *The History of Freemasonry* Vol. I, Albert Mackey, The Masonic History Company, London, 1906
6. *A History of Secret Societies*, Arkon Daraul, Citadel Press, NYC, 1989
7. *From Scythia to Camelot*, Littleton and Malcor, Garland Publishing Inc.
8. *The Dream and the Tomb, A History of the Crusades*, Robert Payne, Cooper Square Press, NYC, 2000
9. *Anacalypsis*, Godfrey Higgins, A&B Books Publishers, Brooklyn, NY
10. *A History of Secret Societies*, Arkon Daraul, Citadel Press, NYC, 1989
11. ***Chronicles of the Crusades***, Joinville and Villehardouin, Penguin Books, NYC, 1986
12. *The History of Freemasonry* Vol. I, Albert Mackey, The Masonic History Company, London, 1906
13. *From Scythia to Camelot*, Littleton and Malcor, Garland Publishing
14. Ibid
15. Ibid

Chapter 2

1. *The Holy Grail, **Its Legends and Symbolism***, Arthur E. Waite, Rider & Co.,
2. *The Templars and the Grail: Knights of the Quest*, Karen Ralls, Quest Books, Theosophical Publishing House, Wheaton, IL, 2003
3. *The Holy Blood and The Holy Grail*, Baigent, Leigh & Lincoln, Delacorte Press, NYC, 1982
4. *Parzival*, Wolfram von Eschenbach, Penguin Books, London, 1980
5. *The Templar Revelation: Secret Gaurdians of the True Identity of Christ*, Lynn Picknett & Clive Prince, Touchstone Books, NYC, 1998

Chapter 3

1. *The Grail Legend*, Emma Young, Sigo Press, Boston, MA, 1986
2. *Glastonbury, Maker of Myths*, Frances Howard-Gordon, Gothic Image Publications, Glastonbury, England, 1997
3. *The Holy Grail, The Legend, The History, The Evidence*, Justin E. Griffin, Mcfarland & Co. Inc. Publishers, Jefferson, NY, 2001
4.Ibid
5. Ibid
6 *Mary Magdalene, Myth and Metaphor*, Susan Haskins, Riverhead Books, NYC 1993.
7.Ibid
8. *The Holy Blood and The Holy Grail*, Baigent, Leigh & Lincoln, Delacorte Press, NYC, 1982
9. *The Templar Revelation: Secret Gaurdians of the True Identity of Christ*, Lynn Picknett & Clive Prince
10. *Lost Cities of Atlantis, Ancient Europe & The Mediterranean*, David Hatcher Childress, Adventures Unlimited Press, Kempton, IL, 1996
11. *The Holy Grail, The Legend, The History, The Evidence*, Justin E. Griffin
12 Ibid
13 Ibid
14 Ibid
15. *The Heart of Asia*, Nicholas Roerich, Inner Traditions, Rochester, VT, 1990
16. *The Holy Grail, Its Legends and Symbolism*, Arthur E. Waite, Rider & Co.,
17. Ibid
18. *The Heart of Asia*, Nicholas Roerich, Inner Traditions, Rochester, VT,
19. Ibid
20 Ibid

Chapter 4

1. *Parzival*, Wolfram von Eschenbach, Penguin Books, London, 1980
2.*The Templars and the Grail: Knights of the Quest*, Karen Ralls, Quest
3.*Wolfram von Eschenbach's Parzival, An Attempt at a Total Evaluation*, Kratz & Bern, Switzerland, 1973
4.*The Holy Grail, Its Legends and Symbolism*, Arthur E. Waite, Rider & Co.
5.*The Grail Legend*, Emma Young, Sigo Press, Boston, MA, 1986
6.*The Sufis*, Idries Shah, Anchor Books, NYC, 1964
7.*Shambhala*, Nicholas Roerich, Nicholas Roerich Museum, NYC, 1985
8. *Beasts, Men and Gods*, Ferdinand Ossendowski, E.P. Dutton & Co.

NYC, 1922
9. *Rule by Secrecy*, Jim Marrs, HarperCollins, NYC, 2000
10. *The Holy Blood and The Holy Grail*, Baigent, Leigh & Lincoln
11. Ibid

Chapter 5

1. *The Krater and the Grail, Hermetic Sources of the Parzival*, Henry and Renée Kahane, University of Illinois Press, Chicago, IL 1984

Chapter 6

1. *From Scythia to Camelot*, Littleton and Malcor, Garland Publishing Inc.
2. Ibid
3. Ibid
4. *Parzival*, Wolfram von Eschenbach, Penguin Books, London, 1980
5. *The Holy Grail, Its Legends and Symbolism*, Arthur E. Waite, Rider & Co.
6. *Parzival*, Wolfram von Eschenbach, Penguin Books, London, 1980
7. Ibid
8. *The Sufis*, Idries Shah, Anchor Books, NYC, 1964
9. *The Sword and the Grail*, Andrew Sinclair
10. *The Sufis*, Idries Shah

Chapter 7

1. *The Grail Legend*, Emma Young, Sigo Press, Boston, MA, 1986
2. *The Holy Grail*, Norma Lorre Goodrich, Harper Collins, NYC, 1992
3. *The Sufis*, Idries Shah, Anchor Books, NYC, 1964
4. *The Templar Revelation: Secret Gaurdians of the True Identity of Christ*, Lynn Picknett & Clive Prince, Touchstone Books, NYC, 1998
5. *The Trail of the Templars*, Malcolm Barber, Cambridge U. Press, London, 1978
6. *The Guilt of the Templars*, G. Legman, Basic Books Inc. Publishers, NYC, 1966
7. *Genisis:The First Book of Revelations*, David Wood, The Baton Press, Kent, England, 1985
8. Ibid

Chapter 8

1. *The Golden Bough,* James G. Frazer, Avenel Books, NYC, 1981
2. *The Grail, A Casebook,* Edited by Dhira B. Mahoney, Garland Pub., Inc. NYC, 2000
3. *An Encyclopedic Outline of Masonic, Hermetic, Qabbalistic, and Rosicrucian Philosophy*, Manly P Hall
4. *Bloodline of the Holy Grail: The Hidden Lineage of Jesus Revealed*, Laurence Gardner, Barnes and Noble Books, NYC, 1996
5. *The Golden Bough*, James G. Frazer, Avenel Books, NYC, 1981
6. Ibid
7. Ibid
8. Ibid
9. Ibid
10. *Parzival*, Wolfram von Eschenbach, Penguin Books, London, 1980
11. *The Realm of Prestor John*, Robert Silverberg, Doubleday & Co. Inc., Garden City, NY, 1972
12. *Lemurian Scrolls, Angelic Prophecies Revealing Human Origins*, Satguru Subramunyaswami, Himalayan Academy, India, 1998
13. *Ponder on This*, Alice A. Bailey, Lucis Publishing Co, NYC, 1980
14. *The Secret Doctrine*, H.P. Blavatsky, Theosophical University Press, Pasadena, CA, 1977
15. *The Way to Shamballa*, Edwin Bernbaum, Jeremy Tarcher, L.A.
16. *Beasts, Men and Gods*, Ferdinand Ossendowski, E.P. Dutton & Co. NYC, 1922
17. *The Secret Doctrine*, H.P. Blavatsky, Theosophical University Press, Pasadena, CA, 1977
18. *Genesis Of The Grail Kings*, Laurence Gardner, Element Books, Boston, MA, 2000
19. Ibid
20. Ibid
21. *The Twelfth Planet*, Zecharia Sitchen, Avon Books, NYC, 1976
22. *Genesis Of The Grail Kings*, Laurence Gardner
23. *The Book of Hiram*, Christopher Knight and Robert Lomas, Century, London, 2003
24. *The Secret Doctrine*, H.P. Blavatsky
25. An Encyclopedic Outline of Masonic, Hermetic, Qabbalistic, and Rosicrucian Philosophy, Manly P Hall
26. *The Woman's Dictionary of Symbols and Sacred Objects*, Barbara Walker, HarperSanFrancisco, CA, 1988

27.*The White Goddess*, Robert Graves, 1972, Octagon Books, NYC
28.*The History of the Kings of Britain*, Geoffrey of Monmouth, Penguin Books, NYC, 1966
29. *From Scythia to Camelot*, Littleton and Malcor, Garland Publishing Inc., NYC 1994
30. *The Holy Blood and The Holy Grail*, Baigent, Leigh & Lincoln
31. *The Spear of Destiny*, Trevor Ravenscroft, Samuel Weiser, York Beach, ME, 1997
32. *The Sufis*, Idries Shah, Anchor Books, NYC, 1964
33. *The Grail, A Casebook*, Edited by Dhira B. Mahoney, Garland Pub., Inc. NYC, 2000

Chapter 9

1. *The Hiram Key*, Christopher Knight & Robert Lomas, Element Books, Rockport, MA, 1996
2. *Pistis Sophia*, G.R.S. Mead, Kessinger Publishing Co, Montana, USA
3. *The Essene Odyssey*, Hugh Schonfield, Element Books, England, 1984
4. *Anacalypsis*, Godfrey Higgins, A&B Books Publishers, Brooklyn, NY
5. Ibid
6. *Journey of the Magi*, Paul William Roberts, 1995
7. *John the Baptist and Jesus: A Report of the Jesus Seminar*, W. Barnes Tatum, Polebridge Press, Sonoma, CA, 1994
8. *The Templar Revelation: Secret Gaurdians of the True Identity of Christ*, Lynn Picknett & Clive Prince, Touchstone Books, NYC, 1998
9. *John the Baptist and Jesus: A Report of the Jesus Seminar*, W. Barnes Tatum, Polebridge Press, Sonoma, CA, 1994
10. *Mandeans of Iraq and Iran*, E.S. Drower, Leiden, 1962
11. *The Essene Odyssey*, Hugh Schonfield, Element Books, England, 1984
12. *Mandeans of Iraq and Iran*, E.S. Drower, Leiden, 1962
13. Ibid
14. Ibid
15. Ibid
16. *The Cup of Destiny: The Quest for the Grail*, Trevor Ravenscroft, Samuel Weiser, York Beach, Maine, 1997
17. *Mandeans of Iraq and Iran*, E.S. Drower, Leiden, 1962
18. *The Templar Revelation: Secret Gaurdians of the True Identity of Christ*, Lynn Picknett & Clive Prince
19. Ibid
20. *Gnosis, Character and Testimony*, Robert Haardt, E.J. Brill Publishers,

Leider, Netherlands, 1971
21. *Gnosis, The Nature and History of Gnostics*, Kurt Rudolph, Harper San Francisco, 1987
22. *Gnosis, Character and Testimony*, Robert Haardt, E.J. Brill Publishers, Leider, Netherlands, 1971
23. *Mary Magdalene, Myth and Metaphor*, Susan Haskins, Riverhead Books, NYC 1993
24. Ibid
25. Ibid
26. *The Templar Revelation: Secret Gaurdians of the True Identity of Christ*, Lynn Picknett & Clive Prince, Touchstone Books, NYC, 1998
27. *Mary Magdalene, Myth and Metaphor*, Susan Haskins, Riverhead Book
28. *The Holy Blood and The Holy Grail*, Baigent, Leigh & Lincoln
29. *Isis Unveiled*, Madame Blavatsky, Theosophical University Press, Pasadena, CA, 1976
30. *History of Magic*, Eliphas Levi,
31. *The Holy Land of Scotland*, Barry Dunford, Sacred Connections, Scotland, 2002
32. *The Templar Revelation: Secret Gaurdians of the True Identity of Christ*, Lynn Picknett & Clive Prince, Touchstone Books, NYC, 1998
33. *The Holy Blood and The Holy Grail*, Baigent, Leigh & Lincoln, Delacorte Press, NYC, 1982
34. *The Templar Revelation: Secret Gaurdians of the True Identity of Christ*

Chapter 10

1. *The Sword and the Grail*, Andrew Sinclair, Crown Publishers Inc., NYC, 1992
2. *The Templars and the Assassins: The Militia of Heaven*, James Wasserman, Inner Traditions, Rochester, Vermont, 2001
3. *A History of Secret Societies*, Arkon Daraul, Citadel Press, NYC, 1989
4.*History of Magic*, Eliphas Levi,
5. *The Guilt of the Templars*, G. Legman, Basic Books Inc. Publishers, NYC, 1966
6. *A History of Secret Societies*, Arkon Daraul, Citadel Press, NYC, 1989
7. *The Templars and the Assassins: The Militia of Heaven*, James Wasserman, Inner Traditions
8. *A History of Secret Societies*, Arkon Daraul
10. *The Knights Templar and Their Myth*, Peter Partner, Destiny Books, Rochester, Vermont, 1990

11. *The Guilt of the Templars*, G. Legman, Basic Books Inc. Publishers
12. *Secret Societies and Subversive Movements*, Nesta H. Webster, Boswell Printing & Publishing Co., London, 1924
13. *The Trial of the Templars*, Edward Martin, George Allen & Unwin Ltd, London, 1928
14. Ibid
15. Ibid
16. Ibid
17. *The History of Magic: Including a Clear and Precise Exposition of Its Procedure, Its Rites, and Its Mysteries*, by Eliphas Levi, Red Wheel Weiser
18. *The Trial of the Templars*, Edward Martin, George Allen & Unwin Ltd
19. Ibid
20. *The Holy Grail, Its Legends and Symbolism*, Arthur E. Waite, Rider & Co.,
21. *Rosslyn, Guardians Of The Secrets Of The Holy Grail*, Tim Wallace-Murphy & Marilyn Hopkins, Barnes and Noble Books, NYC, 2000
22. *The Penguin Book of the Middle Ages*, Morris Bishop, Great Britain, 1978
23. *The Mabinogion*, Translated by Gwyn Jones, Charles E. Tuttle Co., Rutland, VT 1949

Chapter 11

1. *The Sword and the Grail*, Andrew Sinclair, Crown Publishers Inc., NYC
2. *Pirates & The Lost Templar Fleet*, David Hatcher Childress, Adventures Unlimited Press, Kempton, IL, 2003
3. *The Temple and the Lodge*, Michael Baigent and Richard Leigh, Arcade Publishing, NYC, 1989
4. *The History of Freemasonry* Vol. I, Albert Mackey, The Masonic History Company, London, 1906
5. Ibid
6. *The Temple and the Lodge*, Michael Baigent and Richard Leigh, Arcade Publishing, NYC, 1989
7. *The Sword and the Grail*, Andrew Sinclair, Crown Publishers Inc., NYC, 1992
8. *Pirates & The Lost Templar Fleet*, David Hatcher Childress
9. *The Templars and the Grail: Knights of the Quest*, Karen Ralls, Quest Books, Theosophical Publishing House, Wheaton, IL
10. *The Hiram Key*, Christopher Knight & Robert Lomas, Element Books
11. Internet website: Rosslyn Chapel and the Masonic Legacy
12. *The Mark of the Beast*, Trevor Ravencroft & Tim Wallace-Murphy,

Samuel Weiser, York Beach, Maine, 1997
13. *Rosslyn, Guardians Of The Secrets Of The Holy Grail*, Tim Wallace-Murphy & Marilyn Hopkins, Barnes and Noble Books
14. *The Hiram Key*, Christopher Knight & Robert Lomas, Element Books
15. Ibid
16. *The Head of God*, Keith Laidler, Weidenfeld & Nicolson, London, 1998
17. *The Book of Hiram*, Christopher Knight and Robert Lomas, Century, London, 2003
18. *Green Man, The Archetype of our Oneness with the Earth*, William Anderson, HarperCollins, San Francisco, 1990
19. *The Trail of the Templars*, Malcolm Barber, Cambridge U. Press
20. *Rosslyn, Guardians Of The Secrets Of The Holy Grail*, Tim Wallace-Murphy & Marilyn Hopkins
21. *The Sword and the Grail*, Andrew Sinclair, Crown Publishers Inc.
22. *Rosslyn and the Western Mystery*, Robert Brydon, Rosslyn Chapel Trust, Rosslyn Chapel, Roslin, Scotland
23. *Rosslyn, Guardians Of The Secrets Of The Holy Grail*, Tim Wallace-Murphy & Marilyn Hopkins, Barnes and Noble Books, NYC, 2000

Chapter 12

1. *Supremely Abominable Crimes: The Trail of the Templars*, E. Burman, Allision & Busby, London, 1994
2. *The Temple and the Lodge*, Michael Baigent and Richard Leigh, Arcade Publishing, NYC, 1989
3. *The Templars and the Grail: Knights of the Quest*, Karen Ralls, Quest Books, Theosophical Publishing House, Wheaton, IL, 2003
4. *The History of Magic*, Eliphas Levi
5. Ibid
6. *The Origins of Freemasonry, Scotland's Century 1590-1710*, David Stevenson, Cambridge University Press, Cambridge, England, 1988
7. *Born in Blood, The Lost Secrets of Freemasonry*, John J. Robinson, M. Eveans & Co., NYC 1989
8. *A Concise History of Freemasonry*, Robert Freke Gould, Gale & Polden Ltd, London, 1904
9.*The Knights of Malta*, H.J.A. Sire, Yale University Press, New Haven, CT, 1994
10. *A Concise History of Freemasonry*, Robert Freke Gould, Gale & Polden Ltd, London, 1904
11. *The Templar Revelation: Secret Gaurdians of the True Identity of Christ*,

Lynn Picknett & Clive Prince
12. *An Encyclopedic Outline of Masonic, Hermetic, Qabbalistic, and Rosicrucian Philosophy*, Manly P Hall
13. *Rule by Secrecy*, Jim Marrs, HarperCollins, NYC, 2000
14. *The History of Freemasonry* Vol. I, Albert Mackey

Bibliography

Anacalypsis, Godfrey Higgins, A&B Books Publishers, Brooklyn, NY, 1992

Arab Historians of the Crusades, Franceso Gabrieli, University of California Press, Berkeley, CA, 1984

ARKTOS, The Polar Myth in Science, Symbolism, and Nazi Survival, Jocelyn Godwin, Phanes Press, Grand Rapids, MI, 1993

The Assassins, A Radical Sect in Islam, Bernard Lewis, Basic Books Inc. Publishers, NYC, 1968

Babaji And The 18 Siddha Kriya Yoga Tradition, M. Govindan, Kriya Yoga Publications, Montreal, 1991

Beasts, Men and Gods, Ferdinand Ossendowski, E.P. Dutton & Co. NYC, 1922

Bloodline of the Holy Grail: **The Hidden Lineage of Jesus Revealed**, Laurence Gardner, Barnes and Noble Books, NYC, 1996

The Book of Hiram, Christopher Knight and Robert Lomas, Century, London, 2003

Born in Blood, The Lost Secrets of Freemasonry, John J. Robinson, M. Eveans & Co., NYC 1989

The Complete Dead Sea Scrolls in English, Geza Vermes, Penguin Books, NYC 1997

A Concise History of Freemasonry, Robert Freke Gould, Gale & Polden Ltd, London, 1904

The Cup of Destiny: The Quest for the Grail, Trevor Ravenscroft, Samuel Weiser, York Beach, Maine, 1997

Chronicles of the Crusades, Joinville and Villehardouin, Penguin Books, NYC, 1986

The Dream and the Tomb, A History of the Crusades, Robert Payne, Cooper Square Press, NYC, 2000

An Encyclopedic Outline of Masonic, Hermetic, Qabbalistic, and Rosicrucian Philosophy, Manly P Hall, The Philosophical Research, Society, L.A., 1979

The Essene Odyssey, Hugh Schonfield, Element Books, Dorset, England, 1984

From Scythia to Camelot, Littleton and Malcor, Garland Publishing Inc., NYC 1994

Genesis Of The Grail Kings, Laurence Gardner, Element Books, Boston, MA, 2000

Genisis:**The First Book of Revelations**, David Wood, The Baton Press, Kent, England, 1985

Glastonbury, Maker of Myths, Frances Howard-Gordon, Gothic Image Publications, Glastonbury, England, 1997

Gnosis, Character and Testimony, Robert Haardt, E.J. Brill Publishers, Leider, Netherlands, 1971

Gnosis, The Nature and History of Gnostics, Kurt Rudolph, Harper San Francisco, 1987

The Golden Bough, James G. Frazer, Avenel Books, NYC, 1981

The Grail Legend, Emma Young, Sigo Press, Boston, MA, 1986

The Grail, A Casebook, Edited by Dhira B. Mahoney, Garland Pub., Inc. NYC, 2000

Green Man, The Archetype of our Oneness with the Earth, William Anderson, HarperCollins, San Francisco, 1990

The Guilt of the Templars, G. Legman, Basic Books Inc. Publishers, NYC, 1966

The Head of God, Keith Laidler, Weidenfeld & Nicolson, London, 1998

The Heart of Asia, Nicholas Roerich, Inner Traditions, Rochester, VT, 1990

The Hiram Key, Christopher Knight & Robert Lomas, Element Books, Rockport, MA, 1996

A History of Gnosticism, G. Filoramo, Basil Blackwell Inc., Cambridge, MA, 1991

The History of Freemasonry Vol. I, Albert Mackey, The Masonic History Company, London, 1906

The History of Magic: Including a Clear and Precise Exposition of Its Procedure, Its Rites, and Its Mysteries, by Eliphas Levi, Red Wheel Weiser, 1999

A History of Secret Societies, Arkon Daraul, Citadel Press, NYC, 1989

The History of the Order of Assassins, Enno Franzius, Funk & Wagnalls, NYC, 1969

The Holy Blood and The Holy Grail, Baigent, Leigh & Lincoln, Delacorte Press, NYC, 1982

The Holy Grail, Norma Lorre Goodrich, Harper Collins, NYC, 1992

The Holy Grail, Its Legends and Symbolism, Arthur E. Waite, Rider & Co., London 1933

The Holy Grail, The Legend, The History, The Evidence, Justin E. Griffin, Mcfarland & Co. Inc. Publishers, Jefferson, NY, 2001

The Holy Koran, A. Yusef Ali, Hafner, Publishing Co., Cambridge, MA, 1946

The Holy Land of Scotland, Barry Dunford, Sacred Connections, Scotland, 2002

The Immerser: John the Baptist within Second Temple Judaism, Joan E. Taylor, William B. Eerdmans Publishing Co., Grand Rapids, MI, 1997

Isis Unveiled, Madame Blavatsky, Theosophical University Press, Pasadena, CA, 1976

The Jesus Party, Hugh Schonfield, Macmillan Publishing Co., NY, 1974

John, The Son of Zebedee, **The Life of a Legend**, R. Alan Culpepper, University of South Carolina Press, Columbia, S.C., 1994

John the Baptist and Jesus: A Report of the Jesus Seminar, W. Barnes Tatum, Polebridge Press, Sonoma, CA, 1994

Journey of the Magi, Paul William Roberts, 1995

The Knights of Malta, H.J.A. Sire, Yale University Press, New Haven, CT, 1994

The Knights Templar and Their Myth, Peter Partner, Destiny Books, Rochester, Vermont, 1990

The Krater and the Grail, **Hermetic Sources of the Parzival**, Henry and Renée Kahane, University of Illinois Press, Chicago, IL 1984

Lemurian Scrolls, Angelic Prophecies Revealing Human Origins, Satguru Subramunyaswami, Himalayan Academy, India, 1998

Lost Cities of Atlantis, Ancient Europe & The Mediterranean, David Hatcher Childress, Adventures Unlimited Press, Kempton, IL, 1996

The Mabinogion, Translated by Gwyn Jones, Charles E. Tuttle Co., Rutland, VT 1949

Mandeans of Iraq and Iran, E.S. Drower, Leiden, 1962

The Mark of the Beast, Trevor Ravencroft & Tim Wallace-Murphy, Samuel Weiser, York Beach, Maine, 1997

Mary Magdalene, Myth and Metaphor, Susan Haskins, Riverhead Books, NYC 1993

The Murdered Magicians, Peter Partner, Oxford University Press, NYC, 1982

A New Encyclopaedia of Freemasonry, Arthur Edward Waite, Wings Books, NYC 1996

One Hundred Thousand Years of Man's Unknown History, Robert Charroux, Berkeley Publishing Co., NYC, 1971

The Origins of Freemasonry, Scotland's Century 1590-1710, David Stevenson, Cambridge University Press, Cambridge, England, 1988

Parzival, Wolfram von Eschenbach, Penguin Books, London, 1980

The Peacock Angel, E.S. Drower, Butler and Banner Ltd, London, 1941

Perceval or The Story of the Grail, Chrétien de Troyes, translated by Ruth Harwood Cline, Pergamon Press, NYC, 1983

Pirates & The Lost Templar Fleet, David Hatcher Childress, Adventures Unlimited Press, Kempton, IL, 2003
Pistis Sophia, G.R.S. Mead, Kessinger Publishing Co, Montana, USA
Ponder on This, Alice A. Bailey, Lucis Publishing Co, NYC, 1980
The Realm of Prestor John, Robert Silverberg, Doubleday & Co. Inc., Garden City, NY, 1972
Rosslyn, Guardians Of The Secrets Of The Holy Grail, Tim Wallace-Murphy & Marilyn Hopkins, Barnes and Noble Books, NYC, 2000
Rule by Secrecy, Jim Marrs, HarperCollins, NYC, 2000
The Secret Doctrine, H.P. Blavatsky, Theosophical University Press, Pasadena, CA, 1977
Secret Societies and Subversive Movements, Nesta H. Webster, Boswell Printing & Publishing Co., London, 1924
Shambhala, Nicholas Roerich, Nicholas Roerich Museum, NYC, 1985
Sir Gawain And The Green Knight, Translated by Marie Borroff, W.W. Norton & Co. NYC, 1967
The Spear of Destiny, Trevor Ravenscroft, Samuel Weiser, York Beach, ME, 1997
The Sufis, Idries Shah, Anchor Books, NYC, 1964
The Sword and the Grail, Andrew Sinclair, Crown Publishers Inc., NYC, 1992
The Templar Revelation: Secret Gaurdians of the True Identity of Christ, Lynn Picknett & Clive Prince, Touchstone Books, NYC, 1998
The Templars and the Assassins: The Militia of Heaven, James Wasserman, Inner Traditions, Rochester, Vermont, 2001
The Templars and the Grail: Knights of the Quest, Karen Ralls, Quest Books, Theosophical Publishing House, Wheaton, IL, 2003
The Templars' Legacy in Montréal, the New Jerusalem, Francine Bernier, Adventures Unlimited Press, Kempton, IL, 2001
The Temple and the Lodge, Michael Baigent and Richard Leigh, Arcade Publishing, NYC, 1989
The Trail of the Templars, Malcolm Barber, Cambridge U. Press, London, 1978
The Trial of the Templars, Edward Martin, George Allen & Unwin Ltd, London, 1928
The Twelfth Planet, Zecharia Sitchen, Avon Books, NYC, 1976
The Way to Shamballa, Edwin Bernbaum, Jeremy Tarcher, L.A.
The White Goddess, Robert Graves, 1972, Octagon Books, NYC
Wolfram von Eschenbach, James F. Poag, Twayne Publishers, NYC, 1972

Wolfram von Eschenbach's Parzival, An Attempt at a Total Evaluation, Kratz & Bern, Switzerland, 1973

The Woman with the Alabaster Jar, Margaret Starbird, Bea & Co, Santa Fe, NM 1993

The Woman's Dictionary of Symbols and Sacred Objects, Barbara Walker, HarperSanFrancisco, CA, 1988

The International Order of Gnostic Templars

A Division of

The Scottish Knights Templar

Dedicated to the Revival
of the
Holy Grail Mysteries

Before thier mas arrest in 1307, the Knights Templar observed both the Christian rites of the West, as well as the rites of Gnosticism, Alchemy, and those of the Goddess/Nature religions of the East. It is the goal of the International Order of Gnostic Templars to ervive the Templar rites of the East, amalgamate them to the Christian Mysticism of the West, and thereby complete the unfinished work of the Templar Knights which was *to unite East and West spirituality.*

Within the IOGT religious fundamentalism and patriarchal control are absent and there is a perfect balance of male/female membership. The Order is goverened equally at all levels by both men and women.

Patron Saints of the IOGT

Mary Magdalene
John the Baptist
John the Apostle
Saint Germain
Hughes de Payen
The Sinclairs
Past Grand Master Templars

The Three Levels of the IOGT and their Mysteries

Squire or Lady in Waiting

The Mystery of the Holy Chalice

Knight or Lady Templar

The Mystery of the Holy Sword

Fisher King or Fisher Queen

The Mystery of the Holy Spear

The Curriculum of the IOGT

* The Holy Grail Mysteries
* The Secret History of the Knights Templar
* The Mysteries of the Black Madonna
* The Secrets of John the Baptist and Gnosticism
* The Mystery of Baphomet, the Head of Wisdom
* The Practices of Alchemy, Yoga, & Meditation
* The Secret Mysteries of the Goddess Tradition
* The Secrets of the Sinclairs and Rosslyn Chapel
* Martial Arts, Sword Fighting, Tai Chi, etc.

Plus...

* Pilgrimages to ancient sacred sites of the IOGT, the Knights Templar and the Goddess Tradition including:
    * Rosslyn Chapel
    * Rennes le Chateau
    * Black Madonna sites in France
    * Sri Lanka

visit www.BodyMindSpiritJourneys.com.

The Headquaters of the IOGT

Noss Head, Scotland

The Scottish headquarters of the IOGT is the Prince Henry St. Clair Preceptory and Study Centre in Noss Head, Scotland. *See facing page.*

Sedona, Arizona, USA

The North American Headquarters of the IOGT is in Sedona, Arizona. This centre is run by Mark and Andrea Pinkham.

Ian Sinclair, K.C.Tpl
The Inititiator and Worthy Commander of the IOGT.

Prince Henry St. Clair Preceptory and Study Centre.
Sinclair-Girnigoe Castle is in the background.

The Preceptory

Statue of Prince Henry St. Clair

Sacred Travel

In conjunction with ***Body Mind Spirit Journeys***, Mark Amaru Pinkham and his wife, Andrea Mikana-Pinkham, National Director, lead Sacred Journeys to the power points, temples and enlightened Masters around the world. In these places Mark and Andrea teach yoga and meditation, initiations are received, and dramatic and uplifting spiritual experiences are common.

Please visit the following websites to get up-to-date information regarding upcoming tours: **www.BodyMindSpiritJourneys.com.**
www.SerpentsOfWisdom.com.

The Author

Mark Amaru Pinkham is the author of a series of books distributed by Aventures Unlimited Press that cover the mystery traditions associated with the Goddess spiritual tradition. They include: ***The Return of the Serpents of Wisdom, Conversations with the Goddess,*** and ***The Truth Behind the Christ Myth: The Redemption of the Peacock Angel.*** With his wife, Andrea, Mark is a co-Director of both the ***7 Rays of Healing School*** and the North American branch of the ***International Order of Gnostic Templars*** in Sedona, Arizona, U.S.A. In association with ***Body Mind Spirit Journeys***, Mark leads spiritual tours to sacred locations around the globe, including Scotland, France, Peru, Egypt, and India; and he also leads local vortex tours in the Sedona area. Mark can often be heard on radio or seen on television as he continues to spread the wisdom of Gnostic Templarism.

PHILOSOPHY & HISTORY

GUARDIANS OF THE HOLY GRAIL

by Mark Amaru Pinkham

While in the Holy Land the Knights Templar succeeded in their quest of finding a "missing link" that unites the spiritual traditions of the east and west. They discovered it in the form of a very ancient manifestation of the Holy Grail from Asia. Although the Templar Knights had been schooled in the legend of Jesus Christ and his famous chalice while in their homeland of France, during their one hundred years in the Holy Land they discovered that Jesus's Holy Grail was but one of a long line of Holy Grail manifestations, and that a lineage of Guardians of the Holy Grail had existed in Asia for thousands of years prior to the birth of the Messiah. This book presents this extremely ancient Holy Grail lineage from Asia and how the Knights Templar were initiated into it. It also reveals how the ancient Asian wisdom regarding the Holy Grail became the foundation for the Holy Grail legends of the west while also serving as the bedrock of the European Secret Societies, which included the Freemasons, Rosicrucians, and the Illuminati. Also: The Fisher Kings; The Middle Eastern mystery schools, such as the Assassins and Yezidhi; The ancient Holy Grail lineage from Sri Lanka and the Templar Knights' initiation into it; The head of John the Baptist and its importance to the Templars; The secret Templar initiation with grotesque Baphomet, the infamous Head of Wisdom; more.

248 PAGES. 6X9 PAPERBACK. ILLUSTRATED. BIBLIOGRAPHY. $16.95. CODE: GOHG

RETURN OF THE SERPENTS OF WISDOM

by Mark Amaru Pinkham

According to ancient records, the patriarchs and founders of the early civilizations in Egypt, India, China, Peru, Mesopotamia, Britain, and the Americas were the Serpents of Wisdom—spiritual masters associated with the serpent—who arrived in these lands after abandoning their beloved homelands and crossing great seas. While bearing names denoting snake or dragon (such as Naga, Lung, Djedhi, Amaru, Quetzalcoatl, Adder, etc.), these Serpents of Wisdom oversaw the construction of magnificent civilizations within which they and their descendants served as the priest kings and as the enlightened heads of mystery school traditions. *The Return of the Serpents of Wisdom* recounts the history of these "Serpents"—where they came from, why they came, the secret wisdom they disseminated, and why they are returning now.

400 PAGES. 6X9 PAPERBACK. ILLUSTRATED. REFERENCES. $16.95. CODE: RSW

PIRATES & THE LOST TEMPLAR FLEET

The Secret Naval War Between the Templars & the Vatican

by David Hatcher Childress

Childress takes us into the fascinating world of maverick sea captains who were Knights Templar (and later Scottish Rite Free Masons) who battled the Vatican, and the Spanish and Italian ships that sailed for the Pope. The lost Templar fleet was originally based at La Rochelle in southern France, but fled to the deep fiords of Scotland upon the dissolution of the Order by King Phillip. This banned fleet of ships was later commanded by the St. Clair family of Rosslyn Chapel (birthplace of Free Masonry). St. Clair and his Templars made a voyage to Canada in the year 1298 AD, nearly 100 years before Columbus! Later, this fleet of ships and new ones to come, flew the Skull and Crossbones, the symbol of the Knights Templar. They preyed on the ships of the Vatican coming from the rich ports of the Americas and were ultimately known as the Pirates of the Caribbean. Chapters include: 10,000 Years of Seafaring; The Knights Templar & the Crusades; The Templars and the Assassins; The Lost Templar Fleet and the Jolly Roger; Maps of the Ancient Sea Kings; Pirates, Templars and the New World; Christopher Columbus—Secret Templar Pirate?; Later Day Pirates and the War with the Vatican; Pirate Utopias and the New Jerusalem; more.

320 PAGES. 6X9 PAPERBACK. ILLUSTRATED. BIBLIOGRAPHY. $16.95. CODE: PLTF

CLOAK OF THE ILLUMINATI

Secrets, Transformations, Crossing the Star Gate

by William Henry

Thousands of years ago the stargate technology of the gods was lost. Mayan Prophecy says it will return by 2012, along with our alignment with the center of our galaxy. In this book: Find examples of stargates and wormholes in the ancient world; Examine myths and scripture with hidden references to a stargate cloak worn by the Illuminati, including Mari, Nimrod, Elijah, and Jesus; See rare images of gods and goddesses wearing the Cloak of the illuminati; Learn about Saddam Hussein and the secret missing library of Jesus; Uncover the secret Roman-era eugenics experiments at the Temple of Hathor in Denderah, Egypt; Explore the duplicate of the Stargate Pillar of the Gods in the Illuminists' secret garden in Nashville, TN; Discover the secrets of manna, the food of the angels; Share the lost Peace Prayer posture of Osiris, Jesus and the Illuminati; more. Chapters include: Seven Stars Under Three Stars; The Long Walk; Squaring the Circle; The Mill of the Host; The Miracle Garment; The Fig; Nimrod: The Mighty Man; Nebuchadnezzar's Gate; The New Mighty Man; more.

238 PAGES. 6X9 PAPERBACK. ILLUSTRATED. BIBLIOGRAPHY. INDEX. $16.95. CODE: COIL

THE CHILDREN OF THE SUN

A Study of the Egyptian Settlement of the Pacific

by W.J. Perry

A reprint of the groundbreaking work of Professor W.J. Perry, an early diffusionist who believed that civilization spread throughout the world via transoceanic voyaging—an idea that most historians still fail to accept, even in the face of mounting evidence. First published in 1923, this classic presents the fascinating evidence that envoys of the ancient Sun Kingdoms of Egypt and India travelled into Indonesia and the Pacific circa 1500 BC, spreading their sophisticated culture. Perry traces the expansion of megalithic building from its origin in Egypt through Indonesia and across the Pacific all the way to the Americas. These early mariners searched for gold, obsidian, and pearls in their incredible explorations from island to island—they were the Children of the Sun! Includes: The Coming of the Warriors; Rulers and Commoners: The Sky World; The Indo-Egyptian Alliance of Builders; The Oceania-Indonesian Alliance of Explorers; more.

554 PAGES. 6X9 PAPERBACK. ILLUSTRATED. BIBLIOGRAPHY. INDEX. $18.95. CODE: CSUN

THE CANOPUS REVELATION

Stargate of the Gods and the Ark of Osiris

by Philip Coppens

The identification of the constellation Orion with the Egyptian god Osiris has become engrained in human consciousness, yet is one of the biggest misunderstandings dominating the understanding of Egyptian mythology. Rather than the constellation Orion, it is the star Canopus that is linked with Osiris. Canopus, for Egypt the South polar star, is the second brightest star in the sky and interplays with Sirius in such a way that ancient accounts say they control time. Furthermore, Canopus is also the star of the navigators, both ancient and modern, and was believed to allow access to the Afterlife—the domain of Osiris. Canopus was specifically identified with Osiris' Chest, the Ark in which he was transformed from mere mortal to resurrected supergod—an image that has inspired mankind ever since. Canopus was therefore literally a "stargate," where man could communicate with and aspire to become gods—and enter into other dimensions. This book will reveal what the Egyptians actually believed as to what happened to the soul after death and how they coded this knowledge into their mythology. At the same time, it unveils how ancient accounts and modern physics use the same symbolism to describe the structure of the universe, the playground of the Egyptian gods and the souls of the deceased.

204 PAGES. 6X9 PAPERBACK. ILLUSTRATED. BIBLIOGRAPHY. $17.95. CODE: CANR

24 hour credit card orders—call: 815-253-6390 fax: 815-253-6300
email: auphq@frontiernet.net www.adventuresunlimitedpress.com www.wexclub.com

PHILOSOPHY & RELIGION

THE CHRIST CONSPIRACY
The Greatest Story Ever Sold
by Acharya S.

In this highly controversial and explosive book, archaeologist, historian, mythologist and linguist Acharya S. marshals an eno amount of startling evidence to demonstrate that Christianity and the story of Jesus Christ were created by members of various societies, mystery schools and religions in order to unify the Roman Empire under one state religion. In developing such a fa tion, this multinational cabal drew upon a multitude of myths and rituals that existed long before the Christian era, and rew them for centuries into the religion passed down to us today. Contrary to popular belief, there was no single man who was genesis of Christianity; Jesus was many characters rolled into one. These characters personified the ubiquitous solar myth, and exploits were well known, as reflected by such popular deities as Mithras, Heracles/Hercules, Dionysos and many others throu the Roman Empire and beyond. The story of Jesus as portrayed in the Gospels is revealed to be nearly identical in detail to that earlier savior-gods Krishna and Horus, who for millennia preceding Christianity held great favor with the people. *The Christ spiracy* shows the Jesus character as neither unique nor original, not "divine revelation." Christianity re-interprets the sam tremely ancient body of knowledge that revolved around the celestial bodies and natural forces.

436 PAGES. 6X9 PAPERBACK. ILLUSTRATED. $16.95. CODE: CHRC

THE AQUARIAN GOSPEL OF JESUS THE CHRIST
Transcribed from the Akashic Records
by Levi

First published in 1908, this is the amazing story of Jesus, the man from Galilee, and how he attained the Christ consciou open to all men. It includes a complete record of the "lost" 18 years of his life, a time on which the New Testament is stra silent. During this period Jesus travelled widely in India, Tibet, Persia, Egypt and Greece, learning from the Masters, see wisemen of the East and the West in their temples and schools. Included is information on the Council of the Seven Sa the World, Jesus with the Chinese Master Mencius (Meng Tzu) in Tibet, the ministry, trial, execution and resurrection of

270 PAGES. 6X9 PAPERBACK. INDEX. $14.95. CODE: AGJC

CONVERSATIONS WITH THE GODDESS
by Mark Amaru Pinkham

Return of the Serpents of Wisdom author Pinkham tells us that "The Goddess is returning!" Pinkham gives us an alter history of Lucifer, the ancient King of the World, and the Matriarchal Tradition he founded thousands of years ago. The Lucifer means "Light Bringer" and he is the same as the Greek god Prometheus, and is different from Satan, who was based Egyptian god Set. Find out how the branches of the Matriarchy—the Secret Societies and Mystery Schools—were forme how they have been receiving assistance from the Brotherhoods on Sirius and Venus to evolve the world and overthro Patriarchy. Learn about the revival of the Goddess Tradition in the New Age and why the Goddess wants us all to reunite wi now! An unusual book from an unusual writer!

296 PAGES. 7X10 PAPERBACK. ILLUSTRATED. BIBLIOGRAPHY. $14.95. CODE: CWTG.

THE TRUTH BEHIND THE CHRIST MYTH
The Redemption of the Peacock Angel
by Mark Amaru Pinkham

The Peacock Angel of the Catholic Church is Murrugan's symbol, the peacock, a bird native to southeast Asia. Murrugan evolved into the Persian Mithr evolved into Jesus Christ. Saint Paul came from Tarsus, the center of Mithras worship in Asia Minor; he amalgamated the legend of the Persian Son of Go Jesus' life story. Topics include: The Three Wise Men were Magi priests who believed that Jesus was an incarnation of Mithras; While in India, Saint T became a peacock before he died and merged with Murrugan, the Peacock Angel; The myth of the One and Only Son of God originated with Murrug Mithras; The Peacock Angel has been worshipped by many persons world-wide as The King of the World; Hitler, the Knights Templar, and the Illuminati to use the power of the Peacock Angel to conquer the world; more.

174 PAGES. 6X9 PAPERBACK. ILLUSTRATED. BIBLIOGRAPHY. $14.95. CODE: TBCM

THE BOOK OF ENOCH
The Prophet
translated by Richard Laurence

This is a reprint of the Apocryphal *Book of Enoch the Prophet* which was first discovered in Abyssinia in the year 1773 by a Scottish explorer named James Bruce. In 1821 *The Book of Enoch* was translated by Richard Laurence and published in a number of successive editions, culminating in the 1883 edition. One of the main influences from the book is its explanation of evil coming into the world with the arrival of the "fallen angels." Enoch acts as a scribe, writing up a petition on behalf of these fallen angels, or fallen ones, to be given to a higher power for ultimate judgment. Christianity adopted some ideas from Enoch, including the Final Judgment, the concept of demons, the origins of evil and the fallen angels, and the coming of a Messiah and ultimately, a Messianic kingdom. The *Book of Enoch* was ultimately removed from the Bible and banned by the early church. Copies of it were found to have survived in Ethiopia, and fragments in Greece and Italy.

224 PAGES. 6X9 PAPERBACK. ILLUSTRATED. INDEX. $16.95. CODE: BOE

THE WORLD'S SIXTEEN CRUCIFIED SAVIORS
Christianity Before Christ
by Kersey Graves, foreword by Acharya S.

A reprint of Kersey Graves' classic and rare 1875 book on Christianity before Christ, and the 16 messiahs or saviors who are known to history b Christ! Chapters on: Rival Claims of the Saviors; Messianic Prophecies; Prophecies by the Figure of a Serpent; Virgin Mothers and Virgin Gods; Stars Point Out the Time and the Saviors' Birthplace; Sixteen Saviors Crucified; The Holy Ghost of Oriental Origin; Appollonius, Osiri Magus as Gods; 346 Striking Analogies Between Christ and Krishna; 25th of December as the birthday of the Gods; more. 45 chapters in all

436 PAGES. 6X9 PAPERBACK. ILLUSTRATED. $19.95. CODE: WSCS

24 hour credit card orders—call: 815-253-6390 fax: 815-253-6300
email: auphq@frontiernet.net www.adventuresunlimitedpress.com www.wexclub.com

CONSPIRACY & HISTORY

TEMPLARS' LEGACY IN MONTREAL

The New Jerusalem

by Francine Bernier

Designed in the 17th century as the New Jerusalem of the Christian world, the people behind the scene in turning this dream into reality were the Société de Notre-Dame, half of whose members were in the elusive Compagnie du Saint-Sacrement. They took no formal vows and formed the interior elitist and invisible "heart of the church" following a "Johannite" doctrine of the Essene tradition, where men and women were considered equal apostles. The book reveals the links between Montreal and: John the Baptist as patron saint; Melchizedek, the first king-priest and a father figure to the Templars and the Essenes; Stella Maris, the Star of the Sea from Mount Carmel; the Phrygian goddess Cybele as the androgynous Mother of the Church; St. Blaise, the Armenian healer or "Therapeut"- the patron saint of the stonemasons and a major figure to the Benedictine Order and the Templars; the presence of two Black Virgins; an intriguing family coat of arms with twelve blue apples; and more.

352 PAGES. 6X9 PAPERBACK. ILLUSTRATED. BIBLIOGRAPHY. $21.95. CODE: TLIM

THE STONE PUZZLE OF ROSSLYN CHAPEL

by Philip Coppens

Rosslyn Chapel is revered by Freemasons as a vital part of their history, believed by some to hold evidence of pre-Columbian voyages to America, assumed by others to hold important relics, from the Holy Grail to the Head of Christ, the Scottish chapel is a place full of mystery. The history of the chapel, its relationship to freemasonry and the family behind the scenes, the Sinclairs, is brought to life, incorporating new, previously forgotten and heretofore unknown evidence. Significantly, the story is placed in the equally enigmatic landscape surrounding the chapel, which includes features from Templar commanderies to prehistoric markings, from an ancient kingly site to the South to Arthur's Seat directly north of the chapel. The true significance and meaning of the chapel is finally unveiled: it is a medieval stone book of esoteric knowledge "written" by the Sinclair family, one of the most powerful and wealthy families in Scotland, chosen patrons of Freemasonry.

124 PAGES. 6X9 PAPERBACK. ILLUSTRATED. $12.00. CODE: SPRC

NOSTRADAMUS AND THE LOST TEMPLAR LEGACY

by Rudy Cambier

Rudy Cambier's decade-long research and analysis of the verses of Nostradamus' "prophecies" has shown that the language of those verses does not belong in the 16th Century, nor in Nostradamus' region of Provence. The language spoken in the verses belongs to the medieval times of the 14th Century, and the Belgian borders. The documents known as Nostradamus' prophecies were not written ca. 1550 by the French "visionary" Michel de Nostradame. Instead, they were composed between 1323 and 1328 by a Cistercian monk, Yves de Lessines, prior of the abbey of Cambron, on the border between France and Belgium. According to the author, these documents reveal the location of a Templar treasure. This key allowed Cambier to translate the "prophecies." But rather than being confronted with a series of cataclysms and revelations of future events, Cambier discovered a possibly even more stunning secret. Yves de Lessines had waited for many years for someone called "l'attendu," the expected one. This person was supposed to come to collect the safeguarded treasures of the Knights Templar, an organization suppressed in 1307. But no-one came. Hence, the prior decided to impart the whereabouts and nature of the treasure in a most cryptic manner in verses.

204 PAGES. 6X9 PAPERBACK. ILLUSTRATED. BIBLIOGRAPHY. $17.95. CODE: NLTL

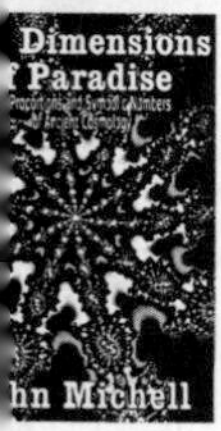

THE DIMENSIONS OF PARADISE

The Proportions & Symbolic Numbers of Ancient Cosmology

by John Michell

The Dimensions of Paradise were known to ancient civilizations as the harmonious numerical standards that underlie the created world. John Michell's quest for these standards provides vital clues for understanding: The dimensions and symbolism of Stonehenge; The plan of Atlantis and reason for its fall; The numbers behind the sacred names of Christianity; The form of St. John's vision of the New Jerusalem; The name of the man with the number 666; The foundation plan of Glastonbury and other sanctuaries and how these symbols suggest a potential for personal, cultural and political regeneration in the 21st century.

220 PAGES. 6X9 PAPERBACK. ILLUSTRATED. BIBLIOGRAPHY. INDEX. $16.95. CODE: DIMP

THE HISTORY OF THE KNIGHTS TEMPLARS

by Charles G. Addison, introduction by David Hatcher Childress

Chapters on the origin of the Templars, their popularity in Europe and their rivalry with the Knights of St. John, later to be known as the Knights of Malta. Detailed information on the activities of the Templars in the Holy Land, and the 1312 AD suppression of the Templars in France and other countries, which culminated in the execution of Jacques de Molay and the continuation of the Knights Templars in England and Scotland; the formation of the society of Knights Templars in London; and the rebuilding of the Temple in 1816. Plus a lengthy intro about the lost Templar fleet and its connections to the ancient North American sea routes.

395 PAGES. 6X9 PAPERBACK. ILLUSTRATED. $16.95. CODE: HKT

SAUNIER'S MODEL AND THE SECRET OF RENNES-LE-CHATEAU

The Priest's Final Legacy

by André Douzet

Berenger Saunière, the enigmatic priest of the French village of Rennes-le-Château, is rumored to have found the legendary treasure of the Cathars. But what became of it? In 1916, Sauniere created his ultimate clue: he went to great expense to create a model of a region said to be the Calvary Mount, indicating the "Tomb of Jesus." But the region on the model does not resemble the region of Jerusalem. Did Saunière leave a clue as to the true location of his treasure? And what is that treasure? After years of research, André Douzet discovered this model—the only real clue Saunière left behind as to the nature and location of his treasure—and the possible tomb of Jesus.

116 PAGES. 6X9 PAPERBACK. ILLUSTRATED. BIBLIOGRAPHY. $12.00. CODE: SMOD

ARKTOS

The Myth of the Pole in Science, Symbolism, and Nazi Survival

by Joscelyn Godwin

A scholarly treatment of catastrophes, ancient myths and the Nazi Occult beliefs. Explored are the many tales of an ancient race said to have lived in the Arctic regions, such as Thule and Hyperborea. Progressing onward, the book looks at modern polar legends including the survival of Hitler, German bases in Antarctica, UFOs, the hollow earth, Agartha and Shambala, more.

220 PAGES. 6X9 PAPERBACK. ILLUSTRATED. $16.95. CODE: ARK

CONSPIRACY & HISTORY

SAUCERS OF THE ILLUMINATI

by Jim Keith, Foreword by Kenn Thomas

Seeking the truth behind stories of alien invasion, secret underground bases, and the secret plans of the New World Order, *Saucers Illuminati* offers ground breaking research, uncovering clues to the nature of UFOs and to forces even more sinister: the secret cabal planetary control! Includes mind control, saucer abductions, the MJ-12 documents, cattle mutilations, government anti-gravity testi Sirius Connection, science fiction author Philip K. Dick and his efforts to expose the Illuminati, plus more from veteran conspira UFO author Keith. Conspiracy expert Keith's final book on UFOs and the highly secret group that manufactures them and uses th their own purposes: the control and manipulation of the population of planet Earth.

148 PAGES. 6X9 PAPERBACK. ILLUSTRATED. $12.95. CODE: SOIL

TECHNOLOGY OF THE GODS

The Incredible Sciences of the Ancients

by David Hatcher Childress

Popular *Lost Cities* author David Hatcher Childress takes us into the amazing world of ancient technology, from computers in antiquity "flying machines of the gods." Childress looks at the technology that was allegedly used in Atlantis and the theory that the Great Pyra Egypt was originally a gigantic power station. He examines tales of ancient flight and the technology that it involved; how the ancien electricity; megalithic building techniques; the use of crystal lenses and the fire from the gods; evidence of various high tech weapons in th including atomic weapons; ancient metallurgy and heavy machinery; the role of modern inventors such as Nikola Tesla in bringing technology back into modern use; impossible artifacts; and more.

356 PAGES. 6X9 PAPERBACK. ILLUSTRATED. BIBLIOGRAPHY. $16.95. CODE: TGOD.

THE ORION PROPHECY

Egyptian & Mayan Prophecies on the Cataclysm of 2012

by Patrick Geryl and Gino Ratinckx

In the year 2012 the Earth awaits a super catastrophe: its magnetic field reverse in one go. Phenomenal earthquakes and tidal waves will completely dest civilization. Europe and North America will shift thousands of kilometers northwards into polar climes. Nearly everyone will perish in the apocalyptic h ings. These dire predictions stem from the Mayans and Egyptians—descendants of the legendary Atlantis. The Atlanteans had highly evolved astror knowledge and were able to exactly predict the previous world-wide flood in 9792 BC. Orion and several others stars will take the same 'code-position 9792 BC! For thousands of years historical sources have told of a forgotten time capsule of ancient wisdom located in a mythical labyrinth of secret ch filled with artifacts and documents from the previous flood. We desperately need this information now—and this book gives one possible location.

324 PAGES. 6X9 PAPERBACK. ILLUSTRATED. BIBLIOGRAPHY. $16.95. CODE: ORP

THE HISTORY OF THE KNIGHTS TEMPLARS

by Charles G. Addison, introduction by David Hatcher Childress

Chapters on the origin of the Templars, their popularity in Europe and their rivalry with the Knights of St. John, later to be known as the Knights of Malta. Detailed information on the activities of the Templars in the Holy Land, and the 1312 AD suppression of the Templars in France and other countries, which culminated in the execution of Jacques de Molay and the continuation of the Knights Templars in England and Scotland; the formation of the society of Knights Templars in London; and the rebuilding of the Temple in 1816. Plus a lengthy intro about the lost Templar fleet and its connections to the ancient North American sea routes.

395 PAGES. 6X9 PAPERBACK. ILLUSTRATED. $16.95. CODE: HKT

DARK MOON

Apollo and the Whistleblowers

by Mary Bennett and David Percy

- Was Neil Armstrong really the first man on the Moon?
- Did you know that 'live' color TV from the Moon was not actually live at all?
- Did you know that the Lunar Surface Camera had no viewfinder?
- Do you know that lighting was used in the Apollo photographs—yet no lighting equipment was taken to the Moon?

All these questions, and more, are discussed in great detail by British researchers Bennett and Percy in *Dark Moon,* the definitive book (nearly 600 pa the possible faking of the Apollo Moon missions. Bennett and Percy delve into every possible aspect of this beguiling theory, one that rocks the very four of our beliefs concerning NASA and the space program. Tons of NASA photos analyzed for possible deceptions.

568 PAGES. 6X9 PAPERBACK. ILLUSTRATED. BIBLIOGRAPHY. INDEX. $25.00. CODE: DMO

WAKE UP DOWN THERE!

The Excluded Middle Anthology

by Greg Bishop

The great American tradition of dropout culture makes it over the millennium mark with a collection of the best from *The Excluded Middle,* the critically acclaimed underground zine of UFOs, the paranormal, conspiracies, psychedelia, and spirit. Contributions from Robert Anton Wilson, Ivan Stang, Martin Kottmeyer, John Shirley, Scott Corrales, Adam Gorightly and Robert Sterling; and interviews with James Moseley, Karla Turner, Bill Moore, Kenn Thomas, Richard Boylan, Dean Radin, Joe McMoneagle, and the mysterious Ira Einhorn (an *Excluded Middle* exclusive). Includes full versions of interviews and extra material not found in the newsstand versions.

420 PAGES. 8X11 PAPERBACK. ILLUSTRATED. $25.00. CODE: WUDT

ARKTOS

The Myth of the Pole in Science, Symbolism, and Nazi Survival

by Joscelyn Godwin

A scholarly treatment of catastrophes, ancient myths and the Nazi Occult beliefs. Explored are the many tales of an ancient race s have lived in the Arctic regions, such as Thule and Hyperborea. Progressing onward, the book looks at modern polar legends inc the survival of Hitler, German bases in Antarctica, UFOs, the hollow earth, Agartha and Shambala, more.

220 PAGES. 6X9 PAPERBACK. ILLUSTRATED. $16.95. CODE: ARK

24 hour credit card orders—call: 815-253-6390 fax: 815-253-6300
email: auphq@frontiernet.net www.adventuresunlimitedpress.com www.wexclub.com

CONSPIRACY & HISTORY

LIQUID CONSPIRACY

JFK, LSD, the CIA, Area 51 & UFOs

by George Piccard

Underground author George Piccard on the politics of LSD, mind control, and Kennedy's involvement with Area 51 and UFOs. Reveals JFK's LSD experiences with Mary Pinchot-Meyer. The plot thickens with an ever expanding web of CIA involvement, from underground bases with UFOs seen by JFK and Marilyn Monroe (among others) to a vaster conspiracy that affects every government agency from NASA to the Justice Department. This may have been the reason that Marilyn Monroe and actress-columnist Dorothy Kilgallen were both murdered. Focusing on the bizarre side of history, *Liquid Conspiracy* takes the reader on a psychedelic tour de force. This is your government on drugs!

264 PAGES. 6X9 PAPERBACK. ILLUSTRATED. $14.95. CODE: LIQC

INSIDE THE GEMSTONE FILE

Howard Hughes, Onassis & JFK

by Kenn Thomas & David Hatcher Childress

Steamshovel Press editor Thomas takes on the Gemstone File in this run-up and run-down of the most famous underground document ever circulated. Photocopied and distributed for over 20 years, the Gemstone File is the story of Bruce Roberts, the inventor of the synthetic ruby widely used in laser technology today, and his relationship with the Howard Hughes Company and ultimately with Aristotle Onassis, the Mafia, and the CIA. Hughes kidnapped and held a drugged-up prisoner for 10 years; Onassis and his role in the Kennedy Assassination; how the Mafia ran corporate America in the 1960s; the death of Onassis' son in the crash of a small private plane in Greece; Onassis as Ian Fleming's archvillain Ernst Stavro Blofeld; more.

320 PAGES. 6X9 PAPERBACK. ILLUSTRATED. $16.00. CODE: IGF

MASS CONTROL

Engineering Human Consciousness

by Jim Keith

Conspiracy expert Keith's final book on mind control, Project Monarch, and mass manipulation presents chilling evidence that we are indeed spinning a Matrix. Keith describes the New Man, where conception of reality is a dance of electronic images fired into his forebrain, a gossamer construction of his masters, designed so that he will not—under any circumstances—perceive the actual. His happiness is delivered to him through a tube or an electronic connection. His God lurks behind an electronic curtain; when the curtain is pulled away we find the CIA sorcerer, the media manipulatorÖ Chapters on the CIA, Tavistock, Jolly West and the Violence Center, Guerrilla Mindwar, Brice Taylor, other recent "victims," more.

256 PAGES. 6X9 PAPERBACK. ILLUSTRATED. INDEX. $16.95. CODE: MASC

THE ARCH CONSPIRATOR

Essays and Actions

by Len Bracken

Veteran conspiracy author Len Bracken's witty essays and articles lead us down the dark corridors of conspiracy, politics, murder and mayhem. In 12 chapters Bracken takes us through a maze of interwoven tales from the Russian Conspiracy to his interview with Costa Rican novelist Joaquin Gutierrez and his Psychogeographic Map into the Third Millennium. Other chapters in the book are A General Theory of Civil War; The New-Catiline Conspiracy for the Cancellation of Debt; Anti-Labor Day; 1997 with selected Aphorisms Against Work; Solar Economics; and more. Bracken's work has appeared in such pop-conspiracy publications as *Paranoia*, *Steamshovel Press* and the *Village Voice*. Len Bracken lives in Arlington, Virginia and haunts the back alleys of Washington D.C., keeping an eye on the predators who run our country.

256 PAGES. 6X9 PAPERBACK. ILLUSTRATED. BIBLIOGRAPHY. $14.95. CODE: ACON.

MIND CONTROL, WORLD CONTROL

by Jim Keith

Veteran author and investigator Jim Keith uncovers a surprising amount of information on the technology, experimentation and implementation of mind control. Various chapters in this shocking book are on early CIA experiments such as Project Artichoke and Project R.H.I.C.-EDOM, the methodology and technology of implants, mind control assassins and couriers, various famous Mind Control victims such as Sirhan Sirhan and Candy Jones. Also featured in this book are chapters on how mind control technology may be linked to some UFO activity and "UFO abductions."

256 PAGES. 6X9 PAPERBACK. ILLUSTRATED. FOOTNOTES. $14.95. CODE: MCWC

NASA, NAZIS & JFK:

The Torbitt Document & the JFK Assassination

introduction by Kenn Thomas

This book emphasizes the links between "Operation Paper Clip" Nazi scientists working for NASA, the assassination of JFK, and the secret Nevada air base Area 51. The Torbitt Document also talks about the roles played in the assassination by Division Five of the FBI, the Defense Industrial Security Command (DISC), the Las Vegas mob, and the shadow corporate entities Permindex and Centro-Mondiale Commerciale. The Torbitt Document claims that the same players planned the 1962 assassination attempt on Charles de Gaul, who ultimately pulled out of NATO because he traced the "Assassination Cabal" to Permindex in Switzerland and to NATO headquarters in Brussels. The Torbitt Document paints a dark picture of NASA, the military industrial complex, and the connections to Mercury, Nevada which headquarters the "secret space program."

258 PAGES. 5X8. PAPERBACK. ILLUSTRATED. $16.00. CODE: NNJ

MIND CONTROL, OSWALD & JFK:

Were We Controlled?

introduction by Kenn Thomas

Steamshovel Press editor Kenn Thomas examines the little-known book *Were We Controlled?*, first published in 1968. The book's author, the mysterious Lincoln Lawrence, maintained that Lee Harvey Oswald was a special agent who was a mind control subject, having received an implant in 1960 at a Russian hospital. Thomas examines the evidence for implant technology and the role it could have played in the Kennedy Assassination. Thomas also looks at the mind control aspects of the RFK assassination and details the history of implant technology. A growing number of people are interested in CIA experiments and its "Silent Weapons for Quiet Wars." Looks at the case that the reporter Damon Runyon, Jr. was murdered because of this book.

256 PAGES. 6X9 PAPERBACK. ILLUSTRATED. NOTES. $16.00. CODE: MCOJ

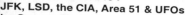

24 hour credit card orders—call: 815-253-6390 fax: 815-253-6300
email: auphq@frontiernet.net www.adventuresunlimitedpress.com www.wexclub.com

PHILOSOPHY & RELIGION

JESUS, LAST OF THE PHARAOHS
Truth Behind the Mask Revealed
by Ralph Ellis

This book, with 43 color plates, traces the history of the Egyptian royal family from the time of Noah through to Jesus, comparing bibli historical records. Nearly all of the biblical characters can be identified in the historical record—all are pharaohs of Egypt or pharaohs in ex Bible depicts them as being simple shepherds, but in truth they were the Hyksos, the Shepherd Kings of Egypt. The biblical story that has cir around the globe is simply a history of one family, Abraham and his descendants. In the Bible he was known as Abram; in the historical reco the pharaoh Maybra—the most powerful man on Earth in his lifetime. By such simple sleight of hand, the pharaohs of Egypt have hidden their i but preserved their ancient history and bloodline. These kings were born of the gods; they were not only royal, they were also Sons of God.

320 PAGES. 6X9 PAPERBACK. ILLUSTRATED. $16.00. CODE: JLOP

TEMPEST & EXODUS
by Ralph Ellis

Starts with the dramatic discovery of a large biblical quotation on an ancient Egyptian stele which tells of a conference in Egypt discussing the way i the biblical Exodus should be organized. The quotation thus has fundamental implications for both history and theology because it explains why the Tab and the Ark of the Covenant were constructed, why the biblical Exodus started, where Mt. Sinai was located, and who the god of the Israelites was. T dramatic discovery is that the central element of early Israelite liturgy was actually the Giza pyramids, and that Mt. Sinai was none other than th Pyramid. Mt. Sinai was described as being both sharp and the tallest 'mountain' in the area, and thus the Israelite god actually resided deep within the of this pyramid. Furthermore, these new translations of ancient texts, both secular and biblical, also clearly demonstrate that the Giza pyramids are ol the first dynasty—the ancestors of the Hyksos were writing about the Giza pyramids long before they are supposed to have been constructed! Incluc Sinai, the Israelite name for the Great Pyramid of Egypt; the biblical Exodus inscribed on an Egyptian stele of Ahmose I; the secret name of God re Noah's Ark discovered, more.

280 PAGES. 6X9 PAPERBACK. ILLUSTRATED. COLOR SECTION. BIBLIOGRAPHY & INDEX. $16.00. CODE: T

THOTH
Architect of the Universe
by Ralph Ellis

This great book, now available in paperback, is on sacred geometry, megalithic architecture and the worship of the mathematical constant pi. Ellis contemplates Ston the ancient Egyptian god Thoth and his Emerald Tablets; Atlantis; Thoth's Ratios; Henge of the World; The Secret Gate of Knowledge; Precessional Henge Planisphere; Kufu's Continents; the Ma'at of the Egyptians; ancient technological civilizations; the Ark of Tutankhamen; Pyramidions; the Pyramid Inch and Pi; mo illustrated with color photo sections.

236 PAGES. 6X9 PAPERBACK. ILLUSTRATED. BIBLIOGRAPHY. $16.00. CODE: TOTH

K2—QUEST OF THE GODS
by Ralph Ellis

This sequel to *Thoth, Architect of the Universe* explains the design of the Great Pyramid in great detail, and it appears that its architect specified a structure that contains a curious blend of technology, lateral thinking and childish fun—yet this design can also point out the exact location of the legendary 'Hall of Records' to within a few meters! The 'X' marks the spot location has been found at last. Join the author on the most ancient quest ever devised, a dramatic journey in the footsteps of Alexander the Great on his search for the legendary Hall of Records, then on to the highest peaks at the top of the world to find the 'The Great Pyramid in the Himalayas'; more.

280 PAGES. 6X9 PAPERBACK. ILLUSTRATED. COLOR SECTION. BIBLIOGRAPHY. $16.00. CODE: K2QD

THE DIMENSIONS OF PARADISE
The Proportions & Symbolic Numbers of Ancient Cosmology
by John Michell

The Dimensions of Paradise were known to ancient civilizations as the harmonious numerical standards that underlie the created world. John Michell's quest for these standards provides vital clues for understanding:

- the dimensions and symbolism of Stonehenge
- the plan of Atlantis and reason for its fall
- the numbers behind the sacred names of Christianity
- the form of St. John's vision of the New Jerusalem
- the name of the man with the number 666
- the foundation plan of Glastonbury and other sanctuaries
- and how these symbols suggest a potential for personal, cultural and political regeneration in the 21st century.

220 PAGES. 6X9 PAPERBACK. ILLUSTRATED. BIBLIOGRAPHY. INDEX. $16.95. CODE: DIMP

A HITCHHIKER'S GUIDE TO ARMAGEDDON
by David Hatcher Childress

With wit and humor, popular Lost Cities author David Hatcher Childress takes us around the world and back in his trippy finalé to the Lost Cities serie off on an adventure in search of the apocalypse and end times. Childress hits the road from the fortress of Megiddo, the legendary citadel in northen where Armageddon is prophesied to start. Hitchhiking around the world, Childress takes us from one adventure to another, to ancient cities in the dese the legends of worlds before our own. Childress muses on the rise and fall of civilizations, and the forces that have shaped mankind over the mil including wars, invasions and cataclysms. He discusses the ancient Armageddons of the past, and chronicles recent Middle East developments an ominous undertones. In the meantime, he becomes a cargo cult god on a remote island off New Guinea, gets dragged into the Kennedy Assassination of the "conspirators," investigates a strange power operating out of the Altai Mountains of Mongolia, and discovers how the Knights Templar and th shoots have driven the world toward an epic battle centered around Jerusalem and the Middle East.

320 PAGES. 6X9 PAPERBACK. ILLUSTRATED. BIBLIOGRAPHY. INDEX. $16.95. CODE: HGA

FREE ENERGY SYSTEMS

LOST SCIENCE

by Gerry Vassilatos

Rediscover the legendary names of suppressed scientific revolution—remarkable lives, astounding discoveries, and incredible inventions which would have produced a world of wonder. How did the aura research of Baron Karl von Reichenbach prove the vitalistic theory and frighten the greatest minds of Germany? How did the physiophone and wireless of Antonio Meucci predate both Bell and Marconi by decades? How does the earth battery technology of Nathan Stubblefield portend an unsuspected energy revolution? How did the geoaetheric engines of Nikola Tesla threaten the establishment of a fuel-dependent America? The microscopes and virus-destroying ray machines of Dr. Royal Rife provided the solution for every world-threatening disease. Why did the FDA and AMA together condemn this great man to Federal Prison? The static crashes on telephone lines enabled Dr. T. Henry Moray to discover the reality of radiant space energy. Was the mysterious "Swedish stone," the powerful mineral which Dr. Moray discovered, the very first historical instance in which stellar power was recognized and secured on earth? Why did the Air Force initially fund the gravitational warp research and warp-cloaking devices of T. Townsend Brown and then reject it? When the controlled fusion devices of Philo Farnsworth achieved the "break-even" point in 1967 the FUSOR project was abruptly cancelled by ITT.

304 PAGES. 6X9 PAPERBACK. ILLUSTRATED. BIBLIOGRAPHY. $16.95. CODE: LOS

SECRETS OF COLD WAR TECHNOLOGY

Project HAARP and Beyond

by Gerry Vassilatos

Vassilatos reveals that "Death Ray" technology has been secretly researched and developed since the turn of the century. Included are chapters on such inventors and their devices as H.C. Vion, the developer of auroral energy receivers; Dr. Selim Lemstrom's pre-Tesla experiments; the early beam weapons of Grindell-Mathews, Ulivi, Turpain and others; John Hettenger and his early beam power systems. Learn about Project Argus, Project Teak and Project Orange; EMP experiments in the 60s; why the Air Force directed the construction of a huge Ionospheric "backscatter" telemetry system across the Pacific just after WWII; why Raytheon has collected every patent relevant to HAARP over the past few years; more.

250 PAGES. 6X9 PAPERBACK. ILLUSTRATED. $15.95. CODE: SCWT

QUEST FOR ZERO-POINT ENERGY

Engineering Principles for "Free Energy"

by Moray B. King

King expands, with diagrams, on how free energy and anti-gravity are possible. The theories of zero point energy maintain there are tremendous fluctuations of electrical field energy embedded within the fabric of space. King explains the following topics: Tapping the Zero-Point Energy as an Energy Source; Fundamentals of a Zero-Point Energy Technology; Vacuum Energy Vortices; The Super Tube; Charge Clusters: The Basis of Zero-Point Energy Inventions; Vortex Filaments, Torsion Fields and the Zero-Point Energy; Transforming the Planet with a Zero-Point Energy Experiment; Dual Vortex Forms: The Key to a Large Zero-Point Energy Coherence. Packed with diagrams, patents and photos. With power shortages now a daily reality in many parts of the world, this book offers a fresh approach very rarely mentioned in the mainstream media.

224 PAGES. 6X9 PAPERBACK. ILLUSTRATED. $14.95. CODE: QZPE

THE TIME TRAVEL HANDBOOK

A Manual of Practical Teleportation & Time Travel

edited by David Hatcher Childress

In the tradition of *The Anti-Gravity Handbook* and *The Free-Energy Device Handbook*, science and UFO author David Hatcher Childress takes us into the weird world of time travel and teleportation. Not just a whacked-out look at science fiction, this book is an authoritative chronicling of real-life time travel experiments, teleportation devices and more. *The Time Travel Handbook* takes the reader beyond the government experiments and deep into the uncharted territory of early time travellers such as Nikola Tesla and Guglielmo Marconi and their alleged time travel experiments, as well as the Wilson Brothers of EMI and their connection to the Philadelphia Experiment—the U.S. Navy's forays into invisibility, time travel, and teleportation. Childress looks into the claims of time travelling individuals, and investigates the unusual claim that the pyramids on Mars were built in the future and sent back in time. A highly visual, large format book, with patents, photos and schematics. Be the first on your block to build your own time travel device!

316 PAGES. 7X10 PAPERBACK. ILLUSTRATED. $16.95. CODE: TTH

THE TESLA PAPERS

Nikola Tesla on Free Energy & Wireless Transmission of Power

by Nikola Tesla, edited by David Hatcher Childress

David Hatcher Childress takes us into the incredible world of Nikola Tesla and his amazing inventions. Tesla's rare article "The Problem of Increasing Human Energy with Special Reference to the Harnessing of the Sun's Energy" is included. This lengthy article was originally published in the June 1900 issue of *The Century Illustrated Monthly Magazine* and it was the outline for Tesla's master blueprint for the world. Tesla's fantastic vision of the future, including wireless power, anti-gravity, free energy and highly advanced solar power. Also included are some of the papers, patents and material collected on Tesla at the Colorado Springs Tesla Symposiums, including papers on: •The Secret History of Wireless Transmission •Tesla and the Magnifying Transmitter •Design and Construction of a Half-Wave Tesla Coil •Electrostatics: A Key to Free Energy •Progress in Zero-Point Energy Research •Electromagnetic Energy from Antennas to Atoms •Tesla's Particle Beam Technology •Fundamental Excitatory Modes of the Earth-Ionosphere Cavity

325 PAGES. 8X10 PAPERBACK. ILLUSTRATED. $16.95. CODE: TTP

THE FANTASTIC INVENTIONS OF NIKOLA TESLA

by Nikola Tesla with additional material by David Hatcher Childress

This book is a readable compendium of patents, diagrams, photos and explanations of the many incredible inventions of the originator of the modern era of electrification. In Tesla's own words are such topics as wireless transmission of power, death rays, and radio-controlled airships. In addition, rare material on German bases in Antarctica and South America, and a secret city built at a remote jungle site in South America by one of Tesla's students, Guglielmo Marconi. Marconi's secret group claims to have built flying saucers in the 1940s and to have gone to Mars in the early 1950s! Incredible photos of these Tesla craft are included. The Ancient Atlantean system of broadcasting energy through a grid system of obelisks and pyramids is discussed, and a fascinating concept comes out of one chapter: that Egyptian engineers had to wear protective metal head-shields while in these power plants, hence the Egyptian Pharoah's head covering as well as the Face on Mars! •His plan to transmit free electricity into the atmosphere. •How electrical devices would work using only small antennas. •Why unlimited power could be utilized anywhere on earth. •How radio and radar technology can be used as death-ray weapons in Star Wars.

342 PAGES. 6X9 PAPERBACK. ILLUSTRATED. $16.95. CODE: FINT

24 hour credit card orders—call: 815-253-6390 fax: 815-253-6300

email: auphq@frontiernet.net www.adventuresunlimitedpress.com www.wexclub.com